T4-ADN-696

{ The Play's the Thing }

The Play's the Thing

*Fifty Years of Yale Repertory Theatre
(1966–2016)*

James Magruder

FOREWORD BY ROCCO LANDESMAN

PHOTOGRAPHS EDITED BY
MARGUERITE ELLIOTT

Yale UNIVERSITY PRESS | NEW HAVEN & LONDON

Published with assistance from the David Geffen School of Drama at Yale University.

Copyright © 2024 by Yale University. Foreword copyright © 2024 by Rocco Landesman. All rights reserved.
This book may not be reproduced, in whole or in part, including illustrations, in any form (beyond that copying permitted by Sections 107 and 108 of the U.S. Copyright Law and except by reviewers for the public press), without written permission from the publishers.

Yale University Press books may be purchased in quantity for educational, business, or promotional use. For information, please email sales.press@yale.edu (U.S. office) or sales@yaleup.co.uk (U.K. office).

Designed by Amber Morena.
Set in 11/14 Garamond Premier type by Motto Publishing Services.
Printed in China.

Library of Congress Control Number: 2024930731
ISBN 978-0-300-21500-7 (hardcover : alk. paper)

A catalogue record for this book is available from the British Library.

This paper meets the requirements of ANSI/NISO Z39.48-1992 (Permanence of Paper).

10 9 8 7 6 5 4 3 2 1

This book is dedicated to the spirit of actor Reginald E. Cathey (1958–2018), Yale School of Drama class of 1981, who taught me in our one meeting all there is to know about staying in the moment.

You don't see a tree grow.
—HENRY CHAUNCEY, 2017

CONTENTS

Foreword: In the beginning . . . **ix**
Preface: An Account of My Conduct **xv**

CHAPTER ONE — Robert Brustein (1966–1979) **1**

CHAPTER TWO — Lloyd Richards (1979–1991) **95**

CHAPTER THREE — Stan Wojewodski Jr. (1991–2002) **157**

CHAPTER FOUR — James Bundy (2002–) **227**

Production History **319**
Bibliographic Essay **347**
List of Interviewees **349**
Acknowledgments **351**
Index **353**

FOREWORD: IN THE BEGINNING . . .

We must take the theater out of the hands of the grocer.
—ANTON CHEKHOV

Talk about Chekhovian economy! There it is, in a single sentence: the mission statement of the American not-for-profit theater. Chekhov, writing to his publisher Suvorin in 1895, knew nothing of the Ford Foundation. Or the National Endowment for the Arts. Or capital campaigns. Or naming opportunities. But he did know that if theater in Russia was ever to be taken seriously, to take its place in literature among the poems of Pushkin and the novels of Tolstoy, it would need to be protected from the vicissitudes of the marketplace. Dramatic productions seeking the broadest appeal, the largest audiences, and the highest profit might qualify as entertainment but not necessarily as art. No ambiguity on this point, no nuance: great theater is art, not commerce.

When Robert Brustein, in 1966, founded the Yale Repertory Theatre (a.k.a. Yale Rep), a professional theater with a professional company performing plays in repertory, and connected it to a legendary conservatory, both under the protective umbrella of Yale University, his intent was to create a theater that would never, ever, under any circumstances, fall into the hands of the grocer. Fifty years later? So far, so good.

A history of any theater is a history of the work it presents. Yale Rep is the sum total of its productions. With this project, James Magruder took on a formidable challenge: to write a history of something ephemeral, that exists for a moment and then disappears into the ether. The audience walks out, the stage is struck, and nothing is left but our recollection of the event. Somehow he does it, with exhaustive research, his own and other people's memories, pictures and videotapes, and reviews—anything and everything he could find. Sometimes he writes about the play, sometimes about the reaction of audiences and critics, and sometimes about the circumstances of individual productions, such as casting issues, difficulties with the playwright's commission, and ensuing controversies (Brustein, Sondheim, and *The Frogs* is a drama unto itself, not to be missed). Occasionally, he even slips in his own minireview: "Unfortunately, Richards allowed Soyinka to direct his own play."

Of course, the productions were performed in a context, and Magruder constantly widens the lens. There have been, in the fifty years of Yale Rep, only four artistic directors, and each also served as dean of the Yale School of Drama. Their aesthetic ambitions, their personalities and management styles, informed every season and set the tone for the daily life of both the theater and the school. And the supporting cast is large; so many people played vital roles in the life of this place that a true index of important names would be longer than the book. Finally, the unique structure of the Rep and its longevity warrant an assessment of its place in the history of the American theater. How Magruder accounts for all of this without letting the massive amount of information gum up a highly readable, sometimes dishy narrative, I'm not quite sure. But he does, masterfully.

We now take subsidized theater in the United States for granted. Every major city, and many smaller ones, have at least one resident, not-for-profit theater. But it wasn't always so. My hometown of St. Louis has a dozen not-for-profit theaters, many of them substantial ongoing enterprises with endowments and strong development departments. When I was growing up there in the 1950s and early 1960s there were none. Zero. You could watch summer stock musicals at the Muny Opera or touring Broadway at the Fox or American Theaters, but there was no permanent institution. There were a few scattered across the country: the American Conservatory Theater in San Francisco, the Arena Stage in Washington, DC, Theater 47 in Dallas, and the Public Theater in New York, among others. Something like the League of Resident Theatres (LORT), which now represents seventy-five theaters, was unimaginable.

In the 1960s the landscape changed, and it changed fast. In 1961, W. McNeil "Mac" Lowry, the president of the Ford Foundation, decided that seeding and funding American resident theaters would be a Ford priority, and with follow-up support from the newly created National Endowment for the Arts and the Rockefeller Foundation, the money started to flow. As Magruder points out, "Within five years some twenty-six new theater companies were born." We can look back and speculate that there was something in the ethos of the egalitarian, anticapitalist spirit of those years that made creating a substantial alternative to commercial theater seem like a good idea. Whatever the reason, a sea change was underway. And today the American theater is dominated by not-for-profit institutions.

My generation included the iconic names of the 1960s counterculture. Robert Brustein was a generation older but was in his way a card-carrying antiestablishmentarian. A dropout from the Yale School of Drama (YSD; Magruder has that story!), he was one of a small number of theater critics, writing mostly in the more serious magazines, who have been described as "adversarial." They stood in opposition. Opposed to the theater of the boulevard, that is, Broadway, opposed to the middlebrow, opposed to the meretricious, opposed to the commercial theater factory that tells people what they already know and confirms what they already believe. Along with Richard Gilman, Stanley Kauffmann, John Simon, and his colleague at Columbia, Eric Bentley, Brustein venerated the great playwrights of European modern drama. Bentley's *The Playwright as Thinker* was the bible, and the approach was intellectual, generally skeptical, and politically left. Brustein's reviews, published in the *New Republic*, could be counted on to be Broadway unfriendly. His signature book, *The Theater of Revolt*, grouped Chekhov, Ibsen, Strindberg, Shaw, Brecht, Pirandello, Genet, and O'Neill not as political revolutionaries but as in revolt against the norms of bourgeois culture and conventional forms. Artaud, Büchner, and Beckett were worthy of attention, Neil Simon and Arthur Miller not so much. So when Kingman Brewster, the president of Yale, offered Brustein the job of dean of the YSD, he knew he would be bringing into a dusty and forgotten corner of academia someone who would turn it upside down.

Which he proceeded to do. I was there. I remember some of it.

When I arrived in New Haven in 1969, newly admitted to the doctoral program in dramatic literature and criticism at the drama school, I saw a place that was indeed being suddenly upended. There was a sense of the ground moving under our feet. Symbolically, the green room adjoining the University Theatre (UT) had been painted a bright red. A new venture was under way and we had been selected to be a part of it. The *New York Times*—in fact, press across the country—reported Brustein's every hire, every provocative speech, every controversial new production. The visit of the newly confrontational Living Theatre and Brustein's response to the demands of the Black Panthers made news. Being students, we expressed dissatisfaction with everything, but we had drunk the Kool-Aid and aspired to careers above and beyond and superior to the expedient compromises of the commercial theater.

When Brustein described what he envisioned to President Brewster, he offered the example of the Yale Medical School and the Yale New Haven Hospital. The professional/teaching hospital. The established doctors teach and mentor and supervise the students and residents. The young doctors in training, in turn, with their energy and ambition, keep the place feeling new and in-process, implicitly challenging their superiors. Brustein's models were the great European theaters that had both a company of professional actors and a conservatory: The Moscow

Foreword

Art Theatre. The Comédie-Française. The Old Vic. There was nothing like that in America then, and there is nothing quite like that now. The professional actors, with their cohort of professional directors, designers, and musicians, would present world-class productions. Those productions would play in repertory, with members of the company assuming different roles, growing as actors as they became different people from one night to the next. The audience, becoming familiar with the permanent company, would grow along with them as they saw familiar faces inhabiting new characters. The members of the company would bond with each other and the audience with the company. Brustein called this the repertory ideal.

The biggest shock to the hallowed YSD under Brustein was that a new professional company displaced the old drama club. Tenured professors were sidelined as working actors and directors and designers became teachers with no conferred authority other than their accomplishments in the professional theater. Their names may have been legendary in New York—Bobby Lewis, Stella Adler, Carmen de Lavallade—but in academia they were uncertified nobodies. The professors in my department, the critics Richard Gilman and Stanley Kauffmann, didn't have a graduate degree between them. The revolution didn't go down smoothly, and Brustein's impatience and imperious manner didn't help. His sole focus was on the work. Everything would be professionalized. What he did with the old PhD program was typical. He wanted to train real-world critics and dramaturgs, not future teachers. So the doctoral students would study dramatic literature and criticism but also work with drama school and Rep productions. He felt that theater critics should actually know something about dramatic literature (it wasn't unusual for a newspaper, when the theater critic job opened up, to promote the restaurant reviewer) and also have the experience of being inside a production.

The complexities of Brustein's personality are critical to consider. Why? Because he imagined, shaped, and personified Yale Rep. In the early years, all the major theaters were commanded by icons. Yes, this model is obsolete now; it's not collaborative, it's top-down. The room where it happens now includes staff: the managing director and the marketing, communications, HR, and idea people. But in the early years of what we now call the Resident Theatre Movement, the theaters were indistinguishable from their founders. The Public Theater was Joe Papp. The Arena Stage was Zelda Fichandler. Theater 47 was Margo Jones. The Alley Theatre was Nina Vance. The Guthrie Theater was, yes, Tyrone Guthrie. And the Yale Rep was Robert Brustein.

Yale Rep is unique among resident theaters because of one man's idea and his determination to bring that idea into being. So who was the Robert Brustein of those formative years?

Bob was my teacher, employer, colleague, champion, and friend for a span of over fifty years. I owe him gratitude. But I also think he would have wanted me to present a full picture of the man I knew during those heady early days at the drama school. I think.

In the final years before his death at the age of ninety-six in 2023, he became a teddy bear: affectionate, nostalgic, generous in spirit. But in earlier years... let's just say that Bob Brustein was not easy-listening radio. Every coin of the realm of the Brustein personality was two-sided. Even gold coins have two sides. He was an eloquent public speaker and convincing debater. And a poor listener. He was a cutting, acerbic critic; yet when criticized, he could be thin-skinned. I always knew him to be fiercely loyal. But he remembered slights and held grudges. He was idealistic, a crusader for the cause. He was also the embodiment of that cause, so he could be self-referential. He was fearless about telling the truth and insistent on being right. He spoke passionately about community, the collective, the company, collaboration, common purpose. But he had little patience for process and could quickly become dictatorial. I wish we could have always selected from column A on that menu, but is there a menu with only a column A?

Bob was charismatic; he tended to dominate the room with a kinetic intelligence that was impossible to resist. He was tall, and he was handsome, with a deep voice and seemingly limitless energy. His style was intellectual but not academic. Kingman Brewster could see what everyone else saw. He made the right choice.

I have tried to convey some sense of the founding spirit of Yale Rep and of the man who willed it into existence. I have made no mention of the physical manifestation of the dream: the production of plays. During my ten years in New Haven (I came in a year after the premiere of the Weinstein-Bolcom musical *Dynamite Tonite!* and left a year after its revival), I saw most of the productions at the Rep and many in the Yale Cabaret. I would agree with Jim Magruder that a fair review of the Brustein era, based on his own ambitions and standards, could be characterized as mixed. The productions were usually provocative, not generally audience friendly, often relevant, occasionally popular. The quality was wildly inconsistent. The Rep under Brustein was a director's theater. Three of his favorites, Andrzej Wajda, Andrei Serban, and Andrei Belgrader, were high-concept Eastern Europeans who presented visually arresting but not always accessible productions. Generally, planning a Brustein production began with the Idea, not the star or even the play. Classics could be done if reinterpreted, and sometimes the play itself was

Foreword

the Idea. If I had to sum it up in one sentence, I'd say that the purpose of Yale Rep during the Brustein years was to contravene theater critic Walter Kerr's statement that good theater gives you "the warm feeling of being at home." If you didn't leave the theater feeling at least somewhat unsettled, the production had failed.

What happened to Brustein's repertory ideal? Over the years the foundational blocks of the original edifice have been chipped away. Even the name, Yale Repertory Theatre, is misleading now, since there is no repertory and no permanent company. Those vanished in the next regime, as did the ban on Broadway transfers. But over the next four decades there were many changes for the better. The Rep became a modern theater, with up-to-date sales, subscription, and fund-raising functions. And more importantly, it became a friendly theater. It found that it could provoke, challenge, and even upset without being—what's the word?—adversarial. In Brustein's view, the audience was privileged to be invited to attend a production. Today the artistic director, James Bundy, makes every effort to embrace his audience; he invites their opinions and responds to them. Rather than standing as a reproof to every other theater, the Rep values its connections with them. One of its signature initiatives, a new play funding program at the Binger Center, was conceived as a collaboration with other theaters. Planning is under way for a new, more welcoming main stage theater.

The intimate connection between the school and the professional theater, physically proximate and spiritually intertwined, has played out in ways that even Brustein had not imagined. James Bundy, speaking of the financial support provided by the Yale endowment, said to Magruder, "Our relative level of stability compared to our sibling theatres is phenomenal." That kind of protection, that financial security, enables theater artists to pursue their craft with confidence. The marketplace of Broadway is just down the road, yet far away. Yale Rep remains out of the hands of the grocer.

Magruder quotes the director Robert Woodruff: "Someone once said the DNA of an institution is planted the moment that it is born. And it can never ultimately change radically from that idea." The Rep has never, as Brustein feared, become deprofessionalized, and the rationale of merging a world-class theater and a conservatory is as singular and powerful today as it has ever been. Despite the passage of all these years and the many transformations, the founding ideal endures.

ROCCO LANDESMAN
MFA '72, DFA '76

Foreword

PREFACE: AN ACCOUNT OF MY CONDUCT

When you go to theater, recollect that you are to give an account of your conduct at the last day.

—YALE PRESIDENT TIMOTHY DWIGHT, CLASS OF 1769

Evan Yionoulis (Yale College BA, 1982; Yale School of Drama MFA, 1985), the first woman to direct at Yale Repertory Theatre (or Yale Rep), for twenty-one years a professor in the practice of acting and directing at the Yale School of Drama (YSD), and a resident director who helmed fifteen shows at Yale Rep before leaving in 2018 to become the Richard Rodgers dean and director of Juilliard's drama division, more than qualifies as a YSD / Yale Rep observer with a long view. She notes of the culture: "There is the students' desire for revolution and dissatisfaction with the status quo, whatever that status quo is. Whoever is running the place they want to tear it down and make their own thing, and whatever is being done on that [Rep] stage is not interesting enough. What they're doing in their own theater is more interesting and will always be more interesting to them."

In 1985, I defected from the Yale graduate school, where I was listlessly pursuing a doctorate in French literature, to the dramaturgy and dramatic criticism program at YSD and swiftly adopted the posture that Evan describes. It was midway through the Lloyd Richards administration, and the Rep was . . . dead. Athol Fugard—all that exposition. August Wilson—all that repetition. Winterfest—oh, please. (One did, however, get *paid* to work Winterfest over intercession, so I did—twice—as a student dramaturg.) The essential work was happening at the Cabaret, or in the annex space, where the student directors staged their second-year verse projects and their third-year thesis productions.

Like all graduate students, dramaturgs possibly more than most, I was an exasperating mix of arrogance, insecurity, entitlement, and dissatisfaction. Today, nearly forty years after my YSD matriculation, after teaching translation and adaptation there for more than a decade, after having had two of my adaptations produced at Yale Rep (a musical version of Marivaux's *The Triumph of Love* and Molière's *The Imaginary Invalid*), and after five years of researching and writing this chronicle, I rue my twenty-something posture of indifference. Would that I again could experience the heart-stopping, act-closing Juba in the original *Joe Turner's Come and Gone*, bend over with laughter at Guare's *Moon Over Miami*, thrill to the middle-aged romantic sparks between Elizabeth Wilson and George Hearn in *Ah, Wilderness!*, watch Pamela Payton-Wright make spellbinding choices thirty feet in the air on a rope ladder in *Little Eyolf*. What did I know? What did I know? One resists quoting the refrain of "Big Yellow Taxi."

Writing a history of Yale Rep was a challenge for someone who claims no experience in long-form nonfiction, journalism, or systems analysis. I haven't mastered the art of the spreadsheet. I don't have the visual imagination of the designer. Or the interest in control of the director. Or the plangent needs of the actor. Or useful technical know-how. The drama school trained me to read and to analyze plays, to attempt to improve new plays in vitro, and to assess them in performance. In other words, if this account seems overly weighted to the play, and to the evolving roster of Yale Rep literary managers and resident dramaturgs, and less to subscription packages and advances in lighting board technology, blame my training.

In winnowing more than three hundred productions by roughly two-thirds, down to a manageable and absorbable number of titles, I sought patterns set in motion by the four artistic directors. Part of me wishes I could have covered every last production and interviewed *everyone* and digested every piece of archival material pertaining to Yale Rep. In covering the most salient "fingerprints"—the image is Barbara Damashek's—that Robert Brustein, Lloyd Richards, Stan Wojewodski Jr., and James Bundy pressed into play at Yale Rep, I have tried to be fair, thorough, and accurate, and to write decent sentences. The need to do so slowed me down and led to a first draft far longer than what you presently read. Interspersed through the text are thirty-six (from an original fifty-one) sidebars; they are intended both for visual relief and for more concentrated looks at significant events, essential and sometimes underknown personnel, and larger narrative arcs in the first half century of the theater.

The Play's the Thing begins with Arnold Weinstein and William Bolcom's musical, *Dynamite Tonite!*, in 1966 and ends with Sarah Ruhl's *Scenes from Court Life; or the whipping boy and his prince* in the fall of 2016. At the time of publication, two things have significantly altered the American theater ecosystem: a forceful calling out of its ingrained, systemic racism, itemized in *We See You White American Theatre* (#WESEEYOU), and the far-reaching disruptions of the COVID-19 pandemic.

Dean Bundy and I anticipate that *The Play's the Thing* will disgruntle a core portion of its readership—YSD alumni—for manifold reasons. Production A was a

xvi *Preface*

complete disaster. Actor B was terrible in that show. Why did you include Show X? Why did you ignore Show Y? Why didn't you interview Z (me)?

Again, where I trained my gaze was informed by my education and taste, set in motion by Robert Brustein and his first disciples, who essentially created the position of dramaturg for the American theater. Poorly mounted and received or not, a production of Gogol's *Marriage* held more interest for me a priori than a production of Lanford Wilson's *Talley's Folly*. It's also possible that individual alumni favorites were, as they say, "cut during previews." Finally, a reminder that, however inextricably linked the two institutions have always been, *The Play's the Thing* chronicles Yale Repertory Theatre, not the newly rechristened David Geffen School of Drama at Yale, about to attain its centenary in a few short years with a chronicle of its own.

JAMES MAGRUDER
MA '84, MFA '88, DFA '92

CHAPTER ONE

Robert Brustein (1966–1979)

One of the most valuable achievements of anyone's life is the creation of a good Idea, and I think this has been a damn good Idea. Plato has told us that an Idea—being of the mind and spirit—can outlive any institution, because an institution is physical and therefore fleeting.

—ROBERT BRUSTEIN

THIS MUCH IS TRUE: in January 1966, Yale University president Kingman Brewster contacted Robert Brustein by phone in New York and offered him the position of dean of the Yale School of Drama (YSD). Brustein, then teaching at Columbia University and reviewing theater regularly for the *New Republic*, was not unaware of the institution, having left it in 1949 before taking a degree. Decades later, when Yale was searching a third time for a dean / artistic director, Brustein recalled for the *Hartford Courant* why he had lasted only a year. "I didn't learn much. I found it not only mostly nonintellectual, but certainly antiprofessional."

What led Brewster to call Brustein? What led Brustein to accept?

The answers depend on the story's teller. When asked to summon events that occurred a half century ago, living subjects are apt to burnish, self-edit, rearrange, and enhance their recollections. The truth everyone tells is *their* truth. Theater artists don't testify like witnesses under oath do. They hold their memories close to their chest like Amanda Wingfield displaying for Tom and Laura her cotillion dress in *The Glass Menagerie*, releasing some—or all—of them to flattering advantage. In remembering the negatives, scores are settled, grudges held, slights remembered, reputations scorched. In remembering the positives, encomia proliferate and superlatives scintillate, and why not? A life spent in the theater is ephemeral, writ large in glitter and mood swings, and generates memories to match.

Back in 1966, did Brustein's neighbor, Pulitzer Prize–winning man of letters Robert Penn Warren, really say, "You've been shooting off your mouth about the theatre, Bob. Why don't you do something about it?" Or did Warren, a member of the English faculty at Yale, suggest Brustein to Brewster first? Did the drama students and faculty really go on record with the choices of newspaper critics Walter Kerr or Howard Taubman to replace Dean W. Curtis Canfield? Why was there no search committee? Did Brewster's recent fact-finding mission to Minneapolis, during which he saw serious plays in repertory at the newish Guthrie Theater influence his thinking? Had he read Brustein's just-published jeremiad, *The Theatre of Revolt*, or only the glowing reviews? Did Brewster go to playwriting professor John Gassner in his Madison Tower apartment on Park Street and say that he was thinking of asking Walter Kerr to be the new dean, and did Gassner say that was a bad idea? Did Brustein, taking a first call from New Haven, instead suggest British actor-manager-director-teacher George Devine at the Royal Court Theatre in London for the post? Did Devine, who expired precipitously on January 20, ever get a transatlantic call? Did Brewster reoffer the job to Brustein in a second call?

One question is easy to answer. In 1966, formal search committees were a characteristic of the future. Twelve years later, the names of the eleven-member committee to replace Brustein were released ("Theatrically undistinguished and very

Robert Brustein (1966–1979)

Old Blue," grumbled at least one drama student.), and five rumored finalists were parsed in the pages of the *New York Times*. In 1990, the successor to Lloyd Richards, Stan Wojewodski Jr., was selected in October from an initial list of more than 150 candidates. A decade later, during the search that led to the appointment of James Bundy, Trinity Repertory Company (a.k.a. Trinity Rep) artistic director Oskar Eustis had only to step off the Amtrak from Providence before the American theater community knew via phone and email that he was under serious consideration for the deanship.

All this to say that (1) the cloak-and-dagger method of hiring arts leaders has gone the way of Kingman Brewster's landline telephone, and (2) the dean of the YSD and the artistic director of Yale Repertory Theatre (a.k.a. Yale Rep)—a dual position Brustein willed into being for himself—has become, in the span of fifty years, a very prominent one.

One thing was certain in January 1966. The drama students were clamoring for change, and it needed to happen yesterday. "If we decide to hire him and we get him, there's going to be a revolution," said Brewster to his assistant, Henry "Sam" Chauncey, who feels to this day that his boss, despite his social pedigree, was a revolutionary at heart. In 1939–1940, as a Yale undergraduate, Brewster had stood alongside Sargent Shriver, who would eventually establish the Peace Corps, and future US Supreme Court justice Potter Stewart as a very visible student leader in the America First Committee, which opposed the war. "For that day and age," says Chauncey, "that was like being Jerry Rubin or Abbie Hoffman. Kingman always struggled about the degree to which he could be a radical *and* remain president of Yale."

Brewster, who had been provost under his mentor, Alfred Whitney Griswold, inherited a Yale College, the metaphorical trunk of the university tree, in good shape. He could shift focus to its branches, the graduate and professional schools. According to Chauncey, two of Brewster's overriding interests when he began his presidency were the growing field of interdisciplinary scholarship and what he considered the greatest jewel in Yale's crown—its arts schools. Yale was the only private university at the time to have all four: art, architecture, music, and drama. (Technically there were three in 1966. The School of Art and Architecture officially split into separate entities in 1972.)

Brustein "shrewdly knew he had to get what we call in the academic world, 'a huge dowry,'" says Chauncey. "Bob had the wit and wisdom to make Kingman squirm with his extraordinary and costly demands." Money would be needed for new hires and to buy out the faculty members who would be more or less forced into retirement. Brustein asked for tenure in the English department as well as

Robert Brustein (1966–1979)

A CALL TO ARMS

The Yale School of Drama (YSD) began in 1925 when George Pierce Baker, unable to persuade Harvard to offer a degree in playwriting, defected to Yale to teach his Drama 47 workshop to tyro playwrights. The University Theatre was built in the same year with money from Edward Harkness (Yale College [YC] 1897). The department awarded its first MFA degree in 1931, and in 1955, it was reorganized into a separate professional school, the first such in the Ivy League.

Institutions of every stripe flourish or wither from a combination of internal forces and external pressures. As it approached its fifth decade of operation, the YSD was in a state of desuetude. Its acting dean, Edward Cyrus Cole, covering for W. Curtis Canfield, was not a scholar but a theater technician. Some original faculty members were still in the classroom. A playwriting professor had begun repeating his lectures verbatim. The head of acting was confusing her students with past graduates. Playwrights weren't guaranteed productions of their work. Many notable names in American theater, including Paul Newman, Elia Kazan, Richard Foreman, Julie Harris, *and* Robert Brustein, elected not to finish their degrees there. The "Yale mafia," as it then existed, was there more to help graduating students obtain their first teaching posts rather than their first professional theater jobs.

Playwright John Guare ('63) recalls watching a rehearsal of *Macbeth* in which the director had the cast listen to Maurice Evans recordings in order to find their parts. John Conklin ('66), now one of America's foremost stage designers, recalls the atmosphere at YSD under Canfield as fossilized, uninteresting, and out of touch. "Canfield did his blocking with golf tees on set models; everything was worked out ahead of time. There was no sense of intersection with the text or meaning of the play." New hire Nikos Psacharopoulos was a breath of fresh air for the students, but Conklin felt that drama school productions "were impossibly retrograde and complacent, in the old Theater Guild manner."

Irene Lewis was a third-year directing student in the fall of 1965. She'd begun in the acting program; a fellow student told her she was "taking a man's place" when she switched programs. The time for institutional change was overdue. "We were incensed at how things were being run, and remember, this was a time of protest. The Vietnam War was getting closer and closer to the middle class. The young people who came in my third year were very vocal, because a lot of them were running from the draft."

> Your presence is urgently requested at a meeting of representative interested students, to present and collect a consensus of ideas concerning a reform in course system and general aims of Yale Drama School. We would appreciate your bringing suggestions concerning your dept (General, not specific) to add to the basic format drawn up.
>   Student Center, 11:00 P.M. Tuesday Nov. 21.
>   Thank you.

"Let's get these people out!" (1965)

One night in November, seven students—Lewis; another third-year director, Alan Leicht ('66); and five first years—met at designer Robert E. Taylor's house. The agenda was swiftly established: "Let's get these people out!" The group of seven invited the entire student body to a late-night meeting on November 21 (see above), and the fuse of a revolution was lit.

Lewis brushes aside the notion of risk. "They might have stopped me from graduating, but it was the sixties and the thing about being that age, it's like 'Screw you, we're paying a thousand dollars a year here, and there's no one in the building connected to professional theater except the 'O' [Donald Oenslager] and Nikos [Psacharopoulos]!'"

Newsweek would later report, "A year ago, 154 students out of 194 signed a petition to Kingman Brewster calling for radical changes in the drama school's curriculum and practices and hinting at mass withdrawals." The dissidents found it surprisingly easy to set up a meeting with a receptive president. "Kingman Brewster knew Yale," says Lewis. "He was a fancy man, a patrician who could nevertheless listen to us, *hear* us, but still pass with the bow-tie crowd running the place."

Brewster agreed to look for a new dean. Some months later, Brustein came to New Haven and made a presentation for the entire school. "Whether he had been hired for the job or not," says Lewis, "we didn't know, but no one else came up. It was thrilling; *he* was thrilling."

The Brustein transition wouldn't be easy, but it was safe to say that a second act had been given to the YSD. So, from little slips of paper great things can happen. Decades later, Irene Lewis, class of 1966, kept that mimeographed invitation on her desk at Center Stage in Baltimore, where she was artistic director for twenty years, as a reminder that change *is* possible and that any and all emperors might be wearing no clothes. ◆

the freedom to abolish tenure in the drama school and to lure and hire a host of practitioner-teachers to New Haven. Brustein, his wife Norma, and their son Daniel needed an appropriate place to live, so an Eero Saarinen house was located for them on St. Ronan's Terrace.

But what Brustein wanted most of all was to start his own theater.

Western theaters, broadly speaking, come into being either top-down or bottom-up. In ancient Greece, the Athenians held annual play competitions designed to stabilize the economy of the city-state through the use of private wealth for public good. The *choregoi*, the earliest arts philanthropists, underwrote the production costs of preparing the choruses and sponsored a feast if their plays won the competition. To be a *choregos* was a duty and an honor that rotated from festival to festival among the wealthiest citizens, a designation restricted to male property holders.

Centuries before episodic television, there were the medieval mystery cycles. For roughly five hundred years, until the final third of the sixteenth century, trains of pageant wagons, each one dramatizing a story from the Old Testament or a slice from the life, miracles, and death of Jesus Christ, would move through an English town during the Feast of Corpus Christi, stopping first to perform before the mayor's house and then proceeding on to other stations. Each play wagon in the mystery cycle was supported, built, and enacted by a different guild—the cobblers, the glovers, the chandlers, and so on. In *A Midsummer Night's Dream*, the Rude Mechanicals, Bottom especially, are eager to shine in "Pyramus and Thisbe" before Theseus and his court because they're stagestruck. (Many scholars believe Shakespeare encountered the last hurrah of the mystery plays in his youth.)

The rise of nation-states in the late Middle Ages led to the beginning of the top-down theaters. Kings and nobles endowed the original German *Hoftheater*, a status symbol for every court. Some 150 or so remain in place to this day as a publicly funded *Stadttheater*, one for every decent-sized German city. The Comédie-Française, proclaimed into being in 1680 when Louis XIV merged the only two legal Parisian acting troupes; Austria's *Burgtheater* in Vienna (1741); and the Royal Danish Theater (1748) are other enduring civic institutions.

Beginning in the nineteenth century, several important theaters sprang bottom-up in reaction to the mechanical formulas of the bourgeois well-made play. These include the Saxe-Meiningen Troupe, founded in 1866 by the duke of Saxe-Meiningen, with a director-focused aesthetic; Le Théâtre Libre in Paris, of short duration (1887–1896) but lasting influence; and Stanislavski and Nemirovich-Danchenko's Moscow Art Theatre (1898–).

As for the New World, Alexis de Tocqueville hit yet another (among dozens) prescient bull's-eye when he wrote in "Some Observations on the Drama amongst Democratic Nations" in *Democracy in America* (1840) that "people who spend every day in the week making money, and the Sunday in going to church, have nothing to invite the Muse of Comedy." In other words, the Puritan ethos, which spies the hand of Satan in all forms of Platonic imitation, and "Follow the money" were, and will remain, foundational roadblocks to artmaking in the United States of America.

From Portland, Maine, to Portland, Oregon, nineteenth-century playhouses were bursting with theater, but serious American *drama* was next to nonexistent, its first genuine crocuses only peeking through the dross in 1915 with the Provincetown Players, which nurtured the young Eugene O'Neill and Susan Glaspell, and then, to a lesser extent, in 1918 with the formation of the Theatre Guild in New York City, a federation of producers and playwrights aiming higher than melodrama and insipid domestic comedy.

Apart from an occasional star-driven production, where could the works of old masters like Goldoni, Shakespeare, and Molière and mind-bending modernists like Ibsen, Strindberg, and Pirandello find purchase? Only the strong-willed Eva Le Gallienne was able to make good on the dream of a rotating classic repertory, opening her thousand-seat Civic Repertory Theatre in 1926 with the watch cry "Not Only for Amusement." Over a ten-year span, Civic Rep presented thirty-seven plays at popular prices, including the American premiere of *Three Sisters*. Wealthy friends and lovers erased years of red ink before the shocks and aftershocks of the Great Depression finally took Le Galienne down. Elsewhere in Manhattan, the Group Theater (1931–1941) matched the spirit of the turbulent 1930s with its synthesis of Stanislavskian technique and social critique, but it dissolved amid clashing egos, the siren call of Hollywood for some of its comelier talents, and the eternal dilemma of how to deploy a nonprofit mission in a commercial biosphere.

Serious playwrights would emerge in America—such as O'Neill, Wilder, Miller, Odets, Inge, and Williams—but, Wilder excepted, their dominant mode of dramatic expression, which came to be known as poetic realism, didn't keep pace with the radical output of their European contemporaries such as Lorca, Cocteau, Sartre, Dürrenmatt, Beckett, Arrabal, and Ionesco. Every so often a deeply strange new American play, like Jane Bowles's *In the Summer House* or Williams's *Camino Real*, would turn up to bewilder Broadway and then swiftly expire.

The rise of off-Broadway in the 1950s would make room for portions of edgy world repertory. Norris Houghton and T. Edward Hambleton's Phoenix Theatre presented for its inaugural 1953–1954 season Sidney Howard's last play, *Madam,*

Will You Walk?; Shakespeare's seldom-seen *Coriolanus*; a new, sung-through comic opera adaptation of *The Iliad* and *The Odyssey* called *The Golden Apple*; and *The Seagull*, starring movie great Montgomery Clift as the doomed Constantin. The theatrical needs of the rest of the nation were met by crisscrossing tours of hit Broadway plays and musicals and the steady output of the "little" (community) theaters that had begun springing up after World War I.

A handful of cities had versions of a German *Stadtheater*, founded not by kings or dukes but by charismatic leaders with access to capital. These theaters included the Cleveland Playhouse (1915), the Goodman Theatre (1925) in Chicago, the Alley Theatre (Nina Vance, 1947) in Houston, Arena Stage (Zelda Fichandler, 1952) in Washington, DC, and the New York Shakespeare Festival (Joseph Papp, 1954). Civic heads were turned in December 1961, when an American *choregos*, W. McNeil "Mac" Lowry of the Ford Foundation, announced a $9 million grant to "strengthen the position of these pioneers and to seed new resident theaters." A second Ford grant that same year launched Theater Communications Group, a centralized advocacy organization for professional American nonprofit theaters devoted to the dissemination of knowledge and research and to the development of standard practices and organizational efficiencies for the field.

Follow the money: within five years, some twenty-six new theater companies were born, with the Guthrie Theater an especially intriguing case. In October 1959, Tyrone Guthrie, Peter Zeisler, and Oliver Rea, disillusioned by the commercial racket, placed a small invitation on the drama page of the *New York Times* seeking responses from cities that would be interested in supporting a resident theater. Of the seven replies, the Twin Cities were most eager, and so began the Minnesota Theater Company. By the time it opened its doors with *Hamlet* in 1963, the Ford Foundation had provided a funding cushion to safeguard the theater against loss for its first three seasons.

The run-up to Kingman Brewster's 1966 job offer was interesting for those, like scholar-critic Brustein, on the theater beat. In 1964, impresario Sol Hurok brought Jean-Louis Barrault's Théâtre de France over for three weeks at City Center. The company performed Beaumarchais's *The Marriage of Figaro* (with costumes by Yves St. Laurent); Racine's consonant-crunching verse tragedy *Andromaque*; a recent Ionesco, *Le Piéton de l'air*; Beckett's contemporary classic *Happy Days*, starring company codirector Madeleine Renaud; and finally, Halévy and Offenbach's comic opera *La Vie parisienne*. The stylistic breadth of their repertory—comedy, tragedy, absurdism, and the cancan—dazzled.

In February 1966, Hurok would import the Comédie-Française for an equally rangy repertory stay. At the end of that September, an act of Congress created the National Endowment for the Arts, "dedicated to supporting excellence in the arts, both the new and established, bringing the arts to all Americans and providing leadership in arts education." American art *legislated* into being? Better late than never.

Once the mortar had cemented the last of the bricks on the Lincoln Center for the Performing Arts, set into motion by John D. Rockefeller, a pressing question on the table was how to fill its cavernous, state-of-the-art 1,700-seat Vivian Beaumont Theatre. The first answer was the launch of the Repertory Theater of Lincoln Center, under the direction of Jules Irving and Herbert Blau. The Beaumont opened on October 21, 1965, with a rare revival of Büchner's massive *Danton's Death*, to be followed by the world premiere of Arthur Miller's *After the Fall*, directed by Elia Kazan. Both productions were loud and public disappointments. Blau left after a year; Irving produced sporadically until 1972.

Pondering Brewster's phone call, Brustein knew that the bumpy ride at Lincoln Center, whose productions he routinely panned in the *New Republic*, was a clear indication that a theater with serious intentions could not be made from scratch. Not in one year. Not in five. Possibly not even in ten. Conversely, how could the work of the Comédie-Française *fail* to dazzle spectators when its traditions and techniques had been passed on for nearly three centuries? Could that be made to happen in New Haven, two hours northeast of the Broadway circus? How long would it take?

Brustein had started theaters before. With six other like-minded refugees from the YSD, Brustein formed Studio 7, acting in an adventurous summer season (Strindberg, Lorca, and Wedekind) at the Provincetown Playhouse in Greenwich Village in 1949. From 1953 to 1959, he was a member of Group 20, one of the earliest classical repertory companies in the country, playing summers at Wellesley College's Theatre on the Green. In thinking about creating a theater to link with the school, Brustein looked to the enduring state theaters with schools attached to them; prime examples were the Moscow Art Theatre School and the National Conservatory of Dramatic Art at the Comédie-Française.

Brewster's thinking couldn't have been that dissimilar from Brustein's. Already he had watched the School of Architecture lure notable practitioners to its faculty with outstanding results. Why couldn't the drama school transform itself into a place where student apprentices would work alongside, and learn from, professionals in the field? Moreover, since the Shubert Theatre on College Street had taken a nosedive in recent years as a Broadway tryout stop, Brewster, contemplating what today are termed quality-of-life issues, was intrigued with the idea of starting a serious theater that would add cultural value to the Yale community and all of New Haven.

Regal in bearing, autocratic as necessary, high-minded, and often high-handed, Robert Brustein was nevertheless neither a king nor an act of Congress. Thirty-nine years old, he had first been an actor. "I loved acting," he recalled fifty years later. "That's really what I wanted to do, more than anything." He directed from time to time. Not yet a playwright, he wrote criticism, often scathing and dismissive of the event at hand and, by extension, the commercial system of a national culture that encouraged no alternatives to bromidic middlebrow pap. No theater in recent or distant memory, certainly not in America, where consciously serious drama had taken root only some fifty years before, had ever been started by a public intellectual.

Could a company with the breadth and depth of Barrault's Théâtre de France be created from the ashes—for there would be fires—of the YSD? Would the university stand the heat? Would it pick up the check? To what extent was Brewster willing to be a latter-day, Ivy League *choregos*? "Kingman had a way of betting on people," concludes Chauncey. "Ten percent of the time he was wrong. He was right about Bob. I don't think he ever looked back." The radical hired the radical.

———

Brustein's appointment was headline news, and his pronouncements always made good copy. Here he opines on the effect of American plays in that summer of 1966: "They exude an ooze of squalid contentment that work[s] like a narcotic on an audience already stupefied by affluence." Remarks like these prompted a *Yale Daily News* interviewer to write in late September that "sometimes, Mr. Brustein seems to speak with righteous anger about the state of American theatre. At others, one wonders if he is exaggerating the glories of European theatre. Will a new American theatre arise from all this activity? It will be an interesting decade before we know."

With the school, Brustein moved swiftly, instantly doubling the faculty to forty-four members with the help of a $350,000 grant from the Rockefeller Foundation. Some faculty were recruited to teach only, while others were hired to teach and work at the Rep. Brustein's first hire was Stella Adler, legendary acting guru and Group Theater alumna. His second was Gordon Rogoff (YC '52), another talent of many hats, whose comprehensive critique of Lee Strasberg in the *Tulane Drama Review* had so impressed Brustein that, spotting Rogoff on a springtime stroll in Central Park, he offered him a job as associate dean. His third was playwright Arnold Weinstein, whose "Arnoldisms" would become legendary. Michael

Posnick ('69) remembers him saying to a playwright in class, "This is the worst writing since the invention of the [*dramatic pause*] hand."

As things turned out, the fires of transition weren't restricted solely to the old regime. Adler would leave after two years, never satisfied with a compromise she had struck with her boss regarding student participation in Yale Rep productions. After moving him to the directing department, Brustein would decide in January 1969 to accept Rogoff's resignation under murkier circumstances caused by escalating strife between the school and the nascent theater. Directing student David Shookhoff ('69) characterizes their clash as an emphasis on product versus process: "Brustein was all about results, powerful visible results. And Gordon was more coming out of the sense of the Open Theatre, Joe Chaikin, 'let's noodle around together and something beautiful will result.'" (For the record, Rogoff returned in 1986 to the dramaturgy and dramatic criticism program and taught Beckett, Shakespeare, and opera, and he led criticism workshops for three decades.)

Conflicts arose between the needs—a Venn diagram of time, space, people, and money—of the drama school and Yale Rep. In the earliest, woolliest years, students received mixed messages about their priorities. For the actor, was an understudy rehearsal for *The Rivals* at the Rep more important to attend than a rehearsal for a school production of *The Flies* or a directing student's thesis project? For the design students, were build crew hours more important than finishing set models for Ming Cho Lee or costume sketches for Jeanne Button? What about Cabaret commitments? What if your instructor was an incompetent/alcoholic/racist/indifferent/predatory/mean-spirited disaster?

For answers to this last question, one complained to Brustein or Administrative Dean Howard Stein or simply cut class after class. Student talents could be pressed into service at the risk of their health and their relations with their classmates. Twenty-three design students and crew members worked round-the-clock for an entire month building the *Prometheus Bound* set. Brustein favored (and produced) certain student playwrights while ignoring others. Ditto student actors. In her final year of training, Meryl Streep ('75) had significant roles in *five* of the six Yale Rep mainstage shows, on top of classwork and school productions.

Three regimes later, matriculants know that their training will include working for Yale Rep, often on multiple occasions and in different capacities. Student actors graduate with an Equity card from a combination of Rep understudy assignments and speaking roles cast by the chair of the acting program in consultation with the professional director and the playwright (if extant). The resident stage manager and the chairs of design slot their students to assistantships on Rep shows, which ideally lead to at least one full professional production credit in their third year. Technical design and production students are lucky to leave the University Theatre (UT) or the Rep for a cigarette break. Dramaturgy students can hold assistant or leading dramaturgy positions at the Rep. Directors assist the professionals. Third-year management students run marketing, ticketing, development, public relations, and education departments in conjunction with their professors. (Third-year playwrights are guaranteed production in the Carlotta Festival of New Plays.)

As part of their financial aid packages, all students complete Rep work-study assignments—they build, run, and strike crews; usher; and so on. Actress Frances McDormand ('82) firmly believes that "you have to learn to sweep the stage before you can be on it." In her second year, a work-study assignment put her backstage at Yale Rep on *Hedda Gabler* as a dresser. She also did laundry for the production as a costume assistant and understudied the role of Mrs. Evsted (a fact she does not recall). During one performance, she was passing the time in the green room with classmate David Alan Grier ('81)—"He told great stories, as you can imagine"—such that McDormand was five minutes late in helping the actress playing the maid, Berta, into her costume. "She gave me such a dressing down. She was right to do it. *She* had an entrance, and I did not."

Classes, which are *not* optional, are held Monday through Friday from 9:00 a.m. until 2:00 p.m. Design, directing, and acting students also have Saturday classes. Yale Rep work assignments have first priority. There are two rehearsal periods: 2:30 to 6:30 p.m. and 7:00 to 11:30 p.m., and cabarets rehearse from 11:00 p.m. to 1:00 a.m. Company day off is Sunday. Motivated students will always work to their utmost—and often beyond—but it is safe to say that the daily triage *necessary* to complete a Yale drama school MFA has, on paper at least, lessened in intensity over the years.

For his new theater, Brustein announced two productions in late September. Jonathan Miller would direct Aeschylus's *Prometheus Bound* in a new adaptation by star American poet Robert Lowell, and the Open Theatre would bring their production of Megan Terry's antiwar musical, *Viet Rock*, to New Haven. Three weeks later he promised *Ubu Roi*; Edward Bond's *Saved*; another musical, *Dynamite Tonite!*; and John Arden's *Armstrong's Last Goodnight*. Strong stuff all.

Lacking a resident company and projects in process, Brustein scheduled two works he or Rogoff had already seen: *Viet Rock* and a production of *Endgame* by Philadelphia's Theatre of Living Arts. As for "actors' opera" *Dynamite Tonite!*, he had already presented it in another medium. In 1960, librettist Arnold Weinstein began writing an examination of what he considered the terminal American "symptom of vanity called winning," something of a companion piece to his

THE THEATRE OF REVOLT

Anyone wondering in 1966 what kind of theater the new dean would be interested in making at Yale needed to look no further than *The Theatre of Revolt: An Approach to the Modern Drama*, published two years before by Atlantic–Little, Brown to widespread acclaim. Brustein's first book is a comparative study of eight "rebel dramatists"—Ibsen, Strindberg, Chekhov, Shaw, Brecht, Pirandello, O'Neill, and Genet—all of whom, through different dramaturgical lenses and in different cultural contexts, break with what he terms the theater of communion—a centuries-old locus of certainty, belief, and transcendence—to forge, with a dissident stance and a rejection of authority, a theater of revolt. In his words, this modern theater is "the temple of a priest without a God, without an orthodoxy, without even much of a congregation, who conducts his service within the hideous architecture of the absurd."

From its inception, Yale Rep has revived (Genet excepted) the works of these vital contrarians. Their claims will always challenge both the artists conducting the service and the audiences that form a sometimes-restive congregation. To this day, *Theatre of Revolt* remains a gauntlet thrown down against the tidy assurances of American drama and is as essential a read for Yale playwrights and dramaturgs as Aristotle's *Poetics*, Shaw's *Ibsenism*, Brecht's *Organum*, Bentley's *The Playwright as Thinker*, and Brook's *The Empty Space*. ◆

Brustein's first broadside (1964)

off-Broadway hit *The Red Eye of Love*. He sent a draft to French composer Darius Milhaud, who suggested he contact his prizewinning former student William Bolcom as a potential collaborator. Bolcom submitted a full first pass of the score to Weinstein in a swift three months.

The Actor's Studio Company produced *Dynamite* off-Broadway in 1964. Brutal notices closed it on opening night, but Brustein caught the one showing on Weinstein's invitation. Charmed by its nonesuch nature, Brustein presented an abridged *Dynamite* with a single piano on a public-television series called *The Opposition Theater* in the spring of 1966. Six months later, for Yale, he reunited director Paul Sills, who had been replaced in the off-Broadway rehearsal period by Mike Nichols, with most of the original cast intact, supplemented by three student actors. The writers were happy for the opportunity to restore a good deal of the original spirit of the piece, and Brustein was happy to expose his students to the "serious fun" working style of Sills and his crew of actors, many of whom had trained with him at Second City in Chicago.

Dynamite Tonite! is set in a supply bunker beneath a battlefield. After twenty years of combat, the sergeant has begun to question his purpose and realizes that he and his prisoner, who speaks a wacky language of Weinstein's invention, are more alike than different. In act 2, unarmed enemy soldiers burst in to celebrate the end of the war, although neither side knows who won. In the mayhem, the prisoner bayonets the captain. The sergeant returns, and the prisoner moves toward a keg of dynamite. They share a standoff—is truce possible? Can humanity trump tribalism? Just as the sergeant drops his bayonet, saying, "I was always for you. I like you," the prisoner drops a match on the dynamite. Postexplosion, everybody is dead, except for the blind, one-handed Private Smiley, who wishes the audience good-night.

Dynamite combines the capitalist critique of *Mother Courage and Her Children*, the "war as daily grind" mood of Sherriff's *Journey's End*, the bitter comedy of Heller's *Catch-22*, and the improvisational spirit of Behan's *The Hostage*. Sharing space with Weinstein's puns, non sequiturs, and Dadaist lyrics and Bolcom's nonpareil musical sampler of everything from Sousa to barbershop to tango is an underlying sense of horror to match that year's CBS News broadcasts showing the destruction of Cam Ne: as old Vietnamese men and women begged them to stop, US Marines ignited the thatched roofs of their village.

Dynamite Tonight! has a tone that is emphatically *silly*. Playwright John Guare ('63), then at Yale on a fellowship, claims to have seen *Dynamite Tonite!* fourteen times, but some critics, audience members, and drama students found its antics tiresomely unsubtle, unaware that one of the *OED* root definitions of the word

Eugene Troobnick and Alvin Epstein in Bolcom and Weinstein's *Dynamite Tonite!* (1966)
PHOTO © GENE COOK

silly is "soulful." Years later, literary manager Michael Feingold ('69) and associate artistic director Alvin Epstein were singing *Dynamite* songs at a cast party. In earshot was Brustein, then contemplating a tenth-anniversary season for the Rep that would include revivals of three Yale Rep "favorites." The return of *Dynamite* in 1975 met with much the same response—delight for its practitioners, daffy soul for its partisans, and a head-scratcher for the unenthused.

No one who has seen it has ever forgotten *Prometheus Bound*. Brustein and many other witnesses point to *Prometheus* as the touchstone production for when the theater first found its identity. MFA playwright David Epstein ('67), who would have four of his works produced at Yale Rep, says that the production was perhaps the greatest piece of theater he has ever seen. "It magnetized my life. I started going every night, *every* night; I can still recite lines from Lowell's adaptation. Later, it took me two weeks to understand why I was depressed—I missed *Prometheus*." Playwriting classmate Lonnie Carter ('69) stood at the back at the closing performance with Epstein. Neither man takes credit for the line, but Carter recalls one of them saying, "There should be a way for us to see this once a week for the rest of our lives."

Boston Brahmin Robert Lowell had won a Pulitzer Prize, the National Book Award, and, in 1961, the Bollingen Poetry Translation Prize. *Old Glory*, his trilogy of one-act verse plays adapted from Hawthorne and Melville stories, won five Obie awards in its 1964 premiere at the American Place Theatre. The NEA gave him time and money for *Prometheus Bound*, awarding Yale Rep its first federal grant of $25,000—Lowell got $10,000 to finish the adaptation in residence, and the theater received $15,000 for production costs.

Aeschylus's static tragedy gave Lowell "a blessed freedom from plot." Half of the lines in his adaptation are his invention, but nothing is modernized. He writes in the published version of the play, "There are no tanks or cigarette lighters. No contemporary statesman is parodied. Yet I think my own concerns and worries and those of the times seep in. Using prose instead of verse, I was free to tone down the poetic eloquence and shove in any thought that occurred to me and seemed to fit."

Lights up. Power and Force drag Prometheus onstage. Zeus is punishing his former ally for giving fire—and hope—to the suffering race of humans. Hephaestus enters with a hammer and chains and binds his cousin to the rock. Left alone to suffer, Prometheus plays surly host to a series of characters urging capitulation: he is to either reveal to Zeus the names of the mother and son who are fated to bring him down or take his eternal punishment, to be repeated every day without surcease. On his final refusal, the horror begins: "Force and Power appear and stand behind Prometheus. Increasing darkness, lightning, thunder. Prometheus and his rock begin to sink and disappear."

There was little question as to who would direct: Jonathan Miller, one-fourth of the male quartet in *Beyond the Fringe*, a British comedy stage revue that had been a smash hit first in London and then on Broadway. After *Fringe*, Miller began a long and far-reaching directing career in theater and opera, gaining an American foothold with Lowell's *Old Glory* trilogy. A doctor by training, Miller was equally steeped in and enthralled by anthropology, sociology, and philosophy. He abhorred unnatural theatrical conventions, most especially the overdramatic Shakespearean voice and manner. His ability to create stage behavior that corresponded to what people actually do was one of the things that impressed Brustein.

Ubiquitous today, "concept" productions of classic works—*The Merry Wives of Windsor* set in a California trailer park, a Third Reich *Richard III*, a Rat Pack *Rigoletto*, and *South Pacific* performed by psychiatric inmates—were a novel development in the mid-1960s. Miller and his set designer, Michael Annals, located

Jonathan Miller, Irene Worth, Robert Brustein, and David Hurst on rehearsal break for *Prometheus Bound* (1967)
PHOTO © SEAN KERNAN

their *Prometheus Bound* in a shattered castle in an unspecified European culture in the first half of the seventeenth century, not because they spun the globe or flipped a calendar in search of a "relevant" transposition for the tragedy, but because a visceral connection, grounded in intellectual exploration, could be made between the concerns of Aeschylus and Lowell and the Zeitgeist under consideration. Whether the audiences or the critics grasped the concept whole cloth was secondary to the collaborative inquiry of the artists. In his program note, Miller writes, "*Prometheus* is all about power and tyranny.... The 17th century saw the rise and fall of peculiarly horrible politics..., the Thirty Years War, regicide and the brief success of military theocracy. I hope we have helped Robert Lowell and Aeschylus to release new images and ideas... as human beings continue their lethal efforts at survival."

Miller rehearsed his cast, whose ranks included Kenneth Haigh, the original Jimmy Porter in *Look Back in Anger*, as the doomed hero, Irene Worth as Io, and a young Ron Liebman as storm trooper Hermes, in the basement of an all-night restaurant where the Yale Center for British Art now stands. Student actor David Clennon ('68) sat in on rehearsals whenever he could: "I associate my consciousness of the Viet Nam horror with *Prometheus Bound* and Robert Lowell and Jonathan Miller and those four or five actors who were bringing this quaint old Greek myth to extraordinary life in ways that I didn't even comprehend. I just knew it was hypnotic to watch. I could feel, in this evolving play, a faint reverberation from what was going on just outside the theater, thirty feet away, on the streets of New Haven. Robert Lowell had, somehow, somewhere, expressed the view that America's war in Vietnam was morally wrong. Five months after *Prometheus* closed, after a lot of other awakenings, I turned in my draft card at a resistance ceremony in the Arlington Street Church in Boston."

Over at the University Theatre, after removing the stage floor, students and technical crew members built a sixty-three-foot-high set that began in the basement, a series of platforms with niches for decaying statues made to suggest an endlessly vertical lighthouse. David Shookhoff ('69) remembers "being dragooned late-night into the aisles in the University Theatre with sheets of Styrofoam, and we were carving them with torches to make them look decayed. . . . We were given a general idea of what they were supposed to look like and we were going crazy, free-forming."

The response to *Prometheus Bound* was as monumental as its design. With the biggest advance in the forty-one-year history of the YSD, *Prometheus* drew a starry audience up from New York for opening, including Robert Motherwell, Stephen Spender, Philip Roth, George Plimpton, Susan Sontag, and Broadway Mephistopheles David Merrick. Peter Brook said to Rogoff at intermission, "Gordon, I suppose this means it's time to get back to the word," and Merrick instantly piped up behind them, "The name of the game is still entertainment."

Walter Kerr reviewed *Prometheus* favorably in the *New York Times*, a cue for Brustein to begin his dance of the seven veils—"Now you review us, now you don't"—with the New York press. Brustein would never really come to terms with Yale Rep coverage. The reliable scourge was now in the line of critical fire and took things personally. Good reviews he might hang in the lobby; pull quotes would pepper promotional materials; bad reviews he never forgot. Critics who wouldn't make room to assess an individual production or performance in the context of the theater's mission or against a season of performances especially drew his wrath. In the case of Kerr on *Prometheus*, Brustein announced, "We're grateful for the review. We hope he never comes again."

Jonathan Miller once wrote, "Classics are simply residues, maps left over from earlier cultures; they invite you to make some sort of imaginative movement." As the history of Yale Rep and American theater unfolds, the imaginative movements intuited by directors would lead, in less intellectually probing or overtly sensationalizing hands, to a generation of concept productions that were relevant at their best and arbitrary or gimmicky at their worst. Yale Rep—and its artistic

THE UNIVERSITY THEATRE

In 1924, Edward S. Harkness donated over $1 million to establish a drama department within the Yale School of Fine Arts and to pay for the construction of the University Theatre (UT), where the new department could be housed. The brick and stone Collegiate Gothic–style building was designed by Blackall, Clapp, and Whittemore and constructed from 1925 to 1926. The proscenium theater can seat 654 patrons on the ground floor and in the balcony. Within the building are several design shops, the undergraduate Yale Dramatic Association office, and a portion of the YSD / Yale Rep administrative offices, including that of the dean / artistic director.

The original stone facade of the UT was refreshed with limestone and granite in 1931 by architect James Gamble Rogers, who also designed Sterling Memorial Library, Payne Whitney Gymnasium, and Harkness Tower. Behind the facade, in the center of the building, a tall, windowless rectangular tower—the fly space—rises imposingly.

Acknowledging that a standard proscenium layout can be seen as an obstacle that separates the actors from their audience, former design department cochair Michael Yeargan ('74) appreciates the UT for its classicism: "It has a proper fly loft at the proper height, decent sightlines, and all the things that decades of proscenium plays required when it was built." The UT also boasted at one time one of the first preset lighting boards, invented in 1947 by Yale professor of theater design and technology George C. Izenour.

For his first three seasons, Brustein battled for UT spaces with the Yale Dramat. The repurpose of the Calvary Baptist Church in 1969 alleviated some of that initial pressure, but it is safe to say that room for rehearsals, design studios and shops, offices, classrooms, and storage will always be at a premium for the YSD / Yale Rep complex. ◆

The University Theatre
COURTESY OF YALE
REPERTORY THEATRE

director—would prove no exception. For every positive (Brustein's Black Mass *Don Juan*), there would be a negative (Brustein's Stonehenge *Macbeth*).

Novels and novelists commanded more cultural space in the 1960s. It was news when a ranking member of the boys' club of publishing, which included Norman Mailer, William Styron, John Updike, Philip Roth, Kurt Vonnegut, Saul Bellow, Joseph Heller, and E. L. Doctorow, brought out a new book bristling with the consciousness and authorial ventriloquism native to fiction. Brustein knew many of these men socially and, finding the current state of playwriting nugatory at best, had the notion that they should be encouraged to write plays for his new theater.

In the history of American letters, only Thornton Wilder managed during his lifetime to succeed in both genres. During the Brustein years, crossover opportunities were provided to Jules Feiffer (*God Bless* [1968]), William Styron (*In the Clap Shack* [1973]), and Isaac Bashevis Singer (*The Mirror* [1973] and *Schlemiel the First* [1974]). Joseph Heller's *We Bombed in New Haven*, "a surrealist comedy about all wars," produced in Brustein's second season, was probably the most successful of the five.

American troop buildup in Vietnam was escalating along with the protest movement against "McNamara's war" and organized resistance to the draft. Given the moment, Brustein's politics, and Heller's prominence, how could Brustein not green-light the first act of a first play by the author of the antiwar, antiauthoritarian, antiheroic *Catch-22*? Heller promised to complete act 2 by the fall of 1967, and he began sending six handwritten pages a day to New Haven.

In accordance with his patron's hopes, Heller did not think small. *We Bombed in New Haven* is ambitious, coruscating, and very funny. From the first page of the Yale Rep typescript:

> TIME: always the present, the exact time at which the play is performed.
> PLACE: the theatre, city, and country in which the play is presented.

After two pages of detailed scenic description, symptomatic of novelist-playwrights since Henry James, the script reads, "A large clock on the wall keeps actual time accurately throughout the play." Uh-oh. Real time is a high dramaturgical bar, requiring continuous action, with no scene changes or temporal jumps to gap plot and character development. In terms of action and tone, as more than one viewer remarked, *We Bombed in New Haven* was *Dynamite Tonite!* without the songs and more than a nod to Kubrick's *Dr. Strangelove*. As the play begins, Captain Starkey announces to his men that their mission, just in from high command, is to bomb the nonexistent Constantinople off the map.

Moments later, Ruth, a nurse making rounds with coffee and doughnuts, "breaks" character by saying, "I've got talent, that's what I've got. But they won't let me use it. I don't even have any good lines." This personal interruption introduces the second level of craziness to the proceedings, consonant with the double meaning of Heller's title, which references the tradition of fixing Broadway plays and musicals in tryout cities. New Haven had hosted decades of theatrical bombs at the Shubert.

Metatheater is another high bar. Plays that deliberately acknowledge that they are an imitation of an action happening *right now in front of you* were revitalized as a convention earlier in the century by Luigi Pirandello, whose dramatic output spins countless variations on the philosophical conundrum of illusion versus reality. Heller, giving perhaps the most candidly sour set of rehearsal interviews in Yale Rep history, said, "They told me it was something like *Six Characters in Search of an Author* [Pirandello's masterpiece], but I had never seen or read the play. I finally read it and I don't think much of it." So be it, but Heller—abetted by director Larry Arrick and another nimble company of improvisational actors (and drama students) trained in Second City techniques—makes excellent use of the metatheatrical toolbox.

In act 2, the metascrew is turned to increasingly somber effect. A soldier's stagestruck kid brother, eleven years old, enlists. Sergeant Henderson, who has assumed that his part is too important to get killed off, begins to suspect that the plot is plotting against him and so initiates a rebellion in which the set is destroyed. The major has the theater doors locked. The Huntsman and the Golfer, a pair of drop-ins representing war profiteers, find and kill Henderson "<u>for real</u>" (the underlining is Heller's) and send in a first replacement to Captain Starkey from a list of three hundred.

The new recruit is Starkey's Son, who asks, "Pop, you had nineteen years to save me from this. When I was born, why didn't you do something? Didn't you care?" Starkey lets him escape through a window. Is the exit real, or is it theater? Starkey's Son reenters as the second candidate, who asks this time, "Will you even weep for me?" And the next? All are Starkey's Sons—a grim visual pun on the title of Arthur Miller's first successful play. The captain finally sacrifices his son to the war machine, and brokenly attempts to convince the audience that they've seen only a play before the curtain falls.

A novelist submits his contracted manuscript, edits proofs, and then waits for it to be a book, a process that takes a year on average. Thus Heller wasn't aware that new plays labor mightily in their month before birth and that the expectant father would do well to spend some time in the delivery room. He didn't know until he came to a run-through that his preproduction agreement with Arrick, approved by

Brustein, meant his unfinished text would serve as a springboard for the company to change, cut, or reorder his lines. Or *improvise* new ones. Evidence of its difficult birth—three manila envelopes stuffed with script changes—remain on reserve in the Haas Family Arts Library.

When *We Bombed in New Haven* opened in December, the critical response was, as *Variety* might say, "respectful but mixed." Audience demand, however, was strong enough for Brustein to schedule an additional week of performances. In the UT lobby were sale copies of the first issue of *yale/theatre* and a notice for the next Rep show—Pirandello's (!) *Henry IV*. Brustein's dream of a flexible acting ensemble was gaining contours: Kenneth Haigh, whose Prometheus had been so indelible that student actors imitated his line readings months after the show closed, would play Henry IV. Three actors with prominent roles in *We Bombed in New Haven*—Stacy Keach, Anthony Holland, and Michael Lombard—were featured in *Henry IV* and would turn up again in either *Three Sisters* or *Coriolanus* before the season was over.

Brustein made an early miscalculation in February 1968 when, erroneously assuming himself capable of sharing power, he promoted Larry Arrick to the new position of artistic director. Arrick lasted five times the length of William Henry Harrison's one-month term as president in 1841, but no hard feelings seemed to remain. Arrick stayed on, teaching, developing various *Story Theatre* pieces and productions, and directing the premiere of Terrence McNally's *Where Has Tommy Flowers Gone?* before leaving in 1971.

For Yale Rep's third season, Brustein announced a single theme: violence. In *Making Scenes*, his retrospective account of the "turbulent years" he underwent in New Haven putting his ideals into practice, his chapter title for the 1968–1969 academic year is "Armageddon."

In the fall of 1968, how was a young person to find purpose studying the arts of make-believe in a privileged environment at one remove from a collective, globally spreading struggle for racial and economic justice? In his opening address to the drama school, Brustein said, "Those of you who are in revolt are rebelling not only against something, but on behalf of certain values—courtesy, decency, generosity, peace. It is crucial that no matter how beset you may become, you try to maintain those values in themselves."

Peace? Absolutely. Courtesy and generosity were a taller order for those politicized by the incremental tragedies of the assassination of Martin Luther King and

YALE/THEATRE AND THEATER

The position of theater critic is neither respected nor remunerative, but someone has to do it. In the hands of an iconoclast like George Bernard Shaw, who hilariously ground his axe against the dramatic output of many a London season to devastating effect, theater criticism becomes its own form of art.

Small wonder that Brustein would encourage the earliest generation of dramatic criticism students to establish a magazine in 1968 as a "gathering of responses to real events." Honor Moore ('70), its first managing editor, credits Gordon Rogoff (YC '52) with the title: "Gordon had a real gift for facilitating exploratory conversation among students. And that's why it ended up being called *yale/theatre*.... It wasn't *Yale: Theatre*; it wasn't *Yale, Theatre*; it wasn't *Yale Theatre*; it was yale slash theatre. The name placed the two ideas in tension."

Whether weighing in on the Living Theatre's incendiary visit and *Prometheus Bound*, printing early works by Yale playwrights, introducing readers to important international dramatists or innovative American playwrights, filing reports from festivals, or reviewing books, *yale/theatre* hewed to the proposition that theater making is a symptomatic endeavor of a healthy society.

In its first decades, under the editorships of Michael Feingold ('69), Rocco Landesman ('72, DFA '76), Robert Marx ('72, DFA '74), Joel Schechter ('72, DFA '73; who changed the title to *Theater* in 1978), and Erika Munk, the student-staffed magazine paid closer attention to Yale Rep activities, interviewing and publishing the works of August Wilson, Athol Fugard, and Winterfest playwrights. Today, the simultaneous erosion of print media and the human attention span has reduced the field of mainstream theater criticism to consumer report checklists. Tom Sellar ('97, DFA '03), *Theater* editor since 2003, has responded to these shifts by expanding the reach and focus of the magazine to include more and more international voices. Fifty years on, if theater that genuinely *matters* is in arrears on American shores, Sellar and his discerning contributors cross the globe to find it elsewhere and—with wit and provocation—report back. ◆

The inaugural issue of *yale/theatre* (1968)
COURTESY OF YALE REPERTORY THEATRE

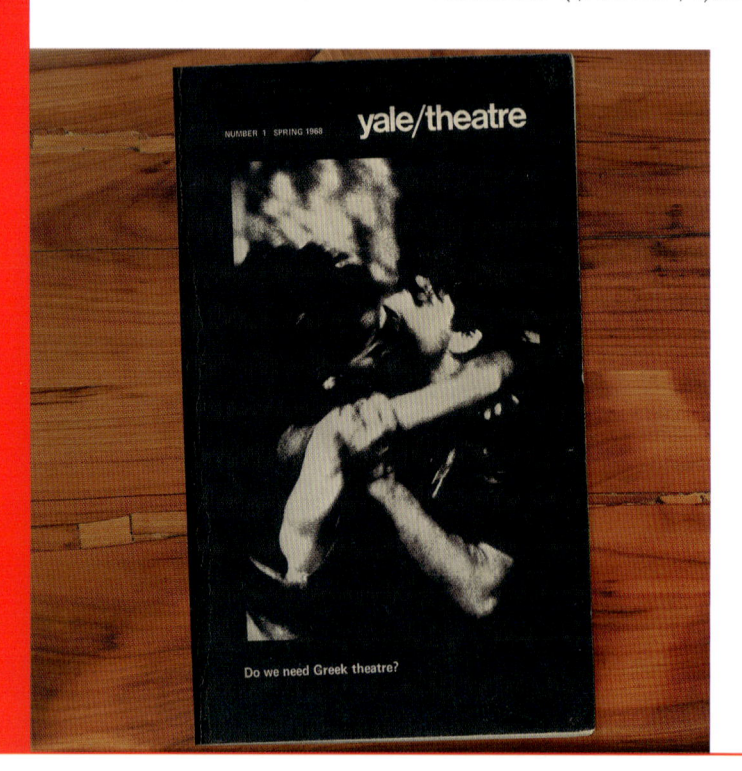

its violent, civic aftershocks; the assassination of Robert Kennedy; the brutality of the Chicago Democratic Convention; and the climbing body counts in Southeast Asia. Alternatives to collegial courtesy were manifest: one could take over buildings, as at Columbia, where students successfully protested both a plan to displace Harlem residents with the construction of a new gymnasium and the university's refusal to resign from a Pentagon think tank. Or one could take to the streets, like the restive Parisian students who struck against capitalism and imperialism, a movement that quickly spread to factories and unions all over France, bringing the economy to a halt and sparking battles complete with barricades and riot police. The objectives and tactics of Mai Soixante-Huit were taken up by students as close as London, Berlin, Madrid, and Rome and as far away as Brazil.

Brustein, whose sympathies were with revolution, had been cast against type in the role of Establishment Figure. Detractors found him to be a neoconservative reactionary. Supporters, observing the queue of students waiting for an audience with demands in hand, knew he was trying to hold his institution together in a Yale-wide maelstrom. Why go to classes? Why was the school even open? Why was the Rep producing *plays*? Why was it charging admission? Why wasn't it donating its income to the Black Panthers, or to local charities, or to the peace movement? Why weren't they taking the theater to the streets?

To this last question, Brustein furnished an answer he would always regret: the Living Theatre (see box). An early fan of Julian Beck and Judith Malina's off-Broadway company, he had not realized that during their recent years of peregrination they had begun, during a time when a central dialectic in the theater was the word versus the body, to eschew text in favor of ritual. *Paradise Now*, a controversy at the Avignon Festival, doggedly foregrounds the body over text. Lonnie Carter ('69) rued that the original poetic mission of the Living Theatre had shifted to become a "theater of underwear." "We playwrights didn't cotton to it. For us, they were like that Texas expression, 'All hat, no cattle.'"

When the Living Theatre departed with, according to the *Yale Daily News*, "their yelps, their rags, their guts and their smell," many were relieved, many experienced loss, and a few went with them. Within six weeks, Richard Nixon was elected president. Responding to growing student complaints about lacking a meaningful forum for their political ideas and aesthetic concerns, Brustein permitted the creation of the Yale Cabaret (see box). It opened with a $2.00 annual membership fee for students, a $3.00 fee for civilians, and no liquor license, and Brustein's season of violence began with the American premiere of Edward Bond's *Saved*, its ten performances alternating in repertory with two new works by drama school playwrights, another Rep first.

THE LIVING THEATRE COMES TO TOWN

So much ink has been spilled about the events of late September 1968 that, peering through the lens of fifty years, one eschews synthesis in favor of a potpourri of salient facts and citations.

- After four years of self-imposed exile, during which their Artaudian brand of theater of involvement played ninety-five cities and ten foreign countries, the Living Theatre, a thirty-two-member company led by Judith Malina and Julian Beck, returned to America to perform from their repertory at Yale Rep before moving on to the Brooklyn Academy of Music and a national tour.
- The works to be performed: *Mysteries and Smaller Pieces*, *Antigone*, *Frankenstein*, and *Paradise Now*. Tickets were free.
- In *Making Scenes*, Brustein wrote, "While in residence at Yale, the Becks proselytized among our students.... During one such meeting... I tried to dispute their assumption, central to anarchism, that human instinct is essentially decent and generous, and twisted only by external social laws... but my professorial arguments proved no match for their Pied Piper appeal."
- The *New Haven Register* commented that "playing and starving together have given [the Living Theatre] ensemble a rapport and awareness that would make the Green Bay Packers envious."
- *Paradise Now*, devised for the 1968 Avignon Festival, was the show that got them into trouble.
- Tom Walker, audience member and Yale College junior in 1968, remembers that "*Paradise Now* was a voyage up an eight-rung ladder to paradise. After the first scene, the actors had stripped to the legal limit. There was no set, but the whole theater space became the set, as the actors often invaded the audience; and the audience was free to invade the stage. Each rung toward paradise contained a ritual, a vision, and an action. The text derived from a scenario of chanted slogans, that is, 'I'm not allowed to travel without a passport.' 'I don't know how to stop the war.' 'I'm not allowed to take my clothes off.' Between each rung on the ladder the actors paused to permit the audience to react, or not. Sometimes these pauses would become scenes or confrontations lasting many minutes that could

Members of the Living Theatre performing *Paradise Now* in the University Theatre (1968)
PHOTO © GIANFRANCO MANTEGNA

overwhelm the play. With the nudity—often audience members would undress completely—the political content, the ritual theater style, and sometimes a good deal of marijuana, the play would slowly take its course. At the end, the company would sound the chant, 'The theater is in the street, the theater is in the street,' and actors would accompany audience members out the doors."

- A police report in the *New Haven Register* on September 27, 1968, read, "25 Naked in Street / Theatre's Outdoor Finale Brings Police on the Run," and "Shortly after midnight, at the conclusion of the three-and-a-half-hour performance of *Paradise Now*, police were sent to York Street where a group of 300–400 people were blocking the street. About twenty-five of them were completely nude and many men were clad only in trousers."
- While bystanders sang "America the Beautiful," six men and four women, including Beck, Malina, performers, and audience members, were arrested

- and charged with indecent exposure, breach of the peace, and resisting arrest.
- Robert Brustein maintained that "the police misunderstood the significance of the event."
- James Ahern, New Haven chief of police, said, "As far as we're concerned, art stops at the door of the theatre, and then we apply community standards."
- Julian Beck testified that "my loincloth was quite adequate and firmly constructed."
- Released on their own recognizance, Beck and Malina promised to keep future performances inside the theater. An estimated two thousand assembled at the UT for the next *Paradise Now*, nearly inciting a riot.
- Beck commented, "We will never reach everybody. Sometimes hundreds of people walk out of our performances, but we will reach some people. If we turn on one or two people each night, that's enough for us."
- Tom Walker, Living Theatre member for forty-plus years and company historian, said, "I was ready to be taken." ◆

Like *Waiting for Godot*, Edward Bond's *Saved* is a twentieth-century classic whose importance was lost on initial critics outraged, in this instance, by a key event in the play—the stoning to death of a baby in its stroller. Despite a warning from the Lord Chamberlain's Office, which had held the power to approve or deny rights of production since 1843, Bond refused to delete the scene. The historic loophole for evading censorship, used by Shaw, Granville-Barker, and other seditious British playwrights, was to mount a private "club" production under the auspices of the "English Stage Society." *Saved* opened "privately" at London's Royal Court Theatre in 1965, but the Lord Chamberlain's Office banned it anyway and brought charges against the Stage Society. A campaign to overturn the prosecution then began. Laurence Olivier, artistic director of the National Theatre, submitted a defense of the play, a portion of which would be printed in the Yale Rep program.

Saved dramatizes the conditioned anomie in a group of South London working-class youth. Bond's method for exposing their violence was realism, a different tack from Golding's social experiment in *Lord of the Flies* (1954) or Burgess's dystopian *A Clockwork Orange* (1962). With the exception of Odets's *Waiting for Lefty* (1935), America hadn't had a tradition of political theater with group protagonists. In an imagined American rewrite of *Saved*, the stoning would function as the dramatic

FIFTEEN FACTS AND SUPPOSITIONS ABOUT THE YALE CABARET

1. Vernon Hall at 217 Park Street was built in 1931 as a fraternity house for Phi Gamma Delta and was returned to Yale in 1950.
2. Brustein originally envisioned the Cabaret as a "place for students and professionals to work together . . . or apart, depending on the project. It was a space that naturally invited experimentation."
3. The doors opened on November 6, 1968, with Yale Rep company member Alvin Epstein and Marthe Schlamme performing *A Kurt Weill Cabaret*.
4. "The Cabaret has remained in continuous operation since then, producing hundreds of new and not-so-new plays, musical revues, skit comedy shows, improv nights, lectures, dance, performance art, and more" (www.cab50.org/wp2/history).
5. With Wooster Square as metaphorically distant to Yalies as the North Pole, early menus *claimed* that the Cabaret had the only working espresso machine in New Haven.
6. Drama students, prideful malcontents, will forever insist that the best work at Yale happens at the Cabaret.
7. Brustein loosened his programming reins in 1973–1974. For decades now, the Cabaret has been student-run. Producing teams submit proposals every spring to run the Cabaret the following year. A committee of faculty advisors, student peers, and the outgoing team review the competing mission statements, budgets, and play ideas and make their choice.
8. The Cabaret presents five performances a weekend, Thursdays through Saturdays, and programs at least eighteen shows a year. The Friday late show is generally considered the one to catch—the evening has found its footing, the actors aren't overly exhausted, and the audience is stoked for fun.
9. Drama students joyfully sever departmental ties to become crossover artists at the Cabaret. Dramaturgs act. Stage managers design. Managers write. Directors . . . direct.
10. MFA acting student Neal Lerner ('87), spotted scrambling eggs at the stove in *Greater Tuna*, his hirsute triceps jiggling in a sleeveless housedress, generated the longest laugh in Cabaret history. Cross-dressing is a constant, mirthful presence in the basement space, so much so that the Cabaret instituted an annual drag show in 2012.

The Yale Cabaret space, awaiting a next transformation
PHOTO © MARGUERITE ELLIOTT

11. With seating configurations and exit patterns changing every week, the New Haven fire marshal is another constant, less mirthful presence at the Cabaret.

12. The venue wasn't designed as a spawning ground for new plays, but early Cabaret versions of OyamO's *The Resurrection of Lady Lester* (1979) and Dick Beebe's *Vampires in Kodachrome* (1983) were later revised and put into Yale Rep Winterfests; Christopher Durang's *'Dentity Crisis* (1975) moved to Yale Rep three years after its premiere at the Cabaret. Bess Wohl's *Cats Talk Back* (2001) and Tim Acito's musical, *Zanna Don't!* (2002), both enjoyed later off-Broadway success.

13. Since 1968, thousands of student artists have moved on to more visible, significant, and remunerated positions elsewhere, but most recall their youthful escapades at the Cabaret with great fondness.

14. Chefs with their own culinary hopes and dreams and hits and flops come and go at the Cabaret, but the beer and wine remain a bargain.

15. Disaster *always* looms—the show is underrehearsed, actors are sick, the set isn't finished, the lights aren't hung, the program has fifteen typos, the fire marshal ruined the design in the name of safety, and so on—but the doors always open at 6:30 on Thursday, and the show goes on. ◆

David Clennon and Mari Gorman in the American premiere of Edward Bond's *Saved* (1968)
PHOTO © SEAN KERNAN

climax of the play. In Bond's hands, infanticide is but one in a series of events calculated to indict the postwar British social and economic policies that created a generation of affectless prisoner-citizens. That Brustein would entrust the premiere of this important play to Jeff Bleckner ('68), a graduate of the directing program (yet another first), indicated that his vision for the drama school as a serious training ground for the profession was bearing fruit.

Sharing the slot with *Saved* was a pairing of David Epstein's two-character

They Told Me You Came This Way and Anthony Scully's ('69) Brechtian *The Great Chinese Revolution*. *They Told Me* is set in a prison cell "in occupied America." A week with belligerent Alex and soft-spoken Peter passes in short scenes; they at last grudgingly acknowledge a bond. Eventually, their cell door opens. A voice asks, "Which one's Cable?" Alex moves to the door, but as he does so, Peter, laughing, pushes him out of the way and says, "I'm Cable," and then he exits. Alex rushes to the door, which slams in his face.

Director Michael Posnick ('69) explains how what could be perceived as an affirming, Christlike sacrifice on Peter's part originated as an in-school joke about a difficult classmate. "David [Epstein] thought: what would it be like to be in a jail cell with this guy? So, he wrote a play about two guys in a jail cell, one a bully and the other a victim. Periodically a loudspeaker calls a name, a door opens, and the person whose name is called goes out to get shot. At the end of this play, they called the bully's name, and the other guy runs out to die in his place."

Posnick first staged *They Told Me* the year before in the Branford College basement, with the pair of prison cots and pillows resting on a grate, lit from below. "We felt we invented theatre with this production," recalls Epstein with a laugh. Epstein would not be the first Yale writer to feel that his play lost something—intimacy and scale in the case of *They Told Me*—in the process of moving from the claustrophobic Branford basement to the 654-seat University Theatre. As *Saved* and the Epstein/Scully double bill played out their December run, Sam Shepard's *Operation Sidewinder* went into rehearsal. It never opened—another migraine in Brustein's Armageddon year (see box).

Edward Bond would never go down easy in New Haven, which would bear witness to four more of his plays (*Passion* [1972], *Lear* [1973], *Bingo* [1976], and *The Bundle* [1979]), making him the most-produced contemporary playwright of the Brustein era. In his preface to *Lear*, the play that most sorely tested the Rep audience, Bond insists, "I write about violence as naturally as Jane Austen wrote about manners. It would be immoral not to write about violence." His aim with *Lear* was to de-aestheticize the poetry and monumentality of Shakespeare's (already violent) text by recasting it as an act of social critique, setting it in a *Mad Max*–style future where even Cordelia, when given her chance to rule, proves herself a barbarous dictator. Violence always begets more violence. Among the accumulating onstage horrors are eardrum punctures via knitting needle, the rape of pregnant women, the bayoneting and visual disembowelment of Lear's other rebellious daughters, and most memorably, the eyeball extractions used on the captured king. Competing with the gore is a densely imagistic text with a Brechtian sweep and a Shavian sense of paradox about law, power, and justice. Walter Kerr's thoughtful *New York*

OPERATION SIDEWINDER

Over the course of Yale Rep history, two productions—*Lear* (1973) and *The Durango Flash* (1977)—did not finish out their scheduled runs due to audience antipathy and/or actor illness. A handful of shows delayed their first previews because of technical complexities. One show, Sam Shepard's *Operation Sidewinder*, closed in the middle of rehearsals in 1968, never to open.

At the time, Shepard was at the beginning of his dramatic career. For the Rep to premiere *Sidewinder*, described in the promotional materials as "a hallucinatory glimpse into our current nightmares," was an artistic coup. In this episodic political allegory, the US Air Force has created a deadly computer in the form of a giant, red-eyed sidewinder rattlesnake. When the snake escapes into the desert, it is hotly pursued by grizzled loners, Native Americans, and Black revolutionaries. The play climaxes in an ecstatic snake ceremony–cum–gun battle between the Hopi Indians and desert tactical troops.

Rehearsals had begun for a late January opening, but on December 23, 1968, the Yale University News Bureau released a statement that Yale Rep had canceled *Operation Sidewinder* "as a result of objections to the play voiced by six of the School's seven Black students." Brustein was quoted in the release saying that the change was involuntary and that Shepard had withdrawn the play against "the will and advice of the School administration."

What happened? The twelve-member play committee, consisting of students and faculty—but no Black students—had selected the play without anticipating that it would offend anyone's sensibilities. The three Black characters in the play, named Blade, Blood, and Dude, appear in two scenes. In the first, they order food from their '57 Chevy and accept the clueless assertions of a blonde carhop about armed struggle and revolution. After she leaves to place their orders, Blood reviews with his pals their part of the plot, which is to put LSD in the water at the air force base and thereby engineer a mass departure of stoned pilots for Cuba. Dude objects: "Sounds pretty shaky to me.... It's like James Bond or something. Why don't we just go in and take the thing over?" Good question.

Act 2 starts with the trio in the middle of the desert. From the trunk of their Chevy, Dude and Blade retrieve the bound and gagged Young Man and his girlfriend, Honey. To stifle their muffled screams, Dude and Blade pull out guns and level them at their heads, execution style. Their plan to poison the air force has gotten screwed up; their new objective is to find the sidewinder computer with the help of their white captives. A solicitous forest ranger enters and becomes suspicious of Honey's gag and wrist restraints; Blood draws his gun. The ranger hesitates and then draws his gun to shoot. Blood fires three shots into the Ranger and kills him. The men free Honey. Blade, Blood, and Dude are never seen, heard from, or mentioned again.

Viewed through the lens of the Black Panther movement, whose volatile political agenda was then inspiring fear and admiration in differing sectors of the American population, it's possible to imagine that the six drama students were offended by the representation of the imprudently named Black characters as trigger happy, befuddled in their revolutionary purpose, forced to rely on white characters to achieve their aims, or all three. It's also possible that the lack of follow-through in their plotline rankled. Worth noting is that the professional actors cast in the roles did not object to their material. The director, recent graduate Jeff Bleckner ('68), felt caught between the duties of his assignment and the feelings of friends still enrolled at the school. The students appealed to Shepard, who withdrew *Operation Sidewinder*, contending that the essential problem was one of bitterness between the Black students and the faculty.

Issues of race, gender, cultural inclusion, and cultural representation reoccurred at Yale Rep in a complicated dance that moved forward and back over the decades. The gay and Latinx content in Terrence McNally's *The Tubs* (1974) would strike most today as offensively stereotypical. In 1975, after *nineteen* seasons in operation, Yale Rep hired its *first* woman director (Evan Yionoulis) to helm *Vampires in Kodachrome*, yet in that very same Winterfest, Anglo student actors Dylan Baker and Christopher Noth were cast to play Cuban revolutionaries in Keith Reddin's *Rum and Coke*. ("It certainly wouldn't happen today," says Reddin ['81].) Two years later, Anglo actor Richard Jenkins was chided in the press for a "garbled Navajo accent" in *Melons*, only one month before Richards premiered a fourth August Wilson play.

Today, Yale Rep, while less than perfect in terms of diversity, equity, inclusion, and belonging (DEIB) issues onstage and backstage, is sufficiently aware and self-critical of the negative assumptions and biases at work in the culture at large and in the art form of theater that it seems impossible that an *Operation Sidewinder* situation could happen again. ◆

WHO'S COUNTING?

Statistically inclined readers might be interested in the tally of the most-produced playwrights in the first fifty seasons of Yale Rep:

1. William Shakespeare: 31 (Two productions apiece of *Troilus and Cressida*, *A Midsummer Night's Dream*, *Hamlet*, *Twelfth Night*, *Richard II*, *The Winter's Tale*, and *As You Like It*)
2. Molière: 11 (Two *Tartuffe*s)
2. Bertolt Brecht, *mit oder ohne* Kurt Weill: 11
3. Anton Chekhov: 10 (Two productions apiece of *Three Sisters*, *Uncle Vanya*, and *Ivanov*)
4. Athol Fugard: 8
5. August Wilson: 7 (Two productions of *The Piano Lesson*)
5. George Bernard Shaw: 7 (Two productions of *Mrs. Warren's Profession*)
6. Henrik Ibsen: 6
6. Sarah Ruhl: 6
7. Edward Bond: 5
7. August Strindberg: 5 (Two productions of *Miss Julie*)

Of Brustein's eight playwrights of revolt, only Jean Genet has never been produced at Yale Rep. Six canonical twentieth-century playwrights made late Rep debuts: Tennessee Williams (*Summer and Smoke*, 1989), Thornton Wilder (*The Skin of Our Teeth*, 1997), Noël Coward (*Hay Fever*, 1999), Harold Pinter (*Betrayal*, 1999), Arthur Miller (*Death of a Salesman*, 2009), and Edward Albee (*A Delicate Balance*, 2010).

Completist patrons might feel the lack to date of any productions of world classics by Seneca, Lope de Vega, Jean Racine, John Webster, Aphra Behn, Georges Feydeau, Friedrich Schiller, Alfred de Musset, Heinrich von Kleist, Gotthold Lessing, Sean O'Casey, Federico Lorca, Maxim Gorky, Marieluise Fleißer, and Johann Wolfgang von Goethe, but they are free to daydream and submit titles to james.bundy@yale.edu. ◆

David Alan Grier and Jane Kaczmarek in Shakespeare's *Love's Labour's Lost* (1982)
PHOTO © GERRY GOODSTEIN

Times review suggested that walking out on *Lear*, a common reaction throughout its run, was practically a moral imperative for the sentient audience member.

Early Yale Rep Company member Betsy Parrish, who had thirty credits in the Yale Rep database, was assigned the role of Bodice, the Regan figure. "She was an excruciatingly evil woman to play, and I went to the director [David Giles] and I said, 'I can fake it, but I'm—just—*moi*? I can't do that. It's just not true.' He said, 'Well, do it in a German accent.'" Parrish made the adjustment in a late run-through and "wound up having a ball; it was the way that I found out what it is not to care—we put your eyes out, not my problem—it's strength *if* you don't care."

One of the most famous stage effects in Yale Rep history, which made patrons faint, scream, and race up the aisles, was the globe luxation apparatus in *Lear*, created by longtime props master Hunter Spence (1934–2013). Spence divulged the secret in 1982. After Lear was laced into a straitjacket, the extractor, painted black and chrome, was affixed to his head. Two syringes on either side of the mechanism were loaded with fake blood. At the right moment, the actor pushed on the syringes, causing the blood to trickle down one side of his face and then the other. The illusion was completed when two plastic grape-like balls fell into a glass, a triumphant combination of graphic language and technical legerdemain that signifies pure theater.

Despite a first performance in 406 BCE, Euripides's *Bacchae*, with its central agon between the irrational ecstasy of Dionysus and his worshippers and the rigidity of King Pentheus of Thebes, seemed fresh for Brustein's season of violence. Its Yale Rep production can be viewed as an undisguised referendum on the Living Theatre's visit five months before.

It helps to be in the right place at the right time. Screenwriter and translator Kenneth Cavander, on a short-term, substitute appointment ("That I didn't deserve," he insists today) with the Yale classics department, found a house to rent next door to the Brusteins. One day, Cavander saw the dean out back with his son and introduced himself. Brustein, always open to hiring new talent, especially if it was British, "said he was interested in doing a new version of *The Bacchae* with André Gregory. I had just done a commission of it for the BBC that had played at the Mermaid for the Old Vic right before I'd come to the States. The play was perfectly coincidental with a lot of the anger and revolutionary fervor at Yale and in the country at the time."

Jerome Robbins famously divided the original Sharks and Jets in *West Side Story* rehearsals into separate camps and encouraged them into a state of mutual animus to draw on in performance. For *The Bacchae*, Gregory agreed to Brustein's idea that the student actors playing the Chorus of Bacchantes, whom he feared were upset at his recent firing of Gordon Rogoff, should be rehearsed separately from the cast of six and with a different director, movement teacher Stanley Rosenberg. Cavander recalls Rosenberg resenting the setup. "It was tense, difficult. I went to a rehearsal, to hear my text, and I made a suggestion to an actor, and Stan said, 'That's not your role here to interfere with my directing.'" Brustein began worrying for the safety of David Spielberg, playing Pentheus, who ultimately is torn to bits by the Chorus and his mother, Agave, played by Broadway veteran Mildred Dunnock.

The halves never jelled, but two positives resulted from the *Bacchae* collabo-

John V. Shea, Joseph G. Grifasi, and Linda Gates in Edward Bond's sanguineous *Lear* (1973)
PHOTO © WILLIAM BAKER

Robert Brustein (1966–1979)

ration: Santo Loquasto and Alvin Epstein. Loquasto, a 2004 inductee into the Theater Hall of Fame who'd been a worker bee on the set of *Prometheus Bound*, was a third-year design student in 1969. In support of Gregory's idea that the play described the process of a mind that is divorced from instinct being blown, Loquasto's *Bacchae* set, described variously as "a womb," "a golden orifice," and "a beautiful oval cage," was an ellipse-mouthed tunnel of iron bars and plexiglass platforms. Concave floors and a web of supports on top of the tunnel created a jungle gym for the Chorus of Bacchantes performing Grotowski-inspired acrobatics to Richard Peaslee's score. Yale College junior Tom Walker remembers a lot of sharp objects on the floor of the set. "I played a Guard and felt lucky to be wearing a pair of boots, but the Chorus had a devil of a time working on it." Photographs of Loquasto's design made the pages of *Life* magazine.

Alvin Epstein (1925–2018) was, like Eva Le Gallienne, one of the undersung titans of the American theater, refractory to the visibility and the big payouts of a film and television career and always reaching to deepen his own art and stretch the boundaries of what the collective art of theater could achieve. A name search for Epstein on the Yale Rep website gets fifty-one hits.

Before Brustein lured him to New Haven, Epstein had been the original Lucky in the English-language premiere of *Waiting for Godot*, the original Clov in *Endgame* in 1958, and the Fool to Orson Welles's Lear; he sang on Broadway in the Richard Rodgers musical *No Strings*; and his first Yale Rep appearance was *Dynamite Tonite!* He joined the company two years later in 1968. Few will forget his magnetic Dionysus in *The Bacchae*, live snakes wrapped around his arms and torso. One critic judged him the sole actor alive who could upstage serpents, but in that same 1968–1969 season, Epstein had already played a 110-year-old statesman in Jules Feiffer's *God Bless* and drawn on his Decroux mime training for the transformational *Story Theatre*. And after Euripides, he would use his singing pipes as the eponymous *Greatshot*, another subversive Bolcom-Weinstein musical.

Encouraged by his boss to expand his talents at the Rep and the school, Epstein was made acting artistic director during Brustein's sabbatical (1972–1973). His meticulously prepared productions of *The Tempest* and *A Midsummer Night's Dream* attracted the notice of the Guthrie Theater, which hired him away in 1977 to be their fourth artistic director, a less than ideal match that lasted only eighteen months. When Brustein left for Harvard in 1979, Epstein joined him there. A decade later Epstein would return to New Haven to direct *The Importance of Being Earnest* and Shaw's *Heartbreak House* during the Richards regime. His final pair of Yale Rep credits were as an actor, in Evan Yionoulis's productions of *Richard II* (2006) and *Black Snow* (2007).

Alvin Epstein as Dionysus in Euripides's *The Bacchae* (1969)
PHOTO © SEAN KERNAN

Upon Epstein's death, Brustein published a loving tribute to him in *American Theatre* magazine, remembering that "some directors—Fellini, for example—achieve their effects through fear and thunder. Alvin threw bouquets. To win Alvin's favor actors were willing to put up with the most difficult procedures, not only because of the satisfying results, but because they might win a hint of a smile or a burst of applause from their director or teacher."

I remember vividly sitting in a class with some of the criticism students who were saying, "What is happening to the Yale Rep? Now we're doing fairy tales!"
—KENNETH CAVANDER

We don't know whether Brustein put out a distress call to Paul Sills in Chicago asking for ideas to fill the *Operation Sidewinder* slot or whether Sills was already in residence leading a student workshop that had so impressed Arnold Weinstein that he brought Sills and his idea directly to Brustein, but we do know that Sills had already created an evening of Grimm's fairy tales performed by a nimble company of Chicago actors who spoke a combination of dialogue and narration. In this technique, developed from the theater games practices started by Sills's mother, Viola Spolin, the actor shifts back and forth from a third- to a first-person perspective—often in a single speech—as a way to theatricalize a heretofore purely narrative story. Gestures, mime, movement, and instrumental and vocal music accompany and embellish spoken narrative in order to establish the circumstances—and uncover the pure, universal reality—of each fable or legend. Props and sets are kept to a minimum; ideally, the actors' bodies transform space as well as objects and also create an environment.

The first iteration of *Story Theater* (1969) was so successful that it generated three more Yale Rep Story Theater productions. After the seven Grimm tales, which were taped and televised by WGBH in Boston, resident director Larry Arrick planned a second helping, readapting Sills and Weinstein's *Metamorphoses*, which had also begun life in Chicago. The eight transformations chosen from Ovid were linked by a common theme—the sexual transgression of a god; examples are "Mars, Venus, and Vulcan," "Jupiter and Callisto," and "Zeus and Europa." Arrick commissioned additional text from Cavander. However broadly playful the results might seem, Cavander maintains that creating Story Theater was a subtle, minimalist calculus. "Some of it is dialogue, but again, the dialogue has to be calculated to the last split second with the movement and the emotional attitude of the actors, and on top of that, the music. When it worked on the simplest level, you thought you saw things that weren't there."

Helming the essential ingredient of music was Barbara Damashek ('69). She'd started Yale as an actor in the first year of the Brustein hurly-burly, where she felt "as green as a traffic light." Because she sang and could play any odd instrument put in front of her, in her second year Damashek was granted a stroll-through with a balalaika in *Three Sisters*. In her final year, Sills needed an onstage musician for *Story Theatre*. "And so she shall provide the music," laughs Damashek today. When not acting in one of the Grimm tales, she was surrounded by instruments on one side of the stage. She underscored the action and the subtler internal movements of the actors using motifs played on guitars and the occasional flute and drums. No piano, however, for the Grimm and Ovid pieces. "It was a rule. Acoustic piano made it sound like *The Fantasticks*. We wanted it to be rawer than musical theatre. Even later on, when we wanted a keyboard for *Olympian Games*, we used an electric harpsichord."

The fast-working Sills was known to lose interest in projects. According to Damashek and Brustein, he came to New Haven that autumn for the first few days

Lydia Fisher, Linda Gulder, Meral Taygun, and Carmen de Lavallade in *Ovid's Metamorphoses* (1969)
PHOTO © SEAN KERNAN

Robert Brustein (1966–1979)

CALVARY BAPTIST CHURCH (1871–1966) AND YALE REPERTORY THEATRE (1969–?)

Cusp and lancet windows. A pair of asymmetrical towers, one with an intact belfry on its third stage. A sweep of horizontal crosses flanking the alternating light and dark voussoirs over a large triple window above the north entrance. Visually, there is no mistaking the ecclesiastical origins of the imposing High Victorian Gothic building at the corner of Chapel and York Streets. Having decided that there needed to be a Baptist presence on the growing western side of the city, nineteenth-century merchant-philanthropist John M. Davis significantly underwrote a place of worship for a second Baptist congregation in New Haven. Designed by Rufus G. Russell and built by Elihu Larkins, the edifice was completed in May 1871, and was dedicated six months later.

Large enough to hold twelve hundred members, Calvary Baptist was partially destroyed by fire and rebuilt in 1882. It then served its faithful until 1966, when the congregation moved. Yale bought the church as part of its planning process for the eventual construction of the British Art Center, and the polygonal spire on the north tower was removed upon deconsecration. Kingman Brewster, aware of the growing pains faced by the Rep and the drama school, offered Brustein the building in a one-year loan, an apt architectural transition considering Western drama had sprung from medieval liturgical practice.

Yale Repertory Theatre
PHOTO © T. CHARLES ERICKSON

Except for the lack of storage and fly space, acoustical challenges, and a massive pipe organ at the back of stage, there was no downside for Brustein. Shows could rehearse onstage; productions could run longer; the planned thrust configuration would provide audiences with a more intimate experience than the UT proscenium; there would no territorial scraps with the Dramat; and best of all, the move was a symbolic and actual separation of the professional company from school activities.

Creating what Brustein would call a "primitive but functional professional theatre" took up the summer of 1969. The organ and the dual balconies running the length of the nave were draped with fiberglass blankets; the pews were replaced with folding chairs; light poles were set up; and a raked stage was constructed. The fire department insisted on a waterproofed basement, which meant that the planned traps for entrances from under the stage floor couldn't be built.

Calvary Baptist Church was thus reborn as Yale Repertory Theatre with the opening of *The Rivals* on October 16. Above the entrance to the theater was an emblem of dual-faced Janus, the Roman patron of beginnings and endings, whose eyes look to the past and to the future, providing a notion of historical continuity for Yale Rep productions. It was understood that the structure was to be demolished within a year. Forty-some seasons and two major renovations later, the church theater shows no signs of disappearing, a clear case of artistic eminent domain, Old Blue entropy, or, more simply, squatter's rights. ◆

Interior of Calvary Baptist Church (1908)
COURTESY OF CALVARY BAPTIST CHURCH

of *Metamorphoses* rehearsals but then returned to Chicago. Free to put more of his own stamp on the Ovid, Arrick asked Damashek to start composing her own score. Damashek and a four-person combo shared the stage with eleven actors, including the first Yale Rep appearance by Carmen de Lavallade, and one enormous metal tree. The program contained a very early instance of "dramaturgy pages"—a two-page layout titled "Animal and Man" featuring a biography of Ovid surrounded by provocative quotes from the likes of Robert Lowell, Georges Bataille, Freud, avant-garde playwright Ronald Tavel, and Konrad Lorenz's "On Aggression."

Sills returned for closing night in the "new" theater and was not pleased with what he felt were overly slick results. Brustein, who agreed in part with Sills's verdict, was nevertheless happy to say to the press, "Going from *The Rivals* to Ovid, that, well, is the sign of a true repertory company." Some critics enjoyed watching Damashek watch and respond to the action. "The instruments were set," she says, "but there were variations from night to night. I was playing for Alvin; I was playing for Carmen; I was listening and watching, and I played for them, following the way the performance breathed, its cadence, how a beat built and finished."

Arrick was now as intrigued as Brustein was in going to the next level. Could the transformation from the literary to the theatrical do more than entertain? Arrick had Cavander look at Flaubert's story "The Legend of St. Julian the Hospitaller." He, Cavander, and the bulk of the company spent a two-month working vacation in 1970 as "Yale Summer Repertory," taking up residence in East Hampton, New York, and working on more Ovid tales; *St. Julian the Hospitaler*; two stories by Philip Roth; Singer's *Gimpel the Fool*; and in the case of *Cops and Horrors*, adaptations of Dashiell Hammett and Stoker's *Dracula*.

As the opener for Yale Rep season six, Brustein scheduled *Story Theatre Repertory*. Although the "conceived by" credit belongs to Sills, the show was all Arrick, Damashek, and Cavander. *Olympian Games* (four new Ovid pieces added to the original three) played in repertory with the double bill of *St. Julian the Hospitaler* and *Gimpel the Fool*. Damashek felt that the work developed in the summer season was critical to the growth of the company. "Discovering ourselves through each other, we were the darlings of East Hampton. Before we hadn't been given the environment to show up on stage with our own youth and our own skills. We hadn't been *seen* at the Rep. *Story Theatre* changed that, and the audience could feel it."

Four years later, Alvin Epstein and third-year directing student Walton Jones ('75) adapted Joseph Conrad's dense, sprawling novel *Victory* (1915) in Story Theater mode. Conrad's multiple narrators posed an interesting challenge, but the psychological mysteries that propel his characters, the interiority of his prose, and the body count at the final curtain weren't a good fit for a theatrical style that prized

THAT *OTHER* THEATER, OR BROWN VERSUS BRUSTEIN

One year before Kingman Brewster hired Brustein to shake things up at Yale, the Long Wharf Theatre opened its doors in a vacant warehouse space in a food terminal facing New Haven harbor with a two-week run of Arthur Miller's *The Crucible*. Today, one stated measure of Long Wharf's success is its thirty Broadway and off-Broadway transfers. Moreover, three plays that originated there were awarded the Pulitzer Prize for Drama.

On Brustein's watch, Broadway transfers and Arthur Miller plays were nonstarters. His disdain for Long Wharf is recorded in *Making Scenes*. First published in 1981, two years after Brustein "moved" Yale Rep to Harvard, the book was subtitled *A Personal History of the Turbulent Years at Yale 1966–1979* and chronicles the learning curve Brustein underwent to put his ideals into practice.

Brustein: "I respected the Long Wharf for its craft and competence, but—and I was hardly in a position to say then (or now)—I didn't find it a very adventurous theatre. The basic style of the Long Wharf was domestic realism—plays in which people discuss their problems over hot meals—and this made it a congenial resting place for the middle-class New Haven population, lulled by the sight of familiar lives on the stage."

In a 2014 interview, Arvin Brown, Long Wharf's artistic director for more than three decades, acknowledges competition between the two young companies: "Bob Brustein was a tremendous enthusiast of Eastern European theater and that was everything to him. It was politically engaged and important and there was certainly a validity to that. The American theater had to look for something different that was engagement on an important American scale. So American naturalism, family drama, I mean, that's at the core of American life. And to completely trash it as being unimportant was, I thought, very narrow."

Mergers and acquisitions, a standard feature of American business, rarely, if ever, occur in the arts. Case in point, from Brustein: "At Yale we found ourselves that first year in the unfamiliar position of attracting most of the press attention and a significant proportion of the audience, despite our controversial season. Possibly for that reason, some members of the Long Wharf board initiated discussions with Kingman Brewster concerning a merger with Yale."

Brown: "The Long Wharf board of directors was in a state of panic, because there was going to be an unanticipated deficit situation. It was so early in the days of the regional theater movement that they hadn't had the education about the fact that a nonprofit institution is going to run a deficit."

Brustein: "I had mixed feelings [about a merger]. The advantage was the acquisition of a much-needed facility. But there were disadvantages, too: the remoteness of the Long Wharf Theatre from the Yale campus, the difficulties of transportation, the implied obligation to provide a more popular season."

Brown: "But the news got out in the press that these conversations were going on, and it caused tremendous upheaval. The fact that Long Wharf had been built, conceived, and proposed as a genuine community operation, and suddenly there it was being absorbed into Yale, certain leaders in the community were really, really unhappy."

No merger then. As time went on, it was never lost on Brustein that Long Wharf was a more popular destination.

Brustein: "We had never had more than 6,000 subscribers, of whom half were usually students on discount passes; Long Wharf had 14,000, including most of the Yale faculty."

Brown: "There was a lot of sort of silly intellectualizing going on about what made plays, what made plays work, and obviously the audience was often left out of the quotient. But that was kind of Brustein's point; why he was so negative about Long Wharf was that anything that was meant to please an audience was outside the realm."

To remain in operation and plan for growth, Long Wharf had to respond to the tastes of its audience, while Brustein had Yale University to absorb the red ink (up to a point) and could afford to program as he saw fit.

Anything left of the hatchet thrown down between Yale Rep and Long Wharf in their early years was buried during the Richards decade. Indeed, Brown had been a member of the search committee that selected Richards as Brustein's successor. ◆

speed, pith, and whimsy. Although not referring to *Victory* in particular, actor Michael Gross ('73) had this to say about Yale Rep during this period: "It was a laboratory. And in a laboratory, you're going to throw away a lot of beakers that just are not the cure for the American theater. Now, sometimes I looked at things with: why can't this be better? And I kept thinking: no, they're experimenting here. And it's not always going to work. But there was a kind of freedom that I loved about the Rep where we felt that you can fail utterly here."

For Damashek, who would leave the company in 1971, *Story Theatre* was the first fingerprint of Brustein's Yale Rep. She and Cavander would collaborate later on a Story Theater *Jason and the Argonauts* for Long Wharf Theatre. Today, Spolin and Sills's games and exercises are thespian building blocks introduced as early as middle school, but fifty years ago, their methodology seemed like a new way to make theater. If *Story Theatre* owes a lot to Brecht, plays like *Peter and the Starcatcher*, *Gross Indecency*, and Mary Zimmerman's *Metamorphoses* and the emergence of "devised" work in the twenty-first century owe a lot to *Story Theatre*. Mercurial shifts in perspective, once novel, are now just another potential tool in a playwright's kit, dramaturgical impulses that performers and directors are now trained to actualize by just skipping a beat.

The works of playwright-poet Bertolt Brecht (1898–1956) and composer Kurt Weill (1900–1950) would be the next fingerprint. The sardonic tone and political stance of Brecht's texts matched to the venomously beautiful sound of Weill's music were a combination that pleased both critics and audiences. Brecht received productions of seven of his works during the Brustein regime, four of them musical collaborations with Weill. Moreover, three of these four—*The Seven Deadly Sins*, *The Mahagonny Songplay* (or *"Little" Mahagonny*), and *Happy End*—would reappear in later seasons. The fourth, *The Rise and Fall of the City of Mahagonny*, would first be seen in its complete version in a 1974 joint collaboration with the Yale School of Music and then again in 1978 in a reduced chamber version that wags referred to as *"Medium" Mahagonny*, or *A Work of Brecht and Weill with the Name "Mahagonny" in the Title*.

The *Mahagonny Songplay* was a six-song cantata set to Brecht poems first heard in 1927. *The Seven Deadly Sins*, their final collaboration, was a dance oratorio commissioned in 1933 for Lotte Lenya and Austrian ballerina Tilly Losch. Together, *Sins* and *Songplay* would create a Yale Rep evening that further extended the range of the company, which had done Weinstein and Bolcom musicals but not Brecht and Weill. "Alvin was involved in the company by then," said Michael Feingold ('69). "Carmen de Lavallade and Betsy Parrish were in the company. Carmen taught movement and Betsy taught singing at the school. And I said to Bob, 'You know, you love Brecht, you should do *Seven Deadly Sins* for them.'"

Sins was one of many adroit Feingold suggestions that Brustein embraced. The production, called *Two by Bertolt Brecht and Kurt Weill*, was presented in association with the Yale School of Music. Professor of Conducting Gustav Meier led the twenty-eight-piece orchestra of student musicians and taught the score to the

Kurt Kasznar, Grace Keagy, and Jeremy Geidt in Brecht and Weill's *The Rise and Fall of the City of Mahagonny* (1974)
PHOTO © DON LOWY

performers. For *The Little Mahagonny*, director Michael Posnick conceived a bitter vaudeville storyline for four Brechtian "sharks" and two prostitutes, dressed in uniform smoking outfits with padded shoulders and little stiff hats à la George Grosz. Epstein, directing *The Seven Deadly Sins*, cast his assignment as a *Pilgrim's Progress* through bourgeois America in *Story Theatre* style. Practical, seen-it-all Anna 1 is performed by a soprano. Creative, impulsive Anna 2 is a dance role. The Annas embark on a journey across the United States, from Memphis to Boston to San Francisco, one sin per city, in order to raise money for her selfish family. Carmen de Lavallade was unable to perform Anna 2 due to a ruptured appendix and was replaced by Stephanie Cotsirilos. The double bill was so successful, however, that Brustein revived the production the following January with de Lavallade assuming the part originally chosen for her.

The *New Haven Register* reported on March 19, 1972, that Yale Rep had gone into rehearsals for the American premiere of a "lost" Weill musical. *Happy End* (1929) had been Brecht and Weill's swift attempt to capitalize on the success of *Threepenny Opera* the year before. Its structure was slipshod, but its closure after two performances was caused more by its politics—"Robbing a bank's no crime compared to owning one" is one of its parting shots—than by its aesthetics. Brecht disowned the piece, and Lenya kept it out of circulation for decades due to its weak book.

48   *Robert Brustein (1966–1979)*

PERSONS OF THE DRAMA: MICHAEL FEINGOLD (1945–2022)

A young theater person is, ideally, a sponge for ideas and experience. Originally from the north suburbs of Chicago, Michael Feingold followed Brustein to New Haven from Columbia University, where he'd been a student in Brustein's senior seminar. He enrolled initially at YSD as a playwright; in his first year (1966) his professor, Arnold Weinstein, appeared to have dammed his creative flow, but he sat in on as many rehearsals of the Open Theatre's *Viet Rock* as he could and got a lot of coffee for the jumped-up Weinstein, who had written *Dynamite Tonite!*

Shifting to the dramatic criticism department, Feingold became Brustein's teaching assistant for his modern drama course and spent his work-study hours manning the drama library. He was a founding editor of *yale/theatre*. He directed plays at the Cabaret and helped curate the Sunday Series at the Rep; he stage-managed in the Drama Annex. When his work-study ran out, he left for New York and found a spot on the theater criticism totem pole at the *Village Voice* and also read scripts for New York Theater Workshop.

One day he got a call from Yale Rep business manager Tom Burrows saying that a score for Brecht and Weill's *Little Mahagonny* had arrived in the mail; Brustein wanted to produce it—but there wasn't a suitable translation. Would Feingold like to take a crack at it?

"I was useful, and I loved the place, and I wanted to be useful," Feingold remembered. He went back to New Haven and got to work. Weill's widow, the imposing, legendary Lotte Lenya, came to the May 1971 opening. During intermission, Brustein, on hearing Lenya gush over Feingold's work, wondered why she wouldn't set Feingold loose on *Happy End*, which had not yet been seen in America.

"Nobody ever asked," said Lenya.

"Well, I'm asking," said Brustein.

In the space of four Yale Rep seasons, Feingold would translate *Happy End*, Ibsen's *When We Dead Awaken*, Molière's *Bourgeois Gentleman*, and Brecht and Weill's pièce de résistance, *The Rise and Fall of the City of Mahagonny*. He also selected and arranged the Shakespeare and Shaw texts for the Aristophanic poolside face-off in *The Frogs*. In 1971 he became the first literary manager of the theater, described in the *New Haven Register* as "a one-man Chautauqua Circuit," splitting his time between New Haven, where he was an institutional ghostwriter and an artistic sounding board and idea generator for Brustein and the company, and New

Michael Feingold, Yale Rep's "one-man Chautauqua circuit" in the late 1980s
PHOTO © STEPHEN PALEY

York, where he continued to review weekly for the *Voice*. "I was one of Bob's adoptive Jewish sons, but I'm not accusing him of paternalism. When he asked a question, I'd have an answer; maybe not the right one, or the one he wanted to hear, but we were in constant dialogue."

Feingold took delight in translating and adapting texts for a specific company of actors—Parrish, de Lavallade, Epstein, Geidt, Joyce, Dempsey, Troobnick, and so on—which he felt had hit its artistic stride with the dual sensibility ("the juicy old-fashioned entertainment forms *and* the critical distance") required of Brecht. His final assignment for Yale Rep was adapting the lyrics for Ron Daniels's production of Brecht's *Mister Puntila and His Servant Matti* (1977).

In his other lives, Feingold remained the lead critic of *The Village Voice* for decades, worked again with Brustein at the American Repertory Theater (A.R.T.), and taught classic drama at NYU and dramaturgical collaboration at Columbia. He dramaturged August Wilson's first plays at the Eugene O'Neill Theater Center. Wilson would always credit him for helping *Ma Rainey's Black Bottom* gain shape and focus. As the go-to Brecht/Weill guy, he went twice to Broadway—first, with another *Happy End*, for which he shared a Tony nomination for Best Book with the pseudonymous Brecht collaborator "Dorothy Lane," and then in 1989 with a new translation of *The Threepenny Opera*, starring Sting as Macheath. He continued to translate and adapt plays from several languages and write about theater with a signature blend of intense erudition, mordant wit, and untrammeled love of live performance. Twice awarded the George Jean Nathan Award for Theater Criticism (1996, 2014), he was also a Pulitzer Prize criticism finalist in 2010. He also resumed the playwriting career that was sidetracked circa 1967 and maintained, as did his life mentor Brustein, that a company of actors in rotating repertory is the ideal situation for the actors, the playwrights, and the audience.

He regarded his decade at Yale with wry enthusiasm. "It wasn't always easy. I was fired three times, and I resigned three times. On six separate occasions." In his case, time healed the pricks and kicks, because he couldn't remember any of the particulars. Theater arouses passion in the young, and Michael Feingold stayed young by welcoming, and sporting, many theatrical hats. He died in Manhattan, at the age of seventy-seven, in November 2022. ◆

Today it is known that Brecht, rather like an Old Master or Andy Warhol at his Factory, supervised an atelier of assistants—in Brecht's case, female admirers who helped generate or revise his works in progress, their contributions subsumed by his ego and his copyright. *Happy End* has a book by "Dorothy Lane," assumed now to be Elisabeth Hauptmann, but what was sent over from Germany was little more than a song catalog, a set of characters, and an incomplete scenario involving a gang of hapless criminals and a Salvation Army lass set in a caricature of Chicago. Feingold got to work, creating his adaptation on and with the actors and director Posnick.

Comparisons between *Happy End* and that acme of American musical comedy, *Guys and Dolls*, are instructive, even if one could not find two more dissimilar love songs than Sarah Brown's exuberant "If I Were a Bell" and Salvation Lil's caustic "Surabaya Johnny." Or Nicely-Nicely Johnson and his crew swinging to Frank Loesser's gospel shout, "Sit Down, You're Rockin' the Boat" versus Bill Cracker and his gang trying to piece together the forgotten lyrics to "The Bilbao Song." The self-conscious title—this is a *song*—reveals that musical moments in Brecht/Weill are action-interrupting "numbers" that announce a situation or illustrate a mood rather than advance the plot or deepen a characterization. Weill's simplified jazz forms with a distinctively dissonant undertow create a uniquely wounded and wounding tone when paired with the jagged, hard-bitten poetry of Brecht's lyrics. The lyrics aren't always set squarely on the melody; they remain at purposeful odds, one more Brechtian strategy designed to create ironic distance between the performance and the listener. Getting carried away by the sound of music, à la Rodgers and Hammerstein, is never the point. Attaching the song to its generative idea is.

Feingold began with the 1958 publication of Hauptmann's script; changes, including structural ones, were worked out with the company in rehearsal, with the understanding that this was the normal procedure for building an American musical, which was essentially what Brecht and Weill had wanted *Happy End* to be, albeit with a somewhat radical attitude. *Happy End* was an unqualified success. Feingold remarked that "we found things that we as a group could do, things that the staff of the theater and the artistic directorate and the businesspeople and the audience and the actors all got excited by." At its opening, *Happy End* earned further praise from Lenya: "They're permanently young, those works. And the music, it speaks to the young people."

The next step was the acme of the Brecht/Weill collaborations, *The Rise and Fall of the City of Mahagonny*. Mahagonny, or "the City of Nets," is a European projection of American freedom, a magnet for human flotsam, a place where anything is possible, and all crimes are pardoned until the money runs out. Yale Rep's

1974 production in the University Theatre, directed by Epstein with a new Feingold translation/adaptation and a thirty-eight-piece orchestra conducted by Otto Werner-Mueller of the Yale Collegium Musicum, would rightfully confer canonical status upon *Mahagonny* in the world opera repertory. It closed on February 23, 1974, having received national press and the highest ticket sales thus far at Yale Rep, the only theater in America for whom Brecht and Weill were the box office equivalent of *A Christmas Carol*.

One year later Brustein revived *Happy End*, which proved popular enough to bring back for four extra performances in May, and in his final season, he allowed Yale Rep associate director Keith Hack to rearrange, retranslate, and direct a "farewell" version of *Mahagonny*. Staged in a boxing ring, the city was renamed "Suckersville"; the orchestra was greatly reduced; spoken dialogue replaced recitative; and a narrator called out the rounds of the boxing match and strung the story along between numbers. Mark Bly ('80), the assigned student dramaturg, recalls a chaotic rehearsal period that included a student actress decking the director in the wings. Despite a strong cast and an evocative Yukon setting by Michael Yeargan, the results seemed to please no one but the audiences—four performances were added to the run.

Through the early 1970s, Brustein made steady progress with his artistic objectives. He had the church theater to himself. His audience was growing, especially among the Yale student population, an essential demographic for him. A true repertory system was in place. Leading American playwrights would send him their new works for consideration, and their nonrealistic dramaturgies were published in the pages of *yale/theatre*. The Yale Cabaret was thriving. Alvin Epstein was proving to be as sensitive and detailed a director as he was an actor. He had a core company of dedicated actor-teachers: character actresses Elizabeth Parrish and Norma Brustein; comics and character men high and low, including Eugene Troobnick, Jeremy Geidt, and Jerome Dempsey; and the quicksilver Carmen de Lavallade. Every year, two or three of the MFA acting graduates would accept invitations to join the company, which had logged enough time together in classrooms, rehearsal halls, and onstage to develop the trust and flexibility to shift from Molière's shaggy *Bourgeois Gentleman* to Ronald Ribman's surreal *A Break in the Skin* to Eric Bentley's docudrama, *Are You Now or Have You Ever Been?*, during the same week. Henry Winkler ('70), who would disappoint Brustein's hopes for his talent when he achieved mass celebrity on the television series *Happy Days*, was thrilled to join the company upon graduation. "Three of us were asked into the company; so here I am, never thinking I could achieve being a professional actor. And I'm getting $173 a week and I'm thinking: I'll buy a coat. The truth is that I used every millisecond of everything that I heard, experienced, learned, [and] lived at Yale in order to create the rest of my life."

Brustein's perpetual hustle was paying for it all. Arts leaders today are habituated to fund-raising, but the landscape was different then. President Brewster never retreated from his commitment to Yale Rep, but university support was not carte blanche. Yale has a central development office to handle donor gifts and alumni bequests and pursue grant opportunities. Brustein would have to woo a separate raft of well-heeled patrons. He was chagrined by the amount of one-on-one glad-handing he had to do on campus, in New York, and during his summer retreats on Martha's Vineyard, nicknamed the Summer White House by students and staff. It helped that he was persistent and persuasive and that the funding climate was conducive to serious artistic exploration. The charge against elitism in the arts was in the future, and the National Endowment for the Arts had yet to shift its focus from general operating support to spreading the wealth geographically and to project-specific granting.

In January 1973, Epstein, subbing for Brustein that season and musing on the operating deficit of $35,000, said, "We have a high flop quotient, particularly due to the risks we take. I'm not ashamed of our flops, though. Obviously, it would be better if they hadn't happened." At the end of the following season, because of the success of *The Tempest*, *Watergate Classics*, and the complete *Mahagonny*, Robert "Rob" Orchard ('72), who had been promoted to the managing director position after assisting Epstein the year before, was pleased to report that the final box office tally was up 30 percent.

In 1975, Yale Rep was one of nine resident theaters awarded money by the Mellon Foundation. Brustein intended to use the $150,000 to create a junior company of professional actors. That May, Brewster earmarked $500,000 to upgrade the theater facility (see box), and within another year, the Ford Foundation gave a $505,586 matching grant to establish an endowment that would improve and stabilize the position of the Rep *and* the school. That same year, in thinking about the distance Yale Rep had traveled, Brustein said, "We're still trying to unearth an American approach to the classics. We're trying to find metaphors in the classics to examine our dreams, nightmares, [and] events so that classics can relate to experiences Americans can recognize, without making them vulgarly relevant."

After *Prometheus Bound*, perhaps the next wholly satisfying "American approach" to a classic text was Molière's *Don Juan*, in a new translation by Cavander.

WHAT IS ROTATING REPERTORY?

The word "repertory" derives from the Latin *reperio*, "to find again." American theaters with "repertory" in their titles—Yale, Berkeley, Seattle, and so on—present a semantic misnomer. A true repertory theater presents several plays from current or past repertory *in rotation* throughout a season, the way the Metropolitan Opera will present *Aida* one night, a matinee of *The Pearl Fishers* the next afternoon, and *Dialogues of the Carmelites* that same night. Rotating rep is a model suited for contracted resident companies of actors who relish the opportunity to play a variety of roles every week through an entire season. Managers can respond to audience demand by scheduling additional performances, sometimes for many years, of successful productions and curtailing the runs of failures. The burdens of true rep fall to stage crews doing the constant set changeovers and, in a certain sense, to audience members, who have to keep closer track of the performance schedule.

In June 1971, Brustein announced an upcoming sixth Yale Rep season of true repertory and made good on the promise: in the same week that December, for example, patrons could see Ibsen's *When We Dead Awaken* in a commissioned translation by Michael Feingold; Lonnie Carter's *The Big House*, a Marx Brothers–style prison farce; and a rare revival of Camus's *Caligula*, starring Christopher Walken as the eponymous Roman antihero.

The following May, Brustein reflected on this first rep year in the *New Haven Register*: "The major problem is the communications problem, which increases your budget greatly by the need for daily ads announcing what's happening at the theatre.... One advantage, which proved to be most important in terms of morale, was the feeling that a play or production didn't ever have to come to an end. That it was somehow always potentially there to be brought back into the repertory.... It makes you feel you're working in something more material than sand."

The chronic challenge for Brustein was keeping a company together in a film and television culture that rewards freelance actors with high paychecks. In 1979, he took a core company of his Yale Rep actors with him to Harvard. Richards retained rotating rep for his first season (1979–1980); lucky audiences could, for example, see James Earl Jones in Fugard's *A Lesson from Aloes* one night and then as Shakespeare's *Timon of Athens* the next night—but a permanent acting company was not critical to his vision for the Rep. For Richards, the play would be the thing: *Winterfest*, launched the following season, was a rotating repertory of three or four plays-in-development not open to critics. Canadian "clowns of horror" Mump + Smoot, who alternated performances of *Caged* and *Inferno* in spring 1994, represent the latest "true rep" situation at YRT. ◆

Fall season eight at Yale Rep—four plays in repertory from October 1973 through March 1974

YALE REPERTORY THEATRE

During the month of February, the Rep will cross the street to the University Theatre for its production of **The Rise and Fall of the City of Mahagonny**, Brecht-Weill's superb song-play, in a new translation by Michael Feingold. Biting, grimly funny, **Mahagonny** is a magnificent musical giant! The spring season at the 'church' will include Sam Shepard's **Geography of a Horse Dreamer** and the Andrzej Wajda version of **The Possessed**, a high point of London's World Theatre Festival.

SCHEDULE INFORMATION

THE TEMPEST
by William Shakespeare
music by Purcell

October 4p, 5, 6m, 6, 9, 10, 11, 12, 13m, 13, 30
November 1, 3m, 3, 7, 9, 27, 30
December 5, 13, 15m, 15

DARKROOM
by David Epstein

October 18p, 19, 20m, 20, 23, 24, 25, 26, 27m, 27, 31
November 2, 6, 8, 10m, 10, 28
December 1m, 1, 6, 7, 11

WATERGATE CLASSICS
November 15p, 16, 17m, 17, 20, 21, 22, 23, 24m, 24, 29
December 4, 14
January 8, 10, 12m, 12, 16, 18, 23, 26m, 26

THE TUBS
by Terrence McNally
December 20p, 21, 22m, 22
January 1, 2, 3, 4, 5m, 5, 9, 11, 15, 17, 19m, 19, 25
March 19, 21, 23m, 23, 27

Watch your newspaper or consult our box office for the following yet to be scheduled dates:
December 8, 12
January 22, 24

p — preview   m — matinee

SEASON SUBSCRIPTIONS WILL BE SOLD THROUGH MID-DECEMBER

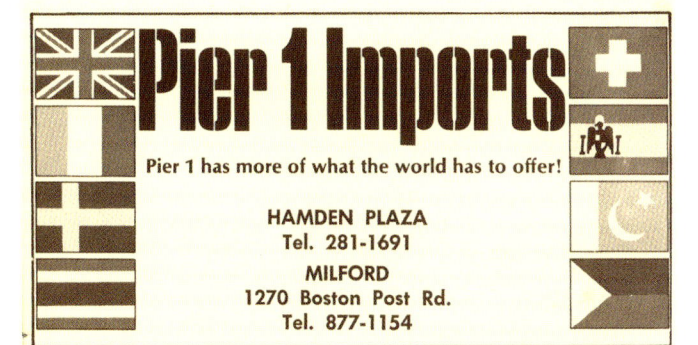

Pier 1 Imports

Pier 1 has more of what the world has to offer!

HAMDEN PLAZA
Tel. 281-1691

MILFORD
1270 Boston Post Rd.
Tel. 877-1154

India Imports
89 howe st.

THE FIRST RENOVATION

There comes a time in the life of every nonprofit theater when it must shed some of its scrappy physical origins and begin to consider the more elaborate dreams of its designers *and* the comfort of its patrons.

The straight-backed folding chairs in the first configuration of Yale Rep were the opposite of comfortable, and the raked stage meant that the actors couldn't wear heels and that the legs on prop furniture had to be cut to the pitch of the floor lest they tip over. In December 1973, Managing Director Rob Orchard ('72) reported that the New Haven fire marshal's office had given the church its final two-year extension: "By the fall of 1975 we must either remodel the existing facility or find a new space to house our productions." In advance of Brustein's tenth-anniversary season, Kingman Brewster allocated $500,000 for the desired renovation.

Half a million dollars went further in 1975. Design faculty Ming Cho Lee, William Warfel, and Michael Yeargan, working with Patricia Tetrault, an architect in Yale's engineering department, were able to create a new raked auditorium floor, a fully trapped stage with a Bayreuth-style orchestra pit, and a new lighting grid. The existing projection booths were moved to the rear. The new thrust was thirty-four feet wide, only two feet less than the UT proscenium. Seating capacity went from 386 to 491, and the new foam-padded chairs were a fund-raising naming opportunity for the princely sum of two hundred dollars apiece. The rear balcony, the side galleries, and the pillars undergirding them were removed, and Yeargan and Lee created a modular-unit set designed specifically to support the quick changeovers required by rotating rep. It was painted black to look like it was an ex-

Molière's subtitle for his play is "Or the Stone Guest"; Brustein, making his Rep directing debut, took his subtitle from Shaw's prefatory epistle to *Don Juan in Hell*—"Or the Enemy of God." Citing Kierkegaard's essay "The Immediate Stages of the Erotic," Brustein announced to the press, "I am planning to treat the character of Don Juan as an example of the corruption of the sexual instinct between the Renaissance health of Rabelais and the Naturalist inversions of the Marquis de Sade."

That was the metaphor, and Brustein loved a metaphor. The praxis: a Black Sab-

tension of the stage. Yeargan recalls the old design: "It had two side balconies that contained the space, as well as a balcony in the alcove to create more storage space. Ultimately, I felt it was too dominant a set that didn't allow enough variety. When it was taken out, I remember it felt like a breath of fresh air."

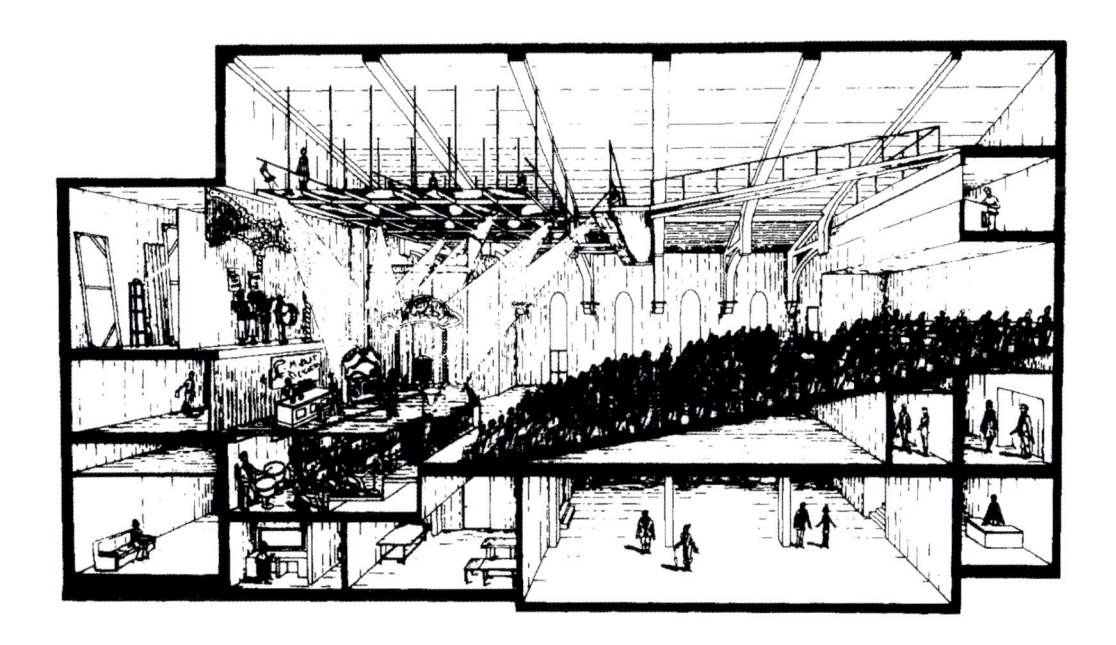

The refurbished Yale Rep, complete with advertising kiosks, opened its doors on October 30, 1975, with a revival of Brustein's "Black Mass" *Don Juan*. In the summer of 1992, at the end of Wojewodski's first season, the last vestiges of Lee's unit set were removed and replaced with the side stages still in use today. ◆

Blueprint cross-section of the first renovation (1975)
COURTESY OF YALE REPERTORY THEATRE

bath in the church theater, with the Molière text serving as a play within the play depicting the life and death of serial seducer Don Juan. When the audience entered, the "Ceremony of the Introit"—the sacrifice of a lamb to Asmodeus—had already begun. A priestess, priest, and two deacons led a chorus muttering sexual incantations over both a sound collage composed by Richard Peaslee and musical blasts from the old Calvary Church pipe organ. Student designer Jeffrey Higgenbottom ('70) had re-covered the windows with pornographic black, white, and gray stained-glass windows; suspended over them were statues of the characters in

Robert Brustein (1966–1979)

Henry Winkler, Alvin Epstein, and Barbara Damashek rehearsing Molière's *Don Juan* (1970)
PHOTO © WILLIAM BAKER

the play in tortured positions. A Gothic altar and altar screen, a sarcophagus, and a pulpit were placed on the stage. Hanging over the altar was an upside-down cross.

Michael Yeargan, then a design student, remembers a terrifying environment. "And then the thing started, and all the lights went out, and all the costumes were black and white and gray except for Don Juan—Alvin Epstein. He came in from upstage and walked downstage, and he was wearing a big, long cape, and as he turned you realized that it wasn't a cape, it was Carmen de Lavallade, one of the most beautiful women in the world. And as she slowly pulled away, you saw this red rosette on his heart."

For Molière, Don Juan is an object lesson of the fearsome power of divine retri-

58 *Robert Brustein (1966–1979)*

bution; in the Rep production, he becomes the next lamb sacrificed to the hooded celebrants. Like Prometheus, he ignores multiple warnings of celestial punishment; his false, hypocritical conversion in front of his father is the last straw. At this point Brustein's veiled Specter of Womanhood (de Lavallade) re-enters and then changes shape and becomes Time, carrying a sickle. Brustein deviated from Molière's denouement: the Stone Guest, instead of sending Don Juan to Hell, forces him to embrace the Specter. Yeargan again recalls, "Carmen threw up this cape, and it looked like the Ivan Albright painting from the end of *The Picture of Dorian Gray*. You see that her body is pustules and rotting organs. And she threw Don Juan down on the altar and she went up over him like she was raping him. The pipe organ started playing so loud you couldn't hear, and all the white statues were lit, and then she slowly pulled back, and he had become one of those white sculptures but dripping with blood. The chorus moved in, repeating their chants, this time over a human sacrifice, and the Specter turned around, her face replaced by a death mask." *Newsweek* deemed *Don Juan* "a landmark in the development of one of the most valuable enterprises in the country."

Sometimes the production metaphor is a magnetic actor giving an unforgettable performance. Albert Camus's *Caligula* (1944) had been a favorite of Brustein's. In the summer of 1971, George Grizzard was originally announced for the title role at Yale Rep but took another engagement. According to director Epstein, Frank Langella dropped out after the first day because the repertory schedule for three plays in rotation would leave *Caligula* without adequate time to rehearse. (Langella's bio remains in the program.) Fortunately, Christopher Walken was, as they say in the casting world, "interested and available."

Caligula is as charmingly self-aware a monster as his dramatic cousins Richard III and Don Juan. He has more than a touch of the poet—and the child—in his nature. He chooses the tyrant's path because who or what is in place to check him? Failing to secure the impossible, he tries through murder, and the systematic perversion of all values, to practice a liberty that he will tragically discover is not the right one. Unlike Don Juan, the supernatural doesn't punish Caligula; he falls victim to the mob, walking to his death with calm. At the close of a climactic melee, he is spotted standing atop a column. He leaps into the fray, crying, "Live in history, Caligula!" They destroy him. There is a final shriek, a gasp, a laugh—"I'm still alive!"

Some of Caligula's flourishes—appearing in a floor show as a wigged Venus on the half shell, painting his toenails, wearing black lipstick, draping himself over a senator or two—could appear today as routine as a compulsory exercise on *Ru Paul's Drag Show*, but in 1971, they had the power to shock, and director Epstein

Christopher Walken as Camus's eponymous *Caligula* (1971)
PHOTO © WILLIAM BAKER

and antihero Walken leaned into the pansexual voluptuousness of the role. Walter Kerr in the *New York Times* wrote of Walken, "He makes philosophy walk." Walken actually mentioned his gait in a rehearsal interview: "I had to get rid of certain aspects of my dance training. I had to learn how to walk again, without quite so much lift. A dancer has a tendency to pose. What in acting is called pose in dancing is called line. In the case of dancing it's an attribute and in acting it's an affectation or would seem to be. So, I had to clean up a little of that."

Walken's virtuosity more than justified the choice of Camus's overlooked play. After its initial repertory run closed on December 8, popular demand led Brustein to schedule it for an additional two-week solo run in January 1972. Walken would return for three other classical roles at Yale Rep: Werle in *The Wild Duck* (1978), Angelo in *Measure for Measure* (1979), and Charteris in Shaw's *The Philanderer* (1982). Asked today about parts he'd still like to play at Yale, Walken mentioned Prospero in Shakespeare's *The Tempest*.

The Tempest opened the Yale Rep 1973–1974 season, incorporating Henry Purcell's score for his seventeenth-century Baroque opera adaptation. A suitable Prospero couldn't be lured to New Haven, so Epstein directed *and* starred, a risky stretch for a demanding play. Although this *Tempest* was not considered a major achievement, the creative triumvirate of Shakespeare, Purcell, and Epstein yielded another transcendent success of the Brustein years. As with *Prometheus Bound*, few who saw it have ever forgotten Epstein's *A Midsummer Night's Dream*, with Christopher Lloyd and de Lavallade leading the charge as Oberon and Titania.

Analyzing the text, Epstein concluded that *Dream* is a martial nightmare. Theseus has won Hippolyta with his sword. Titania and Oberon are warring over possession of a changeling boy. Tangling and untangling the desires of the four young lovers is a protracted skirmish in the woods. Puck seeks manumission from his severe master. Epstein and set designer Tony Straiges ('74) decided that the visual correlative for Athens was a war drop of charging horse cutouts from Paolo Uccello's painting *The Battle of San Romano*. The production began with two armored figures in hand-to-hand combat in front of the cutouts. Lifting their helmets, they are revealed as Theseus and Hippolyta. When the lovers flee to the forest, the horses rise in the air—but not out of sight—to become an abstraction of trees, their spears creating diagonals that disrupt the curves in the set.

One particular curve was a second dominant feature in Straiges's design. Epstein wanted Puck and the fairies to fly in or to hop, slide, and slither. Straiges devised a fifteen-foot wooden wall with a steep, concave slope, or scoop, or slide, at its bottom and with a narrow walkway on top. Angled stage left of the scoop was a giant moon made of popcorn. "I wanted the feeling that everything was happening from the moon," said Straiges at the time. "Like the whole fairy world was rolling down from the moon to confront the literal orchestra." Lizbeth Mackay ('75), who played Peaseblossom, remembers that the fairies entered on lily pads, treated with silicone on the bottom for easier movement. "One performance we slid into the violin section. I've never seen musicians moving so fast to get out of the way."

Epstein and costume designer Zack Brown ('75) eschewed the children-in-gossamer cliché of the fairies in favor of worms, slugs, and horned creatures out of Hans Christian Andersen. The half-naked reptilian Oberon was covered in cobwebs. He and Puck, played by actress Linda Atkinson ('75), shaved their heads and had silver twigs extending from their ears like antennae. The singers were shrubbery in the forest, with long green robes and frizzy green wigs. "We called them 'The Broccoli,'" recalled Feingold some forty years later.

As he had with *Happy End* and *Mahagonny*, Otto Werner-Mueller conducted. His orchestra of twenty-six, plus a sixteen-member fairy chorus, performed nineteen Purcell songs originally composed in 1692 for *The Fairy Queene*. Epstein used Purcell as underscoring and choral interludes for scenic transitions. In one memorable instance, he set Shakespeare's text as if it were the lyrics to Purcell's melody "Remember Me." The speech was Helena's complaint "How happy some o'er other some can be!" The actor was Meryl Streep ('75), then finishing her third year as a drama student. They worked to blend her reading with Purcell's rhythms. In his 2015 memoir, *Dressing Room Stories: The Making of an Artist*, Epstein remembers, "I'm not sure that would have been her instinct initially, but she was able to take a very structured direction and make it her own. We worked alone, with a stage manager and a pianist, going through it line by line, marrying each line of music to each line of text. The challenge was to sustain the emotion yet fit it into the specific rhythmic pattern. Spoken, though, not sung."

Streep believes that the rustics walked away with the production. She remembers business that Joe Grifasi ('75), in the role of Flute the bellows-mender, had with some Bermuda onions he used to supplement his impersonation of the love-struck Thisbe in the play-within-the-play. His costume was empire style, with a waist tied under the bosom. During the court performance, when he discovered Pyramus's corpse, he would raise his hands in tragic alarm, and the onions would fall out and roll down the rake. He was on the horns of a dilemma—would he go after the onions, or would he stay in character? Streep says, "He'd watch them and wait until they almost reached the pit and then he'd run down and—oh, people laughed so hard, when he went offstage, there were undergraduates standing, not on the seats, they were standing on the arms of the chairs, screaming. I've never seen anything like it, before or since. He must have worked on that for hours." What Grifasi remembers, with no small amount of pride, is that Brustein said that his Flute made him weep with laughter. "If I had to erase everything from my résumé," Grifasi said in 1999, "and leave just one thing on, it'd be that *Midsummer Night's Dream* we did."

De Lavallade's Titania is recalled with the same level of superlatives. Before joining the Yale Rep Company in 1969, de Lavallade, like Epstein, had enjoyed a visible career in several fields, beginning with the Lester Horton Dance Theater in Los Angeles. At seventeen, she was in the film version of *Carmen Jones*, which led to her Broadway debut as a dancer in *House of Flowers*, where she met her hus-

Carmen de Lavallade and Philip Kerr as Titania and Oberon in *A Midsummer Night's Dream* (1975)
PHOTO © GENE COOK

band and frequent collaborator, choreographer Geoffrey Holder. By the time she met Brustein, she had had ballets created for her by Horton, Holder, Alvin Ailey, Glen Tetley, and Agnes de Mille. She'd also been the principal dancer for several seasons with the Metropolitan Opera.

One day she decided to take the train to New Haven to see her friends Epstein and Mildred Dunnock in the opening of *The Bacchae*. "I met Bob that night, and he just said, '"Come and teach movement for us."' The dance companies she'd worked with were foundering, and she was and is a woman who goes where things lead her. "I don't plan anything; it just sort of happens, and I say 'why not? Try it out.' Oh my God, next thing I knew, I was in a Strindberg play with eyes as wide as Little Orphan Annie's wondering what I had gotten myself into."

She stayed for eight seasons, teaching movement to the actors, choreographing several shows, and appearing in twenty-six Rep productions of everything from Strindberg's *Crimes and Crimes* to Bond's *Lear* to *Mahagonny* and *Macbett* and Calderón's *Life Is a Dream*. She performed in drama school productions and the Cabaret as well. The premiere of de Lavallade and Holder's "The Creation," in a Sunday Series offering called *The War Show*, generated an audience response to match Grifasi and his tumbling onions (see box).

De Lavallade loved attending rehearsals of everything she could. Her newfound anonymity meant she could take every chance and never be afraid to fail. The inventiveness of the actors—and their pushback in rehearsals—amazed her.

Robert Brustein (1966–1979)

THE SUNDAY SERIES AND *THE WAR SHOW*

In his fourth season, Brustein began the Sunday Series. These were free events, one per Rep offering, for the company, students, and patrons to hear "new plays of quality in search of production." Curated by the literary staff, the readings could be thematic tie-ins to the onstage show, new works in progress by Yale playwrights, complete plays by recent graduates, or a new play by a writer that Yale Rep was interested in. There were oddball occasions like *Classic Pornography* (1971), which traced 3,000 years of porn from Catullus to Twain, compiled by a dramaturgy student, and *She Barged Down the Nile and Sank* (1973), an evening of memorable dramatic criticism.

According to Feingold, one of the Sunday Series masterminds, no event would ever top *The War Show* in 1972. The self-proclaimed procrastinator was too busy adapting *Happy End* to slot a play reading for its April run. President Nixon was then accelerating US bombing in Vietnam, which roiled the Yale community. *Happy End* was a goofy gangster musical, and the company wanted to honor all the soldiers and civilians who had died—and would die—in North and South Vietnam as well as call out the leaders who were responsible for not ending the war.

Feingold got the idea to put together an evening of readings and songs about war. Alvin Epstein would sing "The Cannon Song" from *The Threepenny Opera*; Elizabeth Parrish would sing "Farewell, Goodbye" from *Johnny Johnson*; Nicholas Hormann ('73) would recite the devil's speech from Shaw's *Don Juan in Hell*; and others would recite Siegfried Sassoon and Wilfred Owens poems from World War I, Hecuba mourning her dead grandson in *The Trojan Women*, and so on. The first half would end with a deadpan seated rendition of "Over There."

Carmen de Lavallade casually mentioned to Feingold that she'd been working on a piece with her husband, choreographer Geoffrey Holder, that she thought would be appropriate. It was put in act 2. Chords from Holst's "The Planets" were sounded, and de Lavallade, in a long-sleeved red dress, began speaking and dancing "The Creation." A 1920 poem by James Weldon Johnson, one of his "Negro Sermons," "The Creation" is a retelling of Genesis 1:1–25. After God has made the sun, moon, stars, planets, land, sea, sky, animals, and trees, he is still lonely until...

> Up from the bed of the river
> God scooped the clay;
> And by the bank of the river...

Then into it he blew the breath of life,
And man became a living soul.
Amen. Amen.

Feingold, sitting on the *Happy End* set with the other *War Show* performers, never forgot the reaction to de Lavallade's final transformation from clay to soul. "The audience starts clapping and screaming 'Bravo,' and we can't go on. I didn't know what that was. I had never been onstage when someone stopped the show.

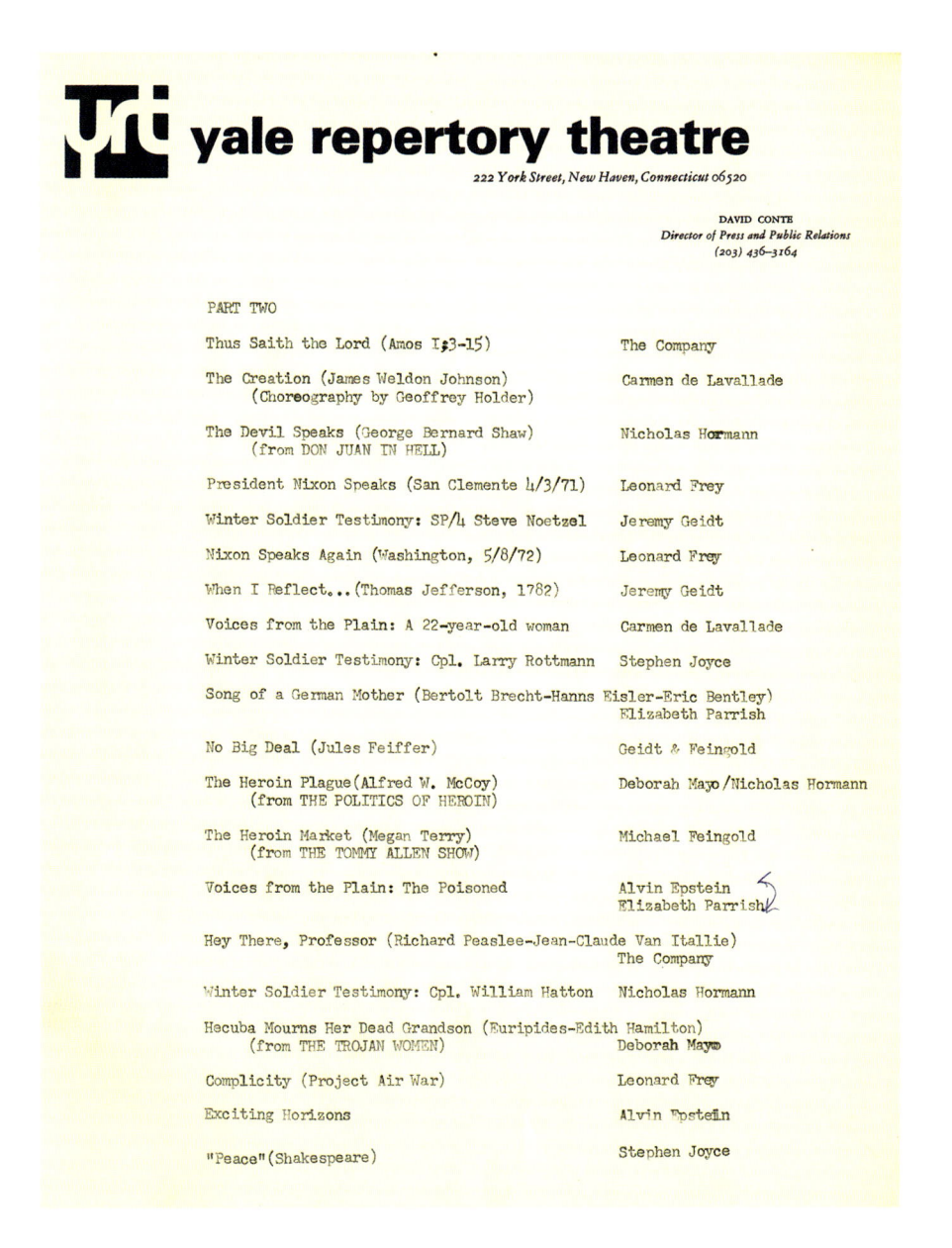

Partial running order for part 2 of the Sunday Series, *The War Show* (1972)

yale repertory theatre
222 York Street, New Haven, Connecticut 06520

DAVID CONTE
Director of Press and Public Relations
(203) 436-3164

PART TWO

Thus Saith the Lord (Amos 1:3-15)	The Company
The Creation (James Weldon Johnson) (Choreography by Geoffrey Holder)	Carmen de Lavallade
The Devil Speaks (George Bernard Shaw) (from DON JUAN IN HELL)	Nicholas Hormann
President Nixon Speaks (San Clemente 4/3/71)	Leonard Frey
Winter Soldier Testimony: SP/4 Steve Noetzel	Jeremy Geidt
Nixon Speaks Again (Washington, 5/8/72)	Leonard Frey
When I Reflect... (Thomas Jefferson, 1782)	Jeremy Geidt
Voices from the Plain: A 22-year-old woman	Carmen de Lavallade
Winter Soldier Testimony: Cpl. Larry Rottmann	Stephen Joyce
Song of a German Mother (Bertolt Brecht-Hanns Eisler-Eric Bentley)	Elizabeth Parrish
No Big Deal (Jules Feiffer)	Geidt & Feingold
The Heroin Plague (Alfred W. McCoy) (from THE POLITICS OF HEROIN)	Deborah Mayo/Nicholas Hormann
The Heroin Market (Megan Terry) (from THE TOMMY ALLEN SHOW)	Michael Feingold
Voices from the Plain: The Poisoned	Alvin Epstein Elizabeth Parrish
Hey There, Professor (Richard Peaslee-Jean-Claude Van Itallie)	The Company
Winter Soldier Testimony: Cpl. William Hatton	Nicholas Hormann
Hecuba Mourns Her Dead Grandson (Euripides-Edith Hamilton) (from THE TROJAN WOMEN)	Deborah Mayo
Complicity (Project Air War)	Leonard Frey
Exciting Horizons	Alvin Epstein
"Peace" (Shakespeare)	Stephen Joyce

People were standing on their seats, screaming and shouting 'Encore! Encore!' I panicked. I turned to Alvin and said, 'What do we do now?' He smiled. 'We wait.' Poor Nicky (Hormann) had to go up next with the Shaw speech. I don't know how he got through it."

The War Show returned at the end of October as a nonpolitical fund-raiser to open the Sunday Series for the 1972–1973 season. New material was added, including poems by Vietnam veterans, songs by Richard Peaslee and Jean-Claude van Itallie, and recent documentation from the Winter Soldier Investigation, which had begun to publicize war crimes and atrocities committed by US armed forces. Proceeds went to Children's Medical Relief International, a hospital in South Vietnam that treated civilians, especially children, requiring plastic surgery as a result of war injuries and burns.

Due to its supplementary nature and to company fatigue, the Sunday Series wasn't consistently programmed from season to season. The last event on record, a reading of *Ophelia Kline* by Richard Lee, was held in 1980. The Sunday Series did fulfill its original mission; at least three plays, Handke's *They Are Dying Out*, Horváth's *Tales from the Vienna Woods*, and Corinne Jacker's *Domestic Issues*, first heard in the Sunday Series graduated to the Yale Rep. It's also worth noting that the words of Athol Fugard were first heard at the Rep in a reading of his *Dimetos* in 1977. ◆

She commented, "Dancers are trained to shut up and do it. They're terrified. Actors question you to death." Her dance training and spatial awareness gave her an edge when it came to creating *Story Theatre* pieces and made the *Midsummer* set easy to navigate. Since dancers take shallow breaths to maintain their line in performance, her biggest challenge was vocal production. De Lavallade worked on her voice by taking private sessions with voice teacher Marjorie Philips and attending her student classes.

Streep paid tribute to her former teacher at the 2017 Kennedy Center Honors, saying, "Her legacy lives on not only in the ineffable single beauty of her own dancing but in the lessons she gives us—the lessons she taught me: forbearance, forgiveness, resilience. That's the secret of the strength in her core from which she soared over so many obstacles in her seventy-year-long career as a dancer."

An alchemical delight for everyone onstage, *A Midsummer Night's Dream* was a fantastic success. That fall, Brustein opened his tenth season with three "retrospective" productions—*Midsummer*, *Don Juan*, and *Dynamite Tonite!* Forty years later, Streep remembers that *Midsummer Night's Dream* was a "production in which all of the elements seemed to come together; in my whole life, I can't figure out why that happens when it does happen. But this time it certainly did." Today, one of Straiges's original cutouts of Uccello's charging horses stands, unattributed, at the top of the first set of stairs in the Cabaret building on Park Street. Few are aware of its provenance, or its significance.

A portion of Brustein's sabbatical (June 1972–June 1973) was spent as a guest critic for the *London Observer*. One of his uncharacteristic raves that year was in response to Polish director Andrzej Wajda's production of *The Possessed*, brought to the World Theater Festival at the Aldwych in the West End by the Stary Teatr of Cracow.

International theater festivals are a combination of open bazaar and trade show. If the resources are in place, one perk of the job of artistic director is the ability to approach an artist or theater organization and invite them to bring their work to New Haven. Brustein lost no time in introducing himself to Wajda and persuading him to come to New Haven and direct *The Possessed* in English at Yale Rep.

Wajda's *The Possessed* has five textual cooks. It is Wajda's adaptation *of* Justin O'Brien's English translation *of* Camus's French adaptation *of* Dostoevsky's novel *The Possessed* (or *Devils*, or *Demons*), further arranged in America by Feingold, who had to coordinate his revisions with the O'Brien, the only version authorized for use in English. The novel would appear, like many great Russian fictions of the nineteenth century, to contain every human crux: good, evil, idealism, conservatism, nihilism, provincialism, nationalism, atheism, faith, love, work, duty, boredom, servitude, revolution, despair, family, state, murder, suicide, sin, punishment—only war seems to go missing in the pages of *The Possessed*.

From such multiplicity one could draft a variety of stagings. Wajda framed the text as an allegorical conflict of the younger generation, embodied chiefly by Pyotr Verkhovensky, a manipulative radical who believes in nothing and who attempts to recruit the charismatic aristocrat Stavrogin into leading his conspiracy to overthrow the government and establish socialism. In 1972, Wajda drew a connection for his students in Cracow between *The Possessed* and "the world of the Black Panthers, the whole world of American social conflicts and the student unrest." The pressure to be progressive unleashes these men possessed by ideas in a fictional town, and the casualties are legion; the last is the heretofore uncommitted Stavrogin, swinging from a noose.

Robert Brustein (1966–1979)

THE RUSSIAN INFLUENCE

"Sorrow is the spiritual genius of Slavic peoples," intones the mopey Comrade Popolitipov in Tony Kushner's *Slavs!*, produced at Yale Rep in 1995. What is it about Russia, its landscapes, its literature, its gestalt, if you will, that has captivated all four of Yale Rep's artistic directors?

Very early on, Brustein programmed Gogol's classic *Government Inspector*, featuring then-student Henry Winkler ('70) as Dobchinsky. In one memorable performance, the actor playing Winkler's twin, Bobchinsky, was a no-show (romantic troubles), whereupon Winkler went on in both roles, whirling around in an instant to indicate the change of siblings and sounding like a madman conversing with himself. Chekhov's four major plays have all been produced, some more than once; also, in 1990, William Hurt starred in a *second* Yale Rep production of Chekhov's *Ivanov*, adapted and directed by Yuri Efremov as part of a cultural exchange between Yale Rep and the Moscow Art Theatre.

In addition to canonical titles, Yale has presented eleven other Russian or Soviet works. Two—*The Black Monk* (2003) and *Rothschild's Fiddle* (2004)—were adapted from Chekhov short stories, the latter by Kama Ginkas and performed in Russian (with English supertitles). Three were drawn from Dostoevsky: the epic *Possessed* (1974) in the UT, which was followed immediately by Christopher Durang and Albert Innaurato's literary burlesque, *The Idiots Karamazov* at the Rep; then, thirty-five years later, the ongoing collaboration between actor Bill Camp and director Robert Woodruff first took flight on their intense *Notes from Underground* (2009). During their tenures, Richards, Wojewodski, and Bundy produced adaptations of Bulgakov's *Black Snow*, Bely's *Petersburg*, Gogol's *Marriage*, and a trio of Soviet-era plays—*An Attempt at Flying*, *The Suicide*, and *Sarcophagus*.

"Joking, through tears" is a famous stage direction in *Ivanov*. Even in moments of high hilarity, a drop into sorrow is often a mere beat away, in Chekhov and in life. Perhaps it is the sheer emotional lability of Russian characters—their capacity to move from comedy to tragedy in an instant—that has made its literature such catnip for the peoples of New Haven. ◆

One of Wajda's chief visual metaphors was mud. The set, by Wajda's wife, Krystyna Zachwatowicz (she also did the costumes and lighting), was a mud-encrusted wasteland. All of the costumes and props had mud applied to them—shoes, dress hems, pant legs. Yeargan, serving as associate set designer at Yale, says, "The mud—*gumowy*, as Wajda called it—was made from rubber and cheesecloth soaked in latex to hold its shape." Surrounding the mudscape was a painted drop of a stormy sky that went wall to wall, with just enough room for actors to get around it. Set pieces included folding screens, practical lamps, tables and chairs with muddy legs, and a large, white neoclassical door. At one point, a bas-relief cutout of a broken

Christopher Lloyd and Meryl Streep in Andrzej Wajda's production of Dostoevsky's *The Possessed* (1974)
PHOTO © WILLIAM BAKER

Robert Brustein (1966–1979)

wagon flew in upstage, silhouetted by the drop, with one of the demons seated on it watching a character's death like a vulture.

Briefly, outside Brustein's office window at the school was a poster that read, "Wanted: Ten tall (6′–6′2″) men for the silent chorus of demons in *The Possessed*." Dressed in black-hooded robes, Wajda's literalized demons began as scene-changers in the style of Japanese *kuroku*. Later they started appearing in scenes as a silent, motionless presence. Still later they began pushing characters into scenes as if to reinforce their destinies. One delivered Stavrogin's suicide note to his young mistress, Lisa (Streep). In the final moment, their hands collectively stopped the mouth of the Narrator attempting to finish the story.

Replicating the Stary production, Wajda knew what he wanted but nevertheless embraced the changes in interpretation new actors brought. In the role of Kirilov, he felt he had, as they say today, "traded up": "Although I thought the way this part was played in Cracow was ideal, at Yale I got a very different Kirilov and which was really superior. [Alvin] Epstein gave him more humor and goodness, which make[s] the character more tragic. This is essential for a man who chooses to kill himself to save humanity."

The full company numbered twenty-seven, plus ten demons. The result was electrifying, the start of a particularly noteworthy Yale Rep season. The prize-winning journalist David Halberstam, who was married to Elzbieta Czyzewska, the actress playing Stavrogin's wife, commented after opening night: "If you had staged this play here a few years ago, the students might have burned the theater the same night."

For an encore, Wajda and Brustein first discussed *Peer Gynt* and then *Macbeth*, until Wajda concluded that his understanding of Elizabethan English was insufficient. Finally, he decided to direct his first comedy, *White Marriage* by Tadeusz Rozewicz, who he felt was the best dramatic writer in contemporary Poland. "If it turns out to be funny," said Wajda to the cast on the first day of rehearsal, "it is our victory; if it is not funny, it will be seen as pretentious, and this will be our misery.... We will try to make it a fairy tale for adults."

"Adult fairy tale" is the logline for Stephen Sondheim and Hugh Wheeler's *A Little Night Music*. By comparison, the explicit *White Marriage*, a collage in thirteen tableaux about the puberty and sexual development of two young girls, Pauline and Bianca, could be misread as an illustrated version of Krafft-Ebing's *Psychopathia Sexualis*.

The set, again by Zachwatowicz, was a false proscenium shaped like a vaginal opening, through which one peered into a bizarre, erotic landscape. The play shifts from the external events of Bianca's upper-class family preparing her for

Carol Willard, Alvin Epstein, and Blanche Baker in Rozewicz's *White Marriage* (1977)
PHOTO © GENE COOK

marriage to Benjamin, to the fantasy lives that the girls imagine for themselves: horse phalluses sprouting between male legs; stinkhorn toadstools appearing as noses; a milkmaid running across the stage, breasts exposed; and a Picassoesque Bull-Father trampling a wedding veil instead of a red rag. In the struggle between social and biological man, animality begins to gain the upper hand. Mother becomes aroused reading Bianca's poetry; Father presses himself against the Cook; the Aunt turns into a cackling hen. The Grandfather reverts to compulsive onanism. In the penultimate tableau, the wedding guests speak with the voices of domestic and wild animals, belching, murmuring, bellowing, toasting.

In the action of the final tableau, the morning after, Bianca, who has convinced Benjamin to agree to a white (unconsummated) marriage, removes all of her clothing facing an upstage mirror and burns her clothes in the fire. She then cuts off

Robert Brustein (1966–1979)

her hair and says to her reflection, "I am." Benjamin enters. Is she ready to go? She says yes and then, more slowly, "I am . . . I am . . . your . . . brother." Whether fantasy or reality, Bianca's final move, as bracingly decisive as Ibsen's Hedda or Nora, is a way forward.

Audiences unmoored in May by *White Marriage*, named a best production of the year by both the *Nation* and *Newsweek*, had the summer months to regain their bearings before a confrontation in September with Strindberg's *Ghost Sonata*, another densely textured, imagistic, nonlinear, continental drama directed by another controversial genius from Eastern Europe. Andrei Serban emigrated from Romania in 1969 to America with assists from a Ford Foundation grant and La Mama impresario Ellen Stewart. He staged three classical productions that are considered high spots in New York theater of the 1970s: *Medea* (1971) and *Fragments of a Greek Trilogy* (1975), both at La Mama, and *The Cherry Orchard* (1977) for Joseph Papp.

A playwright of many moods and modes, Strindberg, according to scholar (and *Sonata* translator) Evert Sprinchorn, "wrote best when dipping his pen into the inkwell of his unconscious." *Sonata*, dated 1907, is Opus Three of his four "Chamber Plays," shorter works that rejected ostentatious theatrical effects, and form itself, in favor of *theme*. For Strindberg, "the theme determines the form," and the result, like a piece of music, asks its audiences to heed theme and development rather than plot and character. Like his dramatic heir, Sam Shepard, Strindberg is a mystical hypnotist whose plays override questions of plausibility and causality with a rush of overlapping visual energies.

The theme of *Ghost Sonata* is vampires. The three settings are different dwellings of the soul. The first scene (Allegro/Earth) takes place on a bench on the street in front of the house, where an Old Man (Mephistopheles, Asmodeus, Thor, a caricatured Jew) has a philosophical conversation with the Student (Jesus, Siegfried, Faust, the Buddha) about the inhabitants of the house—The Dead Man, The Fiancée, The Baron, The Colonel, The Young Lady, The Lady in Black, The Mummy—who appear and disappear from view in a motif-like musical structure.

Scene two (Largo/Hades-Limbo) moves indoors to the Round Room for the Ghost Supper, which has been going on for twenty years, with the same people repeating the same things, their crimes and secrets and guilt binding them together. Tonight, however, the Old Man appears on crutches with a plan to buy the house and give it to the Student. The gathering defeats the Old Man by placing the death screen in front of him.

Scene three (Andante + Coda / The Higher Triad) is an extended duet between Adèle, the Hyacinth Girl, and the Student in front of an enormous Buddha.

Costume sketches of the Woman in Black and the Aristocrat for *The Ghost Sonata* (1977) by Dunya Ramicova, who writes, "It had been my habit, throughout my career, to include a portrait of the director of each production in the designs. The Aristocrat is a portrait of Andrei Serban."
PHOTO © DUNYA RAMICOVA

At a crucial moment, the harp strings begin to move and hum of their own volition, and pure white light pours into the room. The Student repeats a recitation of "The Song of the Sun" as Adèle dies behind the death screen. The room vanishes. In the distance, Boecklin's painting "The Island of the Dead" appears; from the island is heard soft, pleasant, melancholy music.

As much an editor and games-master as director, Serban would lead wordless improvisations in rehearsals or have actors mime their roles while the stage manager read their lines. He often left subsets of the *Ghost Sonata* company to themselves for days at a time and then revised their discoveries with them. First-year actor Kristine Nielsen ('80) remembers, "We were just the peasants in the background, but we spent a whole day in rehearsal with Liz Swados just clinking milk bottles offstage for the Milkmaid's entrance. It was an exciting way to work." The result was another unqualified success for Yale Rep. Where *White Marriage* was explicit, *Ghost Sonata* was allusive, but both productions painted "more truly than

Robert Brustein (1966–1979)

the truth," fulfilling Jean Cocteau's call for "Theatre Poetry"—a coarse lace, a lace of rigging, a ship upon the sea.

At any point in his tenure, Yale Rep subscribers might have felt that Brustein and his literary staff selected violent, abstract, profanity-laced, sexed-up, politically subversive, willfully obtuse works in order to bludgeon them with serious messages and/or drive them from the theater. Whither entertainment? They misremembered (or never knew) that Brustein's cudgel was aimed at the middlebrow. He embraced the highbrow *and* the lowbrow, saying in 2017, "I love burlesque. Zero Mostel, Phil Silvers, Sid Caesar—they were all my heroes. Mel Brooks."

There is something about an Ivy League environment that provokes the pranksters (see box). Several Rep productions in the 1970s were fruitful high-low collisions, Rodin's Thinker landing on a whoopee cushion. Moreover, from June 7, 1972, the evening of the bungled Watergate Hotel burglary, to August 8, 1974, when President Richard Milhous Nixon resigned in disgrace, he and his scrum of felons in the Oval Office and the Department of Justice made an irresistible target. The bloodletting sanctioned in an evening of *Watergate Classics* was a hilarious balm for American citizens rendered anxious, weary, splenetic, or heartsick by daily doses of White House chicanery.

Watergate Classics and its origin story were published in a special issue of *yale/theatre*. A planned *Misanthrope* had fallen through, and a Nixonian *Resistible Rise of Arturo Ui* might have encountered resistance from the Brecht estate. Brustein, on a trip to Greece, was struck by the parallels between Nixon's and Oedipus's reactions to their self-engendered civic blights, and he wrote a sketch called "Oedipus Nix." At the same time, company member Jeremy Geidt and Jonathan Marks (YC '68, '72, DFA '84) had created *The Nixon Show: The Bug Stops Here* for the Cabaret. Its centerpiece was the Shakespearean *Samlet*, in which the Ghost of Uncle Sam (Sam Ervin, chair of the Senate Watergate Committee) haunts a simple country prince. Sensing an opportunity, Feingold drafted and circulated a memo of possible sketches to fill the open slot. The definition of "classic" was extended to include modern plays, music, and American cinema, and potential writers were contacted about providing new or existing material.

On the title page of the program ran the proviso, "Changes in program subject to continuing revelations." A partial rundown of the lineup should demonstrate what the company, critics, and enthusiastic patrons felt was "poetic justice for Richard Nixon." In addition to "Oedipus Nix" and "The Tragical History of

JAPES AND INTERTEXTS

Theatrical parody is at least as old as the trial scene in *The Frogs* (405 BCE), in which Aeschylus mocks Euripides and his style by appending "lost his little bottle of oil" to all of Euripides's verses. Molière, too, never missed an opportunity to ridicule the declamatory bombast of his frenemy Corneille. As a genre, parody requires insider knowledge—the literary target must be familiar in order to be struck—so it shouldn't surprise that a setting like Yale University, steeped in centuries of classical learning, would foster an appetite for parody in its citizens.

Brustein-era parodies came in two forms. There were the genre spoofs: *The Big House* (a Marx Brothers prison movie); *The Shaft of Love* (television soap operas); *General Gorgeous* (comic superheroes); and *The Idiots Karamazov*, a silly symphony of Russian literary tropes. The others were overtly political: *Macbett*, Ionesco's Cold War travesty of *Macbeth*; *Watergate Classics*, an Aristophanic revue of Tricky Dick's deceits; *The Vietnamization of New Jersey*, a Christopher Durang "tragedy" that spoofed David Rabe's *Sticks and Bones* as a way to indemnify an American "dramaturgy of guilt"; and, finally, Edward Bond's cruel revisioning of Shakespeare's *Lear*.

Wojewodski tested the civic reflex for literary foolery by programming a rare revival of Charles Ludlam's *Le Bourgeois Avant-Garde*, a "ridiculous theatre" do-over of Molière reset in the hyperventilating world of "downtown Manhattan aesthetics." He also commissioned Eric Overmyer to create *Figaro/Figaro*, a conflation of Beaumarchais's *The Marriage of Figaro* and Ödön von Horváth's *Figaro Gets a Divorce*. ◆

Sarah Knowlton, Steve Mellor, Reg E. Cathey, and Elijah Alexander in Charles Ludlam's *Le Bourgeois Avant-Garde* (1995)
PHOTO © T. CHARLES ERICKSON

Samlet," there was "Pirate Martha" (Mitchell), a parody of Brecht/Weill's "Pirate Jenny"; "High Shame" (an "Eastern Western"); "Dick's Last Tape" (Beckett); and "Agamilhous Rebound," in which Rosemary Woods's obfuscating palaver seems, by current Washington standards, newly minted. Beckett inspired a second bout of logorrhea when Epstein, the original Lucky in *Godot*, entered to deliver Lickie's monologue "Waiting for G," the rope around his neck held this time by Bebe Rebozo. Lonnie Carter, who provided two other sketches for the show, retained the first four lines from Beckett and then let pour a lunatic torrent that sometimes exhausted Epstein in performance: "Get thee behind me Watergate Water Satan plunging self in spite for reasons imperfectly hazy I resume toughing it out when the going gets bunctious the bunctious get going in spite of the labors lost of Baldeman and Dichlich . . . money Rebozzo Reclown the cheat ethic dollars Abplap Abplop Abadabbaplopplap Planalp . . . Aerosol . . . unfinished."

Closing out the evening, the commander in chief (Brustein), surrounded by portraits of Washington, Lincoln, his family, and Eisenhower, praises the Senate for demanding his resignation and then announces his refusal to abdicate, concluding with "God bless each and every one of you. Good night." He waves and leaves. The audience was left to file out past armed members of the National Guard. *Classics* was scattershot or uneven perhaps, but decades later, late-night comics make room for this brand of up-to-the-minute satire—without, it must be noted, sustained Shakespearean and Aeschylean references.

Concurrent with *Watergate Classics*, two of Brustein's favorite playwriting students, Christopher Durang ('74) and Albert Innaurato ('74), had, by their third year, worked a mini comedy circuit from lunch-table riffs at the Hall of Graduate Studies to the Yale Art Gallery—where they presented a half-hour lecture/reading of counterfeit William Blake and Thomas Gray poems that morphed into Eleanor and Franklin D. Roosevelt saying Mass over a sugar bowl—to musical revues at the Yale Cabaret. Their shared ground zero for comedy seemed to be violent nuns.

In 1973, Innaurato ditched an opportunity to direct *Hedda Gabler* in favor of a cockeyed, allusion-rich improvisation with Durang on what was first titled *The Brothers Karamazov, Starring Dame Edith Evans*. Indisposed that very day by a broken hip, Dame Edith had to cede the central role of Constance Garnett, the ubiquitous translator of nineteenth-century Russian literature, to her understudy (Innaurato). One of many plot strands is the romance between Anais Nin and Alyosha Karamazov (Durang), a love so great that he leaves the monastery, and she makes him a rock star.

Associate Dean Howard Stein found the evening hilarious and sent acting and directing instructor Tom Haas over to see it; Haas fell for it and decided to di-

Robert Brustein as Uncle Sam in *Watergate Classics* (1974)
PHOTO © WILLIAM BAKER

rect an expanded version at the drama school in the spring of 1974. Brustein saw *that* iteration, which included songs like "We Gotta Get to Moscow" and "Totem and Tabu and Toto Too" and a scarcely identifiable Streep as the ancient Garnett, haranguing the audience with bursts of linguistic folderol from a wheelchair. The mania infected Brustein as well, such that potential subscribers to the 1974–1975 Yale Rep season were sent this Russian novel–length blurb for the rechristened *The Idiots Karamazov*: "The authors of this zany assault . . . define it as a 'cereal based on the works of Fyodor Kafka.' We're willing to agree that it snaps and crackles with pop philosophy and if you like your classics scrambled with a little singing, less talk and a lot of no-holds-barred hilarity, then hop on our troika and

Ralph Redpath and Meryl Streep in Christopher Durang and Albert Innaurato's *The Idiots Karamazov* (1974)
PHOTO © WILLIAM BAKER

it's off through the wintry steppes as the four Karamazov brothers meet *The Three Sisters*, Ernest Hemingway, Anais Nin, and Mary Tyrone and practically everyone else on the Mod. Lit. syllabus, in the ultimate satiric musical madness of this or any other season."

A delicious counteragent to *The Possessed*, which had closed the week before,

Idiots concludes with a final rant from Garnett (revised endlessly by Innaurato until Streep put a stop to the changes just before opening night) that begins with a conjugation of the verb "Karamazov." Those who saw both productions, including Brustein and Durang, felt that *Idiots* lost something special in its transfer from the school to the Rep. Brustein thought the new director, William Peters, whose work the writers had admired, scanted the satire in favor of farce. Durang, again playing Alyosha, felt Peters didn't find or make room for the core of gravity inscribed, and previously discovered, in the play.

When asked to summon a trio of unforgettable Yale Rep offerings of the Brustein years, grizzled observers say *Prometheus*, *Midsummer's*, and *Frogs*. The Aeschylus and the Shakespeare were triumphs. Conversely, the Aristophanes–Burt Shevelove–Stephen Sondheim *Frogs*, staged in and around the Kiphuth Exhibition Pool at the Payne Whitney Gymnasium, was . . . a bomb? Not at all. A misfire? Perhaps. A crazy idea? Certainly, but crazy ideas lead sometimes to great achievements. An event? Absolutely. A mistake?

"Mistake" would be the least of Sondheim's epithets for his first creative foray in a resident theater. The passage of thirty-six years and a cultural preeminence to rival that of Goethe, Hugo, or Shaw in their own times did nothing to soften his rancorous perspective on the Yale Rep *Frogs*. He writes in *Finishing the Hat* (2010): "The producer was that worst of both worlds, the academic amateur. The result was a calamity . . . , which, at the producer's insistence, was presented to a paying audience before it was ready to be seen." Ouch. Sondheim goes on this way for paragraphs, the foundation of his asperity traced, in a footnote, to Brustein's negative notice of Sondheim's score for *A Funny Thing Happened on the Way to the Forum* in 1961. (Geniuses never forget.)

Shevelove had directed around the same pool a freewheeling musical adaptation of *The Frogs* with book, music, and lyrics by classmates. It opened a month before Pearl Harbor. He'd chosen *The Frogs* because "Brekekekek Koax Koax," sung by the Frog Chorus, is an old Yale cheer. Brustein, who had admired Shevelove's book for *Forum*, re-made his acquaintance during his London sabbatical. Why not revive *The Frogs* with a new Shevelove book? A projected sold-out run of 1,600 five-dollar seats would help reduce the theater's accumulated $350,000 deficit. The purist in him sidestepped his horror of commercial theater by offering *Frogs* to his 4,000 subscribers first, as a one-week "supplement" to the regular 1973–1974 season.

Shevelove persuaded Sondheim to write a new score, announced as headline news in the *New York Times*. Sondheim, fresh off the triple crown of *Company*, *Follies*, and *A Little Night Music* and as cranky a presence as Brustein, said at the time, "I'm doing it strictly as a favor to Burt. I think it's an awful play . . . ; there's

The Frogs, a poolside potpourri of Aristophanes, Shevelove, Sondheim, Shaw, and Shakespeare (1974)

Yale Repertory Theatre

presents a comedy written in 405 B.C. by
Aristophanes
entitled

THE FROGS

freely adapted in 1974 A.D. by
Burt Shevelove

with music and lyrics by
Stephen Sondheim

The music has been orchestrated and supervised by
Jonathan Tunick

and the orchestra and chorus are directed by
Don Jennings

The scenery has been designed by
Michael H. Yeargan

the costumes by
Jeanne Button

and the lighting by
Carol M. Waaser

The words of William Shakespeare and Bernard Shaw have been selected and arranged from their works by
Michael Feingold

The production has been choreographed by
Carmen de Lavallade

and staged by
Burt Shevelove

no cumulative build to Aristophanes—everything is arbitrary." In the original, Dionysus, god of wine and theater, travels to the underworld with his manservant in order to persuade Pluto to release the shade of the recently deceased Euripides, whose return to Athens will bolster the flagging faith and morals of its citizens. Before this can happen, there is a trial scene in which the words and virtues of Euripides are weighed against those of his earlier rival, Aeschylus. Shevelove's adaptation substitutes Shaw and Shakespeare for the Greek tragedians. Feingold supplied their texts. Shakespeare wins by a voice vote.

A host of unforeseen challenges emerged during rehearsals. The underground boilers at the gym had to be turned off, as the company of sixty-eight actors, singers, dancers, and male swimming frogs (the "Chlorines") were sweltering. The no-smoking policy was waived for the Broadway chain smokers. Jonathan Tunick's orchestrations were very, very expensive. Chorus member Alma Cuervo ('76) remembers that the pool acoustics created an echo chamber. "Nobody could hear *anything*. Sondheim wrote echoes into the lyrics. Burt Shevelove would direct through a megaphone from a dinghy in the pool." No one planned for hazardous water puddles on the tile when the actors and frogs quit the pool after the prologue, so de Lavallade had to modify her choreography, and the actors had to check their speed and watch their footing through the entire show. Songs were late. Because of the chlorine gas in the atmosphere, the flameproofed cheesecloth canopy lit up for the fire marshal as if it were drenched in kerosene and had to be taken down and treated with a different chemical. The gas also made the paint peel on the flats, which were then covered with painted masking tape.

Sondheim recalled there being no dress rehearsals, and fireproofing the set kept the cast from the space for two of the three days before opening. This situation became a madhouse of Gotham celebrities arriving in a rented van and scrambling for seats that hadn't been reserved for them. Trying to have it both ways, Brustein published a sniffy article in the *New York Times* about the hazards of working with the Broadway talents he expressly invited. The show, naturally, extended for a second week.

With hindsight, *The Frogs* seems less a mistake than a case of mistaken expectations. The lunatic premise—an Aristophanic musical aquacade—was embraceable and very Yale Rep. Audiences had a wonderful time; tickets were impossible to procure; the critics were kind enough, carping only about a decline in quality in the final Shaw-versus-Shakespeare third of the evening; the Yale actors, designers, and technicians involved retain fond, head-scratching memories of the experience; and no one broke an ankle on the wet floor.

Today, many of America's leading nonprofit theaters, with Yale Rep a notable exception, offer their facilities and their subscription audience to commercial producers trying out their musicals in vitro in exchange for production "enhancement money" and a percentage of potential future royalties. Brustein was, ergo, years ahead of this curve with *The Frogs*, except Yale didn't accept any enhancement money, and despite a completely sold-out run, the wildly escalating expense budget meant that, when all was said and done, Brustein's wished-for bonanza amounted to seven thousand dollars, barely a dent in the deficit. His final, oddly restrained words on *The Frogs*: "You can't ask major artists to do a lark."

It's possible that, comedy-wise, the lowest twenty minutes in the entire Brustein era was *A Dumb Show*, the final offering in the portmanteau *Sganarelle: An Evening of Molière Farces*. For his second Yale Rep production, Andrei Serban was to direct Bulgakov's *Monsieur de Molière, or a Cabal of Hypocrites*, intercut with some shorter Molière farces. After some initial work with the company, Serban felt the Bulgakov was not worth the effort. Might they just do a selection of farces? Brustein embraced the idea. The company read and reread them all before Serban and Literary Manager (and utility actor) Jonathan Marks hit on the unifying thread of Sganarelle, Molière's answer to the wily, commedia dell'arte clown Scaramouche, who appears in seven of his plays.

Sganarelle reaches his dramaturgical apex as Don Juan's God-fearing sidekick, but Serban drew on a quartet of more lighthearted Sganarelle plays: *The Imaginary Cuckold*, *The Forced Marriage*, *The Flying Doctor*, and *The Doctor in Spite of Himself*. The last, in which Sganarelle, a woodcutter, plays doctor to aid the course of true love was the base text for what became *A Dumb Show*. Serban came back one weekend from New York with eight or nine sets of undefined words from different language groups he had invented with composer Elizabeth Swados. Marks, who was in the show, remembers, "Andrei handed them to us and pronounced all the words. Then he left the whole thing up to us. We went into corners and worked on fitting the words into the various scenes. Then we began assigning meanings to some of them and inventing grammatical rules and exceptions. The grammar, in some instances, included mandatory gestures to accompany certain words."

For example, Sganarelle is identified only as *grzengroho*, "woodcutter." His pals, Lucas and Valère, are known collectively as *schmendriku*. "Sex," which surfaces a lot, is *mooshi-mooshi pooshi-pooshi*, often preceded by *choo-si silkkwit*, which denotes the sighting of a pretty girl. "Doctor" is *ponmnikka*. A great doctor is *omnikka ponmnikka*, with the hands held in a reverential tent. "Apothecary" is *shata pupu*. When a plot point was deemed absolutely necessary for audience comprehension, a title card appeared on Michael Yeargan's all-white set of Mexican home-

Mark Linn-Baker, Michael Gross, and Elizabeth Norment in one of four *Sganarelle* farces by Molière (1978)
PHOTO © GENE COOK

spun and widths of floating cheesecloth, so flexible and ingenious (and inexpensive) it was profiled in *Theatre Crafts* later that year.

A Dumb Show was nearly scrapped until Serban decided to give the cast a half an hour to revisit it before the final run-through prior to tech week. It worked, but where to put it—in the lobby before the play, in the downstairs lobby at intermission, a post–curtain call bonus for remaining patrons?—was decided only at the final dress: *A Dumb Show* would happen onstage at the end, with the company changing costumes from *The Imaginary Cuckold* in full view of the audience.

This last decision explains why, when listening to the audio recording of *A*

Robert Brustein (1966–1979) 83

Dumb Show in Manuscripts and Archives at Sterling Memorial Library, one begins to hear peals of laughter competing with the booming brasses, clavier, and organ chords of a piped-in Baroque canon. From undifferentiated clothing racks on the set, the actors were choosing shabby costume pieces—some period, some contemporary—designed by Dunya Ramicova ('77) in strong, candy-colored reds, oranges, blues, and greens. Once the play begins in Dumbspeak, the peals become howls, shrieks, and cascades of laughter, punctuated by bursts of applause. *The Doctor in Spite of Himself* has a famous scene in which Sganarelle is forced to diagnose the ingenue, Lucinde, who has been feigning a loss of speech to escape an unwelcome engagement. Suddenly, amid the verbal mayhem of his examination, in tones worthy of the Mayfair Eliza Doolittle, one hears Patrizia Norcia ('78) say, "I'm terribly ill. I can't be understood by anybody." It brings down the house. *A Dumb Show*, the high point of *Sganarelle*, demonstrates that humankind's lowest urges don't require language to generate universal laughter.

Sganarelle was brought back for six additional performances in the spring of 1978. A couple of years later, it would be up to Marks, armed with his mimeographed vocabulary sheets, the archival tape, and experiential memory, to write the script down in its original Dumbspeak when Brustein revived it for American Repertory Theatre in Cambridge. "And so *A Dumb Show* was reborn," recalls Marks, "and revived for years on several continents."

Reflecting on Brustein's legacy at the Rep, Gordon Rogoff said in 2017, "What Bob established, entirely to his credit, was the taste. The good taste, the unusual repertory of plays, not cookie-cutter, not from the rest of the country. He believed his taste was going to carry it."

Any repertory theater worth the name produces the contemporary alongside the classic, but for Brustein, over and above whether a new play cleared the bar of his good taste, there were two additional caveats. The play should ideally suit the needs of his acting company, and his theater was *never* going to be a commercial tryout house. The landscape for new American work made an immense shift while he was at Yale. Plays had been moving infrequently from off-Broadway to Broadway since the mid-1950s, but a corner was forever turned in 1969 when Arena Stage's production of *The Great White Hope* moved intact from Washington, DC, to New York and won both the Tony Award for Best Play and the Pulitzer Prize. By 1976, new plays and musicals that had premiered at Arena, Long Wharf, and the Mark Taper Forum in Los Angeles were moving to New York. By the end of the decade, three popular successes from the newly established Humana Festival of New American Plays at Actors Theatre of Louisville (*The Gin Game*, *Crimes of the Heart*, and *Getting Out*) moved east, leading to new subsidies for new American plays, a significant jump in the number of self-designated playwrights across the country, the expansion of literary offices to read their output, and a fierce uptick in telephone calls among agents, producers, and theater managers. Resident theaters with a play that moved to New York got bragging rights and a financial piece of the action and were able to trumpet their hometown pride to audiences and donors. Do enough new plays that transferred to Broadway and your theater might be awarded the Regional Theatre Tony Award, a brand-new noncompetitive category established in 1976.

Brustein never succumbed to premiere-itis. Opening the doors to barbarian producers was mission drift at best and prostitution at worst. He derided the practice in print and attempted to shame his peers at national theater conferences. Only four plays produced on his watch, *We Bombed in New Haven*, Terrence McNally's *Where Has Tommy Flowers Gone?* and *The Tubs*, and Arthur Kopit's *Wings*, were eventually seen in New York but, with one exception, in different stagings. Long Wharf, in comparison, transferred *ten* shows in the 1970s alone, including Jules Feiffer's *Little Murders*, the play intended to inaugurate Yale Rep in 1966 until Feiffer discovered that Brustein had no plans whatsoever to move it.

Brustein occasionally "imported" student plays from school spaces, funded novelists' first dramatic efforts, and premiered work by recent playwriting graduates. A $500,000 fellowship grant from the CBS Foundation that craftily supported both playwrights and their mainstage productions allowed him to enlarge the supply side of the market five years running. The first round of Yale CBS Fellows (1973–1974) included Adrienne Kennedy, only the third woman to have a play done at Yale Rep (after Megan Terry and Italian novelist Natalia Ginzburg) and the sole playwright of color to be produced during the entire Brustein era. Her short play, *An Evening with Dead Essex*, was presented on a double bill in the spring of 1974 with Sam Shepard's "mystery in two acts," *Geography of a Horse Dreamer*.

Kennedy, who came to prominence with *Funnyhouse of a Negro* in 1964, remains to this day an outlier in the landscape of American dramaturgy; her plays are dreamlike, poetic, deeply personal, and uncompromisingly nonlinear. *An Evening with Dead Essex* was a departure for Kennedy inasmuch as it treated, in docudrama fashion, the real-life event of the death of Mark "Jimmy" Essex, a Black, twenty-three-year-old ex-sailor who had been killed after almost thirty-two hours of near-guerrilla warfare with police helicopters on January 9, 1973. Acting alone, Essex shot and killed seven people and wounded twenty-one more from his posi-

Earnest L. Hudson, Darryl Hill, Hannibal Penney Jr., and Carmen de Lavallade in Adrienne Kennedy's *An Evening with Dead Essex* (1974)
PHOTO © MICHAEL SHANE

tion on the roof of a Howard Johnson's Motor Lodge in New Orleans. Coroners found at least one hundred bullets in his body.

Mass shootings were not a weekly event in 1973. What hasn't changed in the decades since the Essex shooting is the lurid post-tragedy media search for possible motives in the sniper's background. Mark Essex grew up in a middle-class, churchgoing family in Emporia, Kansas. While serving in the navy, he apparently developed a hatred for white people. His apartment walls were emblazoned with painted slogans along the lines of "My destiny dies in the bloody death of all racist pigs," and "Revolutionary justice is black justice."

Kennedy conducted her own investigation and said during rehearsals, "I haven't tried to re-create Essex. I feel I understand him. I feel he did what he had to do. I don't think he was crazy. I feel it was a moment in a person's life when they just do what they have to do and they suffer the consequences." *An Evening with Dead Essex* takes place in a screening room in New York. Three Actors, two men and one woman, are rehearsing a play about Mark Essex to be performed the following evening. Also on hand are a Director, an Assistant Director, and a silent Projectionist, the sole white character, who sits upstage facing away from the audience.

In another instance of metatheater, Kennedy wants the live actors to "use their real names and the director should get the actors to play themselves." (Ergo, Carmen de Lavallade's Actress would be addressed as Carmen by the rest of the cast.) In attempting to capture the core of Essex and his story, the actors improvise scenes suggested by media coverage that might shed light on his motivations, discuss their own responses to the tragedy, and exchange ideas of what could be included in the show. Concurrently, the Director searches with the Projectionist for the most effective arrangement of visual slides to play with, or against, the text.

Things take a turn when the Projectionist shows unanticipated slides: a smiling Henry Kissinger entering the Paris Peace Accords, a visual juxtaposition of Vietnam B-52 bombers making their biggest raid on the demilitarized zone in 1972, and the police sharpshooters ripping Essex's body apart with bullets a year later. The collective investigation slows further and grows ever quieter as the company processes its grief. *Dead Essex* concludes with a mournful adagio of hymns, slides, and a faltering recitation of Luke 3:5–6.

A rattled Brustein devotes two pages in *Making Scenes* to his dissatisfactions with the play, the playwright, the director, Andre Mtumi, and the production: "In her own mind, Adrienne had written not a documentary but an activist piece with revolutionary implications, and the director she selected wanted to treat *Dead Essex* as a piece of racial propaganda." A gun not mentioned in the script turned up in rehearsals and was passed around among the actors after they recited Luke but before they left the stage. Brustein attempted to de-escalate its significance by insisting the prop be kept in a holster. At the next rehearsal, the gun was raised in the air as a (muzzled) call to action; Brustein's response, which infuriated Kennedy and Mtumi, was to threaten to cancel the production outright if the gesture was repeated.

The show went on, but audiences fled *Dead Essex* with the zeal they'd brought to Bond's *Lear* the previous season. The play is a fascinating read but a tough sit. Its deliberate slowness, its silences and repetitions, its lack of discernible forward action, its lack of resolution, and its banal dialogue probably taxed the most sophisticated of Yale Rep patrons. It is, like many docudramas in search of truth, both subtly elusive and ham-fisted. As with much of Kennedy's work, its form is *decades* ahead of its time, while its content remains tragically prescient. Dedicated "to the many mothers / of the many sons / who have been recorded as ciphers," *An Evening with Dead Essex* merits serious revival in a more sensitive environment.

Perhaps because of Brustein's disdain, *Dead Essex* has been partially erased from the institutional record. While lauding *Mahagonny*, *Geography of a Horse Dreamer*, *The Tubs*, *Schlemiel the First*, and the CBS Foundation, Brustein mentions neither Kennedy nor her play in his "Message from the Director" in the 1974 Yale Rep spring repertory program. Moreover, the play doesn't have a cover image, and Andre Mtumi, visuals designer Karma Stanley, and the actor playing the character of the Director, Hannibal Penney Jr., all lack program biographies.

The curtain raiser for that evening, *Geography of a Horse Dreamer*, directed by David Schweizer (YC '72), fared better. Both Kennedy and Shepard are musical playwrights who poeticize American mythologies, but Shepard favors action over rumination. His plots boil over with bizarre twists and cultural references. Shepard plays can feel obscure or unfinished, but they always entertain. After the *Operation Sidewinder* debacle in 1968, Yale Rep produced three other Shepards—*Horse Dreamer*, a quasi-Western about a displaced Wyoming cowboy who picks winning horses in his sleep; *Suicide in B Flat* (1976), a "mysterious overture" that draws on jazz improvisation and film noir tropes, and *Buried Child*, which revealed, for cultural pundits at least, a new maturity in the bad boy playwright with its win of the 1979 Pulitzer Prize.

Shepard scored major points with *Buried Child* for pushing the buttons of that hoariest of New World forms: the American family play (AFP). In a country without a titled aristocracy and whose serious drama begins only fifteen years after Freud's "discovery" of the unconscious, it makes sense that American dramatists would turn to the family system for material. (Even Aristotle advocates for characters who know one another very well.) Early modernists such as Ibsen and Shaw and, to a lesser extent, Strindberg, used the revelation of familial secrets and lies as a portal to access larger ideas about the mendacity of bourgeois values. The blended families in Chekhov are their own peculiar society, and to the author's trailblazing credit, the secrets and lies not only are never revealed but are beside the dramatic point.

AFPs trade in the blame game. O'Neill's sad and sorry Tyrones, to take the most famous example, spend four hours ventilating grievances and shifting alliances in a search for a temporary equilibrium. For every worthy antecedent to *Buried Child*—*The Show-Off*, *Long Day's Journey into Night*, *Awake and Sing*, *Death of a Salesman*, *Cat on a Hot Tin Roof*, *The Glass Menagerie*, *A Raisin in the Sun*—there are dozens of overrated or trifling items in the cupboard. Only Wilder's *Our Town* and *The Skin of Our Teeth*, partial AFPs, achieve the existential depth of Ibsen's *Ghosts* or Shaw's *You Never Can Tell*.

In thirteen seasons, Brustein programmed only one other AFP, Christopher Durang's *The Vietnamization of New Jersey*, a spoof that treats David Rabe's prize-winning *Sticks and Bones* as its host organism. *Buried Child* had already been staged in San Francisco and New York before Shepard's agent sent it to Yale and to Adrian Hall at Trinity Rep in Providence. The two artistic directors decided the play might fare better in New Haven, and Brustein offered it to Hall to direct. The relief in Hall's voice was palpable when he said to the *New Haven Register*, "It's the most accessible of Sam Shepard plays. There is a recognizable family story there. It affirms that you did come from some place."

The "some place" in *Buried Child* is as out of whack as the seasons in *A Midsummer Night's Dream*. A family of four coexists in a ruined farmhouse in Illinois where nothing has grown since Dust Bowl days. Father Dodge is an alcoholic who

Ford Rainey, Tony Shalhoub, and Clarence Felder in Sam Shepard's *Buried Child* (1979)
PHOTO © WILLIAM BAKER

Robert Brustein (1966–1979)

89

rarely leaves the couch. Mother Halie is a shrewish siren having an affair with the local minister. Their elder son, Tilden, brings armfuls of fresh vegetables from the dead yard into the house and lays a blanket of corn husks on his sleeping father. Their younger son, Bradley, is a partial amputee who shaves Dodge's head while he sleeps. Tilden's son, Vince, in exile for years, makes a surprise visit with his girlfriend, Shelly, in the second act. Vince's struggle to rejoin the family ignites a chain of bizarre events that eventually recalibrates the system before the needful death of the patriarch.

Shepard's thematics—paternity, inheritance, identity, land, the open range, agriculture, damage and decay, fecundity, and masculinity—play themselves out with a savage surrealism that, because the action creates its own logic, rings true. Shelly the newcomer will also momentarily stake her claim for belonging: "So I'll stay. I'll stay and I'll cut the carrots. And I'll cook the carrots. And I'll do whatever I have to do to survive. Just to make it through this." Shelly's decision—bleak, hilarious, genuine, and, given her surroundings, potentially *sane*—recalls Sonya at the end of *Uncle Vanya*, Beckett's clowns, and anyone ever forced by experience to conclude that any family is better than no family at all. With a cast that included drama student Tony Shalhoub ('79) as Vince, Yale Rep's *Buried Child* was a Pulitzer-worthy shock, because forty years ago the American living room wasn't peopled with such compellingly *recognizable* grotesques. Nearly all of the best AFPs since *Buried Child* have absorbed Shepard's meld of naturalism and abstraction. Playwrights who ignore it might as well write for network television, a point Brustein himself made repeatedly.

Brustein's stand against commercial theater met its most strenuous test with Arthur Kopit's *Wings*, a play that found its final form at Brustein's own suggestion. While under commission by National Public Radio for a radio play, Kopit lost his father to complications from a second stroke. He began writing about the stroke-related language disorder known as aphasia in the room where his father lay dying. *Wings* opened the 1977 NPR Earplay series. Brustein heard a tape of the broadcast, starring Mildred Dunnock, at Kopit's house in Martha's Vineyard that summer, and struck by its poetry and intellectual heft, he suggested to Kopit that he adapt it into a stage play for Yale Rep's upcoming season.

Kopit places us inside the mind of his heroine, Emily Stilson, an aviatrix and stunt pilot in her youth, with no suggestion of clinical disability. The audience must piece together her new world with her as surrogate paramedics. The first part, "Catastrophe," set in a hospital, captures Emily's panic as fragments of language and memory lie scattered in the poststroke debris. Part two, titled "Awakening," charts her linguistic reintegration in a rehabilitative institution. The final, most realistic section, "Explorations," shows Emily's growing responsiveness and recovery in group and private therapy sessions.

Emily is an enormous acting challenge. Dunnock chose not to repeat the assignment, and the part fell to Constance Cummings. Her brilliance in the role—a near monologue of devious half starts, repetitions, and circumlocutions—was a tour de force. The play's overwhelming success led Brustein to take it to the Public Theater, along with *Sganarelle*, the other spring Rep hit, for a month of New York performances that June.

A second set of rapturous reviews for *Wings* attracted a Broadway producer, who wanted the Yale set and sound effects and all of the student actors, four of whom were due back in school. Would Brustein release the Yale hold on the play ahead of its August 31 expiration? As things played out, *Wings* delayed its commercial opening until January 1979, sparing Brustein charges of hypocrisy from his peers. At any rate, there was a far more essential story to cover that summer than Brustein's conscience. On June 21, 1978, the morning after *Wings* began its run at the Public Theater, a teaser on the front page of the *New York Times* read, "Yale Dropping Brustein."

His exit was as newsworthy as his entrance. The official word from Yale University News Bureau chief Stanley Flink was, "This is an appointments story, not a policy story." But it was difficult for anyone to view Yale president A. Bartlett Giamatti's failure to renew Brustein's contract as anything but getting the sack. Officially, no Yale dean was supposed to serve more than two five-year terms, although exceptions did (and still do) happen. Brustein's contract history with Kingman Brewster included extensions, and he claims in *Making Scenes* that Brewster had wanted him to sign for a third five-year term. When Brewster left Yale in May 1977 to become ambassador to the Court of St. James, Brustein had already served eleven of a potential fifteen years. He felt acting president Hanna Gray, Brewster's provost, was responsive to the work of the drama school and the Rep, but Brustein decided to wait for the announcement of the next president of Yale before committing himself to a final three years, which would take him through June 1981.

The presidency was bestowed that December on inside candidate A. Bartlett Giamatti, a professor of Renaissance literature. Giamatti was an enthusiastic supporter of the Yale College Dramat; his wife, Toni, was a satisfied 1960 graduate of the pre-Brustein drama school, and they were Long Wharf subscribers, so Brustein was nervous about Giamatti's sympathies. In three meetings held over several months, their differences were, as later divulged by Brustein to the press, threefold: (1) Giamatti thought tenure for drama school faculty should be reinstated, which ran counter to Brustein's core belief that the best teachers for his mentoring laboratory should have active professional careers outside of the school; (2) Giamatti thought undergraduates should be able to take classes at the school on a nonexceptional basis, but Brustein felt that the resulting variance in the talent level and commitment of the additional students would dilute the efficacy of the conservatory experience for all; and (3) Giamatti thought there should be additional courses offered to actors and directors in the history of drama, stagecraft, costume, and so on, but Brustein had witnessed through trial and error that, apart from the dramaturgy and dramatic criticism students, theater artists in training responded indifferently to purely academic courses. Taken together, these three changes would, for Brustein, result in a deprofessionalization of the school, a realignment that would serve the interests of the university but not the national theater field, nonprofit *and* commercial, which had been steadily hiring Yale MFAs for more than a decade.

On May 24, Giamatti informed Brustein that the following year would be his last. For fear of demoralizing the company, then performing in Boston, Brustein sat on the news for a month. Once the word was out, he spent the summer of 1978 selecting a final season for Yale Rep, plotting how and where to keep his Idea alive, and trying to avoid firebombing Giamatti in the press.

In the annals of American nonprofit theater, Brustein's is a famous pink slip. Firings or contractual nonrenewals are a jolt, but in the slipstream of time, what does one or two or even three additional years signify to a man, or to an institution? Since Brustein's departure was clearly on the horizon, why wouldn't Giamatti honor Brewster's wishes and allow the dean to determine his own timeline? Policy is an easy excuse. How much of it was personality? Charles "Chip" Long, who was an eighteenth-century-English-literature professor before serving in the provost's office under six provosts and four presidents, including Giamatti, has this to say: "Bob Brustein was acerbic. He would never come to meetings. He lambasted the department for being old-fashioned and for not coming to the theater. He couldn't have been more offensive to the English department. When he left, I don't have the sense we lost something we loved and that Harvard now had something we coveted."

Rogoff remembered an early conversation with Brustein about what kind of theater he wanted to create. "Bob said, 'Something like the Royal Shakespeare Company.' I laughed. 'In *New Haven*? Who is our Shakespeare?'" In his years at Yale, Brustein may never have found his Shakespeare—Edward Bond, however accurate his Marxist lens, lacked the Bard's common touch and infinite variety—but armed with vision, will, intellect, *and* enough charisma to attract a cadre of tireless disciples willing to walk through the fires of fund-raising *and* navigate the bureaucratic labyrinths of Yale *and* slog through days and weeks of set changeovers and technical rehearsals and production meetings and school-wide critiques with and for and about him, Robert Brustein did, in the final analysis, manage to start something like the Royal Shakespeare Company in New Haven. Even Long charitably admits, "Robert Brustein put Yale Rep on the map, no doubt. It meant we could hire good deans and attract good students. No matter what local cloud he left under, we had become a place to be reckoned with."

The final Brustein season was dedicated to Brewster, "under whose administration the Yale Repertory Theatre was founded and flourished." Brustein's farewell message to his audience, in the program for season opener Horváth's *Tales of the Vienna Woods*, is worth quoting in part: "For twelve years we have tried to demonstrate that it was possible to fertilize the academic soil of a university with the nutrients of an experimental laboratory theatre—that the imagination and the intellect, art and humanism, could live together in mutual accord." Listed on a separate page of the program are the thirty-four Yale Repertory Theatre Associate Artists, an advisory council of seasoned Yale Rep artists begun in 1977 "to provide continued stability, permanence, and continuity to our theater, and to dramatize how a theatrical institution can continue to draw strength and nourishment from the people who have helped establish its identity." Included among them were actors David Ackroyd ('68); Brustein's beloved wife Norma, who would die suddenly of a heart attack that spring at the age of fifty, three days after completing a run as Arkadina in her husband's production of *The Seagull*; Charles Levin ('74); and Jeremy Geidt. Also included were playwrights Arnold Weinstein, Lonnie Carter, and Isaac Bashevis Singer; directors Larry Arrick and Michael Posnick; designers Tony Straiges, William Warfel, and Michael Yeargan; and dramaturg/adapters Michael Feingold and Jonathan Marks.

In July 1979, Brustein would leave New Haven, taking his Idea and a significant portion of true believers, and do it all over again in Cambridge.

CHAPTER TWO

Lloyd Richards (1979–1991)

The theater's front doors face the university and its back doors face the ghetto in which the university sits. Both have to be opened.

—LLOYD RICHARDS, *VILLAGE VOICE*, JANUARY 1979

AT THE TIME OF HIS APPOINTMENT as dean of the Yale School of Drama and artistic director of Yale Rep, Lloyd Richards was an equally known, if quieter, quantity than Brustein, a man who had also made his mark in several theatrical practices.

Born in Canada in 1919, Richards grew up in Detroit. His Jamaican-born father died when Richards was nine. After his mother went blind, Richards and his brother kept the family together during the Great Depression. He interrupted his studies at Wayne State University to train with the Tuskegee Airmen. When he returned to college after the war, he shifted his focus from law to theater and radio production. Like Brustein, he started a theater group postgraduation, but realizing that decent opportunities were chimerical in Michigan, he moved to New York in 1947 to become an actor.

By the mid-1950s, he had appeared on Broadway in a pair of short-lived comedies, directed off-Broadway, acted on radio, and begun teaching Method acting at Paul Mann Actors Workshop, eventually becoming its chief assistant director. In 1959, he directed Lorraine Hansberry's *A Raisin in the Sun*, the first play by a Black woman to reach Broadway and the first play with a Black director since 1907. (One of its tryout towns before New York was New Haven. Legend has it that Yale College junior Bart Giamatti congratulated Richards in the aisle of the Shubert Theatre.)

Only a few news sources neglected to mention at Richards's appointment in December 1978 that he was the first Black man to head a professional school at the university. In his first interview with the *New Haven Register*, he said, "The fact that I'm black probably is significant to some people, but not to me, and hopefully not to too many other people. I certainly don't believe it was a weighted factor in my choice for the position."

After *Raisin*, he had directed five more times on Broadway; his most recent credit, that same year, was *Robeson*, starring James Earl Jones. He'd directed the television movie *Freeman* and an episode of the groundbreaking *Roots*. After heading actor training at NYU's School of the Arts in 1966, he moved to Hunter College as a professor of theater and cinema. He had already taught a course for Brustein in the management program at the drama school, been the chair of an NEA theater panel, and been an advisor to the Ford Foundation. He was also the president of the Theater Development Fund, a New York nonprofit agency dedicated to bringing live theater and dance to everyone while eliminating barriers to attendance.

Richards's most valuable credit was his stewardship of the O'Neill Playwriting Conference in Connecticut, where he had been artistic director since 1969 (see box). The O'Neill was the one commitment Richards refused to consider giving up when approached by the search committee.

The six months between Brustein's nonrenewal and Richards's appointment weren't quiet. Brustein found time, while negotiating with Harvard for a new home, to wage battle with the *Yale Daily News* over their coverage of his dismissal. The search committee of eleven, which contained not a single Brustein-era drama school graduate, did nothing to dampen Brustein's fear of deprofessionalization and led dramaturgy graduate Rocco Landesman ('72, DFA '76) to ask in a letter to the *Daily News* that September, "If President Giamatti intends no policy change in the administration of the [drama] school, how can he ignore the opinion of those who have made it what it is?"

New artistic leaders quickly establish a tone through the media. Richards gave a series of interviews upon his appointment and once he began work. Most tellingly (and amusingly), James Leverett concludes his interview with Richards in the *Soho Weekly News* (February 1, 1979) by saying, "At least the school will be run by a gentleman." Anyone who had met both men would have gotten Leverett's point. Brustein was a tall, combative, opinionated word wielder who did what he had to to get his own way. "Avuncular" describes him at his most charming. Richards, by contrast, was diminutive, rotund, soft-spoken, and circumspect with his language and in his public interactions. Years of observing and teaching and directing actors made him a listener first and foremost. He habitually evaded the word "I" in favor of "One does or does not." The descriptor "Buddha" or "Buddha-like" comes up often in print profiles and the personal remembrances of collaborators and students.

Brustein's fears of deprofessionalization would prove unfounded; none of his stated sticking points with Giamatti led to curriculum or policy changes. Early on, Richards avoids a straight answer to questions about the future of Brustein's greatest Yale Rep signature: "The concept of a resident company of actors is valid, but economics today mitigate against it. Repertory is a very difficult thing to do. It only adds to the headaches. But there are some good headaches and some bad headaches. Repertory is a good headache." With much of the core company now in Boston, the headache, good or bad, lasted only through Richards's first season. (It should be noted, however, that from 1980 onward, Yale Rep productions have nearly always included MFA acting graduates of every vintage in their casts.)

For Richards, any organization involved with the American theater had to be involved with developing playwrights. Having presided for fifteen years over the growth of the O'Neill conference, he knew that the two most exciting movements in American dramaturgy at that time were the emergence of Black playwrights

THE EUGENE O'NEILL THEATER CENTER

George C. White (YC '57, YSD '61) was another 1960s visionary who thought that America could do better by its writers. Before White founded the Eugene O'Neill Theater Center, a playwright would send their latest script to agents and commercial producers and hope for the best. The emergence of off- and off-off-Broadway and the rise of the regional theater movement in the 1950s made room for riskier forms and edgier content, but it wasn't until 1965, when White invited a group of playwrights to the former Eugene O'Neill estate along the Connecticut shoreline to read and discuss their newest works, that a new *developmental* model for playwrights was born.

The process goes like this: every summer a select number of writers with promising new plays take up residence in Waterford for several weeks. Actors, directors, dramaturgs, and designers are on tap to serve the playwrights' needs as they rewrite. The residency culminates with two script-in-hand readings in front of an audience as well as postreading feedback sessions. Some procedures have changed in the fifty-plus years the O'Neill has been in operation, but the focus on writers in residence has never altered.

Given that Lloyd Richards ran both Yale and the O'Neill Center in the 1980s, the institutional synergy was intense. Only Ted Tally's *Terra Nova* moved from Waterford to New Haven during the Brustein years. During Richards's twelve seasons, nineteen plays headed west to premiere at Yale Rep. White's original brainstorm has since been replicated, with modifications, as necessary, across the country at other organizations such as Sundance, the Playwrights Center in Minneapolis, Powerhouse Theater at Vassar, the Ground Floor at Berkeley Repertory Theatre, the Humana Festival at Actors Theatre of Louisville, and the Ojai Playwrights Festival. ◆

and the emergence of women playwrights. The dearth of supportive, professional venues for them was uppermost in his mind. Yale Rep, which in fourteen Brustein seasons had produced only three plays by women and one by a person of color (with Adrienne Kennedy doing double duty with *An Evening with Dead Essex*), would become a space for their voices.

Lloyd Richards (1979–1991)

With key managers also now in Boston, Richards didn't need a broom to sweep away underperformers or the disgruntled. To improve the morale of the school, whose students described feeling abandoned in the changeover, at the outset of his appointment he hired Edward Martenson, from the McCarter Theatre in Princeton, to be managing director of the Rep and Earle Gister to essentially run the drama school as associate dean and to chair the acting department. With new work foremost on his agenda, Richards would incrementally expand the literary and dramaturgical office. Jonathan Marks (YC '68, '72, DFA '84,), who says Richards told him that he never completely trusted him, remained for two seasons, assisted by Joel Schechter ('72, DFA '73), a political theater specialist who edited *yale/theater* (renamed *Theater* in 1978), and Richards's wife, Barbara Davenport, who was a new play dramaturg at the O'Neill conference. Recent graduate Michael Cadden ('76, DFA '79) replaced Marks and then remained for three seasons.

Richards began wooing Nigerian writer Wole Soyinka for a new play and also announced a musical adaptation of Tirso de Molina's *The Joker of Seville* by West Indian poet/playwright Derek Walcott. He redressed the lack of female playwright mentors at the school by inviting Anne Commire and Corinne Jacker to be in residence that first year. By October 1979, he spoke of a development program for playwrights, which could evolve into a winter festival of new plays within the structure of a Yale Rep season.

Richards's goal for his first season was programming work to "affect the head, the heart, and the spirit of our audience—the head to make us think, the heart to make us feel, and the spirit to make it possible for us to perceive what we are and what we might become." Whether massaged by a press director or not, the inclusion of the words "heart," "feel," and "spirit" in Richards's statement signal a turn toward the theater of communion that Brustein had so obdurately rejected.

When parsed, however, Richards's first season is hardly a break with the past. It opened with John Guare's *Bosoms and Neglect*, an acerbic comedy that had failed in its Broadway debut that same spring. Richards gave Guare, whose work he had nurtured at the O'Neill, the opportunity to revise it for New Haven. Joining *Bosoms* in rotating rep was the American premiere of Peter Handke's *They Are Dying Out*. An existential comedy of manners, the play limns the self-destruction of a business tycoon. Its surrealistic second act, in which furniture is replaced by a boulder, a balloon, a block of ice, and a stream of sand falling from the rafters, made *They Are Dying Out* seem to be the most Brustein-like offering of the entire Richards regime. (Sluggish audience response led some student ushers to nickname it *They Are Dozing Off*.)

Measure for Measure, with a cast that included student actors Kristine Nielsen,

Tony Shalhoub, David Alan Grier, and Polly Draper, lost something special when Christopher Walken, returning to Yale Rep to play Angelo, had to withdraw in the first week of performances because of a street mugging that had left him with a broken nose and a finger that eventually burst from blood poisoning. The February repertory pairing of Shepard's *Curse of the Starving Class* and Alfred Jarry's schoolboy prank, *Ubu Rex* (1898), could also have been taken from the Brustein playbook. *Curse* features the Tates, a West Coast Shepard clan as impoverished, obtuse, and hilarious as the midwestern Dodge and sons in *Buried Child* the previous season.

Ubu Rex was directed by Andrei Belgrader, another Romanian émigré with a powerful visual style, an antipathy to realism, and a lunatic sense of humor. Brustein had brought him to Yale to teach and direct *As You Like It* at the Rep. After the Jarry, Belgrader would direct seven more productions for Richards, including Gogol's *Marriage*, two Molières, and Shakespeare's thorny *Troilus and Cressida*. (He was one of the few "double agents" invited to direct at both A.R.T. and Yale throughout the 1980s.) Belgrader attributed the simultaneous emergence of a quartet of Romanian directing talents—the others being Liviu Ciulei, Serban, and Lucian Pintilie—to state control of the theaters. In Eastern Europe, the theater was a proving ground where a director "has to find a forum which says something without saying it directly. Maybe that's what develops a sense of metaphor."

Both Shalhoub and Nielsen remember Belgrader in the classroom and in rehearsal with a tiny cigarette and rudimentary English, always asking for bigger and crazier choices. "He just opened doors and pushed us through," says Nielsen. "The *Ubu* did exactly what it should do: half the audience left; half the audience was bent double laughing. Tony [Shalhoub] played the General, with multiple missing body parts. A plate in his head. A hook. One leg. A colostomy bag. It was just hysterical. He would march us around and go crazy, starting to dance on one leg—which was just so Andrei."

Promotional materials that spring made much of the fact that *Timon of Athens* had only received twenty or so professional productions since 1833. Richards was directing it with his longtime friend and collaborator James Earl Jones in a trade situation. Jones would play Timon if Richards would let him play Steve in Fugard's *A Lesson from Aloes* in rep.

Had the diagnosis been available to the Elizabethans, *Timon* might have been categorized as the Bard's tragedy of manic depression. Timon begins as a celebrated acme of human generosity who ends up an utter misanthrope who attempts to tear down his city and destroy his friends. Unlike its dramaturgical cousins, *The Tempest* and *The Winter's Tale*, the play moves from light to darkness, tracing the

Lloyd Richards (1979–1991)

descent of rational man to unredeemable beast. *Timon* productions are catnip for Shakespeare "completists" but a tough sell otherwise; yet with Jones and Richards making Yale Rep debuts, it was a challenge worth taking. Jones said at the time, "Timon a tough part? I can't look at it that way. It may be impossible, but it's not tough." Directors and actors undertake *Timon* if they believe they can locate and unleash its mysterious powers. Today, Jones remembers, "Ours didn't. I'm accepting of my fluffs. Not that I can learn a lot from them, but I accept them."

Decades later, as they starred together in a Broadway revival of *You Can't Take It with You*, Nielsen reminded Jones that they had been in *Timon* together—she as a Prostitute with twelve lines—and that he had been her acting mentor during the production period. Jones apologized to her for his Timon: "I was so terrible. I didn't know what that play meant." Nielsen countered with, "No one does."

Evaluating his first season to the press, Richards said, "The wonderful thing about a bumpy road is that the bumps go both up and down." If *Timon of Athens* and *They Are Dying Out* were downs, the biggest up was Athol Fugard's *A Lesson from Aloes*.

On September 3, 1961, at the age of twenty-nine, Athol Fugard made his first mark on world theater with the one-performance Johannesburg premiere of *The Blood Knot*, a portrait of two "colored" (signifying "of mixed race," a legal classification in apartheid South Africa) half brothers, Morris and Zachariah, played by Fugard and Black African actor Zakes Mokae, living in the colored section of Port Elizabeth. It was the first time in South African history that an integrated cast performed onstage together. Additional provocations would soon flow from Fugard's pen and from his vocal support of the anti-apartheid movement—enough for the government to restrict his movements and set up security police surveillance of his multiracial theater, the Serpent Players.

Off-Broadway doyenne Lucille Lortel launched Fugard in America with a production of *The Blood Knot* in 1964, with James Earl Jones as Zachariah. By 1980, Fugard's *Boesman and Lena* had premiered in downtown New York at Circle in the Square, and *Sizwe Bansi Is Dead* and *The Island* (1974), developed in workshops with Fugard by Serpent players John Kani and Winston Ntosha, had received Tony nominations for Best Play and Best Director and a dual Best Actor award for Kani and Ntosha. *A Lesson from Aloes*, Fugard's first play to focus on the repercussions of apartheid on white South Africans, premiered in Johannesburg in 1978, where novelist (and future Nobel laureate) Nadine Gordimer observed "the white audience streaming in week after week to sit as if fascinated by a snake."

After five Fugards in as many seasons, Lloyd Richards recalled in 1985 for the *New Haven Register* the beginning of their collaboration: "One day Jimmy [Jones] called me up and said he had just read a play he had fallen in love with. It was *A Lesson from Aloes*. There was only one script in the country, which Jimmy said I could have for one night. I, too, fell in love with the play, but the rights were owned by the National Theatre in England. Several weeks later, I saw that the National Theatre was on strike and was likely to suspend the rest of their season. They had therefore dropped the rights to the play. So, I had my dramaturg [Marks] track down Athol on the phone in South Africa."

Contemporary playwrights versed in economic reality know to write plays with the fewest number of actors possible. Fugard, however, has always been a

Harris Yulin, James Earl Jones, and Maria Tucci in Athol Fugard's *A Lesson from Aloes* (1980)
PHOTO © GERRY GOODSTEIN

Lloyd Richards (1979–1991)

miniaturist. The number of actors hired for all *eight* Fugard plays produced at Yale Rep totals just twenty-one. (Compare that to the twenty-eight actors required for Bond's eye-extracting *Lear*.) Fugard himself says he is drawn to "the craft of a small situation I can explore in depth." Part of his "smallness" springs from the impoverished, improvisatory nature of the South African theater scene. Shakespeare and Brecht and Bond wrote for large, often subsidized companies. Fugard wrote, directed, designed, and acted in plays for tiny ensembles of nonprofessional practitioners. Physical resources were practically nonexistent, so much so that Fugard was staggered to find himself surrounded at his first Yale *Aloes* rehearsal by an armada of designers, stage managers, dramaturgs, and production assistants eager to do his bidding.

What Fugard achieves with two or three actors and a single set can, in the right hands, equal the sweep of a well-executed Shakespeare. Fugard locates his epic in the struggles of ordinary lives facing the shocks and aftershocks of a dehumanizing political system. Since Fugard is a language playwright raised in a storytelling culture, some patience is required. He can be prolix, his first acts long on exposition, his repeated use of central metaphors a touch obvious, but just as Dickens needs the first six hundred pages of *David Copperfield* to destroy his readers in the final three hundred, Fugard lays the groundwork inside his two, at most three, characters for an eventual shattering detonation. Male or female, white, Black, or colored, his characters, for all their volubility, are mysterious to themselves until the dramatic action yields revelation and resolution. Like Chekhov before him, Fugard is an empathic but dispassionate observer. In an unjust world, he will not judge.

The context for *Aloes* was a 1963 crackdown on political expression after a number of Black and colored townships struck in response to a one-penny bus fare increase, which led to boycotts and rallies. In the play, Afrikaaner Piet Bezuidenhout and his wife, Gladys, are waiting for their colored friend, Steve Daniels, to come to dinner. Gladys is just home from a hospital after suffering a nervous breakdown when security police, in response to Piet's involvement in the "movement," confiscate her diaries. The embittered Steve, released from jail for his subversive activities, has decided to give up the struggle and take his family to England. We learn that everyone in the movement, including, in a dramatic twist, Gladys, believes (erroneously) that Piet was the informer who led to Steve's imprisonment. Gladys, whose weakness is her strength, says to her husband at the end, "You're a good man, Peter, and that has become a terrible provocation. I want to destroy that goodness."

Shouldering the metaphorical lesson is Piet's collection of indigenous aloes that, quoting Fugard, are thorny succulents with "an inordinate capacity for survival under the worst possible conditions." Piet has found an aloe that doesn't appear to fit into any of the twenty-one identified species. Can his new aloe be said to exist if it cannot be classified? For Yale audiences, meeting these totally foreign yet eminently decipherable characters—apartheid magnified, as it were, through Fugard's lens and the sensitive portrayals by Jones, Harris Yulin, and Maria Tucci—was a profound experience.

In August 1979, Richards announced that "regional theatres shouldn't operate with Broadway as their goal." Not ten months later, after its Yale closing, *Aloes* was aiming for a September opening at the Belasco Theatre on Forty-Fourth Street. This initial deal fell through, but three weeks later, *Variety* reported that "[Managing Director] Martenson said Yale is actively looking for another New York management to sponsor a Broadway showing of the Fugard drama."

Broadway? In contemplating this commercial about-face, the term "whiplash" springs to mind. Neil Mazzella ('78), a technical design student who would go on to found Hudson Scenic Studio and later be identified by the *New York Times* as a "Builder of Broadway's World," remembers that under Brustein, "New York was a bad word. We were taught to feel *above* it." Asked today about the shift, Martenson says, "We knew it would be seen as a big deal, given that Brustein previously had been so skeptical about transfers. However, we viewed it as an easy and straightforward decision, not at all threatening to the Rep's independence. I'm sure that there was a discussion or two about it, but I don't remember them. We simply went ahead with transfer plans when they came up, as if they were the normal course of business."

Richards and Martenson, who had supervised commercial transfers from McCarter Theatre to New York, were mindful of protecting Yale's proprietary position over the artistic aspects of the project. The aloes that set designer Yeargan assembled for the production were stored in the interim in the safest of locations, the drama school library. *Aloes* played twelve weeks on Broadway, closing at the beginning of February 1981.

A second Fugard, *Boesman and Lena*, opened at Yale that fall, starring Zakes Mokae and Novella Nelson and directed by Walton Jones ('75), one of the unsung director-teachers of Yale Rep / YSD. Straddling the Brustein and Richards regimes, Jones directed a serendipitous range of assignments—*Tartuffe, Much Ado about Nothing*, Winterfest plays of uneven merit, new works by Durang and Auletta, and Mamet and Shepard—with an improvisational approach honed in the rebellious early days of the Yale Cabaret and in his decade of working for Richards at the O'Neill.

Lloyd Richards (1979–1991)

PERSONS OF THE DRAMA: PAM JORDAN

She was born and raised in New Haven. She wears black on Halloween and on Friday the 13th. Every other day of the year she wears purple. Upon seeing her first Yale Rep show, Edward Bond's *Saved*, she vowed never to set foot there again. Sorry, Molière and Fo and Goldoni, but she eschews clowning, preferring Shakespeare and Shepard, Williams and Wilson. Upon her retirement, alumnus Charles S. "Roc" Dutton ('83) dedicated his performance of Willy Loman in *Death of a Salesman* to her.

Drama librarian from 1976 to 2009, Pamela Jordan presided over a realm where fines weren't collected, where there was no pressure to keep quiet, where there was a full dish of candy at the circulation desk, where students were allowed to eat, drink, and *smoke* (!) as they held thousands of creative meetings, read the *New York Times* or *Backstage*, and hung out between classes. Jordan went to all lengths to help solve research cruxes for dramaturgs on criticism paper deadlines, actors looking for scenes, and Yale Rep designers and craftsmen with special requests: "I remember (Yale Rep prop master) Hunter Spence came in needing pictures of penises, because they were a crucial design element in *White Marriage*. In those pre-Internet days, we had to go to the Mother Lode and comb through stacks of *National Geographic*s." Jordan's domain was also the way station for the aloes between the Rep run and the Broadway opening of *A Lesson from Aloes*.

Two of Jordan's daily activities were recording the volume of foot traffic on a clipboard and attending to her scrapbooks. After she had posted media clippings on a bulletin board for community perusal—with alumni and faculty names circled in ink—she would paste in every news feature, interview, review, or editorial relating to the Rep and the drama school. One can even find mimeographed copies of Brustein's opening-day speeches to the school. "They had been around since the 1920s. I tweaked the practice, expanding their focus by including all the alumni credits I could find. Before me, it was just engagement and wedding announcements."

The drama library was one of the last to be fully computerized, starting with one public terminal in the back, usually with three or four students crowded around it. Jordan says, "Even the Internet the students made into a collaborative project. 'That better not be porn!' I'd shout from the desk." Library brass was never happy about the eating and smoking (!) around the collections and started to crack down; the long-rumored but often postponed Haas Family Arts Library was unveiled in 2008. Jordan happily took her retirement within a year. Her legacy is the Pamela Jordan Scholarship as well as the Pamela Jordan Yale School of Drama Scrapbook Collection (1966–2008), thirty-six boxes taking up forty linear feet of shelf space in Special Collections at Haas. ◆

Pam Jordan at work in 1980
PHOTO © ALLAN HAVIS

Danny Glover, Zakes Mokae, and Željko Ivanek in the world premiere of Fugard's *Master Harold . . . and the Boys* (1982)
PHOTO © GERRY GOODSTEIN

Fugard's next was an act of semi-autobiographical retrospection. *Master Harold . . . and the Boys*, which would be banned in South Africa, made its world premiere at Yale in March 1982. In it, teenaged Hally (Harold), an aspiring writer, spends a rainy afternoon in 1950 in his mother's teashop. With him are Sam and Willy, two middle-aged Black servants who have nurtured Hally's path toward manhood. While teaching Willy ballroom steps for a dance competition, Sam successfully goads Hally into dancing by comparing it to "being in a dream about a world in which accidents don't happen." The spell cast in their makeshift ballroom is shattered by the news that Hally's father, a crippled alcoholic, has managed to get himself discharged from the hospital. Hally disgorges years of pent-up disgust and anger at his father's cruelties. Sam chides the child for mocking the father, and in "an agony of self-hatred," Hally, cathecting his own ingrained racism, turns on his friends, insisting that Sam henceforth call him Master Harold and going so far as to spit in his face. Knowing that Hally is in more pain than they, Sam forgives him. Hally leaves "the boys" to resume their dance lesson as the lights fade.

"Racism is both homicidal and suicidal," said Fugard, whose given name was Harold and whose father had been disabled. As with *Aloes*, a three-person cast (Danny Glover, Željko Ivanek, and Zakes Mokae) on a single set delivered an unforgettable night at the UT. Wesley Fata, who had been brought to Yale by Carmen de Lavallade in 1973 and taught movement to forty-four classes of graduate student actors, assisted with Fugard's staging. "I choreographed four or five little dances throughout the piece. Athol told me, 'You saved my ass, Wesley.'" The production broke existing Yale Rep box office records, and Martenson was more than ready for the Broadway drumbeat that Frank Rich's *New York Times* rave set off. The play opened in New York a mere five weeks after closing in New Haven, with Lonny Price replacing Ivanek as Hally. *Master Harold . . . and the Boys* earned three Tony nominations, including one for Fugard for Best Play, and ran for ten months.

"Saintly" is not an adjective Fugard would approve of in reference to himself, but Martenson recalls his presence at the school as spiritual. (The same was true, Martenson says, of James Earl Jones.) Holding forth at Kavanagh's, the "Sardi's of New Haven," on Chapel Street with student playwrights, collaborators, audience members, and August Wilson when they were both in residence, Fugard was an inspiring model of an engaged artist/activist, always attempting to extend his creative reach.

Yale Rep would produce four more Fugards during the Richards years. Two were revivals: *Hello and Goodbye* (1982) and a twenty-fifth-anniversary production of *The Blood Knot* (1985) with its original Johannesburg cast—Fugard and Zakes Mokae. The other two were world premieres: the disappointing parable *A Place with the Pigs* (1987), which starred Fugard as a World War II Russian deserter who spent a decade hiding in his pigsty, and *The Road to Mecca* (1984), a play as commanding as *Aloes* and *Master Harold* that added a week to its Yale run before it even opened.

Scattered on the classroom walls at the Yale School of Drama are a number of production posters from the 1980s. One room on the first floor of the annex building on Park Street bears an enfilade of dreary snowflake images. Children are taught that every snowflake is unique, yet their parents might claim that in the end, all snowflakes look alike. The tension between individuality and uniformity is apropos when evaluating the subjects of the Annex posters—to wit, the eleven Yale Rep Winterfests of new work, forty-two plays in all, produced during the Richards years.

Richards outlined his idea to the *New York Times* in August 1980: "I plan to take one play out of the repertory and supplant it with what I am calling a Winterfest of new plays. We will do a very short repertory situation. The plays will be done in a fully rehearsed situation and give our audience an opportunity to see the work of developing writers." The initial ground rules called for two-week runs; the plays were performed at the Rep on a flexible unit set designed by Yeargan. To compress the sense of onstage space and provide a more intimate surrounding, the light grid would be dropped and the floor reduced, thereby creating a smaller "theater box." Subscribers would receive tickets to two of the offerings, with discounts for the rest. To protect the works in process and to avoid a scorecard mentality, the press was invited to write rehearsal feature stories that introduced the writers and their plays, but actual production reviews were forbidden.

In many ways—remember the snowflakes—the first Winterfest quartet, which ran mid-January to mid-February 1981, provided a template for the entire decade. First seen at the O'Neill conference, *Sally and Marsha*, by Sybille Pearson, was a funny, well-crafted two-hander tracing a growing friendship between dissimilar women in the same New York apartment building; it was so successful that the Manhattan Theatre Club produced it the following year. *Domestic Issues*, which had graduated from a Sunday Series reading the previous season, was by playwright in residence Corinne Jacker; the play is about a former Weatherman and his wife who attempt to reintegrate themselves into society. Its very title is a Winterfest trope—issues of national interest hashed out in a family setting, in other words, *topical* American realism with real food prepared and eaten onstage. The third Winterfest play, *Rococo*, was a formally inventive, language-drunk play about creativity and success by third-year playwright Harry Kondoleon ('81).

The fourth, OyamO's *The Resurrection of Lady Lester*, had, like *The Idiots Karamazov*, a drama school backstory. Directing student Jim Simpson ('81) adored the music of tenor sax legend Lester Young. He commissioned three short pieces about

Program for Winterfest I, a festival of four new American plays (1981)

Young for the Yale Cabaret in 1979, one each from Keith Reddin ('81), OyamO ('81), and Paavo Hall ('79). After the Cabaret, OyamO, on Brustein's advice, expanded the piece, which was taking on the structure of an extended Young improvisation. Actor Reg A. Cathey ('81) remembered the process: "Jimmy and I used to stay up late and play the sax together. OyamO would come over, and Jimmy literally sat him down and went through record by record by record and told Young's life experience—this happened then; this happened then."

Richards saw a second Cabaret version and put it in Winterfest. *Resurrection* includes thirteen musical interludes composed and arranged by Dwight Andrews. The details of Young's biography—the casual and the violent racism, the white appropriation of Black culture, his bond with Billie Holiday, drug and alcohol abuse—isn't as startling today as it was in 1981, before the advent of MTV's *Behind the Music*, but its vivid poetry and its celebration of the transcendent power of free-form jazz keep it evergreen. As for its post-Yale life, Cathey remembered, sadly, that "OyamO wanted a black director for New York, who then hired Cleavant Derricks as Lester and recast all of our parts. It got terrible reviews, and that was it for *Lady Lester*."

Winterfest I, in sum, presented one play that had already been to the O'Neill and one play that had been read in the Sunday Series. Two were by Yale drama students, one of them currently enrolled. Of the two realistic plays, one bore political overtones; of the two formally experimental works, both foregrounded bravura language, and one of them explicitly investigated the challenges of living with a nonmainstream cultural identity in America. In the seasons to come, Winterfest—"four blind dates," wrote local critic Frank Rizzo—would premiere many more works by Black and women playwrights; two plays by Asian Americans, *Union Boys* by James Yoshimura (1986) and *The Memento* by Wakako Yamauchi (1987); and the first by a Latinx writer, student playwright Edit Villarreal ('86), whose *Crazy from the Heart* dramatized a potlatch, the traditional gift-giving feast celebrated by Indigenous tribes in the Pacific Northwest.

An unanticipated positive to Winterfest was the wealth of collaborative opportunities extended to Yale students. By Winterfest IV, costume, set, and lighting design students were appearing regularly on the program masthead, even though their aspirations consistently pushed back against the original "simple is best" production philosophy. By Winterfest V, the productions began to rotate in the UT as well as at the Rep; each performed every other day, meaning more changeovers for technical and design production students and more work-study money for all. Student directors began getting hired. Third-year director Evan Yionoulis ('85) helmed Dick Beebe's ('85) *Vampires in Kodachrome* for Winterfest V. The first woman to direct a play at the Rep, Yionoulis suspects this institutional milestone flew under the radar because, although she was named for her grandmother, Evanthea, "Evan" reads as a male given name. She said in an interview, "The bottom line is ability, not gender. . . . It's not so much a fear of failure, but a fear of being mediocre. I want to make the audience feel something. And if I'm successful or not, it won't be because I'm a woman." As for Yale writers, Winterfests VI through XI featured at least one, if not two, current student playwrights, usually paired, like Beebe and Yionoulis, with directors with whom they'd already established a fruitful working relationship. Even the criticism students got in on the act,

David Alan Grier, Darryl Croxton, Reg E. Cathey, and Scott Rickey Wheeler in OyamO's *The Resurrection of Lady Lester* (1981)
PHOTO © GERRY GOODSTEIN

Lloyd Richards (1979–1991)

sitting in rehearsals as assistant dramaturgs, writing program notes, and sharing their thoughts for rewrites.

With additional productions every season, student actors had more chances to work alongside the professionals. MFA actors (and future theater, television, and film fixtures) Frances McDormand, Isabell Monk, Jane Kaczmarek, Charles S. "Roc" Dutton, Angela Bassett, Julie Boyd, John Turturro, Patricia Clarkson, Laila Robbins, Jayne Atkinson, Dylan Baker, Courtney B. Vance, Christopher Noth, Amy Aquino, Patrick Kerr, Steven Skybell, Tom McGowan, Michael Potts, and Liev Schreiber all appeared in Winterfest plays, sharing the stage with the likes of Seret Scott, Jan Miner, Frances Conroy, John Seitz, Theresa Merritt, James Earl Jones, Kim Hunter, Jo Henderson, Ching Valdes, Jon DeVries, Delroy Lindo, Sylvia Miles, David Chandler, J. Smith-Cameron, Dan Butler, Mary Louise Wilson, and Debra Monk.

As Winterfest gathered momentum, audiences were provided with opportunities to enrich their knowledge of the development process. In addition to postshow talk-backs with intrepid playwrights ready to face the slings and arrows of the public, the Rep began hosting free seminars and panel discussions in the basement lounge of the Rep. For Winterfest III (1983), there were six, ranging from "Blood, Sweat, and Tears: Directing the New Play," a panel with Richards, Gordon Davidson, and Harold Prince, to "New Plays—Why Bother?," featuring Emanuel Azenberg, George C. White, James Leverett, and Michael Cadden, to "Perspectives on Contemporary Playwriting" with John Guare and recent Winterfest playwrights Harry Kondoleon and Stuart Browne.

How did the three or four plays chosen from literally hundreds of scripts make the cut? Another crucial Richards hire, in 1983, was Gitta Honegger, the first non-drama-school graduate to run the literary management office for the Rep as well as the first woman to teach in the dramaturgy and dramatic criticism program and hold the title of resident dramaturg. An Austrian émigrée with a doctorate on Eugene O'Neill, she lived in Connecticut and had written criticism about Brustein-era productions for German newspapers. Brustein had thought her overqualified to attend the school, but Richards made use of her talents. "Lloyd interviewed me at the O'Neill, but then he took me to Yale and then I sat in this little office and he threw a play on my desk. 'Tell me what you think about this.' It was *Ma Rainey*." Her astute positive appraisal of August Wilson's first play helped her land the job. For Winterfests, she, Joel Schechter, Barbara Davenport, and Michael Cadden would begin reading in September. Richards gave them the O'Neill plays from that summer that he thought might be suitable. The dramaturgy students began reading and reporting on the agent submissions. Honegger and Schechter kept an ear out for promising student plays coming through the department pipeline. Honegger recalls, "I read scripts all the time. Lloyd went to a dinner and somebody, a donor, anybody, would say they wrote a play, and then we had to read it."

Broadly speaking, Davenport was drawn to psychologically detailed character plays, Schechter went for sociopolitical themes, and Honegger advocated for quirky, formally challenging work. When it came time for final selection, the group could sit for hours discussing individual plays and the overall balance of the festival mix, and Richards, Honegger says, "never looked at his watch." Viewed through this collective prism, a deeply strange play like *Rococo* or Adrienne Kennedy's *Ohio State Murders* could share a slot with a realistic *Sally and Marsha* or Sam Kelley's *Pill Hill*.

Amid the Winterfest positives stood two interrelated negatives. The first was expectational: with three weeks of rehearsal and a rudimentary physical production, the offerings shown to the public were caught between two stools—more than an O'Neill workshop reading but less than a finished Yale Rep show. Would the playwright be able to incorporate rewrites generated from variable audience response? Could the play conceivably continue its development through the run? The answers were "no" and "not really." The second was fiscal: in terms of production budgets, the amount of money allocated for one Rep slot (for example, *A Lesson from Aloes*) was divided among four Winterfest plays. As the years went on, increasing student design participation led to increased ambitions that the tiny budgets and the rushed time frame couldn't accommodate. Not for nothing did designers and tech staff often refer to December and January as Winterf*ck.

Technical Director Bronislaw Sammler, who revolutionized budgeting at Yale Rep (see box), maintains a unique perspective on the dozen festivals. "One of the things that we never spent money on [for] Winterfest was a wig, because they cost five hundred dollars. Five hundred out of thirty-five hundred for one wig for one play for one character in one of four plays when you also have to do scenery and costumes and lights and props and everything else was a very large percentage. And so, the director would say, 'Can I have a wig? No, not in our vocabulary.' Lloyd was comfortable with a second stage level. His goal was to hear the play."

While no single play from Lloyd's eleven Winterfests can be said to have entered the permanent repertory, a majority received subsequent productions. Nearly every one of the playwrights has either migrated to television and film or continues to this day to write for the theater and/or teach playwriting. Student Wendy MacLeod ('87), whose comedies *Apocalyptic Butterflies* ('87) and *The My House Play* ('88) were presented at Winterfests VII and VIII, felt that giving four beginning playwrights a full premiere was revolutionary. "The collaborative give and take of

PERSONS OF THE DRAMA: BRONISLAW (BEN) SAMMLER

In the spring of 1974, Ben Sammler was stretched thin. He was a third-year technical design and production student with two Yale Rep shows for which he'd done the lighting design, four remaining Rep shows to tech, and a thesis to write. On commencement day, after marching to get his degree, he took off his cap and gown and headed back to the Payne-Whitney Gymnasium. *The Frogs* was opening that night in the Kiphuth Exhibition pool, and he was the technical director.

The boundaries between student and professional were looser then. The concept-driven shows of the early Brustein years often translated into large physical productions that reconfigured the playing space and required rebuilding the stage several times each season, work that burned through tech students at a fast clip, which all but ensured that a talent like Sammler would have an abbreviated life in the classroom. In his first year, he had been a carpenter for Yale Rep's *Life Is a Dream*. The following year, he was stage carpenter for the season, running and changing over every Rep show, and was then promoted to technical director in his third.

Sammler stayed on. By the time he was elevated to production manager in 1979 and was chairing the technical design and production department, he had begun organizational measures that would allay student burnout, reduce cost overruns, and promote efficiency and interdepartmental collaboration yet still provide flexibility and wiggle room in case of emergencies—or eureka moments—that emerged in rehearsals or during tech. By 1982, he was handing out pencils to students and colleagues printed with the legend "Bringing Order to the Chaos," his description of the role of technical director.

He recalls, "I was one of the first production managers hired to lead the budget process. Prior to that it was often the general manager or managing director. So, Rob Orchard [Brustein's managing director] would run those meetings . . . , and he'd go around the room and ask how much do you need? If you're me as the TD, I say, 'I need 4,000.' How much do you need as the costume shop manager, I need 6,000, et cetera. He looks at his numbers, we only have half that, you get 2,000, you get 3,000, you get whatever. And now you all go and figure out how to make that work. And I thought, I don't think so. Here's my list of how I got to my 4,000; which of those things do you *not* want to do? And that's how we do it now."

Department heads came to Sammler budget meetings, run like a court of law,

Laraine and Bronislaw (Ben) Sammler at his retirement party (2017)
PHOTO © T. CHARLES ERICKSON

with every design item identified, estimated, and tallied. The directors and designers were present; for new works, the playwrights were invited to attend. Incomplete visions were permitted, says Sammler. "'We have a rough idea about such and such, and so we're putting aside about five hundred dollars for that idea. We don't know exactly how it's going to be done, but that's how much we're putting aside for it.' Which is very different from 'We want to do this, we have no idea what it's going to cost, I'll let you know later on,' an approach that leads to everybody running around, scrambling at the last minute, working overtime, and exploding the budget."

Initial budget meeting attendees reunite at the subsequent weekly production meetings during the rehearsal period, a process that Sammler feels is of paramount importance to the students of every discipline, who are compelled to interact with facts and numbers throughout their three years together. They gather production knowledge to apply to their future professional lives.

Another Sammler master achievement was the production calendar, essential to the life and well-being of the YSD / Yale Rep complex and since adopted by theaters across the country. A wealth of detail and a marvel of concision, Sammler's invention may seem at first as runic as the Aztec calendar, but once its code is cracked, a world of duties and deadlines emerges, so much so that the calendar-literate tech student will know on the first day of class in August when he gets a half day off the following March.

That Sammler was able to carve out the time to cowrite *Structural Design for the Stage* (1999) and edit three volumes of *Technical Design Solutions for Theatre*, informally known as "Tech Briefs," is further proof of his bred-in-the-bone sense of analytical industry and his commitment to pedagogy. *Structural Design* and "Tech Briefs," a collection of articles by students of the program and professionals in the field, have become foundational texts for techies around the world.

When he retired in June 2017 as chair of the technical design and production department and designated Henry McCormick Professor in the Practice, Ben Sammler had by his own estimation been production manager at the Rep or the drama school on some seven hundred shows. His favorite of all? Lee Blessing's *A Walk in the Woods*. "I usually don't go back to see plays a second time, because I've already seen them eighteen times during tech, so I go to [the] opening, and thank you very much, eighteen times I've seen it. *Woods* was one of those rare ones where you go back for a really special moment in the theater. Beautifully lit by Jennifer Tipton. It was written at the right time. It stands up."

As will *Structural Design for the Stage* and the production calendar. ◆

those experiences, both in rehearsal and in front of a live audience, laughing and *not* laughing, showed me how to become an adult in the theatre." Doug Wright (YC '85) also had back-to-back Winterfests, *Interrogating the Nude* (1989) and *Dinosaurs* (1990), as his first professional productions. A recent president of the Dramatists Guild of America with six Broadway credits and a Tony Award for his play *I Am My Own Wife*, Wright remembers the tools he gained from *Dinosaurs*: when to intercede, what to ask from a director and a design team, and ways to advocate for the play in rehearsal. "That's the thing about new play festivals like that," he says. "Everyone can look back and assess the success or failure of the play, but what no one can quantify but the people involved are the value of the lessons learned by the artists participating. In the way that Winterfest was designed to be pedagogical, *Dinosaurs* was a total success, which is not to say it was a great play. But it totally served Lloyd's vision of giving the playwright a safe forum in which to learn."

Before investigating Richards's approach to classic repertory, it would be useful to track some institutional growth at Yale Rep under his aegis. Not counting student pass holders, Richards began his tenure with 1,100 subscribers, three-week production runs, and a 1.1-million-dollar budget. Marketing in the nonprofit arts arena was beginning to take hold in the 1980s. Although Managing Director Martenson knew that the university would ultimately absorb the institutional red ink—$455,000 for the 1979–1980 season, for example—audience members are the final collaborators in the theatrical experience, and Richards wanted more of them. When Martenson arrived, "there had been some criticisms we wanted to address. What the Rep needed was a more energized relationship with the audience, a clearer role for the students to play, and a way of organizing a more systematic place for new plays in the [Yale Rep] set-up." When he left after three seasons to chair the National Endowment for the Arts theater program, he felt his work wasn't finished, but Richards said to him, "You don't turn down the chance to serve the field through the government." (Martenson would return decades later to chair the theater management program at the drama school.)

His successor, Benjamin "Ben" Mordecai, began in September 1982. Rather than complete a PhD at Indiana University, Mordecai had cofounded Indiana Repertory Theatre in 1971 with Gregory Poggi and Edward Stern. His widow, Sherry Mordecai, remembers that all three men had directing experience, but because her husband had an actuarial background, he kept the books and assumed the title of managing director. After ten years of nonstop hustle to keep the doors open in Indianapolis, the opportunity to return east, to the Ivy League, and to a theater where, as she puts it, "You were always going to make payroll," proved irresistible.

Mordecai wasted no time spreading good news. After five months on the job, he announced that the Rep had reached 96 percent capacity for *A Doll House* with Dianne Wiest, Fugard's *Hello and Goodbye*, and Shaw's *The Philanderer* with Christopher Walken. After the Broadway transfers of *Aloes* and *Master Harold . . . and the Boys*, Yale Rep would be able to take a "See it here first" angle with its promotional materials. For the 1983–1984 season, which would include the twenty-fifth-anniversary production of *A Raisin in the Sun* as well as the world premieres of *Ma Rainey's Black Bottom* and *The Road to Mecca*, an eight-play subscription ranged from an "unbeatable" $40.00 to $85.00. In January 1984, *Variety* reported that Yale Rep now had 5,050 subscribers and 2,200 student pass holders. Demand was high enough for the following subscription season that the theater added a week of performances to every production run.

Due to the needs of a longtime staff member, Arthur Pepine, Yale Rep was also making significant progress with accessibility issues. Initially hired by Brustein in May 1966 as resident stage manager, Pepine dove into a swimming pool the following summer and broke his neck, leaving him paralyzed except for the push muscles in his hands. After rehabilitation, he returned to Yale to become the director of financial aid at the drama school and faculty advisor to the Yale Cabaret, positions that required the installation of wheelchair ramps at the UT and Cabaret buildings.

The 1990 Americans with Disabilities Act required that all public spaces as well as events advertised to the public be fully accessible, but because of the efforts of Pepine and Director of Theater Safety and Occupational Health Bill Reynolds ('79), blind or visually impaired patrons could listen to a prepared visual description of the production as early as the 1980–1981 season. The following year, special elevators and bathrooms with wheelchair access were installed at the Rep and the UT, and there was a sign-interpreted performance for the deaf and hearing impaired on the second Thursday of each run.

The early Reagan years, when fiscal deregulation led to major reversals in the tax treatment of business income, were awash with money to disburse, even for the arts. In the spring of 1985, producer and theater owner Lucille Lortel gave $300,000 to create the Lucille Lortel Fund for New Drama at Yale Repertory Theatre. The next year went even better: in January 1986, the Exxon Corporation gave a $25,000 operating gift that could be matched up to $75,000. Four months later, the Mellon Foundation awarded Yale one of twenty-seven three-year grants of $125,000 to assist them in "producing earlier work that has survived to become an important part of the theatrical literature or that, whether or not well known, merits revival." Money begets money: the Dana Charitable Trust then gave $150,000 to attract to the Rep "significant American and international directors of real vision, to support the fulfillment of their vision through production and to make the impact resonate through the theatre by supporting talented directing interns to assist in the collaboration of these distinctive artists." Unrestricted funds for productions of classic plays, both known *and* obscure, and for visionary directors *and* interns would be unthinkable today.

Because Richards would make his deepest imprint at Yale with Winterfest, Fugard, and August Wilson, it's easy to forget, when surveying his twelve seasons, that his taste in classic repertory was as eclectic as Brustein's. Consider for starters the revivals of Crommelynck's savage *The Imaginary Cuckold*; Shaw's obscure

CAST EARLY, CAST OFTEN

Where do the actors come from?

Once a play has been given production dates, the director (and the playwright, if it's a new work) creates capsule descriptions for each character in the cast. They send this breakdown to the casting director, who may modify it before forwarding it to actors' agents, printing it in trade papers like *Backstage*, and posting it on the Actors' Equity Association, Playbill, and Breakdown Express websites. The casting director then compiles lists of actors they feel would be right for the roles, solicits additional names from the director, and contacts their agents as to their availability and interest in the role.

Casting lists shrink with the discoveries that actors are already booked, aren't doing theater, are waiting for television pilot season, are up for a movie, won't leave New York, are expecting a child, don't like the role, are offer only and won't come in to audition, or what have you.

Auditions are then held at ten- to fifteen-minute intervals in the casting director's offices or in a rented studio space. The actors have "sides" from the play to read. The auditioners have the actors' headshots and resumes in front of them. Readers hired for the day feed the cues. Actors from the other coast put themselves on tape or a private YouTube channel. Directors will sometimes ask for a second reading, giving the actor an adjustment that can reveal whether the actor is right for the role and whether they can take direction.

Callbacks for the most promising candidates are then held with the playwrights and often the artistic and associate artistic director in attendance. Choices are ranked. The casting director then calls the actors' agents to check their availability, and the managing director initiates the negotiations, which can take days or weeks of back-and-forth about housing, salary, pets, days off, and so on. Casting, a labor-intensive business, can go up to the very last minute.

During the Brustein years, Yale Rep cast throughout the season and during the summer, supplementing its core acting company with MFA students, recent graduates, and actors from New York. In 1976, third-year management student Fran Kumin ('77) said to Brustein that he needed a casting director who shared his artistic sensibility. To get a sense of her taste, Brustein asked her to compile lists for particular shows. Andrei Serban's production of *The Ghost Sonata,* the 1977–1978 season opener, was her first professional casting assignment. "It was terribly naïve of me," Kumin recalls. "I didn't know what I didn't know, but if you could come up with ten or twelve good ideas for each role, you could cast a show. People wanted to come to Yale Rep." After discussing the roles with Serban, she scoured *The Player's Guide* (a massive tome of Equity actor photos and contact information) and, with Brustein's approval, began dialing.

After graduation, Kumin continued casting for Yale, joining forces with Meg Simon, a friend who had begun her career working for Broadway producer Alexander Cohen. They opened a New York office in 1980 with Yale Rep as one of their first clients. Theirs was a good mix. Simon says with a laugh, "Fran is always diplomatic. Always appropriate. I'm rarely diplomatic and often inappropriate." They claim that the only argument they ever had was whether to buy an electric typewriter with a self-correcting ribbon. Sharing a sensibility in terms of taste, values, and treating actors well, they felt lucky to be working with all the young Yale artists. Both remember how exciting it was to be in the room with Athol Fugard when he heard American actors read his words for the first time. Equally thrilling was watching August Wilson's face light up when actors revealed in their auditions more than he had already imagined about the characters he'd put on paper. Richards, by contrast, they said, maintained a poker face.

Yale Rep was an easy sell in the 1980s. The work was challenging. The salary was attractive. The opportunities to do premieres and get reviewed in the *New York Times* were pluses. Simon and Kumin were unfailingly kind to the Winterfest entourages (student directors, assistant directors, playwrights, and dramaturgs) that would come down from New Haven and crowd their office, educating them about how to use the casting process to advantage. They used drama school actors as their readers—an eye-opening, behind-the-scenes look for them. "It's just so hard to be an actor," says Kumin today, decades after she stopped casting. "And so hard to go in there. You want to make it as comfortable as you can for people. And so we just tried to be decent. And honorable. And this is something Meg and I shared."

Casting director Tara Rubin, who with her associate Laura Schutzel has had the Yale Rep account since the 2004–2005 season, says, "When I started my own company, it was important to me to cast plays as well as musicals. When James [Bundy] asked me, it felt like such a great honor. I knew if I could work at a place like Yale Rep, I'd be working with important voices and a lot of early-career people." If actors are mulling a Yale offer, Rubin will tell them that the nature of the work will make for a rich creative experience. Because Broadway is more star driven than ever, the opportunity to originate a role in a new Sarah Ruhl play is not going to come along in New York. Of casting, Bundy says, "We make a lot of offers, and we sometimes won't program a piece until we have an accepted offer. For example, there were no auditions for *The Realistic Joneses* (2012). It was all done on offers only."

The *Players Guide* and the self-correcting typewriter ribbon are ancient history, but casting a show has become even more of a 24/7 endeavor today. Texts and email attachments are time-saving replacements for the phone, the fax, the messenger, and overnight FedEx, but entertainment options unheard of thirty years ago—cable, internet series, YouTube, theme parks, cruise shows—have sped up the casting cycle. Through it all, however, the biggest casting challenge is the same for Rubin today as it was for Simon and Kumin in the 1980s: finding a middle-aged man who can walk and talk who will come to New Haven. Rubin sighs, "Instead of originating a part at Yale, they can do three television shows in the same amount of time and get paid ten times as much."

"Cast early, cast often" is a mantra for Rubin and her professional peers. Everyone breathes a sigh of relief when James Bundy has a final cast sheet posted on the door outside the UT Green Room. ◆

Tara Rubin Casting
311 West 43rd Street, 5th Floor
New York, NY 10036

ALL'S WELL THAT ENDS WELL
By William Shakespeare
Directed by James Bundy

Auditions will be in NY the week of January 2nd, 2006.

"Helena is the orphaned ward of the Countess of Rossillion, a widow with an open heart and a handsome son named Bertram. When this physician's daughter cures the languishing King of France, he grants her Bertram's hand in marriage. But the proud boy runs away to war to escape a match he deems so far beneath him. Humility and ambition collide on the battlefield and in the bedroom, as one of Shakespeare's most resourceful and resilient heroines, embarks on a quest across Europe to win the heart of a man she loves."

This production of ALL'S WELL THAT ENDS WELL will be a play with music set in contemporary times.
All actors should be comfortable singing at some level.

Seeking actors of all backgrounds for the following roles:

BERTRAM – 20s, male. Son of the Countess. A very handsome soldier who behaves badly in his relationship with Helena, who loves him dearly. He is sexy, immature, witty, loving and charismatic, inflamed with honor but undermined by hypocrisy.

LAFEW – 40s – 60s. A secretary of state for Rossillion. He is bluff, crusty, observant, intuitive, faithful, warm-hearted, and has a sense of humor. He is both quick to anger and also quick to forgive.

PAROLLES – late 20s-40s, male. A soldier in name only, handsome, fancy dresser, a womanizing coward, but also warm, charismatic, hypocritical, weak, charming, and in the course of the play, comes to learn how cowardly he is. THIS ACTOR SHOULD BE ABLE TO SING.

LAVATCH the CLOWN – 30s-60s, male. Servant of the Countess who serves as a messenger and gardener. Down to earth and incredibly funny, often in a crude and sexual way.

A portion of the casting breakdown for Yale Rep's production of *All's Well That Ends Well* (2006)
COURTESY OF YALE REPERTORY THEATRE / TARA RUBIN CASTING

riff on Ibsenism, *The Philanderer*; De Filippo's *Neapolitan Ghosts*; Schnitzler's *Intermezzo*; and Ben Jonson's lexically opaque *The Alchemist*. Richards also brought two of Brustein's *Theatre of Revolt* titans—Shaw and O'Neill—to the Rep for the first time and reminded the public that *A Raisin in the Sun* was a first-rate American classic. The distinction to draw, however, is that apart from *Timon of Athens*, Richards entrusted these plays to guest directors. As befits a former actor and revered acting teacher, he gravitated to classics with difficult leading roles—Vanya and Astrov, Hedda, Nora, Major Barbara, Jamie and Josie in *A Moon for the Misbegotten*, and Con Melody in *A Touch of the Poet*.

Ben Cameron ('81) was another regime straddler, arriving in New Haven to study dramaturgy and dramatic criticism in Brustein's final year. When Richards took over, he recalls an immediate shift in the philosophy of acting. "Bob thought actors should be trained in repertory to stretch, I mean really s-t-r-e-t-c-h what they had in order to tackle any role. Lloyd believed in casting actors for what they most likely would be hired to play." Cue the casting director (see box).

Richards brilliantly showed his hand at the end of his second season, with Dianne Wiest and James Earl Jones playing Hedda and Judge Brack in *Hedda Gabler*. Hedda, Ibsen's most inscrutable heroine, is beautiful, intelligent, refined, cold, impulsive, and overtly wicked to friends, family, and her well-intentioned but hapless new husband. She is also, if one pays close attention, pregnant—the fresh crisis, dramaturgically speaking. With energy to burn but nowhere to light, Hedda turns her flame on others, with mortal results. She and Brack, who share an undisclosed past, play cat and mouse with each other throughout the play. Understanding and even relishing her complicated vitality, Brack wants to possess Hedda, but she will belong to no one, even if that means suicide.

Although Karen Schultz's set was a glowing, febrile expressionist red—think Edvard Munch—Gussow's positive *New York Times* review commended Richards's production for its lack of "Brustein-era updating or conceptual framework to over-intellectualize the play." He praised Wiest's audacious choices—hurling herself full-length on the floor in boredom and throwing open the red drapes and emitting a vampire's scream at the sunlight before she burns Lovborg's manuscript. Today, Wiest recalls the freedom Richards gave her in rehearsal and, more than anything else, her physicality. "I remember Jimmy [Jones] at my shoulder, threatening me, and how threatening that was. I remember pointing a gun, very clearly, at my father's portrait, then at myself in the mirror. I remember burning the letters."

Charles S. "Roc" Dutton ('83), then a student, has gone on record saying that repeat viewings of Jones's Brack constituted a master acting class. Jones is charac-

James Earl Jones and Dianne Wiest as Brock and Hedda in Ibsen's *Hedda Gabler* (1981)
PHOTO © GERRY GOODSTEIN

teristically modest about the results of his pairing with Wiest. "It [the play] had in it some primal attraction. A predatory man and a very vulnerable woman. To the extent that she was open to him is a mystery. He sure wanted her. And I didn't have to play that. Dianne and I just walked on the stage and we did our lines. I wasn't playing anything heavy or mysterious. But Henrik Ibsen . . . , he set it up, you know? And that's all I know." Two seasons later, Wiest would team up again

Lloyd Richards (1979–1991)   125

with Ibsen and Richards on *A Doll House*. With hilarious candor, Wiest today describes playing Nora as "dragging around a dead horse. Unlike Hedda, who's right to the target, Nora goes on about things, the whole play does, and I found I didn't have the appetite for Nora that I had for Hedda, and I think it was a bit of a disappointment for Lloyd."

The 1981–1982 season opened with back-to-back classics, starting with *Uncle Vanya*, directed by Richards, with *Aloes* alumnus Harris Yulin as Astrov and a young Glenn Close as the enigmatic beauty Yelena. After the Chekhov, George Bernard Shaw made his belated Yale Rep debut with his 1893 "play unpleasant," *Mrs. Warren's Profession*. Brustein never mentioned why he hadn't programmed Shaw, but one could suppose that, alone among his *Theater of Revolt* peers, Shaw's genius lives in and on the text. He lays out his arguments, his counterarguments, and his paradoxes in playful ribbons of dialogue and mammoth, elegant speeches. In Shaw, thought and plot take precedence over characters that are less, from an Aristotelian standpoint, conveyors of action than vessels of ideas. The Shavian play doesn't foreground psychology and doesn't require directorial metaphor to enrich the staging. What Shaw needs most are actors with nimble minds, verbal dexterity, superior breath control, and enough thespian legerdemain (a.k.a. charisma) to sway an audience into believing that these fluent mouthpieces are also human beings with interior lives and personal motives. ("They aren't people" is a common actor complaint.)

None of this is meant to suggest that Shaw isn't as stageworthy as Brecht or Pirandello or Chekhov or that he is easy to do well. His particular genius is an ability to embed radical social critique inside the efficient mechanism of the well-made play. As with Stoppard or Kushner or Churchill, a well-done Shaw can leave an audience reckless and giddy with thought. *Mrs. Warren's Profession*, its title an impish riff on all the "fallen women" plays Shaw was forced to review as a drama critic, posits that sex work is not a moral failing on the part of its practitioners but the only outcome in a society that offers poor and uneducated women no other viable option except marriage and childrearing, which is itself a form of *un*paid prostitution. Embodying Shaw's thesis is Kitty Warren, whose priggish, Cambridge-educated daughter, Vivie, has been raised in ignorance of the source of her fortune. One of Shaw's "independent women," Vivie discovers the truth about her mother's past but forgives her—admires her pluck, even—once Mrs. Warren lays out the economic reality she'd faced at Vivie's age. Their embrace ends when Vivie discovers that her mother still runs a chain of brothels on the Continent. Why shouldn't she earn an easy 35 percent in the market, just like all decent unidentified English hypocrites? Shaw's ultimate indictment—look to your investments—is crystal clear.

Frances McDormand and Robert Brown in Shaw's *Mrs. Warren's Profession* (1981)
PHOTO © GERRY GOODSTEIN

    To direct, Richards hired Stephen Porter (YSD '48), who had done four successful Shaws in New York. Barbara Baxley, known for film roles in *Nashville*, *East of Eden*, and *Norma*, was cast as Mrs. Warren. The third-year acting student who played Vivie was, to quote Frank Rizzo in the *New Haven Journal-Courier*, "reminiscent of Jane Fonda at her best. This character is not without humor. She can laugh at a witty line, as well as give one herself." Gussow in the *New York Times* praised her for giving "the most forcefully Shavian performance." The actor was future stage and film star Frances McDormand ('82). Provided the company possesses charm, technique, and stage chops to spare, Shaw could succeed at Yale. Richards scheduled four more: *The Philanderer* with Walken and Tandy Cronyn; *Major Barbara*, again with Baxley and with MFA actor Laila Robbins ('85); *Heartbreak House* (directed by Alvin Epstein); and *Pygmalion*. Fifteen years later, *Mrs. Warren's Profession* would be revived at Yale Rep, directed by Liz Diamond and with alumni Caitlin Clarke ('79) and Susan Cremin ('95) as Kitty and Vivie.

    After a quintet of Fugards and a more actor-centered approach to classic plays, the public had ceased comparing the excesses of the Brustein era to the more straightforward taste of Richards. After *The Blood Knot* anniversary revival in 1985, however, the next two productions, both obscure classics, managed to stupefy, enrage, enlighten, entertain, and divide their audiences. The first was Ibsen's *Little Eyolf*. Rarely seen in America since its Chicago premiere in 1910, *Little Eyolf*

Susan Gibney as the Rat Wife, astride Pokey, in Ibsen's *Little Eyolf* (1985)
PHOTO BY WILLIAM B. CARTER

is a mystery that explores love and marriage, jealousy, devotion, and—this being late Ibsen—death and the great beyond.

Director Travis Preston ('78) had staged *Little Eyolf* the previous year at the American Ibsen Theater in Pittsburgh, a theater he had helped found with fellow Yalies. As we've seen, directors often re-set Shakespeare and Molière in other periods and places. A concept production of Shaw is a ludicrous notion; ditto Chekhov (although that hasn't stopped playwrights from moving him to the Texas-Mexico border, or deconstructing him, as in the Wooster Group's *Brace Up!*). Overly faithful Ibsen productions risk exposing to negative effect the creaking coincidences in his tightly wound plots, but unlike Chekhov and Shaw, Ibsen has enough metaphorical space in his works to invite offbeat reinterpretation. Brustein himself attempted it in 1978 with provisional success, directing a production of *The Wild Duck*. Inspired by his reading of Susan Sontag's critical study *On Photography*, he literalized the metaphor of a camera lens that opened and shuttered on the scenes and characters.

A first glance at Preston's *Little Eyolf* provoked immediate speculation: "*What* is that gigantic rocking horse doing onstage? *Who* is that veiled figure astride it? *How* is this Ibsen?" The technically minded might have also wondered, "*How* did they build the horse?" Wanting to change the feel of the Yale Rep playing space and devise "landscapes that suggest the emotional realities" of the three acts, Preston partially rejected Ibsen's scenic suggestions. Student set designer Elina Katsioula ('86) created a domestic space of platforms, battle-scene tapestries, luxurious Persian rugs, large embroidered cushions, and a twelve-foot-high foam and fiberglass horse nicknamed "Pokey" by the stagehands who had to move him. For act 2, tons of white sand were carted onstage to create the dune where the folkloric Rat Wife leads Eyolf to his death. The sand was covered with black cloth in the last act as four rope ladders were dropped from the ceiling. Characters in conversation ascended their ladders, with each subsequent rung appearing to signal an emotional change or discovery for them. In the closing moment, Rita and Allmers, estranged by the tragic drowning of their only child, stretched an arm out to one another from their respective positions twenty feet in the air, Pokey suspended above them. Although quite a climb, salvation *is* possible.

Stephen McHattie and Pamela Payton-Wright, versatile actors game for the challenge, led the company. The acting was expressionist: sometimes overloud, often slow, often uninflected, with enormous pauses. As for Pokey, was he Pegasus? A Jungian symbol of childhood innocence? A Freudian symbol of sexuality? *Big Eyolf*? A deconstruction of this sort was thrilling to some, but for others it read as so much *spaghetti alla Brustein* thrown at the walls of the play.

Eyolf actors couldn't be afraid of heights. For *Marriage*, up next, actors needed trampoline skills. Belgrader, directing Gogol's "absolutely incredible event in two acts," had his cast bounce on- and offstage, complete with amplified "boings," from trampolines set at the edge of the playing area. That was one of his many conceits designed to highlight the social satire of Gogol's world, where form is more important than feeling. *Marriage* asks, existentially, "Why get married?" None of the New World reasons—love, children, companionship, happiness, stability—occur to the gallery of grotesques. The answers are property and status. Everyone is too worried that they are being taken, or worse, taken for appearing ridiculous, which Molière once posited as humankind's greatest fear.

Our hero, Podkoliosin, passive as only a Russian gentleman of the 1840s can be, is urged to the altar by his frenemy, Kochkariev, whose objective, given his own recent alliance, would seem to be misery loves company. He has a first cousin in mind. Agafya, over the hill at twenty-seven, is a merchant's daughter anxious to marry up. When they are finally alone, Podkoliosin and Agafya conduct a stammering, fits-and-starts wooing scene to match Marlow and Kate in *She Stoops to Conquer*. Abruptly Podkoliosin jumps out the window and leaps into a cab he's heard on the street. Agafya runs screaming from the room while a recording of Eddie Cantor's "Makin' Whoopee" plays over the sound system. Curtain.

Belgrader, as ever, reached for extremes. An offstage fiddler provided musical commentary à la *Story Theatre*. Belgrader cinematically sped up or slowed down

THE SCENE AND PROP SHOPS

Where did they build the popcorn moon in *A Midsummer Night's Dream* (1975)? Pokey, the giant rocking horse for *Little Eyolf* (1985)? The wall of bottles in Ralph Lemon's *Geography I* (1997)? The facilities for set construction for YSD / Yale Rep are the woodshop, located on the main level of the UT, and the fabrication shop, which is in the basement. Props are built next door to the woodshop. As with the costume shop upstairs, all scene shop spaces and tools for both Yale Rep and drama school productions are shared. The facilities are well organized but, again, small for the amount of work they do. Yale employs five full-time staff carpenters, two of whom are year-round and three of whom are seasonal. Work for the season begins around the first week of August and ends with the strike of Rep show five in the third week of May. Technical director Neil Mulligan ('01) estimates that professional and university theaters of similar budgets have two to three times the square footage in their shops as Yale does. He considers the shop equipment top-notch: "Tools that we don't own are out of reach because of space, not money."

Over the years, Riccardo Hernández, an alumnus ('92) who is now set design advisor at the Yale Rep and cochair of design and head of the set design concentration at the school, has enjoyed watching student designers and technical design and production students shift aesthetically away from painting and stage illusion toward the use of real materials with a grounded reality. He himself began pushing the envelope with his first show, Suzan-Lori Parks's *The Death of the Last Black Man in the Whole Entire World* (1992). He and director Liz Diamond had wanted to put the play on at the Trinity Church on the New Haven Green. "When that couldn't happen, I decided to create square Gothic columns to create a church nave on which this requiem of a play unfolds. The columns and the back wall were a deep ultramarine blue. Instead of painting the surfaces we used a reflective laminate called Pionite, which gave the world great depth. Liz and I were interested

the action, cast eccentrically sized actors to play the other suitors—one heavyset, one tall and skeletally thin, and one five feet tall. They wore identical courting outfits, with idiosyncratic top hats, designed by Czech-born Dunya Ramicova ('77), then the Rep's resident costume designer. She designed the costumes for twenty-three shows from 1977 to 1990 and is proud today of having always made a lot with

Lloyd Richards (1979–1991)

Current design department cochair Riccardo Hernández's favorite set, for Koltès's *Battle of Black and Dogs*, with Tommy Schrider and Andrew Robinson (2010)
PHOTO © JOAN MARCUS

in championing the reality of the surface itself rather than what it depicts." For Hernández today, the question for his students is how to deal with investigations of structural spaces that allow for poetry but are also real. "Our job is to encourage the students—designers, directors, playwrights, technicians—to demand this world, and fight for it if they have to." ◆

a little. "Small budgets were a fact of life," she says. "And costumes are always the stepchildren, designed by women and gay men." *Marriage*, more a shaggy-dog anecdote than play, received, like *Eyolf*, a mixed response: one reviewer fittingly described the production as "a gold mine for theater arts students, a puzzlement for unsuspecting audiences . . . , and an outrageous nirvana for Gogol fans."

Lloyd Richards (1979–1991)   131

Colleen Dewhurst and Jason Robards Jr. as Mary and James Tyrone in O'Neill's *Long Day's Journey into Night* (1988)
PHOTO © GERRY GOODSTEIN

Eugene O'Neill wrote fifty-two plays from 1919 to 1945 before hand tremors stopped his pen. To mark the centenary of his birth, Yale Rep and Long Wharf jointly announced in August 1987 a coproduction the following spring of his autobiographical masterpiece, *A Long Day's Journey into Night* (1956), and his one comedy, *Ah, Wilderness!* (1933), in rotating repertory at Yale. Three months later, the reported reunion of three of the leading artists in *Long Day's Journey* made the production a must-see event. Jason Robards, who had played Jamie Tyrone in the original Broadway production of *Long Day's Journey*, would now play James Tyrone. Colleen Dewhurst, who had won a Tony Award in 1973 for playing Josie Hogan in the landmark revival of O'Neill's *A Moon for the Misbegotten*, would again play opposite Robards, as Mary Tyrone. Directing them was José Quintero, who had directed both the original *Long Day's Journey* and the *Moon* revival.

Dewhurst and Robards would also play parents Nat and Essie Miller in *Ah, Wilderness!*, to be directed by Long Wharf artistic director Arvin Brown. Dewhurst's son, Campbell Scott, and John Heard would play the Tyrone brothers, tubercular Edmund and wastrel Jamie. Playing Sid and Aunt Lily Miller, the middle-aged couple whose thwarted romance centers the woolly comic plot of *Ah, Wilderness!*, were notable Broadway veterans George Hearn and Elizabeth Wilson.

Wilderness represents the fantasy boyhood O'Neill wished for himself: an intact, loving family that forgives the lovestruck, Omar Khayyám–quoting Richard Miller (O'Neill) for a mildly drunken spree in a New Haven public house. *Long*

Day's Journey presents the reality of a family trapped in an endlessly repeating cycle of guilt and recrimination, Greek in its intensity. Both plays are set in New London, Connecticut, where O'Neill spent his childhood summers at Monte Cristo Cottage. Reinforcing the linkage, designers Ben Edwards and Michael Yeargan created sets that would change over from the fog-enshrouded, poorly laid-out nonhome that Mary Tyrone despises in *Long Day's Journey* (Edwards) to the bright, laughter-filled sanctuary of the Millers (Yeargan).

The *Long Day's Journey* company savored the opportunity to move from tragedy to comedy on successive rehearsal days. Quintero and Robards gave interviews that leaned on how the passage of time had affected their understanding of the play, with Robards attempting to exorcise Fredric March's original rhythms in his head and Quintero, adjusting to a mechanical voice box after losing a battle with throat cancer, feeling a kinship to O'Neill in his final decade, unable to write or dictate dialogue. The only distress during the rehearsal period was replacing John Heard as Jamie with Jamey Sheridan. Casting director Meg Simon remembers, "John acted out and was fired. He was a tortured soul, and when you do that particular play, the father issues can't help but surface. He substituted José for his dad. To the end of his life, whenever I saw John, he would say that that was his biggest regret."

Richards's farewell production at Yale Rep was *A Moon for the Misbegotten*, with Frances McDormand, Roy Cooper, and David Strathairn. In response to McDormand's question about why Richards would make his exit with a play at the center of the repertory, Richards replied, consciously or unconsciously connecting August Wilson to O'Neill, that *Moon* was a play about "people who have a musical language of the oppressed."

In the winter of 1981, Connie Grappo ('95), working the grueling levers of a freelance directing career in New York, was looking for ways to supplement her income. Jean Passanante, the literary manager of the O'Neill Playwrights Center, gave her sixty scripts to read for the 1982 conference. She separated wheat from chaff at eight dollars per script. "A lot of them weren't even plays," Grappo remembers. "If you were on the fence about one, you were told to pass it forward." She estimates she sent ten scripts on to a second round, but easily the best of the sixty was *Ma Rainey's Black Bottom* by August Wilson. "It had *everything*. The world was so unique—and new to me. I remember thinking whatever happened to it, this play was going to have a life."

As his career skyrocketed and Wilson gave more interviews, the number of times he claimed that he had failed to get into the O'Neill shifted. Lloyd Richards eventually made it official: *Ma Rainey* had been Wilson's fifth attempt. The copy that landed on Richards's desk initiated an artistic partnership that would enrich and enlarge American literature. Wilson's project to dramatize the daily experience of marginalized Black Americans throughout the twentieth century, one play per decade, has become as essential to our culture as Walt Whitman's *Leaves of Grass*, Philip Roth's *Zuckerman* novels, or the film output of Preston Sturges. Kenny Leon, who has acted in or directed nearly all of Wilson's plays, said, "What he's done for Blacks is make them feel that the stories of their grandfathers and grandmothers are worthy to be told and belong in America." Not only has Wilson's achievement provided a permanent place on the world stage for the Black diaspora, it has launched a next generation of playwrights, actors, directors, and scholars. Timothy Douglas ('86) understudied roles in the first three Wilsons while still in drama school. Nearly twenty years later, directing the world premiere of Wilson's final work, *Radio Golf*, at Yale Rep, he said in an interview, "There's a joke among black actors. We all know we will be working during the month of February [Black History Month] because of August Wilson. We say it in a good-natured way, but it's a reality."

Born in 1946, Frederick August Kittle Jr. was the son of a largely absent German immigrant baker. His mother cleaned houses to raise their six children. Growing up in Pittsburgh's Hill District, Wilson ended his formal education his sophomore year of high school after a teacher accused him of plagiarizing a term paper on Napoleon. An early and inveterate reader, he immersed himself in the classics of Black literature, spending so much time in the Carnegie Library of Pittsburgh that they awarded him an honorary high school diploma.

After his father's death in 1965, Wilson took his mother's name, discovered Bessie Smith and the blues, and, shaped by the teachings of the Nation of Islam and the Black Power Movement, began submitting poetry to literary journals. When a sister sent him a check for twenty dollars for writing a college paper for her about Frost and Shelley, he went downtown and bought a secondhand typewriter. "The first thing I typed was my name. I wanted to see how it looked in print," Wilson recalled for the *New York Times* in 1987.

In 1968, Wilson and his friend Rob Penny cofounded the Black Horizon Theater in the Hill District. Wilson took on the function of director and, true to form, checked out a book in order to find out how to stage a play. A director friend, Claude Purdy, persuaded him a decade later to move to St. Paul, Minnesota. In an interview published in *Theater* at the time of the Yale Rep opening of *Ma Rainey's*

Black Bottom, Wilson tells Kim Powers ('84) that he came to playwriting through arrogance and frustration. "My ideas no longer fit in the poems, or they fit in a different way, for myself only. I needed a larger canvas that would include everyone." According to Wilson, *Ma Rainey* depicted one of the only two avenues for success—music—open to Blacks in 1927, when the play is set. Gertrude "Ma" Rainey (1882–1939) was among the first Black singers to get a recording contract with a white company, Paramount, which dubbed her "Mother of the Blues." Wilson, finding her singing more poignant than Bessie Smith's, wanted to "go into the studio on the day they were making the record and find out what the costs were, what indignities she had to suffer."

As the play begins, Ma is late. Waiting for their temperamental meal ticket, her four sidemen swap stories. The distinctively voiced, leisurely byplay of Cutler,

Charles S. "Roc" Dutton, Leonard Jackson, Robert Judd, Theresa Merritt, and Joe Seneca in the world premiere of August Wilson's *Ma Rainey's Black Bottom* (1984)
PHOTO BY WILLIAM B. CARTER

Lloyd Richards (1979–1991)

Toledo, Slow Drag, and Levee is its own piece of music, by turns painful and hilarious. Wilson's poetic vernacular for his characters is a dramatic hallmark that lends their workaday, anecdotal existences a bravura richness. Wilson said of *Ma Rainey*, "Blacks in America have so little to make life with compared to whites, yet they do so with a certain zest, a certain energy that is fascinating because they make life out of nothing—yet it is charged and luminous and has all the qualities of anyone else's life." In play after play, Wilson composes deceptively meandering symphonies from groups of men (and less frequently, women) shooting the breeze over apparent nothings that, in a flash, become everything. These symphonies, Richards later remarked, reminded him of the barbershop conversations he heard in his youth, "language full of vivid images, inventive forms, and deep feeling."

The conflict in *Ma Rainey* is over a musical arrangement. The career-minded trumpet player, Levee, wants Ma to consider his re-setting of "The Black Bottom" into something jazzier for the public. Tensions escalate between the old and the new order; Levee and Cutler eventually come to blows, and in the climax, Ma fires Levee, who, overcome with rage and humiliation, fatally stabs Toledo. Charles S. "Roc" Dutton, a year out of the drama school, who had been in the initial reading at the O'Neill and would go on to New York with the production, earning a Tony nomination for Best Featured Actor, related to his character. "The thing about Levee is that he's a guy waving a knife at God, calling everyone a fool but himself."

The other avenue to success for Blacks in the twentieth century for Wilson was sports, which he addresses in *Fences*, set in the 1950s. After an enthusiastic response to *Ma Rainey* at the O'Neill conference, Wilson immediately began another play, writing the first scene on a bus leaving Waterford. Plays usually came to Wilson via an image or a line of dialogue, or sometimes both. *Fences* began with the image of a Black man holding a baby. "I saw him there in the yard and he was saying, 'I'm standing here with my daughter in my arms,' and I wondered who he was talking to. Then, I decided it was his wife and I invented a series of situations and circumstances that would allow him to say those words to her."

The man became Troy Maxson, a fifty-something garbage collector who had held hopes of breaking into major league baseball but grew too old waiting for the color barrier to be broken. The failure of his dream has embittered him and leads him to belittle his son, Cory, undermine his athletic aspirations, and eventually kick him out of the house. In the final coda, seven years have passed. Cory, who has joined the Marines, is convinced by his mother, Rose, to attend Troy's funeral. In the closing moment, Troy's brother, Gabriel, whose war experiences have damaged his mind, blows on a trumpet he carries around his neck and opens the gates of heaven for the great but flawed soul of his brother.

Courtney B. Vance and James Earl Jones in *Fences*, the second installment in the August Wilson Century Cycle (1985)
PHOTO © PAUL J. PENDERS

Courtney B. Vance ('86) recalls reading the O'Neill draft of *Fences* in the drama library. "I thought, *they'll get some big football player type for this*, and I went on to class." But as a second-year student, he was cast as Cory in the premiere at the Yale Rep. When the play was remounted and taken to the Goodman Theatre in Chicago the following year, his third, there was something of an uproar when he was granted a leave of absence from school to reprise his role. "Lloyd was a master director and dramaturg, so when he cast you, he assumed you can do the role. So he gave me very little direction, but I do remember him telling me after the play was pre-Broadway and being remounted a third time, this time at the Curran Theater in San Francisco, 'Take two physical gestures of James Earl Jones and

Lloyd Richards (1979–1991)

work them into your performance.' He never told me which ones, or where to put them. But he didn't have to. After living with the play on and off for two years and watching almost 150 performances, I knew what to do." Vance's choices were to hit his chest on the line, "I don't wanna be like Troy Maxson! I wanna be ME!!!," and to point his finger to the side at [little sister] Raynelle to say, "Go on in there and tell Mama we going to Papa's funeral." "Both of these physical gestures, like James Earl Jones, let the audience see that Cory was very much the son of Troy Maxson—whether he wanted to admit it or not. It was a genius move by the master. And boy, did it work!"

Wilson said of *Fences* in a contemporary interview, "I wrote the play out of a concern that my generation of blacks in particular did not know very many things about their parents in terms of choices that they made and the reasons for making them. Very often our parents hid from us the indignities that they suffered." New Haven audiences seeing *Fences* for the first time in 1985—with Jones, Mary Alice, and Vance as Troy, Rose, and Cory, respectively—encountered an American family with the particularized heft of the Lomans, the Youngers, and the Tyrones. Rose's decision to raise Troy's child by his mistress, Alberta, as her own—"From right now this child got a mother, but you a womanless man"—would elicit vociferous shouts of approval and sustained applause from women of all means and every race wherever *Fences* played.

Ben Mordecai used to claim that the initial reviews of *Fences* were weak, and that's when Richards told him to get more productions after Yale Rep. In a novel production-sharing arrangement hammered together by Mordecai and peer managing directors across the country, *Fences*, its cast and physical production intact, went to the Goodman in Chicago, Seattle Repertory Theatre, and the Geva Theater in Rochester. Then it went to a commercial San Francisco house under the auspices of independent producer Carole Shorenstein Hays. It opened last in New York at the 46th Street Theatre (now the Richard Rodgers) on March 26, 1987. Within four months, the play had won the Pulitzer Prize, the Drama Desk Award, Tony Awards for Best Play, Best Leading Actor, Best Featured Actress, and Best Director, and it had recouped its $655,000 investment. Moreover, Wilson was ready to purchase a newfangled "word-processing computer" for three hundred dollars.

An essential theme in the Wilson cycle is the choice between embracing or denying one's African past. The Great Migration of Blacks leaving the South in the first third of the twentieth century to escape the depredations of Jim Crow laws is the context for *Joe Turner's Come and Gone*. The play shared its original title, "Mill Hand's Lunch Bucket," with a boardinghouse collage by Romare Bearden that

THE TONY IN THE PARKING LOT

Since 1948, the Antoinette Perry Awards have been given annually in recognition of excellence on the Broadway stage. Since 1976, a noncompetitive Tony Award has been awarded to a regional theater. In 1991, Lloyd Richards and Ben Mordecai accepted the regional Tony for Yale Rep. It was Lloyd's final year as artistic director, and during his tenure at least eight Rep productions had moved to Broadway.

Four years earlier, on another big night for New Haven theater, *Fences* won four Tony Awards, for August Wilson, for Richards, and for actors James Earl Jones and Mary Alice. Long Wharf Theatre won a Best Revival Tony for their production of Arthur Miller's *All My Sons*. There was a viewing party for interested fans from both theaters at Kavanagh's on Chapel Street, the closest thing New Haven had to a sports bar. Because Yale Rep press director Robert Wildman and his Long Wharf colleague David Mayhew were ever avid for coverage, the *New Haven Register* sent a reporter to cover the party.

The next morning, Wildman convinced the local ABC-TV affiliate, WTNH, to do a live interview with Richards on the steps of the Rep for their afternoon "Newsmakers" segment. Richards, in New York, readily agreed, and Wildman cheekily told him not to forget to bring his Tony with him.

"I don't have it," said Richards. It had been whisked from his hands backstage for engraving.

Oops. Thence began Wildman's daylong, pre-Internet search for a Tony that Lloyd could hold in his hands. After a couple of dead ends, he remembered that Long Wharf Theatre kept its 1978 regional Tony Award in a case in Executive Director Edgar Rosenblum's office. He cajoled Mayhew into springing their Tony for a good cause.

"They insisted that David present it to me in the Long Wharf parking lot with all of the staff members watching. They even took pictures of the

Long Wharf press director David Mayhew lends the Antoinette Perry Award to his Yale Rep peer Robert Wildman (1987)
PHOTO © DAVID SHIMCHICK

transfer. Later in the day, when Lloyd was standing on the Rep steps getting mic'd up, it was rush hour; cars were honking, and people were waving and shouting their congratulations. WTNH interviewed Lloyd that night with Long Wharf's Tony, although the award's pedigree never came up. I hung onto the award for three days before giving it back."

Word of the substitute Tony leaked out; in the week to come, the "truer" story got additional print mileage, from the *New Haven Register* and then from *Variety*. Wildman and Mayhew still think of it as "the story that kept on giving." ◆

Wilson had seen in an exhibition in Washington, DC. He described it this way: "A man coming downstairs with a lunch box. A woman in a dress, with a little purse, ready to go out. A child at the table, drinking milk. And, seated at the table with a hat and coat on, a man—black, like all the others—who seemed utterly defeated."

Seth Holly's boardinghouse in *Joe Turner's Come and Gone* is a way station for people starting over. Young men and women fresh off the farm find work, flirt, bicker, tell stories, profess their faith, and claim a freer space. Into their midst comes the fearsome Herald Loomis and his daughter, Zonia. Loomis has been released from seven years of peonage on Joe Turner's plantation and is looking for his wife, who didn't wait for his manumission. Loomis's journey in the play is to find his individual song with the assistance of Bynum, a conjure man and "binder of what clings." The supernatural surround to the boardinghouse, as realistic a setting as Ma Rainey's recording studio and Troy Maxson's backyard, includes imagery and practices associated with African mysticism. Loomis talks in tongues and experiences sudden paralysis, visual hallucinations, and spiritual possession. His climax is a renunciation of his Christian faith followed by a self-cutting that cleanses his identity and frees him to start his life over. Wilson's ability to credibly meld these two worlds marked an advance in his dramatic powers.

Kimberly Scott ('86) played Molly Cunningham, an independent woman up for anything except returning to the South. A second-year student at the time, Scott initially read for Richards and Wilson as a favor to a male classmate auditioning for another role. "So, I go in, we go in, and then I didn't think anything about it. The cast list comes out and I get cast in it. I was shocked, gobsmacked, all that stuff, you know. I'd go to classes and then I'd go work with Lloyd and August Wilson." She remembers Richards as a patient, brilliant dramaturg in the rehearsal process. As for Wilson, "He was a soft-spoken guy. He was a playwright who loved

Kimberleigh Aarn, Kimberly Scott, and Ed Hall in Wilson's *Joe Turner's Come and Gone* (1986)
PHOTO BY WILLIAM B. CARTER

and respected actors. If you stumbled on a line more than once, he'd lean forward and take the pencil from behind his ear and scribble something on a piece of paper and go, 'Try that next time.' And he'd be around town, he'd write in longhand on legal pads. And I had lunch with him once where he was talking about process, [and] he said, 'I just listen. They talk to me and I just listen.'"

After closing in New Haven at the end of May 1986, *Joe Turner's Come and Gone* played four other regional theaters before opening in New York, where it won

Lloyd Richards (1979–1991)   141

Wilson his third New York Drama Critics Circle Award for Best Play (and a Tony nomination for Scott in her Broadway debut). Not since Tennessee Williams and Elia Kazan began supplying Broadway with plays every other year had an American playwright and director collaboration generated such excitement. Going on the road to noncommercial regional theaters gave Wilson, Richards, and Mordecai a safer environment in which to refine the plays and, most important, reduce their running times to no more than three hours. (After three hours, Broadway union workers are guaranteed overtime.) Mordecai and his colleagues structured their deals so that even if the show did not succeed on Broadway, Yale incurred no financial risk: much of the New York transfer costs were earned through guaranteed income from the tour of the nonprofit theaters. The financial rewards for Yale Rep, a fixed royalty percentage from Broadway and post-Broadway regional productions, were considerable. In 1991, for example, the $250,000 generated from Yale Rep's participation in *Fences* and *The Piano Lesson* helped balance the operating budget. *Fences* alone ended up making Yale Rep $1 million, which Richards leveraged with the university provost to increase the salaries of leading faculty.

Richards and Wilson were loyal to their student actors and designers. With rare exceptions, their work was seen at every stop from New Haven to New York. Wilson met his third wife, Constanza Romero ('88), on *The Piano Lesson* (1987), for which she designed the clothes. In this play, Wilson's theme of denying or accepting one's African past takes literal form in an heirloom piano ornately carved with portraits and historical symbols of the enslaved ancestors of recently widowed Berniece Charles and her brother, Boy Willie, a sharecropper visiting Pittsburgh from Mississippi. Boy Willie wants to sell the piano and purchase the land, which belongs to the deceased Sutter, that the Charleses originally worked as slaves, while Berniece refuses to sell their heritage. Several sightings of Sutter's ghost force her to open the keyboard and call on her ancestors for help. The ghost is exorcised, and Boy Willie heads back south, lesson learned. Several months after *The Piano Lesson* closed, Yale University awarded August Wilson an honorary doctorate; when it moved to Broadway in 1990, Wilson won a second Pulitzer Prize for Drama.

The title for *Two Trains Running* (1990), the fifth and final Wilson premiere during Richards's leadership, comes from an old blues song that says, "There's two trains running, but neither one's going my way." Audience members expecting Wilson's 1960s play to center on the struggles of the Civil Rights and Black Power Movements were surprised to witness another "barbershop" gathering of middle-aged male customers telling tales in Memphis Lee's restaurant, slated for demolition. With Jim Crow putatively legislated out of existence, overt racism takes a back seat to economic decline and urban redevelopment. Enter Sterling, a hothead released from jail, who tries to interest the old-timers into going to a rally to celebrate Malcolm X's birthday. The generational conflict reflects the shift from Martin Luther King's policy of peaceful nonviolence to the more confrontational positions of Malcolm X and Stokely Carmichael.

With the opening of *Two Trains Running*, the Wilson cycle was half completed. Richards had one year left in his Yale contract. Asked by the *New Haven Register* what might happen next, Wilson said, "I'm going to go where Lloyd goes. I'm hoping that whoever comes in will let me and Lloyd work on my plays here." It was not to be; the new artistic director, Stan Wojewodski Jr., championed other contemporary playwrights, but there were half a dozen other theaters on the Wilson production circuit eager to develop and present *Seven Guitars*, *Jitney*, *King Hedley II*, and *Gem of the Ocean*. Things would come full circle, however, when Wilson's final play, *Radio Golf*, composed as he was dying of cancer, premiered at Yale Rep in 2005.

Dean/Artistic Director Lloyd Richards, Managing Director Benjamin Mordecai, and August Wilson on a rehearsal break from *Two Trains Running* (1990)
COURTESY OF BEINECKE RARE BOOK AND MANUSCRIPT LIBRARY, YALE UNIVERSITY

Lloyd Richards (1979–1991)

A Yale Rep milestone of sorts was achieved on May 15, 1988, when the *New York Times* listed six plays that had originated in New Haven that were concurrently playing in New York. *Fences, Joe Turner's Come and Gone, The Road to Mecca*, and *Long Day's Journey into Night* in rep with *Ah! Wilderness* at the First International Festival of the Arts in New York City, and Lee Blessing's *A Walk in the Woods*.

Blessing, who has workshopped *nine* different plays at the Eugene O'Neill Theater Center, remembers the *Times* arts section declaring, in 1984 or 1985, that there were too many family plays. He decided to look for an international front-page story and then write from the outside in. There had been an event, kept from the public, about two nuclear arms negotiators, an American and a Soviet Russian, who had taken an unofficial walk in the woods during the 1982 Geneva talks on reducing intermediate-range nuclear missiles in Europe. A compromise was reached whereby the Americans would not deploy any missiles in Europe if the USSR would reduce its arsenal, but the deal ultimately fell through.

The challenge for Blessing was crystal clear: "How do you write a play that most people don't even want to read about in a newspaper?" Using Strobe Talbott's *Deadly Gambits* (1984) as primary research, Blessing set *A Walk in the Woods* over the course of one year, during which an experienced Soviet negotiator attempts to teach a newly appointed American the intricacies of the summit process. Andrey Botvinnik is a playful, charming, continental realist, and John Honeyman is a stiff and humorless idealist. The plot is political, but the story is personal.

Shaw or Brecht or Bond would have filled the play with arms dealers and capitalists, politicians, journalists, and protestors as a way to arouse and educate the audience. Blessing instead walks the tightrope of a two-character play, a dramaturgical choice that historically leads either to violence (*Zoo Story*; *'Night, Mother*; *Oleanna*; *Topdog/Underdog*) or to romantic commitment (*Tally's Folly*; *Frankie and Johnny in the Clair de Lune*). Blessing achieves a hybrid with *A Walk in the Woods*. Andrey and John are quick, funny characters with lively geopolitical observations. Their growing friendship is the bait that hooks the audience into paying attention to what is happening offstage. The Russian knows the talks are futile, but when Honeyman brings an unauthorized treaty to their park bench for a work session, and Botvinnick goes through it with a marking pen, using technical arms terms for the first time in the play, the stakes get real for the men, and for the audience; hope for a way out of the stalemate is nearly ignited.

But the president rejects their agreement. The two decide that their special handicap as negotiators is a *conscience*, and the play ends with them silently sitting on their historic bench. *A Walk in the Woods* dramatizes the attractive idea that world problems might be solved if the right people just sat down and talked things through. This inherent naïveté is mitigated by its ability to make an audience feel smart and informed, not about specific nuclear capabilities but about the geopolitical reality of the US-Soviet dyad that fuels arms races and dooms global peace to this day.

Its world premiere was a coproduction between Yale Rep and La Jolla Playhouse, headed by Des McAnuff, who served as director. Audiences and critics in both locations were drawn to Blessing's ability to wring humor, nuance, and, yes, a modicum of hope from the depressing subject matter. Special praise was given to Bill Clarke's ('87) realistic design of trees and the earth changing through the sea-

Josef Sommer and Kenneth Welsh in Lee Blessing's *A Walk in the Woods* (1987)
PHOTO BY WILLIAM B. CARTER

Lloyd Richards (1979–1991)

sons. Blessing remembers, "There was so much mulch on the set that mushrooms started growing on it." Teresa Eyring ('89), now the executive director of Theater Communications Group (TCG), recalls learning how to drop leaves from the flies at just the right tempo for the autumn scene as her work-study assignment.

George S. Kaufman famously said, "Satire is what closes on Saturday night." Chancier still is *political* satire. Three were presented at Yale Rep in the 1980s: Wole Soyinka's *A Play of Giants* (1985), Dario Fo's *Elizabeth: Almost by Chance a Woman* (1987), and John Guare's *Moon Over Miami* (1989). All stood about as much chance of reaching New York as a star-driven revival of *Gammar Gurton's Needle*, but each illustrated the prerogative of theater to vent communal spleen and provoke mindful outrage.

As early as 1969, Richards had attempted to get Soyinka to the O'Neill. The Nigerian Civil War had only just ended, and the writer-activist had been released from two years of solitary confinement. It took three years to raise the money to bring over a troupe of Nigerian actors, but *Madmen and Specialists*, a play written from his prison notes, did make it to Connecticut.

It would take five years of gentle pressure for Soyinka to complete *A Play of Giants* for Yale Rep. In this "Fantasia on the Aminian Theme," Soyinka gathers together thinly veiled caricatures of four brutal African presidents for life. Leading the pack, representing Uganda's Idi Amin Dada, is El-Hadj Dr. Kamini of Bugara. (To provide some context, it is estimated that 350,000 people were killed during Amin Dada's eight-year reign.) Joining Kamini onstage are Gunema (Francisco Macías Nguema of Equatorial Guinea), Kasco (Jean-Bédel Bokassa of the Central African Republic), and Barr Taboum (Mobutu Sese Seko of the Congo).

Field Marshal Kamini is in his New York embassy, getting a bust made to give to the United Nations. Kicking off the plot is the World Bank's refusal to give him $100 million, so he tells his bank administrator to return home and print some more money. The administrator's comparison of Bugaran currency to toilet paper so enrages Kamini that he stuffs the administrator's head into a toilet, which flushes periodically throughout the play, an act of torture as juvenile and terrifying as Idi Amin Dada, who had only a second-grade education.

Kamini then decides on having a group sculpture with his three fellow experts in political repression, nepotism, corruption, ethnic persecution, economic mismanagement, and "the diversionary scarecrow of human rights." Since Kamini is not on Bugaran soil, things spiral downward: the rest of his delegation bolts, leaving Kamani without a speechwriter; his ambassador flees the compound; a Telex announces there's been a coup in Bugara; and finally, "First World" agents—Soviets, Brits, and Swedes—call on the jittery psychopath, whose Achilles heel / homicidal trigger is the phrase, "You don't understand." Not a complete buffoon, Kamini begs for an atom bomb to destroy South African apartheid and accurately compares the hypocrisies of the USSR and its Cuba policy with the United States and its relations with Nicaragua and El Salvador. At the climax, the embassy is blown open, with Kamini backing everyone into a corner. Lights fade on a freeze, except for the Sculptor, already beaten mercilessly by his subject, who continues his work in slow, pained motion.

A Play of Giants is caustically funny on the page. Soyinka's use of the word "fantasia" in the title leads to Shaw and Kushner, who employ the term for *Heartbreak House* and *Angels in America*. Like those two utterly serious comedies, *Giants*, which Soyinka stated in his introduction is structurally modeled on Genet's *The Balcony*, is brilliant in its analysis of geopolitical complicity on the left *and* the right, as well as of the process by which the brutality of manifest power warps and dehumanizes even the most rational men and women. Unfortunately, Richards al-

Leon Morenzie, Michael Rogers, Herb Downer, Roger Robinson, Avril Gentles, Lloyd Hollar, Dwight Bacquie, L. Scott Caldwell, and Ray Aranha in the world premiere of Wole Soyinka's *A Play of Giants* (1984)
PHOTO © PAUL J. PENDERS

Lloyd Richards (1979–1991)   147

lowed Soyinka to direct his own play. Harold Pinter and María Irene Fornès excepted, the practice did not prove a sound one in the twentieth century. Despite a talented acting company led by Roger Robinson as Kamini, *A Play of Giants* in production was ponderous, muffled, static, and repetitive. In other words, not at all funny. Today, Africa and the rest of the globe still support a growing share of presidents for life / dictators, and the global realignment of China, the Middle East, and post-Soviet Russia has not dulled the edge of geopolitical opportunism. The sleeping *Play of Giants* is ready for serious revival.

Another leader beset by paranoia is Great Britain's virgin queen in Fo's *Elizabeth: Almost by Chance a Woman*. Yale Rep's initial Fo encounter was giving him his American print debut, publishing *Accidental Death of an Anarchist* in Yale's *Theater* in 1979. In 1983, Yale Rep presented the English-language premiere of *About Face*, a comedy about police brutality, fondly remembered for a torture scene in which a plutocrat is force-fed food through his nose via a meat grinder.

Fo—a political clown with the verbal wit of Molière and the physical dexterity and mime chops of Charlie Chaplin—and Franca Rame, a sharp-eyed monologist à la Ruth Draper and Lily Tomlin, were married in 1954. After years together onstage and on television, they had become, in Fo's words, "the Alka-Seltzer of the bourgeoisie." In reaction to their mainstream success, they founded Nuova Scena, a touring theater for working-class audiences that performed in factories, stadiums, and gymnasiums all over Europe. Their short-lived association in the late 1960s with Soccorso Rosso (Red Aid), a leftist organization that helped people imprisoned for politically motivated crimes, led the US State Department to brand them as "sympathetic to the terrorist movement" and deny them visas in 1980 and 1983.

Fo and Rame were at last permitted to tour the United States in 1986 with an evening of their work. From May 13 to 17, 1986, the pair took over the UT with Fo's *Mistero Buffo*, Rame's *Tutta Casa, Letto, è Chiesa* (*All House, Bed, and Church*), and Fo's "Lecture on the 'Origin' of the Mask,'" a visual and interpretive retrospective of masks from commedia dell'arte to the present. In *Mistero*, the clown impersonates sundry saints and popes and, in a vertiginous climax, reenacts the resurrection of Lazarus, a crowd scene with a cast of sixteen, including a ticket seller, a wench, a sardine vendor, and a bookie laying odds on whether Lazarus can pull off his stunt. A high spot in Fo's mask lecture was his logorrheic use of "grammelot," an invented gibberish with the cadence of, depending on the satiric target, Italian or French or English.

Their success led Richards to schedule the American premiere of *Elizabeth* the following spring. After losing the original director, Richards flew to San Francisco

Joe Morton, Mary Lou Rosato, Tom Mardirosian, and Joan McIntosh in Dario Fo's *Elizabeth: Almost by Chance a Woman* (1987)
PHOTO BY WILLIAM B. CARTER

to meet Tony Taccone, who had already produced three Fo works at the Eureka Theatre. Taccone recalls, "Lloyd saw something I'd done, asked me to direct *Elizabeth*, and of course I said 'yes.' I was a kid going to make his East Coast debut."

After Olympia Dukakis had to withdraw from the project, casting Elizabeth took them right up to the day before rehearsals began. "Seven actresses were called that morning," says Taccone. "Six dropped out, leaving Tammy. It seemed a little planned on Yale's part, if you know what I mean." Two-time Tony Award–winner Tammy Grimes seemed an ideal virgin queen: a more-than-regal presence, a sui generis voice and manner, and a comedic brilliance. It was star casting à la James Earl Jones or Christopher Walken. In recalling the first week of rehearsals, Taccone hesitates. "She was honestly . . . bonkers. I gathered the cast after about four days. We all agreed that the situation was untenable. It was one of the hardest decisions I've ever made in the theater." In the pre-Internet era, the *Elizabeth* press release hadn't yet gone out, so they held it until Joan MacIntosh came in to replace Grimes.

Fo's monarch is a basket case with enemies ranging from the Puritans to the pope to her aging skin. Dreading a palace coup, she believes that she is being lampooned nightly in a play called *Hamlet*; the specter of the beheaded queen Mary of Scotland still haunts her; and finally, she cannot face the thought of losing the love of her oft-treacherous favorite, Robert Deveraux. Enter Madame Zaza, witch doctor, beautician, and factota. In play after play, Fo sends (and usually plays) a clown

Lloyd Richards (1979–1991)

like Zaza into a corrupt world to unleash the truth. Whether stinging Elizabeth's breasts with bees to enlarge them, performing a scat version of "To Be or Not to Be," or directly acknowledging the house, the demented Zaza, chattering away in a dubious Italo-English, represents the people, who ultimately cannot be fooled. By the close of the play, the rebellion has been quashed and Deveraux is sentenced to the headman's axe, and as the lights fade, Elizabeth relives the decapitation of her Catholic cousin.

For Fo, the parallels were obvious. Performances began with a lengthy letter to Ronald Reagan titled "Dear Friend and Fellow Actor": "Just because my play is about an aging leader whose advisors don't tell her what they're doing behind her back, a leader who tends to be confused and forgetful about certain details, don't think for a minute that it has anything at all to do with you." Despite a fine cast of comic actors, including Mary Lou Rosato, Tom Mardirosian, and Joe Morton as Zaza, the production was only fitfully funny. According to both Taccone and production dramaturg Schechter, Fo seemed more focused on the simultaneous rehearsals of *Archangels Don't Play Pinball* up at Brustein's A.R.T. Schechter humorously recalls, "Dario showed up a few nights before opening. It was a surprise. He wanted to give notes. My Italian is not so good, so he sat next to me throughout rehearsal and drew pictures of what the set should be like, not knowing that these kinds of changes were impossible." In hindsight, Taccone feels that he was trying too hard to please Richards and Fo rather than trusting his own instincts about the play. He also wasn't the first director to find the moat separating the Rep stage from its audience inhospitable to comedy. "It was a great learning experience. The script couldn't change. Fo performed some of it for us in Italian, but the inflections are not the same; the nuances of his comedy were built for his bravura gifts as a clown, but they didn't necessarily translate to our company."

With the exceptions of Bond's *Saved* and Kennedy's *An Evening with Dead Essex*, one would be hard-pressed to find a play in its fifty-year history that drove Yale Rep patrons out of the theater in such numbers as did *Moon Over Miami*, John Guare's madcap farce about the pornography of American politics. "To be offended by it is to show good taste," sniffed Markland Taylor in the *New Haven Register*. "It is the Rep's first X-rated production."

Moon was the only play Guare had yet written that came from reading the front page of the *New York Times*. Inspired by the 1980 Abscam sting, in which the FBI hoodwinked several US congressmen into accepting payoffs from bogus Arab sheikhs, *Moon Over Miami* began as a screenplay for comedians John Belushi and Dan Ackroyd; but Belushi died, and film director Louis Malle suggested Guare turn it into a play. Williamstown Theater Festival produced *Moon* in 1987, where,

Stanley Tucci and Tony Shalhoub in John Guare's *Moon Over Miami* (1989)
PHOTO © GERRY GOODSTEIN

according to Guare, it so offended a major donor that the individual withdrew a $100,000 pledge to the theater.

Guare grew up loving Kaufman and Hart but had never written a full-out farce. *Moon Over Miami* runs six concurrent plots, shifting locales (as screenplays do) from several hotel locations to the Everglades to an offshore yacht to fantasy sequences involving a chorus of singing mermaids. "The more balls in the air, the better," Guare laughs today. An FBI agent, Otis Presby, is investigating links between corrupt politicians and an array of drug and gun merchants, chief among them the brutal pig Shelley Slutsky and his triple-crossing moll Giselle, of the untraceable accent. Oswaldo, a "Jewban" (Jewish and Cuban) congressman, is trying to raise money for reelection commercials. The sheik of Akhbaran wants to purchase US citizenship and rebuild Israel in Florida, and Special Agent Wilcox, who has a shrine to J. Edgar Hoover in his home, wants to videotape more congressmen trading favors for briefcases of cash. On the romance front, Otis falls for Corleen, a born-again Christian and president of the Everglades Light Opera.

Roosting in the hotel's Boom Boom Room—and wading dangerously into the audience with her microphone—is Fran Farkas, a foul-mouthed, platinum-blonde chanteuse à la Belle Barth and Rusty Warren. All of her material is basically unprintable; it was her excretory riff on Ellington's "Don't Get Around Much Anymore" that ignited the first steady rush for the exits. Those not offended by scatology might have left for the culturally insensitive observations about Jews, Arabs,

Lloyd Richards (1979–1991)

Italians, Cubans, Republicans, and J. Edgar Hoover. Those impervious to all offense had a marvelous time as *Moon Over Miami* flew higher and faster into the realm of pure, illogically logical farce. As with *Ubu* nine years before (also directed by Belgrader), half left and half laughed themselves sick.

Moon's principals formed the kind of thespian dream team seldom seen outside of New York: Julie Hagerty (Corleen), Oliver Platt (Otis), Lewis J. Stadlen (Oswaldo), Stanley Tucci (Slutsky), Tony Shalhoub ('80; the Sheik), Sally Kellerman (Giselle), and Lauren Cronin (Fran). The average new American play is from 110 to 125 pages long. *Moon Over Miami* was 185 pages, with thirty-one scene changes, several musical numbers, and a cast of twenty-four, so Richards's announcement of a postponed opening due to enormous technical demands was not a shock. When it did open, Frank Rich wrote in the *New York Times* that *Moon* was "a completely uninhibited comic mess." He meant it as a compliment. Today, Guare rues that the stars never aligned correctly for *Moon*. His final word on the subject: "The play has a gift for making the audience insanely self-righteous."

There would be no pink slip for Lloyd Richards. In September of 1988, Yale president Benno C. Schmidt extended his contract for an additional two years. In 1989 he was inducted into the Theater Hall of Fame; the following year, Yale University awarded him an honorary degree.

As his final season began, Richards, a Reagan appointee to the National Council on the Arts, which was the advisory board to the National Endowment for the Arts, wisely weighed in on a First Amendment issue involving controversial grants to the "NEA Four"—Karen Finley, John Fleck, Holly Hughes, and Tim Miller. Three weeks before his contract was up, Yale Rep was awarded the regional Tony, an apt tribute for a theater that, apart from its many transfers to New York, had developed an August Wilson pipeline with peer institutions across the country. Accepting the award with Associate Dean Gister and Managing Director Mordecai, Richards thanked his staff, President Schmidt, and "the people of greater New Haven, who are real theatergoers." Citing Fugard, Wilson, and Blessing in particular, he also thanked "the angels of the theater, those wonderful artists . . . who have done it for us."

In considering the quantitative legacy of Lloyd Richards at Yale Rep, one easily points to audience involvement. During his tenure, subscriptions tripled to 7,500; overall attendance nearly doubled, and during his final four seasons, roughly 100,000 people came to the theater. With fifty-four premieres produced during

THE NEA AND ITS FORTUNES

Since 1965 the National Endowment for the Arts (NEA) has been "dedicated to supporting excellence in the arts, both the new and established, bringing the arts to all Americans and providing leadership in arts education."

Both the unrestricted operating funds and the seal of approval that an NEA grant afforded were valuable for Yale Rep in its earliest shoestring years. Receiving one wasn't a foregone conclusion, but Brustein's mission was usually persuasive. By the time of the Carter administration (1976–1980), rumblings had begun that the NEA had become too elitist, with an overly large percentage of its grants going to East Coast institutions. Brustein's public response to this charge—excellence must always, as the original charter is worded, come first—was vexing, but the NEA did begin to shift focus in the 1980s to include the "established" (for example, local and folk) arts, "all" Americans, and "education" initiatives.

Lest anyone get excited about the numbers, note that President Reagan allocated more money in the 1982 federal budget for military bands than for the NEA and the National Endowment for the Humanities combined. By 1995, after a second rabid wave to abolish the NEA had surfaced, the annual public arts expenditure was calculated to be six dollars per US citizen. In Germany, by contrast, the amount was eighty-five dollars per person.

In 1989, religious fundamentalists, led by Pat Robertson and Jerry Falwell and abetted by North Carolina senator Jesse Helms, made a sustained ruckus over the work of grant recipients Robert Mapplethorpe (homoerotic photographs) and Andres Serrano ("Piss Christ," a piece that submerged a crucifix in urine). Congress swiftly amended the agency's yearly budget to ban federal support of "depictions of sadomasochism, homoeroticism, the sexual exploitation of children or individuals engaged in sex acts." NEA chairman John Frohnmayer stuck by this obscenity pledge. The controversy, centered on free speech, escalated quickly, even extending to the two public seminars offered at Winterfest X: "For God, for Country, and for Art," and "Theatre: A Haven for Misbehavin'."

Richards, about to finish his term on the National Council on the Arts, was eloquent in his defense of the agency. "Throughout the world, the United States is looked to as the repository of freedom. To withdraw (funding) altogether is an announcement to the world that we no longer trust freedom. That we are threatened because a person speaks his mind. This is the exact obverse to the basis on which this country evolved." Richards's thoughts were especially salient in light of the anticommunist revolution then spreading from Romania and Czechoslovakia through the rest of the Soviet bloc.

Fifty-some years after its charter, it's clear that the ways and means of the NEA will always remain a flash point. Depending on who is in the White House and which party controls Congress, the fight to save or deauthorize the NEA waxes and wanes. Cultural warriors against the endowment cherry-pick previous "obscene" recipients and invoke an unholy terror of deficit spending. Partisans weave together the high road (a nation is best judged by the quality of its creative expression, artistic freedom is an inalienable right, and so on) with the low (the arts are a proven engine for economic growth in any and all communities). ◆

his twelve seasons, Richards exceeded his promise to focus on new plays and playwrights. Qualitatively, he will always be revered, in tandem with his savvy, sensitive managing director, Ben Mordecai, for discovering and shaping the talent of August Wilson. Some thirty years after the premiere of *Ma Rainey's Black Bottom*, the list of artists who began—or enriched—their stage careers by working on the ten plays in the Wilson cycle, is staggering. The same can be said for a next generation of Black playwrights who continue, by his example, if not his aesthetics, to expand the American dramatic repertory.

It seems beside the point to mention his race. Richards, who had broken several color barriers before coming to Yale, never made much of it publicly. The late Reg A. Cathey ('81) commented that "you felt the difference, and he didn't talk about it. It was taboo, almost. Being Black had nothing to do with anything, but you were proud of it." Martenson, his first managing director, says, "We can't ever lose sight of the fact that Lloyd was the first Black artistic director. Diversity at the school began to expand when Lloyd arrived. He just did it. Lloyd never needed to talk about diversity. He just did it."

Director and translator David Chambers ('71) studied under Brustein but came back to direct four very different assignments for Richards (*Neapolitan Ghosts, Sarcophagus, Kiss of the Spider Woman*, and *Search and Destroy*) and also became a pillar of the YSD directing department for thirty years. Comparing Brustein and Richards, Chambers recalls, "Brustein did very little Shakespeare. I once had lunch with a rabbi in New Haven who said, 'Well, Bob Brustein doesn't do Shakespeare because he's not interested in people. He's interested in ideas and forces.' As for Lloyd, I don't think he had much in the way of theatricalism. I don't think he was interested in the body; I don't think he was really interested in the words; I think he was interested in psychological action inside social content."

Chambers is correct inasmuch as Richards was sensitive first and foremost to the needs of playwrights and actors. Kimberly Scott says, "Lloyd said one thing to me that has stayed with me my whole career, my whole life, and continues to be part of my mission as an actor. *Serve the play*. When I am the most befuddled or frustrated or in the thick of it, his voice saying, 'Serve the play' is what comes to me. That always sees me through." Courtney B. Vance has never forgotten Richards saying, "At a certain point, the playwright knows the most about the play. At a certain point, the director knows the most. At a certain point, the actors know the play more than anyone else. And finally, the audience knows more than anyone else, and know[s] *everything* about the play."

Whenever asked what is the best piece of writing advice he's ever received, Pulitzer Prize–winning playwright Doug Wright "flashes to a meeting with Lloyd in his office at the drama school where he was concerned about certain aspects of my Winterfest production. He just looked at me, in a consoling, wise way, and said, 'Always remember, you must write for an audience that is *smarter* than you are.' And that's been my beacon ever since; it really has."

CHAPTER THREE

Stan Wojewodski Jr.
(1991–2002)

What does the school have to do with the Rep? What does the Rep have to do with the school? That remains, in theory, very simple for me, and I would like to evaporate the questions rather than define the differences.

—STAN WOJEWODSKI JR., 1991

IN JANUARY 1990, an eight-member search committee for Richards's successor was formed; the committee included YSD faculty members Gister, Mordecai, and Lee as well as Yale College Theater Studies professor Thomas Whitaker.

Four months later, Brustein, reviewing *The Piano Lesson* in the *New Republic*, could hold his tongue no longer. In a piece titled "Broadway Tail Wagging Yale Rep Dog," he panned the play: "When ghosts begin resolving realistic plots, you can be sure the playwright has not mastered his material." With faint praise he damns the audience for Wilson's works: "It is comforting to find a black playwright working the mainstream American realist tradition of Odets, Hellman, and early Miller." (All writers he would never schedule.) He is ham-handed and obtuse when he suggests that Wilson has focused too much on the Black experience.

In a *Variety* follow-up, Brustein, referencing Trevor Nunn's forced resignation as artistic director of the Royal Shakespeare Company for his years of financial involvement with the global contagion of *Cats* and *Les Misérables*, goes on to say, "I will simply ask how much attention can such an artistic director pay to his own institution when he has spent the last three years staging a single play in six different theaters, before producing it and directing it on Broadway?" (Lest anyone accuse Brustein of hypocrisy, A.R.T. had sent *'Night, Mother*, *Mastergate*, and *Big River* to Broadway, but A.R.T. was not a Broadway partner.)

In an interesting twist, Rocco Landesman ('72, DFA '76), who, as the head of Jujamcyn Theaters, was both the Broadway landlord of *The Piano Lesson* and one of its principal investors, agreed with his Yale mentor: "When the focus of your energy is developing one property as fully as you can with the culmination being Broadway, then you're in a different business than [Yale Rep]." Richards held *his* tongue until he left New Haven. In an "exit interview" with *American Theatre*, he said, "There are people who believe that what they do is the be-all and end-all. There are people who think they are the guardians of ethics and artistry and that the muse speaks only to them. I can't really accept that."

The search committee, reviewing a first round of 150 applicants, must have been aware of this flap. Richards had left the drama school in the skilled hands of Gister. Unlike his two successive deans, who would attend every school production, Richards was rarely spotted among student audiences. An acting graduate from the Richards years, Kate Burton ('82), acknowledges a disconnect between Dean Richards and Artistic Director Richards. Says Burton, "I was in Lloyd's first class at YSD; I never quite got him, as he seemed disconnected, and I assumed I drove him crazy as I was always banging the drum about getting better teachers. Then, postgraduation, I went to the O'Neill for the summer of '85, and I discovered: 'Oh, this is where his heart is. This is his home.' And from then on, I loved

Stan Wojewodski Jr. (1991–2002)

him to pieces, and I totally got him. During my time at Yale I didn't think he was as effective as he could have been as dean of the drama school. I thought he was an extraordinary artistic director of the Rep, and, in hindsight, his deanship has taken on a different sheen. There was a method to his madness."

By 1986, the growing number of *Fences* productions across the country requiring Richards's presence (with *Joe Turner's Come and Gone* on deck) led to frustration across much of the school regarding the level of attention paid to the students. The dean's office held a series of one-on-one meetings, each with a department representative. Amy Aquino ('86), selected by her peers to represent the actors, recalls saying to Richards, "'Look, you have too many things going on. You're the artistic director of one of the major regional theaters in America. You have shows on Broadway. You're running the preeminent new playwrights' festival every summer. And you're the dean.' He said, 'Well, that's the fun part.' To which I respectfully replied, 'It's not a joke. We're not getting the education that we thought we were going to get when we came here.' I can't say anything came out of the meeting, but he listened."

There was no question that it was time to recalibrate the needs of the drama school with the purpose of the theater. By mid-October, the names David Chambers, Jon Jory, Ming Cho Lee, Lynne Meadow, Jennifer Tipton, Stan Wojewodski Jr., and Garland Wright were mentioned as finalists in the press. Chambers ('71), Lee, and Tipton were on the drama faculty; Jory ('66), Meadow ('71), Wojewodski, and Wright were running, respectively, Actors Theatre of Louisville, the Manhattan Theatre Club, Center Stage in Baltimore, and the Guthrie Theater in Minneapolis.

On January 10, 1991, Yale president Benno C. Schmidt announced the job had gone to Wojewodski, "a leader of the American theater with a passionate dedication to young artists and creativity in drama. He is also a first-rate, proven administrator, under whose direction Center Stage has become one of America's leading theaters, in terms of its artistic vision, resources, performance facilities, and innovative productions."

Born in Scranton, Pennsylvania, to a father who worked in state government and a mother who was a homemaker, Wojewodski earned a full scholarship to the Jesuit University of Scranton, getting a BA in English, with minors in philosophy and education. He received his MFA in theater/directing from Catholic University in 1973. Two years later, he became the assistant to Artistic Director Jacques Cartier at Center Stage. Two years after that, Wojewodski replaced Cartier and began a partnership with Managing Director Peter C. Culman and a board of trustees sufficiently indoctrinated in the endeavor to pursue artistic excellence and in the idea that art has no bottom line. (Lest that last point sound fiscally cavalier, Center Stage always balanced its operating budgets.) Center Stage had recently experienced a period of tremendous growth: an endowment was launched as well as an associate artists program; also, a $13 million capital campaign to raise actor, director, and designer salaries, build a completely flexible second theater, and transform a block of brick row houses into state-of-the-art housing for visiting artists was completed the year before Wojewodski left for New Haven.

His taste, supported by his resident dramaturg Rick Davis ('83, DFA '03) and a sequence of dramaturgy fellows fresh out of Yale, could be termed "adventurously anticommercial": plays by Ramón de Valle-Inclán, Antonio Buero Vallejo, Vaclav Havel, Kleist, Gertrude Stein, Beckett, Horváth, David Hare, Büchner, and Wallace Shawn were spread liberally across his seasons. The house playwright was Eric Overmyer, whose premieres there included *On the Verge, or the Geography of Yearning*, *Native Speech*, and *In Perpetuity Throughout the Universe*.

If Richards had been tantalized by the thought of running a theater after years in the classroom, the opposite was true for Wojewodski, quoted here in an introductory brochure for Yale: "The union of professional theater with conservatory training has long been my ideal. Yale's achievement—and potential—in this regard are unique. . . . I am aware of the enormity of the challenge and energized by the scale of possibility."

A man of erudition and wit, he answered questions, according to an early interviewer in the *Hartford Courant*, "in essay form: analytical, complex, almost footnoted." Overmyer, a close friend, said, "Anyone with his intelligence can be formidable for other people. He can be impatient with foolishness, and as you know, there is occasional foolishness in theater. And he doesn't coddle actors or treat them like semipsychotic children. He's very sensitive, but I've heard him say he's nobody's father."

Wojewodski made this announcement to the *Register* ten days after his appointment: "Briefly stated, the theater is to train students." One step toward striking down what he considered artificial barriers between the Rep and the school was to chair the directing department. Another was to double down—even in a weak economy and another period of Yale-wide belt tightening—on finding the funds to upgrade the inadequate classroom spaces and rehearsal studios. (Before taking office, he had received a letter from the provost directing him to cut $500,000 out of his first budget.) Another way to further the growth of specific artists was Wojewodski's launch of an associate artists program, another initiative transplanted from Center Stage; he modified the program to include ongoing projects at Yale Rep and teaching commitments to the students.

ASSOCIATE ARTISTS AT YALE REP

Many freelance theater makers long for a home base where their talents might be purposed for aims larger than a suite of short-term gigs in the rehearsal room. One feature that Wojewodski brought to Yale Rep from Baltimore's Center Stage was his version of an associate artists program. He had launched the effort—something of an R&D apparatus for the theater—in Maryland to bring the perspectives of playwrights, designers, dramaturgs, and directors to institutional planning efforts.

Given the breadth of YSD / Yale Rep resources, Wojewodski's program goals shifted in New Haven, such that his associates were fully engaged in the classroom. Among his initial batch of eight were Eric Overmyer and Suzan-Lori Parks, who taught playwriting in his first season. Actor Byron Jennings played the eponymous *Edward II* in a rare revival of the Marlowe tragedy and staged the fights for *Hamlet* the following season. As time went on, Paul Schmidt would translate Molière and Chekhov for the Rep, act there, and teach translation to the dramaturgy students; by 1997, Ralph Lemon was generating some of his *Geography* in residence, while the 52nd St. Project was sharing future MacArthur genius Willie Reale's pedagogical strategies to help launch the Dwight/Edgewood Project.

Composer Kim Sherman first worked with Wojewodski on *Hamlet* at Center Stage. She jokes, "Stan taught me about dramatic action, and I taught him the twelve-tone row. There were many dinners. And many martinis. He ushered me in to becoming a theater artist." Wojewodski brought her to Yale, where she scored

As Richards's final production, *A Moon for the Misbegotten*, was completing its run in May, Wojewodski had staked out more territory. For his first season, in order to give more time to the design and rehearsal process, there would be three, not four, *fully produced* Winterfest productions. The loss of one Winterfest meant that the first Wojewodski season had seven shows instead of ten: Overmyer's *On the Verge, or the Geography of Yearning*; Fugard's latest, *My Children! My Africa!*; the three Winterfests; Marlowe's *Edward II*; and S. J. Perelman's *The Beauty Part*.

Fifteen years post-Yale, Wojewodski recalls, "Looking back, the first season at the Rep was a template for everything I did that followed. Either more of, or less

Composer and Yale Rep associate artist Kim D. Sherman (1991–2002)
JAMES SHUBINSKI

(and sometimes performed in) at least one show a season for live musicians. For ten years she also taught a course on collaboration for composers / sound designers and directors. "In my case, being an associate artist was about bringing my 'classical music' language into the aesthetic of the theatre, bringing musicians onto the stage, and bringing musical concepts into the collaborative language among design disciplines." ◆

of, maybe abandoned for a while to move in another direction or attempt to reincorporate." The Overmyer had been seen everywhere since its Baltimore premiere in 1985. A daft play about three Victorian "lady explorers" time-traveling forward through the American century to Terra Incognita, *On the Verge* is a giddy fantasy that depends more on environment, tone, and point of view than on plot or character development. The Yale Rep revival could be read as an artistic declaration of principles from its new leader. Language is the sine qua non of the theatrical event; linearity—not so much. Powerful, abstract visuals are ascendant. Cerebration is celebration.

Riccardo Hernández ('92), then a third-year set designer, remembers the liberation of the Rep space. "The first thing Stan did was remove the catwalks at the Rep, which Ming had put in. It lifted the whole thing." Creating the large and wide open "found" space for *On the Verge* led the design, directing, and playwriting students to think more about visual text. Yeargan seconds the idea: "It was such a relief—like suddenly being liberated from prison. The catwalks had been useful for storage space, and they masked upstage to downstage entrances, but that was about it."

Just as Handke's *They Are Dying Out* was perceived in Richards's first season as a throwback to Brustein, Fugard's *My Children! My Africa!* (1989) would feel like an *ave atque vale* to the tidy dramaturgy and sociopolitical content of the Richards years. *Edward II* (1594) aligned with both Wojewodski's taste for difficult plays and Yale Rep's history of producing neglected classics. Perelman's satire *The Beauty Part* had opened and closed during a 1962 newspaper strike and was considered a lost play. Of the Marlowe and the Perelman, more will be said. For now, we turn to the last Winterfest.

Wojewodski announced on November 4, 1991, that *Fefu and Her Friends*, by María Irene Fornès, would be produced at the Rep and that *The Death of the Last Black Man in the Whole Entire World* by Suzan-Lori Parks would play in repertory at the UT with *Democracy in America* by YSD dramaturgy alumna Colette Brooks ('79). Photos of the playwrights replaced the snowflake on the program cover, which also bore the label "Experiments in Form." For subscribers and reviewers—Wojewodski was willing for Winterfest to take the rap from the critical community—the label could be viewed either as a skull-and-crossbones warning or as a "Drink me" invitation straight out of *Alice in Wonderland*. Further bucking tradition, neither the Fornès nor the Parks was a new work.

By 1992, Cuban American María Irene Fornès had written (and often directed) two dozen works for the stage, winning seven Obie awards as well as NEA, Rockefeller, and Guggenheim Foundation grants. In terms of output, stylistic range, experimental audacity, and sheer talent, her plays matched those of her contemporary peer, Sam Shepard; yet in her lifetime (1930–2018) she earned few of the cultural and monetary benefits that accrued to him. Was it her gender? Was it because she didn't forge and flog a thematic mythology, like Shepard's father-son-horse-cowboy-manhood-decline-of-the-Wild-Wild-West matrix? Or was it that she never visited the living room of the AFP?

The entirely female cast of *Fefu and Her Friends* provides one clue to her relative obscurity. Plays without male characters almost never enter the canon. The few that do—*The Women, for colored girls who have considered suicide / when the*

Pippa Pearthree as Julia in Fornès's *Fefu and Her Friends* (1992)
PHOTO © GERRY GOODSTEIN

rainbow is enuf, and *The House of Bernarda Alba*—do not exactly ace the Bechdel-Wallace Test, a standard contemporary measure of equity and gender representation. To wit, does the work at hand (novel, film, play) feature at least *two* women with *names of their own* who talk *to each other* about *something other* than a *man*? (Graphic novelist Alison Bechdel created this test in 1985 in her comic strip "Dykes to Watch Out For.")

Although men are discussed in *Fefu and Her Friends*, the play shares the highest possible Bechdel score with Caryl Churchill's *Top Girls*. On a spring day in 1935, Fefu invites friends over to rehearse a presentation for their charity. She interrupts a chat with the first arrivals by shooting her husband, Phillip, out in the garden, through the living room window. He feigns death—that is their game—but he's begun threatening to replace the blanks in her gun with real bullets. The rest arrive, including Julia, Fefu's symbolic, wheelchair-bound adversary.

For part two of the play, "Afternoon," four scenes take place simultaneously in four separate locations: (1) on the lawn, Emma and Fefu play croquet, Fefu confessing to an undefined "spiritual" pain; (2) in the study, Cindy and Christina sit and read aloud to each other; (3) in a bedroom, Julia lies alone, hallucinating about being attacked by strangers; and (4) in the kitchen, Paula and Sue discuss love and celibacy. Sue leaves with Julia's soup, and Cecilia, whose affair with Paula is on the wane, enters. During this part of the play, the divided audience tours the theater, experiencing the scenes in a different order.

Stan Wojewodski Jr. (1991–2002)

The audience reassembles for part three, "Evening." At one moment, Fefu alone observes Julia out of her wheelchair. As dusk settles in, everyone except Fefu and Julia go outside to observe the stars. When Julia says that she cannot walk, Fefu, failing to goad her into a physical altercation, takes her gun outside. A shot rings out, and Julia's head falls back. She is dead. Fefu reenters with a dead rabbit. On the surface, a Sam Shepard climax. Underneath, more like late Ibsen.

Fefu and Her Friends demands that its audiences watch women engaging in female activities in female spaces. Forcing the audience to displace itself four times undermines the authority of the playwright to form a time-driven, Aristotelian plot. The audience makes the play *with* the cast, embracing or disdaining its portrait gallery of female isolation and entrapment. In "killing" Julia, Fefu destroys the internalized weakness that bourgeois expectations—of marriage, children, homes, and social lives—instill in women and exorcises Julia's semiarticulated pain.

Fefu had first been performed in New York apartments and lofts with real kitchens and libraries. For director Lisa Peterson (YC '83), the greatest challenge with this first major revival was carving playing spaces out of Yale Rep for part two. Audiences, color-coded by a dot on their programs, followed student ushers in matching-colored sweatshirts and hats. A kitchen set was built in the green room behind and below the main stage. The study was a ledge extending out from the lighting booth: patrons eavesdropped on Cindy and Christina's feet high above them. Fefu and Emma played croquet on an Astroturf lawn set up in the downstairs lounge. For Julia's bedroom, the audience stood onstage and stared down a hole at the tortured, mesmerizing Pippa Pearthree, hallucinating on a tilted bed through a layer of plexiglass.

Decades later, Peterson suspects the audiences didn't appreciate the fun of the tour and that the production puzzled Fornès, whom she'd personally brought up to New Haven. "Irene always believed her work was 'real'—when for most of us her plays read like glorious poems. I think for her, pretending that these invented spaces in the theater were real made the play more abstract than she was comfortable with. I didn't see the play as real. I felt I was creating a visual poem about female friendship."

As the twenty-first century has witnessed the rise of immersive or interactive stagings in which the audience moves, randomly or in regiments, around the theatrical space, the procedural novelty of *Fefu and Her Friends* has worn off. Its thematics of female perception and experience, however, are evergreen. In terms of Yale Rep history, Peterson's production of the Fornès can be seen as a rebuttal to Wajda's *White Marriage* in 1977, which seemed to mansplain the fears of budding female sexuality on a set crowded with penises. (It should be noted that *White Marriage* has since become the province of female directors.)

Parks's *The Death of the Last Black Man in the Whole Entire World* began previews at the UT the week after *Fefu* opened. It began with a cascade of screaming whispers in the dark; then, a shaft of light struck a bier covered with white gauze. Riccardo Hernández's set of square, slickly lacquered blue columns flanking the stage with stairs reaching down into the house presages a ceremony. There is a bright-red spiral staircase stage right. An actor says, "The black man moves his hands," but, holding a watermelon, he cannot move his hands. (His character is called Black Man with Watermelon.) A bell sounds twice. The rest of the cast introduce themselves: Black Woman with Fried Drumstick, Lots of Grease and Lots of Pork, Queen-Then-Pharaoh Hatshepsut, And Bigger and Bigger and Bigger, and so on. Constructed from scraps of stereotypes and misperceptions of African and Black American history and culture, the eleven figures in *Death of the Last Black Man* are a timeline stretching from the Biblical Ham, cast out in Genesis by his father Noah to beget a race of slaves, to Voice on Thuh Tee V, the "Broad Caster" whose headline news is the death of Gamble Major, the "absolutely last living Negro man in the whole entire known world."

If August Wilson had been the most exciting new Broadway playwright since David Mamet, Suzan-Lori Parks was the most exciting new "downtown" (read: nonlinear) playwright since, well, Shepard and Fornès. When Winterfest XII began, the twenty-seven-year-old Parks had written six other plays and had won an Obie, two grants from the NEA, and one grant each from the Rockefeller Foundation, Ford Foundation, and New York State Council for the Arts. Parks's work so excited the editors of Yale's *Theater* that they published a draft of *Death of the Last Black Man* in a special "New Writing" issue *before* the play premiered in September 1990 in Brooklyn. A literal student of James Baldwin, and influenced by James Joyce and dramatic outliers Gertrude Stein and Adrienne Kennedy, Parks said to interviewer Alisa Solomon ('81, DFA '95): "Why does everyone think that white artists make art, and black artists make statements? Why doesn't anyone ever ask me about *form*?"

If poetry is, according to *Black Man* director Liz Diamond, "the radical condensation of meaning in form," then early Parks plays behave like poems in which form and content are inseparable. They are fugue-like, jazz-influenced, intensely musical, call-and-response poems built from what she terms rep and rev (repetition and revision). A word like "history" becomes "his tree" in a next iteration and then "his story" in a third. The Black Man with Watermelon experiences a succession of near deaths in the play, yet may never actually die. His greatest mortal risk

Leon Addison Brown as Black Man with Watermelon and Fanni Green as Black Woman with Fried Drumstick in Suzan Lori-Parks's *The Death of the Last Black Man in the Whole Entire World* (1992)
PHOTO © T. CHARLES ERICKSON

is to have been erased from history. The injunction that the characters repeatedly return to is "You should write this down. You should hide this under a rock." The last words of the play are "Hold it," repeated seven times. The characters attempt to fix themselves, but nothing holds in the flux of the present moment. For critic Marc Robinson ('90, DFA '92), they are negotiating with time itself. "They long for

168 *Stan Wojewodski Jr. (1991–2002)*

endlessness and yet hope to root themselves in history. The tension is not meant to be reconciled."

Catherine Sheehy ('92, DFA '99), current chair of the dramaturgy and dramatic criticism department and Yale Rep resident dramaturg, was a third-year student for Winterfest XII. She wryly recalls that *Death of the Last Black Man* was the first time she willingly saw a Rep production more than once. "I was transfixed. I particularly remember Michael Potts ('92) as And Bigger and Bigger and Bigger dangling from a noose dozens of feet above the stage, and Fanni Green as Black Woman with Drumstick bending over the altar/casket during the final invocation to 're-member me.' And Reg Cathey ('81) as Ham, costumed as a homeless man against that pristine set, yelling 'Ham is not tuh blame!'"

What is time-stopping for some is time-killing for others, a hazard for any experiment in form. *Death of the Last Black Man* bewildered some and perplexed others; at ninety minutes without an intermission, it may have seemed too long to sustain its intellection, but the critical establishment recognized an important new voice for the theater. Brustein himself reviewed it favorably from his rostrum in Boston, writing, "She will be even more exciting once she clarifies her vision."

To *Democracy in America*, a collage of movement, image, original prose in several languages, and passages from Descartes, Walter Benjamin, Adam Smith, and de Tocqueville, the critics were merciless. "It shifts between a Victorian illustrated lecture and a very dated modern dance recital. . . . [There is] no cumulative effect except mounting exasperation," a reviewer from *Variety* claimed. A *New York Times* article declared the play to be "a self-conscious, uneasy mixture of jangling nerves, shrillness, whispering, and droning." And Jonathan Kalb ('85, DFA '87) wrote in the *Village Voice* that "*Democracy in America* is an enormous, prolix, unwieldy, doleful monstrosity of a production . . . for which I am deeply grateful. A triumphal failure."

No one deliberately sets out to make *Spiderman: Turn Off the Dark*. After Yale, where she had served as production dramaturg for Wajda and Serban, Colette Brooks worked with avant-garde director JoAnne Akalaitis and taught at Harvard, the New School, and Playwrights Horizons. *Democracy* was her first theatrical piece, initially developed in two workshops at Center Stage with Travis Preston ('78) and a group of actors with singular perspectives on the United States. Preston said at the time, "One's father worked with Che Guevara; one's father was second-in-command in Ceaușescu's Romania; another's grandparents were from Germany." Preston asked them to bring biographical material and began to shape the event with Brooks. Wojewodski brought the project to Yale, where additional

The ensemble of *Democracy in America* in *La Via Dolorosa* (1992)
PHOTO © GERRY GOODSTEIN

actors, including four Yale students with their own baggage, were folded into the process.

With the exception of Preston's own *Little Eyolf*, intently avant-garde stagings at Yale Rep had taken a hit during the Richards regime. Preston and Brooks were avid followers of the works of Robert Wilson, Ariane Mnouchkine, Peter Stein, Giorgio Strehler, Richard Foreman, and Pina Bausch. They knew their German expressionists and their Wooster Group. Theater made as an act of collective creation inspired them. The result of their de Tocqueville fantasia on "Americanness" was a Mount Everest of free-associative, multimedia information. As the play began, a light fell on a lone suitcase stage left. Hernández's turquoise *Black Man* set had been switched out for Christopher Barreca's ('83) expanding and contracting proscenium in blacks and grays, beautifully lit by Stephen Strawbridge ('83). Scene titles and thematic koans were projected on wide pieces of scrim that rolled up and down on the set. An ensemble of thirteen, each dressed in black and carrying a suitcase, entered and began traveling at that agonizingly slow pace invented by Robert Wilson and directors of Baroque opera exhumations.

The program and the scrims presented a schema: act 1, *La Via Dolorosa*, and act 2, *The Past Is Readied for the Future*. As can happen with brain-first projects, however, the links between events known only to the creatives risk striking the audience as infuriatingly capricious. In act 1, as part of a section called "Meditations," an actor facing *up*stage recites a long passage from René Descartes. This is followed immediately by a spirited group samba. Five minutes later, a Mexican editorial denouncing the United States is delivered in Spanish. To close the act, a Romanian fairy tale with supertitles. After a point, why ask why?

The theory thickens in act 2 as Adam Smith and Walter Benjamin join the conversation, which has shifted to the shocks of the Industrial Revolution. De Tocqueville's words appear only in a projected coda to the performance, after a personal account of the life and suicide of a character's disabled brother—a segment acknowledged by all the carping critics as the high point of the evening, in both its writing and its performance.

In addition to playing Ham in *Black Man*, actor Reg E. Cathey ('81) was one of the *Democracy* travelers. He remembered it as being "one crazy show" but respected its process. One night after the show, Cathey heard a patron ask her companion in the lobby, "What kept you awake?" Today, in considering the reception to *Democracy*, it's facile to cite the wiseacre who said, "Everything changes except the avant-garde." But it's equally useful to keep in mind Jonathan Kalb's last words in *The Village Voice*—"a triumphal failure." Any forward-thinking, noncommercial theater should strive to outpace audience expectations. Yale Rep, with its considerable resources, should expect certain productions to falter with integrity. Spectacular misfires had happened in the past and would certainly happen again. Two months after *Black Man* and *Democracy* had played their final performances, Wojewodski announced the 1992–1993 season. Winterfest had melted faster than a snowflake.

After a decade-long revolving door of disgruntled department chairs and master teachers, Brustein, whose ideal was that any actor leaving with a Yale MFA would be able to play *any* role, managed to establish an intelligible acting curriculum by 1976. First-year students would study "realism," meant here to foreground the works of Chekhov, Ibsen, and Strindberg. The second-year actors would focus exclusively on verse drama, that is, Shakespeare and the Jacobeans. Everyone else, from Brecht to Maeterlinck, was reserved for the third year.

Stan Wojewodski Jr. (1991–2002)

In November 1991, Wojewodski announced to *Variety* a structural change to the Rep: a verse project, featuring the class of third-year acting students, would be part of the following season. This decision to devote one mainstage slot to the graduating actors would satisfy several objectives. Improving the practice of Yale Rep as a "teaching hospital" for the students was a core value of Wojewodski's mission. Chair of the acting department Gister also invoked the hospital image: "We're training professionals in nonprofessional spaces. It's like having an operating room in a tennis court." He meant that the acting students may have had many production experiences in the school and at the Cabaret in their first two years, but they hadn't experienced the professional conditions of working on a large stage with different spatial and acoustic demands. Neither had they experienced the discoveries to be made in performing a role during a three- or four-week run. Further, they hadn't experienced playing to a paying, *nonstudent* audience. (Drama students are irritatingly, vocally partisan when watching their peers perform.)

Why start small? Wojewodski began with *Hamlet*. The leading female parts, Gertrude and Ophelia, were double cast. A white man, Brendan Corbalis ('93), and a Black woman, Melody Garrett ('93), played Hamlet in alternate performances. Hidebound patrons objecting to a distaff Dane were treated to program photos of Bernhardt, Le Gallienne, Judith Anderson, and Diane Venora in the role.

Wojewodski maintains that the process for third-year Rep projects was no different from other shows in a given season. Since he had been watching the class perform for two years, they weren't auditioned. He might consult with Gister or subsequent chair of the acting department Evan Yionoulis ('85) as to whether an actor could handle a specific part, but the play wasn't chosen for the class. For the text of *Hamlet*, he relied on his first important hire: the tireless Mark Bly ('80), rumored to have read a new script every single day of his working life. In the twelve years since his Yale graduation, Bly had been a dramaturg at Arena Stage, the Guthrie Theater, and Seattle Repertory Theatre, working on dozens of classics and new plays. His Yale job would be a triple handful: associate artistic director of Yale Rep and cochair of playwriting *and* dramaturgy and dramatic criticism.

Hamlet was publicized, in a slight fib, as the first all-student cast at the Rep in a decade. (Fifteen of the seventeen actors in *Love's Labour's Lost* in 1982 had been currently enrolled, one was a recent grad, and the last was a British ringer.) The house aesthetic, one that would obtain for Wojewodski's tenure and beyond, was postmodern. The practice of combining striking visual details from different eras in sets and costumes to create unique stage environments for classic plays spread across the United States in the 1990s, not only because Yale MFAs, mentored by Lee, Yeargan, Jane Greenwood, and Jess Goldstein, were hired to design everywhere but also because they had begun chairing their own design programs. For *Hamlet*, student set designer Todd Rosenthal ('93), who would win a Tony Award fifteen years later for *August: Osage County*, created a spare, neutral space, an obvious stage. Flats and the occasional scrim moved constantly to create an unstable, shifting ground; a domed glass ceiling rose and fell to vary the vertical space and intensify Hamlet's claustrophobia. Several panels were painted an intense red and hung with royal portraits from van Dyck to Reynolds to Gainsborough.

Katherine Roth's ('93) costumes—modern white fencing suits for the act 5 duel; exotic, Persian-influenced costumes for the Players in "The Murder of Gonzago"; a bulky sweater and dark contemporary slacks for Garrett's Hamlet; and hand-painted dresses for Ophelia and Gertrude—were "period, with a spin," designed not for any *Hamlet* but for this *Hamlet*. Or these two different *Hamlets*. Critics covering both casts found Corbalis's Hamlet athletic and inward. Garrett's prince, by contrast, was given to "secret and startling rages" that transformed Hamlet's melancholia to anger and frustration. Both delivered the text beautifully.

Melody J. Garrett as Hamlet and Sean Haberle as Laertes (*center*), with Craig Mathers, Earl Baker, Enrico Colantoni, James Hallet, and Tom McCarthy (1992)
PHOTO © T. CHARLES ERICKSON

Stan Wojewodski Jr. (1991–2002)

Wojewodski's *As You Like It* the following season was notable for the male trio of Bo Foxworth, Tony Ward, and Paul Giamatti as, respectively, Orlando, Touchstone, and a vibrantly sour Jaques. For the class of 1995, Wojewodski engaged recent graduate Mark Rucker ('92) to direct *Twelfth Night, Or What You Will*. Bly says today that he and Wojewodski chose outside directors "who wouldn't pander to the idea of the conservatory, but who would embrace the two-way street of it. Mark [Rucker] had been out in the world for a few years and knew what the actors needed to succeed on the outside." Rucker excelled at creating theatrical events. His directing thesis had been a cross-gendered version of Kaufman and Ferber's screenplay for *Stage Door*, and he was still remembered for his blitzkrieg condensations of *Sweet Charity* and *Chicago* at the Cabaret.

For *Twelfth Night*, Rucker took Orsino's plaintive "Give me excess" speech as a guiding principle. Growing up in Southern California, he remembered the glossy spreads of famous people in his mother's *Photoplay* magazines. "These are young, wealthy, self-obsessed people," he noted. "Elitists without a care who manufacture their own little dramas at their own risk, and at the risk of people around them." Rucker and set designer Ritirong Jiwakanon ('95) wanted an East Hampton beach house out of a 1960s issue of *Architectural Digest*. "When you're a student, you have to beg for a table or a roll of tape," Rucker said at the time. With Wojewodski's expanded production budgets, the Rep provided an elevator, a spiral staircase and balcony that extended the width of the stage, rain, and an in-ground swimming pool. Three musicians played Kim Sherman's original score in an alcove on the second level. The concept wasn't the psychedelic, let-it-all-hang-out American 1960s but rather Fellini's chic, bored-with-it-all Rome in *La Dolce Vita* or mod London in Antonioni's *Blow-Up*. The clothes by Sarah Eckert ('95) referenced Courrèges and Mary Quant.

As the lights went down, Michael Strickland ('95), playing the shipwrecked Sebastian, slipped into the downstage pool and held his breath for as long as he could. Then he popped up with a gigantic gasp—a surprise entrance matched every night by gasps in the audience. As with *The Frogs* twenty years before, water was an unforeseen hazard. The first time, in tech, when the Sea Captain carried Viola in his arms out of the rainy alcove, the deck was the proverbial banana peel. A first solution was surfboard wax, which, when wet, creates a surface that grips. In the interest of safety, the entire deck was coated with the wax. No one realized that under hot stage lights, surfboard wax becomes slippery. So the wax was stripped and the deck redone once more. A preview was lost in the process.

The nuptial pairings at the end of Shakespeare's comedies can be perfunctory at best. Rucker's *Twelfth Night* made room for ambiguities that the Bard skips

John Bland and Mercedes Herrero in *Twelfth Night* (1995)
PHOTO © T. CHARLES ERICKSON

over. When Viola's trick was ultimately revealed, the principals were draped on an enormous white couch. Orsino began matching them up. Olivia hesitated; she leaned first toward Viola, making it evident that Sebastian was not her first choice, before she finally reached over to him in assent. "What you will" indeed.

Wojewodski's production of *Richard III* in 2000 took place on a set of two giant, curving, rusted pieces, rather like a Richard Serra sculpture. Wanting the men to be monolithic, rooted, *and* skirted, costume designer Roth stole the skirt of the Minoan snake goddess figure. A lot of time was spent on them in the costume shop: "In order to hold their conical shape and to avoid using hoops, we padded and rigged them from the waist with tapes so we could adjust them as they stretched on various biases in various fabrics. I wanted them to open all the way up the front (men's parts need to be seen), which was a nightmare—the center front edges swung in and crossed each other from the knee down, making them look sort of pigeon-toed and dangerous to walk in. We had to recut the center front edges to trick gravity. When they figured out the sword fighting, the swirling, flying, flipping skirts were more than worth the trouble."

Four of the ten third-year projects weren't by the Bard. Another of Wojewodski's objectives was to bring drama students in sustained contact with uniquely different artists. For Farquhar's *The Beaux' Stratagem*, a Restoration look at fashionable fortune hunters, he hired Everett Quinton, a "self-styled male actress and director," to direct. Quinton and his partner, the late, great Charles Ludlam (1943–1987), had created the Theater of the Ridiculous in Greenwich Village, making antic hay by adapting high-toned texts to their downtown aesthetic, one in which theatrical excess, camp, and burlesque commingled with the flagrantly amateur and the visibly tacky. For *Beaux' Stratagem*, the newspapers advertised, "Today's best actors attack a time-tested romp," but applying Ridiculous Theater techniques to Farquhar's linguistic filigree and plot convolutions in a four-week rehearsal period proved in the end to be putting a hat on a hat on a hat—in other words, excess to an excess.

On the occasion of his centenary in 1998, a work by Thornton Wilder, son of New Haven and also a famous Bulldog (YC '20), at last graced a Rep stage, with Liz Diamond's production of *The Skin of Our Teeth* (1942). Its three eon-stretching acts with the Antrobus family of Excelsior, New Jersey, spiral from the hilarious (the Ice Age) to the alarming (the Flood) and, finally, the tragic (the [Latest] War to End All Wars). A final stage gesture—Mrs. Antrobus closing the book in her napping husband's hand—was a lovely directorial twist, reminding the audience that the women who toil as the ancillaries to history are equally, if not more, responsible for saving the planet as the men who daydream its improvements.

THE COSTUME SHOP

Among the tightest, busiest, and most colorful of Yale Rep spaces is the costume shop, a suite of rooms located on the second floor of the UT. Dress dummies lined up like Chinese tomb soldiers flank a perpendicular hallway that leads to the dressing rooms. Laid out for maximum efficiency, the costume shop has two glass-fronted rooms for drafting, draping, stitching, and fitting; a laundry and dyeing room; an emergency eyewash station in case of accidents; a closet with hanging rolls of muslin; eleven sewing machines; plenty of mirrors; and everywhere, bolts of cloth and meticulously organized boxes of passementerie.

Things weren't always so organized. Originally there were separate costume shops for the Rep and the school. Retired design faculty member Jess Goldstein ('78) says, "In the 1970s, we were all still more than willing to stay up all night and do whatever it took to get the work done. It was very much the attitude of the time, even in much of the professional theater." Soon after Goldstein's graduation, the two shops were combined under the leadership of Lisa Logan, who had begun as a

Brennan Brown (*center*) as Shakespeare's *Richard III*, with Harvey Gardner Moore, Joe Tantolo, Robert Libetti, Lael Logan, and John Woo Taak Kwon (2000)
PHOTO © T. CHARLES ERICKSON

stitcher and, close in age to the students, was empathetic in regard to their needs. During her decade there, Logan expanded the professional personnel of the shop so that student designers had little to do besides be designers, an important goal of their faculty.

The shop has a current workload of eleven public productions: five Yale Rep shows, the MFA directing thesis series, and three Carlotta Festival plays. (During Richards's tenure, there had been fourteen.) Six full-time employees work on every show. Costume project coordinator Linda Kelley-Dodd assists student designers with their additional assignments, like the Shakespeare Rep and commedia projects. For large-scale shows there is also a smaller annex shop at 1156 Chapel Street for overhire help. As opposed to drawing from available stock, the shop staff take pride in building as many costumes as possible, both to advance their own artistry and to pass hands-on technical knowledge to the students.

Tom McAlister, who retired in 2019 after thirty years of teaching and working in the shop, has excellent recall. Creatively tough costumes to build: Kathy Chalfant as Elizabeth I in *Passion Play* (2008); the Yeti for *On the Verge*; and the "insanely creative mermaid dress, which fully lit up," made for B. J. Crosby in *King Stag* (2004). Technically challenging costumes: The silk chiffon and organza evening gowns designed by Jane Greenwood for *Hay Fever* (1999). "You need deft, skilled hands to make dresses look 'effortless.'" Favorite look: "The clothing the shop made for Laila Robbins as Alma in *Summer and Smoke* (1989), designed by Melina Root ('90), was the most period-perfect 1910s silhouette I have ever seen onstage." Favorite achievements: "I am most proud of two productions where the shop built every piece, and in doing that, created specific worlds—Wojewodski's *Way of the World* (2001), costumes designed by Katherine Roth ('03), and Harold Scott's *King Lear* (2004), designed by Jessica Ford ('04)." ◆

Clowning teacher Christopher Bayes so inspired the class of 2001 that they wanted to work with him on their third-year project. Wojewodski and Bly felt associate artist Len Jenkin's sensibility matched the satiric outrage of Aristophanes and commissioned him to adapt *The Birds* (414 BCE). Jenkins repurposed Athenians Pisthetaerus and Euelpides into Venable Smoke, a down-at-his-heels comic, and Arnold Sand, his sleazy agent. Fleeing Las Vegas, they are taken to a realm in the sky run by showgirl-peacock Queen Popsy (the hilarious Kathryn Hahn ['01]), and they convince her to dethrone the original Olympians and create a new paradise—Cloudcuckooland. Some find *South Park*, *Young Frankenstein*, and *The Id-*

iots Karamazov deeply hilarious. Others deeply do not. So it was with Yale Rep's avian *Hellzapoppin.'*

The toughest challenge of all the third-year projects was Caryl Churchill's anti-Thatcher *Serious Money*, directed in 2002 by Jean Randich ('94). Dramatizing the aftermath of the "Big Bang," when Great Britain deregulated its capital markets, *Serious Money* is written in rhymed couplets and paced as fast as Chopin's "Minute Waltz," with simultaneous scenes saturated with overlapping dialogue, Britishisms, and financial jargon. The experience is as unruly and relentless as the clamor of the trading floor. Among the many high spots in Randich's production was the opening of act 2, a monologue delivered by a suave Peruvian businesswoman, Jacinta Condor. The actress, Jeanine Serralles, who was afraid of heights, spent the entire first act high up in the flies. In an entrance to rival Sebastian's in Rucker's *Twelfth Night*, Serralles dispensed her craven economic doctrines while standing on a swing that was slowly lowered to the stage floor.

Shortly after his appointment, incoming dean / artistic director James Bundy and his administrative staff conducted market research during the fall and winter of 2001–2002 and discovered that, among other perceptions, patrons were confused by the conflation of YSD and Rep work in promotional materials, so much so that 40 percent of nonattenders thought it was *all* educational theater. Low ticket prices contributed to this misperception, so the Rep raised prices closer to those at Long Wharf and Hartford Stage. Bundy excised the third-year acting slot from the season faster than Richards discontinued Brustein's rotating repertory in 1980, and Wojewodski eliminated Winterfest in 1992.

For arts institutions, the 1990s were a decade in which assumptions about the subscription model were challenged. The aging, predominantly white middle-class audience members who had supported civic theater for thirty-plus years were dying out and not being replaced. Although Wojewodski had stated right from the start that "finding a commercial audience is definitely not a priority of mine," Yale Rep was not immune to the marketplace. Richards had taken subscriptions to an all-time high, but after Wojewodski's first season, one-third of the Rep's subscribers failed to renew. Winterfest XII had certainly been one shot across the bow. Further, the nation was in the middle of a recession initially caused by a doubling of gas prices after Iraq invaded Kuwait. After the 1992–1993 season, the Rep lost another third of its subscriber base, going down to 3,950.

As Wojewodski put it, he wasn't worried about attracting ten thousand people

PERSONS OF THE DRAMA: VICTORIA (VICKI) NOLAN

Retiring in 2020 after twenty-seven years, Victoria Nolan was the longest-serving managing director in Yale Rep history, and the first to disbelieve it. She came to New Haven in 1993 after six seasons at Indiana Repertory Theatre; before that, she'd spent a decade working with Wojewodski as associate managing director at Center Stage. The decision to follow him to New Haven was an easy one.

Having moved Indiana Rep out of a bankruptcy position, she found the lack of cash-flow problems at Yale Rep a sweet surprise, as was an operating budget where earned income accounted for less than 10 percent of the total. The shocks were teaching at the school and coming to a hierarchical academic environment where change was like "moving glaciers." Although she didn't miss having to satisfy a board of trustees, she did miss the level of community engagement and civic involvement she'd experienced in Indianapolis and Baltimore, and so she began interacting with the mayor's office and the chamber of commerce and began an arts industry coalition with the other players in town.

Wojewodski remembers that among Nolan's many astonishing gifts was "her commitment to the continual revision and rebuilding of the management model in the service of artistic impulse. The cross-cultural, interdisciplinary work of Ralph Lemon is one of many, many examples of work that enjoyed the benefits of her steadfast dedication to an environment that prizes original dramaturgy and the pursuit of those resources that make its creation possible."

from three zip codes. Theater was an elite activity but not one tied to social class. For the 1992–1993 season, he had initiated, as he had in Baltimore, pay-what-you-can performances. Yale Rep also introduced a flex-pass subscription, in which subscribers could choose four out of the six shows. In its first year, 1,100 flex passes were sold, doubling projections.

In the fall of 1992, after a decade as managing director, Mordecai changed positions to become associate dean of the YSD. Among his new tasks was becoming a de facto Hollywood ambassador; in this role he would shake the trees for alumni

When Bundy became dean / artistic director in 2001, Nolan asked for a title that the university would understand. Once she was designated a deputy dean, Yale magically knew who she was and what she did, and she found the hierarchy easier to navigate. Before Yale, Bundy had spent eight years working for companies where cash flow was an almost daily concern, and so he was inclined to look very closely at the Yale Rep artistic budgets to nickel-and-dime his way to savings, but he quickly learned to trust Nolan's sound instincts and practices with the artistic budget, where her conservative approach made it possible to make several nimble adjustments every year in the face of inevitable surprises. "Her ability to deal with the complexity of negotiations with artists, agents, and Yale's counsel—sometimes lasting over a year—was most admirable; in this, as in so many other tasks, her signature and reassuring communiqué 'I'm on it!' always gave me comfort."

Before her retirement, Nolan had a quick response when asked what had kept her in the game so long: the students. "I love them. I love the training. The day-to-day engagement. Not only do I love helping them out after they graduate, but I love the fact that they become my colleagues." ◆

Managing Director Victoria Nolan
PHOTO © T. CHARLES ERICKSON

money to upgrade the deteriorating facilities and increase the comparatively spartan artist salaries. His alumni solicitations on both coasts were also successful in the area of scholarship gifts.

In April 1993, Wojewodski announced his appointment of Victoria Nolan as managing director (see box). She would teach in the theater management department and work at cracking the nut of finding the resources and an audience for the boundary-stretching kinds of theater makers Wojewodski was keen on bringing to New Haven. Given its fiscal position under the university umbrella, Yale Rep

Stan Wojewodski Jr. (1991–2002)

didn't need an audience to keep its doors open, but an audience is the final collaborator in the experience of live theater, and drama students in every discipline needed the experience of working with them or for them or of playing to them.

One genus of boundary-stretching artist that interested Wojewodski was the solo performer. His time at Yale coincided with the dawning of the Age of American Confession and a concomitant flowering of the one-person show. Yale Rep / YSD took full advantage of what was out there. Bly remembers the process of what were called "special events": "Vicki and I supervised a third-year administration student with an eye toward producing or curating in their post-Yale lives. The student would research ideas based on scouting he or she had done in New York, or looking at nationwide festivals. Stan, Vicki, the student, and I would meet and add or subtract names to the list. The student would then do artist interest and availability checks. The list would shrink, and we'd pick our season." For its first season, during the break between *Hamlet* and *The Colored Museum*, the comic Paula Poundstone and the ranting scold Reno each performed on the same November day in 1992, one at the UT and the other at the Rep. The idea took permanent hold.

The activist impulses in the Brustein years had, with the exception of a one-night benefit performance of Bernard Pomerance's *Melons* in 1987 with the mayor's task force on AIDS, gone silent under Richards. Amid the waves of reaction and counterreaction to the NEA obscenity funding flap, the Rep invited two of the NEA Four, Holly Hughes and Tim Miller, to perform as special events. One week of the run of *The Baltimore Waltz*, Paula Vogel's marvelous, seriocomic response to the AIDS epidemic, was designated to be part of *7 Days of Action: A Community Response to AIDS*, culminating in a benefit performance and party organized by YSD students and staff in cooperation with local organizations and businesses. Proceeds were distributed among AIDS Project New Haven, the AIDS Interfaith Network, Hispanos Unidos Contra El Sida, and Broadway Cares / Equity Fights AIDS. The Rep also participated in *Hearts for Life*, a benefit concert at the Shubert that drew acts from arts organizations all over the city.

For the first time since the Living Theatre's visit in 1968, Yale Rep welcomed an entire company of artists in residence. Bly was a fan of the six-member ensemble Le Théâtre de la Jeune Lune, darlings of the Minneapolis theater scene who had produced nearly forty shows in thirteen years. Five of the six had trained with Jacques Lecoq in Paris, so their work, which they often wrote, depended as much on the physical and gestural as on the verbal and visual. Their mission was to be a boisterous theater of emotion and event, combining vaudeville, commedia dell'arte, street theater, musical theater, and Brecht's alienation effect. In addition to the Bly connection, Wojewodski had sat on an NEA granting panel with Jeune Lune

GUEST COMPANIES/SPECIAL EVENTS/ NO BOUNDARIES

All four artistic directors made room at the Rep for visiting artists. When contemplating how to jump-start Yale Rep in 1966, Brustein invited two companies to perform works he had admired as a critic: Philadelphia's Southwark Theatre Company (producing Beckett's *Endgame*) and New York's Open Theatre (producing Megan Terry's polemical musical *Viet Rock*). He also invited Irene Worth and John Gielgud to perform *Men and Women of Shakespeare*, a master class in acting if ever there was one.

The Living Theatre visit in 1968 was infamous, but few recall that Brustein also imported France's foremost theatrical couple, Jean-Louis Barrault and Madeleine Renaud, that same season to perform Beckett's *Happy Days* and a piece about Louis XIV's court at Versailles. As time went on, while continuing to bring in troupes like the Negro Ensemble Company and Liviu Ciulei's Bulandra Theatre Company from Bucharest, Brustein allowed his acting company and students to devise admittedly lighter, midseason "holiday" events. These included Walton Jones's ('75) *The 1940's Radio Hour*, a musical whose several summer Cabaret iterations led eventually to a Broadway run in 1978; a Jacques Brel evening; and *The Banquet Years*, an evening of words, music, song, and dance celebrating Belle Époque Paris.

Richards scheduled two special events, and special they were. In 1986, Dario Fo and Franca Rame brought their first US tour to Yale Rep. Two years later, Lee Breuer and Mabou Mines installed a portion of their massive, cross-cultural *The Warrior Ant* in the UT: two master Bunraku puppeteers, five American puppeteers, seven narrators, ten dancers, and four musical bands dramatized an epic-sized ant (eighteen feet tall) on his journey from miraculous conception to life and death in an all-female colony of ants. In both instances, while in residence, the artists conducted workshops, master classes, and Q and A sessions with the drama students.

A partial roster of artists who came to Yale Rep for one- or two-performance stints in the 1990s for Wojewodski reads like a Who's Who of brilliant solo work: Spalding Gray, David Cale, Holly Hughes, Eric Bogosian, Diamanda Galas, Lisa Kron, Rhodessa Jones, Meredith Monk, and many others.

Special events at Yale Rep went global with Bundy. In 2006, Yale College theater studies professor Joseph Roach was awarded a five-year Mellon grant for the

A scene from Breuer and Mabou Mines's *The Warrior Ant* (1988)
PHOTO © T. CHARLES ERICKSON

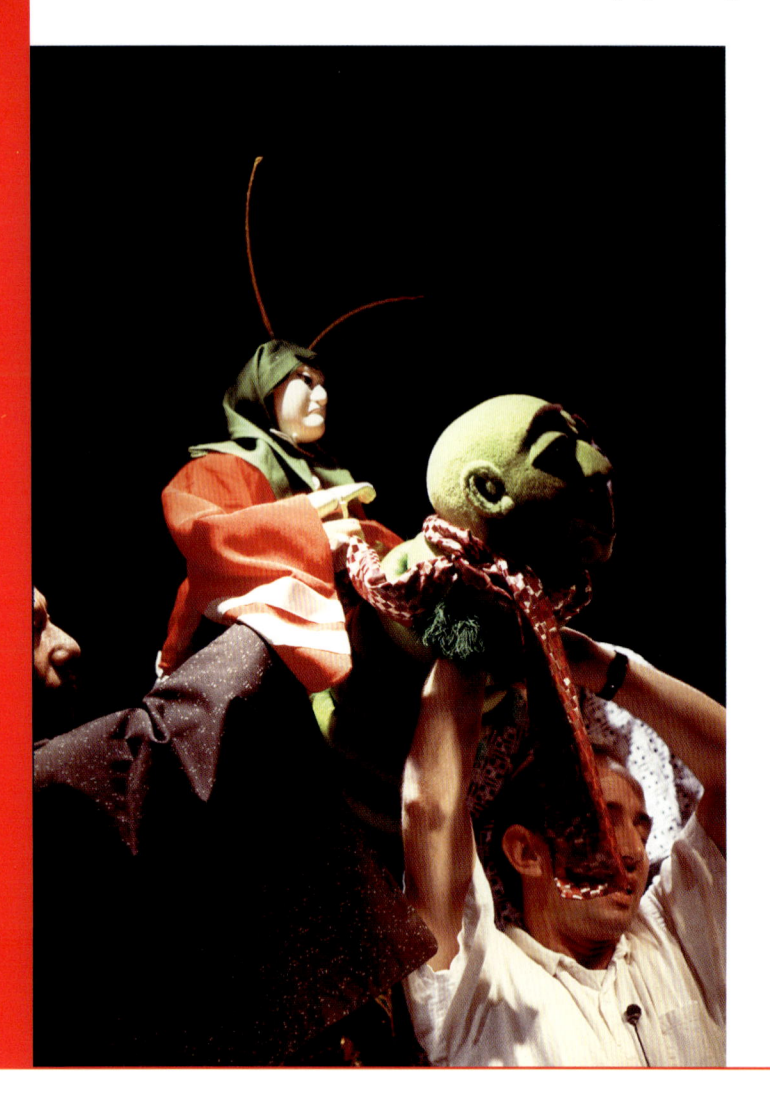

World Performance Project (WPP), one of whose tenets was the idea that performance is a vehicle of communication more holistically human and emotionally felt than many other forms of knowledge exchange. WPP collaborations with the Whitney Humanities Center, several undergraduate departments, and Yale Rep during the grant period led to, among other things, the Festival of International Dance at Yale, a first for the university.

The collaboration between the WPP and Yale Rep was formalized in the performance series currently known as No Boundaries. In addition to running the Binger Center for New Theatre, Yale Rep associate artistic director Jennifer Kiger curated and produced No Boundaries. Realizing that there is more to live performance than plays, she attended presenting conferences and festivals in foreign countries "where playwriting is not necessarily the center of the generative process. Sometimes the artists don't label themselves as writers; they call themselves theater makers." Noteworthy offerings in recent years include *Refuse the Hour*, a Dadaist chamber opera–cum–lecture with a libretto by William Kentridge and music by Philip Miller; Guillermo Calderón's *Escuela*, a performance in which a masked cadre of left-wing Chilean activists gather in 1987 to receive paramilitary instruction aimed at overthrowing Augusto Pinochet's military dictatorship; *Super Night Shot* by the German/British artists' collective the Gob Squad, in which the audience becomes costars in a four-camera film being simultaneously shot and screened; and an early taste of MacArthur genius Taylor Mac in *The Be(a)st of Taylor Mac*.

As with all extra events, time and space must be found in the jam-packed production calendar along with the material and human resources to market, advertise, load in, and tech the projects. To date only *one* company has visited or been produced at Yale during all four artistic regimes: Mabou Mines, with *The B. Beaver Animation* (1977), *The Warrior Ant* (1988), *Peter and Wendy* (1998), and *Mabou Mines Dollhouse* (2006). ◆

member Robert Rosen and learned that the company had been devising a play about Marcel Carné's cinema classic, *Les Enfants du Paradis* (1945). The troupe had discovered after years of research that many events surrounding the making of the film in Nazi-occupied France mirrored plot developments in the movie, such that Jeune Lune couldn't decide whether *Les Enfants du Paradis* is the escapist work of a proto-Collaborator or a subtle tribute to French resiliency. (This complicity crux divides film historians to this day.)

Through its long gestation, the four cowriters (company members Steven Epp, Felicity Jones Latta, and Dominique Serrand and dramaturg Paul Walsh) elected to tease out the reverberations between the fictional world of the screenplay, Paris's "Boulevard of Crime" in the 1830s, and the historical reality of shooting the movie in the 1940s. A blurring of the two in this "study in docu-fiction"—the term is Walsh's—would, using all the performative whizbang in the Jeune Lune wheelhouse, celebrate the power of the artist to overcome all manner of exterior pressures to pursue, and sometimes achieve, a dream.

Wojewodski scheduled the unscripted project sight unseen, saying to the press, "Jeune Lune is an artist-run company, and the work is chosen by the artists for the artists. I wanted to offer the company to the students of the Yale School of Drama as an example of something that can be done in that way." Jeune Lune's model of collective ownership meant that all member / coartistic directors had an equal say in what went onstage. All acted, directed, and designed. Each project generated its own needs, challenges, and production calendar. Dominique Serrand joked at the time, "The arguing ends when someone gives up."

The writing team held a first reading of act 1 in September 1992. In a scant two months, the huge, intricately layered *Children of Paradise: Shooting a Dream* was to christen Jeune Lune's new home. Keeping a production diary, later to be edited by Bly and published by TCG, Walsh quipped that the objective was to "bring the show in under twelve hours." They got it down to three and a half. *Time* magazine raved, and the play won the American Theatre Critics Association's New Play Award.

For Yale, Jeune Lune had to reduce the Minneapolis design to fit into the UT. In the prologue, half of the audience were led (*Fefu*-style) from the lobby through a side alley and then onto the crowded stage to participate in the raffish street life of the Boulevard of Crime. At a signal, the drop lifted, and the half-filled house was revealed to the onstage audience, a coup de théâtre replicating Carné's famous shot of the "Children of Paradise" (the seats furthest from the stage). The play begins with a projection on a flat screen against the back wall of the theater of a French street in 1943. A life-sized cutout locomotive belches steam, and the worlds converge. Latta, who portrayed the inscrutable love interest Garance in the movie, played Arletty; she remembers January in New Haven: "A gloomier time could not be imagined. We were told never to go anywhere by ourselves. We only had a week to put it in. The most amazing thing I remember is the first preview and it was all Yale undergraduates. They were the most vocal audience we ever had; they were with us every second; they went crazy. Of course, that never happened again."

Another emerging development in American theater in the late 1980s and early 1990s was New Vaudeville. Following the lead of heroes like Fo and the Bread and Puppet Theater, new vaudevillians such as Bill Irwin, the Pickle Family Circus, Geoff Hoyle, and the Dell'Arte Company invested their clowning with intellectual content and a political perspective, such that some wags referred to New Vaudeville as "old vaudeville with a college degree."

Michael Kennard and John Turner had met in 1987 in a Second City workshop in Toronto and then enrolled in a clown workshop taught by the legendary, Lecoq-trained Richard Pochinko. Within seven hours, they had created their clowns: bossy, irritable, two-horned Mump (Kennard) and jumpy, puckish, one-horned Smoot (Turner). In clown terminology, Mump is the "Joey" (manipulator) and Smoot is the "Auguste" (victim). Starting off in fringe shows, Mump + Smoot made their American debut in *Caged* at the American Place Theatre in 1991. Yale Rep brought in another piece, *Ferno*, as a special event in the 1992–1993 season. Wojewodski then made Kennard and Turner associate artists and put them in the mainstage Rep season, where they rotated performances of *Caged* and *Ferno*.

They sport red rubber noses, but Mump + Smoot instantly lay to rest the shades of their mirth-generating ancestors. Self-designated "clowns of horror," whose print ads caution "Not suitable for children," they explore and exploit the primal childhood fears that adults attempt to suppress, the fears that Freud postulated as the true engine of the comic: Hunger. Pain. Torture. Death. Abandonment. Humiliation. Ineptitude. Ignorance. Betrayal. Under garish lights, to an assaultive soundscape, Mump + Smoot enact their scenarios in desolate, postapocalyptic settings, a cross between *Waiting for Godot* and an asylum playroom. Ramping up the glee factor is the fact that they speak their own language, a gibberish called Ummonian. At one point in *Caged*, Smoot teaches the audience key terms like "twingle" (rope), "pooleps" (fishing pole), and "pugs" (tongs). They keep track of their sacred book, *Boolibah*, and their god, Ummo, a cone-shaped object that looks suspiciously like a lava lamp.

As strange as they sound and behave, the action never confuses, and the pair instantly bond with the customers. *Ferno* sends the pair on a vacation that goes literally to hell. They make a plane of boards, fans, and a big inner tube. They wait

Smoot (John Turner) indulges his dream of becoming a television chef with Mump (Michael Kennard) in *Something Else with Zug* (2000)
PHOTO © JOAN MARCUS

for it to take off. They decide to fly it themselves. They crash in a storm. They suffer horrible deaths. They pull out their guts (spaghetti) and eat their dismembered limbs. The power of Ummo intervenes and rescues them.

In *Caged*, the clowns, and Ummo, are imprisoned by evil sorcerer Tagon (played by Rick Kunst). At a critical point, Smoot betrays Mump, and the audience, deeply invested in their bond, turns on him. The more Smoot enjoyed his betrayal—getting out for an instant from under the thumb of his bossy partner—the louder the shock and disapproval from the house. Kennard spoke of their golden rule in an interview in *Theater*: "We both always love each other. No matter what, if we're in an argument, or he's betraying me, still[,] deep underneath, he loves me."

The shows varied every night, depending on the audience. Unwrapping candies and ringing cell phones provoked confiscation and humiliation. Mump + Smoot were invited back to Yale twice more following the same pattern—a successful weekend run of *Something Else with Zug* led to them opening the thirty-fifth-anniversary season in September 2000. Releasing the id, then containing it, and then purging collective human fears through the generation of laughter via a shower of blood or a flying limb is serious, hilarious, healing business. For those

Stan Wojewodski Jr. (1991–2002)   **187**

who grasped their purpose and laughed hardest or longest, Mump + Smoot had as much to say—in Ummonian, no less—as Shakespeare, Shaw, or Brecht.

The transition from Richards to Wojewodski provided no disruption to foundation support. After the Supreme Court ruled against the NEA's obscenity clause in 1993 and awarded compensatory damages to the NEA Four, the agency revised its application criteria: rather than underwrite basic operations, grants would be allocated to specific projects that would advance the art form *and* build audiences. Yale Rep continued to score well, getting grants for, among other offerings, Brecht's *Galileo* (1998), which led North Carolina senator Jesse Helms to showboat thusly on the Senate floor on September 15, 1997: "Yale University—I am not going to let them get off the hook—with a total endowment fund of $3.5 billion[,] which it had gotten from private sources, received $100,000 from the NEA for the Yale Repertory Theater for—I want you to guess what for—a celebration of the one-hundredth birthday of a Marxist playwright, Bertolt Brecht." Some Southern neighbors of Helms might respond to this performative wrath with a "Bless his heart!"

By mid-decade, arts organizations around the country, faced with declining audiences, began devising special subscription series, with pre- or postshow events. Preshow gatherings usually meant a chablis-and-cheese-cube reception hosted by an in-house talking head. Postshow events tended toward "Touch an Actor" Q and A sessions. Yale Rep was no exception. In 1994, patrons could subscribe to *Re: Play*, a series led by production dramaturgs on the first Saturday matinee after the opening. Or *Technically Speaking*, hosted by stage technicians on the first Monday night performance after opening. Or *Tuesday Night Discussions* with cast members and, as available, directors and playwrights. In 1995, two additional series options were launched, the *Rainbow Series* for gays and lesbians and their friends (the first such in Connecticut) and the *Singles Series*. In 1997, a new membership package for Yale faculty and staff was offered along the lines of what Lincoln Center and the Manhattan Theatre Club had begun doing in New York. Rather like a student passbook for adults, a membership differed from a subscription insofar as members paid an initial fee of $25 and then in turn could purchase a $10 ticket to as many as twelve Yale Rep or YSD productions during the season. Whatever the effort, whatever the pitch, Yale Rep averaged 4,600 subscribers between 1992 and 2002.

Healthy audience numbers in the seats are not equivalent to engagement in the community. Wojewodski and Nolan were more intent on attempting the latter than were their predecessors. Early in 1995, Wojewodski met Willie Reale, the founder of New York's 52nd Street Project, whose mission is to bring together children, ages ten and up, from Hell's Kitchen and theater professionals to create original theater and, not incidentally, foster literacy and long-term life skills. "I'd heard about their work in NYC from theater friends, including some YSD alums, who were working with the kids in Hell's Kitchen," Wojewodski said. So he met with Reale about the possibility of a New Haven replication in the Dwight and Edgewood neighborhoods and then made him an associate artist. After extended consultation, the Dwight/Edgewood Project was launched under the leadership of managing director Victoria Nolan and management student Ricardo Morris ('97), a former high school teacher from Tennessee who spent the summer of 1995 with Reale in New York developing strategies to pitch a playwriting project to the educators and also, critically, to the parents of sixth graders at the Augusta Lewis Troup School. In New York, Reale had access to professional artists; in New Haven, Morris had drama students, but with some cajoling and a tiny honorarium, he recruited several peers for the initial spring and summer of 1996. It was an instant success, so much so that Morris was the first drama student to be designated a Yale presidential fellow, and twenty-five years later, drama students currently fight for mentoring positions on the project (see box).

Wojewodski's most sustained act of patronage led to the first two parts of Ralph Lemon's *Geography* trilogy (1997, 2000). After a decade of success as a dancer and choreographer, Ralph Lemon dissolved his company in 1994. He wanted to shift to a new way of making multidisciplinary, project-specific work. At the same time, Wojewodski was following his path in bringing other kinds of work and other ways of working to the Rep and school. Artistic matchmakers Sam Miller, executive director of the New England Dance Foundation, and Cynthia Mayeda, Dayton Hudson Foundation chair, both suggested to Wojewodski that he and Lemon should meet.

Lemon, who would be awarded a MacArthur "genius grant" in 2020, remembers, "I felt like I walked into his office and his arms were open." As a Black man who had been working in a nearly all-white modern dance environment, Lemon wanted to meet performers of his generation who were doing what he was doing—American modern dance: "I grew up Black and knew what that meant. My parents were from the South. So, there was a particular kind of locus to a Black American reality in my center. But as an artist, it was mostly a white world. So, here's this Black/white artist, maybe, going to have a conversation with some Black West Africans, which is a culture I don't know."

Wojewodski, as he had with Willie Reale, Jeune Lune, and Suzan-Lori Parks, said yes, in this instance giving Lemon carte blanche to develop his project on its own timetable. Over the next seventeen months, with assistance from the AT&T

THE DWIGHT/EDGEWOOD PROJECT

Since its inception in 1996, the Dwight/Edgewood Project (D/EP), a joint endeavor of Yale Rep and YSD, has grown into an annual mid-May to mid-June afterschool program for eight New Haven middle school students who spend time with YSD student mentors learning about theater, engaging in playwriting exercises, and writing not one but two original plays. After an overnight retreat at Camp Wightman in Griswold, Connecticut, one play per student is then rehearsed for a week with Yale actors, designers, and directors and is presented in a standing-room-only performance for parents, friends, and the Yale community at the 120-seat off-Broadway theater in the alley behind Mory's eating club and Toad's concert venue on York Street. Two MFA students, in the roles of producing director and general manager, run the D/EP. In recent years, as more and more drama students have identified as theater activists committed to fostering social change, the competition to become a program mentor has grown significantly.

Nahuel Telleria ('16, DFA '21), who participated in D/EP from 2014 to 2017 as a mentor, director, and teaching artist, has this to say about working with middle-schoolers: "Young people inherently carry a joy about them. When they imagine, they commit themselves to their visions. When they share their happiness or their sadness or their ambivalence, they are truthful. Some of the most rewarding moments in Dwight/Edgewood are those moments of utter transformation in which a young person believes not only in her vision (the artistic object) but begins to believe in herself (the artist, the human being)."

Chad Kinsman ('18) seconds these thoughts: "One of my favorite moments of D/EP was watching the final dress rehearsal and appreciating each play for all its complexity. Yes, seeing a one-armed octopus perform lifesaving surgery on an orphaned cloud person while an EKG bleeps in the background is silly and funny, but there's a lot happening below the surface too. Mixed up in the strange and the inexplicable are shockingly guileless discussions of big, big questions. . . . These young playwrights put their fears, doubts, hopes, and dreams into the mouths, beaks, and snouts of their creations. During D/EP, all creatures, big and small, real or imagined, can be wise. And weird. And wonderful."

D/EP returns agency in imagination to the playwrights, to the professionals in training, and to the experienced YSD/Rep staff members who facilitate the an-

Steven Koernig and Chalia La Tour read a scene by fledgling playwright Jamiah Green (2015)
PHOTO © EMALIE MAYO

nual summer magic. As with all areas of theater outreach, funding for the project, which derives from a combination of university and foundation support and a half dozen or so individual donors, is an ongoing challenge.

In recognition of their distinguished service to the community through the D/EP, Wojewodski, Nolan, and cofounder Ricardo Morris ('97) received the Seton Elm and Ivy Award, given jointly by Yale University and the City of New Haven. ◆

Foundation and other granting organizations, Yale Rep sent Lemon to Ghana once and to the Côte d'Ivoire twice for research. Lemon convened a month-long workshop of *Geography I: Africa* in New Haven in late May 1997. None on his roster of collaborators had a purely theater-based background. Solo performer and slam poet Tracie Morris would provide a text inspired by *The Oresteia*. Led by Lemon, a nine-member company of seven male actor-dancers and two percussionists of African descent from Côte d'Ivoire, Guinea, and the United States would perform. Jamaican sculptor and installation artist Nari Ward created the physical environment. Francisco López and Paul D. Miller, a.k.a. DJ Spooky, provided soundscapes. Also essential to the process were student dramaturgs Peter Novak ('98) and Katherine Profeta ('99), the latter with a dance background and enough French to serve as a backup translator with the Francophone company members.

On the first day of rehearsals, as Profeta recorded in her production journal, Lemon said he wouldn't know where he was going until right before he got there. *Geography* would be very much about the process of its own making, about how the ensemble, from divergent backgrounds, would create a path between the continents and cultures. In her book *Dramaturgy in Motion*, Profeta recalls constant movement among different languages, musical styles, and dance vocabularies. "There was no single person in the room, however, who understood all the words spoken there, all the time. That was the work's chaos, and joy."

Morris wanted her words to provide context and reference, while Lemon eschewed the overly literal. Of the twenty-one pages of her original submission, Lemon selected three and a half "aural footfalls," as Morris called them in the program. *The Oresteia* was lost between the first and second workshops. What remains is an Aeschylean schema divided into Map, Crime, Trial, and Divination. Among many sequences in *Geography*, several stood out. In "Circle Dance with Satellites," Lemon physicalized the separation that exists between the two Black worlds, African and American: four different traditional dances are repeated by the African performers in a contained, inward-facing circle and interrupted by bouts of improvisational walking. Concurrently, Lemon and the other American in the company, Carlos Funn, dance "Western," in unison facing the audience but separated from each other by the circle. In the Trial section, there are multiple versions of a minuet. In a duet set to—or against—a Bach prelude on harpsichord, elegant steps turn violent as one partner hurls the other into the air. The aggressor then helps their target up from the floor, they return to the minuet, and the sequence is repeated, with the aggressor and the target switching roles. The duet becomes a quartet, then a sextet split into two trios. For Profeta, Lemon and his crew "developed an image that refers, quite succinctly, to the dynamics of violence in a post-colonial state" (*The Production Notebooks*, volume 2, edited by Mark Bly). In the Divination section, there was a heart-stopping "Endurance" duet between Côte D'Ivoirians Djédjé Djédjé Gervais and Akpa Yves Didier in which a loop of three or four West African steps was repeated over and over at full energy for nearly eight minutes, building, building, building. Toward the end, Didier would dance offstage, ceding his place to Gervais. The soundtrack, now at a cacophonous level, would suddenly cut out, bolero-like, leaving Gervais caught in midair.

Few who saw *Geography* would forget Ward's physical installation. A-frame ladders wrapped in fabric. An oversized ceiling fan made of ladders. Three screens of mattresses stripped of casings and stuffing, leaving their frames and springs exposed. And finally, in the Divination section, rising by electric winches from the stage floor, a half-ton curtain, twenty-eight feet high and thirty feet across, of dangling, tinkling bottles—clear, green, yellow, and brown—strung together with thin steel cable. Eight hundred to eleven hundred wine and liquor bottles had

Djédjé Djédjé Gervais, Djeli Moussa Diabaté, Kouakou Yale "Angelo," and Nai Zou in Ralph Lemon's *Geography* (1997)
PHOTO © T. CHARLES ERICKSON

Stan Wojewodski Jr. (1991–2002)

been collected from New Haven bars and eateries for over a year. (Five restaurants and two bedding companies got special thanks in the program.)

Wojewodski remembers that "Ben [Sammler] and his team during that period of time were just heroic. They were somewhat liberated by Ralph's complete lack of experience of production at that level." For Lemon, "they were just trying to figure out: what is this thing? For them it was always: how do we make it? How do we DO this? And you just see the lights going off in their heads and being really excited about the challenge of doing it."

Unless they followed postmodern dance, how prepared could a subscriber be for an episodic, multilayered, nonlinear event with only the barest hints of narrative? Profeta grew accustomed in talkbacks to assuring patrons that there were no right answers. Whether *Geography* enthralled you or you wound up counting bottles from boredom, everybody loved the drumming. Because it spoke primarily in movement, *Geography*, another collage of commonality and difference in a particular cultural diaspora, was not as frustrating as the formally similar *Democracy in America*. In other words, drumming trumped Descartes.

The logistics of putting on *Geography* were complicated. Nolan remembers paying the drummers' salaries to their village and hiring the brother of one of the actors to walk to the village where the drummers were in order to take them to a town with an airstrip. As Part I toured to four other venues, tightening its transitions and attracting more positive notices and more discerning critics as it went along, Lemon was thinking ahead. If Part I treated race and Africa, Part II would investigate faith and Asia. Lemon would move, in his words, from the "energy and sound of Africa to the supposed Asian 'quiet,' a perceived body politic of restraint," tracing the origins of Buddhism in northern India and tracking its spread through southern India, Bali, China, and finally, Japan. Did the belief system generate its own cultural art aesthetic? Did belief originate in artistic ritual and discipline?

Multiple funders signed on for his second journey, which began in India in February 1998 and would ultimately be titled *Tree, Part 2 of the Geography Trilogy: Asia/Belief*. As with *Geography*, there was an initial Yale workshop in August 1999 before the final push of rehearsals in March 2000. For *Tree*, Lemon brought Ward back to create the environment and hired Profeta as dramaturg and hunter-gatherer of scientific texts about natural disasters. She remembers that the bits of material that made it all the way into the performance were the Mercalli Scale, a discarded way of characterizing the strength of earthquakes; an account of a pilot who fell through a hurricane outside his plane; and a cast member's own narration of her memory of a Japanese earthquake in her childhood.

Of the twelve-member *Tree* cast, four were women, hailing from Asia and West Africa. Three men were retained from *Geography I*, and five more were added from India and the Yunnan province in southern China. Add seven or eight translators to the mix of performers on any given rehearsal day and you get what Wojewodski remembers as a latter-day Tower of Babel on York Street. Lemon, a cultural outsider this time around, was sensitive to the pitfalls inherent in generalizing Asia and focused on creating, in his words, "a dialogue of diverse traditions."

To its partisans, *Tree* felt less tethered to the weight of Lemon's history and identity and was therefore a freer, more relaxed, and less personally beholden event than *Geography I*. Its harshest critics found it an example of overfunded cultural piracy. Audience members vexed by *Tree*'s manifest illustrations of how things, ideas, utterances, and movements can never fully cohere somewhat missed the Buddhist impulse behind it all, closure being an occidental fixation.

Regarding the classics, Brustein had been drawn to plays titanic in thought and dialectic. Richards favored plays with great parts for great actors. This is an oversimplification. *Volpone* and *Hedda Gabler* are great plays *and* great parts; they achieve their status as classics because they teem with complex meanings and characters, posing large questions they decline to answer. Neither do they stint on Aristotle's sine qua non: plot. During his time in New Haven, Wojewodski would give equal weight to a fourth feature from *The Poetics*, selecting classics massive in thought, character, plot and . . . *diction*.

A habitual reader of verse, whose desert island poets would be (for starters) Bishop, Heaney, and Glück, Wojewodski was attracted to playwrights who deployed language idiosyncratically in form, pattern, and lexical reach. If he scheduled lexicon-drunk American writers like Overmyer, Parks, Mamet, Kushner, and Guare, he made room at the Rep for their forebears: Congreve, Farquhar, Williams, and Marlowe. If existing translations of a foreign classic were judged outdated, he would commission a new one. A stickler for language, his notes to actors in his productions were as often technical—missed operative words, muddy consonants, front-loaded speeches, misplaced breaths—as they were qualitative. Emotion, meaning, and action could spring only from proper delivery of the text.

It's not surprising, then, that Wojewodski would choose for his first Rep classic not a Shakespeare but, as he says today, a play by "his next-door neighbor, with enough lyricism to swing on." First performed in 1592, Christopher Marlowe's *Ed-

Thomas Gibson as Gaveston and Byron Jennings as Marlowe's eponymous *Edward II* (1992)
PHOTO © GERRY GOODSTEIN

ward II is a cornerstone of Elizabethan drama, considered the first mature English history play. (The Bard would shortly catch up to his friendly rival with *Richard II* and *Richard III*.)

Henry IV's line "Uneasy lies the head that wears a crown" is a watchcry for the entire history play genre, one that, reduced to its essentials, is as formulaic as any *Star Wars*–franchise entry: A king ascends his throne. Eventually a usurper, often a relative, leads an insurgency to unseat the monarch. He succeeds or fails, and the cycle begins again, either with the old king or a new king and a fresh upstart. Marlowe's full title for the play is *The Troublesome Reign and Lamentable Death of Edward the Second, King of England, with the Tragical Fall of Proud Mortimer*. The plot is simple, and the body count is high; the splendors of this rich and brutal play are found in the motivations and machinations of Mortimer and Queen Isabella and in the character arc of the king—and in the verse. *Edward II* remains relevant today for its insights on corporate decision-making, self-serving government advisors, feminism, and political torture, but its human draw, and what launches the plot and plotters, is Edward's infatuation with Piers Gaveston. Mortimer makes it clear early in act 1 that Gaveston's crime is not sodomy but his access to royal patronage.

Initially petulant, misogynistic, and negligent, Edward, once taken captive, wrestles with his identity in an extraordinarily poetic way. "But what are kings when regiment is gone / But perfect shadows in a sunshine day," he says, and the audience begins to understand him as a figure worthy of tragedy. Wojewodski chose *Edward II* specifically for associate artist Byron Jennings. A classical actor with stature and tremendous vocal chops, Jennings had already played Benedick and a youngish Prospero for Wojewodski as well as Hamlet, Coriolanus, and Richard III. To physicalize a medieval world spinning out of control, Wojewodski chose Yeargan for the set, the scale of which was another indication of a new aesthetic for a new Rep regime. Its central feature was an enormous iron drawbridge. The cast of twenty-four learned to navigate their entrances upon it as it was simultaneously being lowered. "It felt so powerful to deliver the actors into the space that way," remembers Wojewodski. Yeargan placed climbing footholds in the back wall for the plotters and counterplotters. Historically, Edward II was murdered by having his bowels burned out by a hot poker to avoid external marks. In the theater, the murder was conducted below the stage; the audience watched it happen via a mirror tilted over the "moat" such that the violence was presented as an image and not a bodily enactment. Countering the rigid metal set were Tom Broeker's ('92) costumes, which drew on the nineteenth-century pre-Raphaelite idealization of the Middle Ages—rich, flowing velvet and brocade robes for the nobles, ermine-trimmed cloaks and miters for the clergy, and coarse doublets and hose for the commoners. As a nod, perhaps, to their private relationship, Edward and Gaveston were clean-shaven, while the rest of the court sported beards.

Wojewodski's open-door policy was especially welcome to the dramaturgy students, malcontents by training whose liminal collaborative position might be summed up as "No glory, no blame." In the months between his appointment and his arrival, Wojewodski had Gordon Rogoff ask his students to propose plays for the Rep. Second-year student Catherine Sheehy suggested Perelman's *The Beauty Part*. Once in place, Wojewodski created the student position of associate resident dramaturg, hired Sheehy, and announced *The Beauty Part* as the closing production of his first season. Sheehy's classmate, Canadian Stephen Haff ('92), shared his enthusiasm not only for Mump + Smoot but also for the hopped-up, mordant comedies of Toronto playwright George F. Walker. Yale Rep coproduced Walker's *Escape from Happiness* with Center Stage in 1993 and *Heaven* seven years later.

After two years in the wilderness as a freelance dramaturg and associate editor of *American Theatre* magazine, Sheehy returned to Yale as resident dramaturg, replacing Gitta Honegger, who had begun chairing the theater program at Catholic University. (Longtime literary manager Joel Schechter had left the previous season for San Francisco State University.) Sheehy, who has remained in her position since 1994 and who has chaired the dramaturgy and dramatic criticism program for more than a decade, made another early, fruitful suggestion. Repelled in a seminar by Brecht's misogynistic *Baal*, she made an about-face the following week with *St. Joan of the Stockyards*. Rogoff told her to suggest it, even in poor translation, to Wojewodski. On Bly's advice, Wojewodski commissioned a new version from actor-scholar-poet-translator Paul Schmidt, but who should direct it? Sheehy and Wojewodski independently hit upon Liz Diamond, who had done such a masterly job with *Death of the Last Black Man* the year before.

"After Suzan-Lori's play opened," recalls Diamond, "Stan invited me to come teach a master class in directing. A couple of weeks later, the phone rings; it's Stan again, and he says, 'I think you need to be directing larger-scale classical work, and I would like to create that opportunity for you. I would like you to become resident director of Yale Repertory Theatre and teach in the directing program.' It took me .001 second to say yes." Diamond had directed a lot of Brecht with minimal production budgets. That would change with *St. Joan of the Stockyards*, Brecht's return to Yale Rep after thirteen seasons.

Conceived during Germany's catastrophic hyperinflation, *St. Joan of the Stockyards* marks a turn in Brecht's thinking. In this, his first of several parables of goodness in a corrupt society, he synthesizes his fascination with Upton Sinclair's *The Jungle*, his readings of Marx in order to understand Chicago's grain market, his observations of the viciousness of urban living, his interest in the mission of the Salvation Army, and the martyred figure of St. Joan, idealized in the European consciousness. Goethe's *Faust*, Shaw's *Major Barbara* (1905), and Frank Norris's *The Pit* (1903) are additional influences. Published in 1932, *St. Joan* was outlawed shortly after Hitler was appointed chancellor in January 1933. Brecht left Germany within weeks and never saw it performed.

If the poor will *really* always be among us (John 12:8), how are we to deal with them? Brecht's Joan Dark struggles to restore faith in irreligious, early twentieth-century Chicago. In her naïve quest "to know," she gets swept into the cyclical boom-and-bust combat waged between livestock workers and commodities magnates. The dialectic between religion, embodied by Joan and her circle of benevolent Black Straw Hats, and capitalism, in the persons of meatpacking king Pierpont Mauler and his ruthless peers, is reinforced by Brecht's use of classical German verse forms to describe iniquitous contemporary content. Joan eventually learns that the haves and the have-nots are locked in a game of materialist seesaw and that force is the only useful tool in a world where force rules. The police club her to death. Mauler emerges richer than ever, and Joan is canonized by both Big Business and the Church.

The God-versus-Mammon messages in *St. Joan* remained current for turn-of-the-millennium Connecticut. Life in New Haven, a poor city mired for decades in a fractious town-gown relationship with its chief employer, was then at its grittiest, the burgeoning crack cocaine epidemic having led to a wave of teen shootings and related acts of violence. Bolstering the play's currency was Schmidt's translation. Another chameleon of the American theater, Schmidt presented to Wojewodski, in their first meeting, his two significant credentials: "My PhD in comparative literature from Harvard, and my Equity card." His scholarship, his own poetic gifts, and what he considered his translator's ear, which was linked to his love of the spoken word and to an actor's ability to listen, would serve him well with Brecht. He could distinguish, for example, between Brecht's fictional "American" dialect and his verse parodies of Goethe, Schiller, and Shakespeare. The results were supple, lucid, and, unusual for Brecht in English, *funny*.

Diamond now had the resources to mount a Brecht epic epically. Amy Brenneman and a white-faced, pomaded David Chandler as Joan and Mauler led a cast

Sarah Knowlton, Nicky Paraiso, Amy Brenneman, David Chandler, and Alessandro Nivola in Brecht's *St. Joan of the Stockyards* (1993)
PHOTO © T. CHARLES ERICKSON

Stan Wojewodski Jr. (1991–2002)

199

of twenty-two, supported by Brendan Corbalis ('93), Camryn Manheim, and Ben Halley Jr. ('77) in key roles. A high, black, menacing, multileveled set of platforms and ramps, designed by Adam Scher ('93), included an industrial staircase and a private elevator for Mauler to take him to the top platform, above which scene titles, plot synopses, news flashes, and ticker tape quotations were projected in red neon. The environment shifted from black to gold when the Livestock Exchange was revealed. A gridded floor that could be pierced by Jennifer Tipton's lighting, cold and white, or shadowy and expressionistic, as the occasion required.

With *St. Joan*, Diamond brilliantly made the case that "you cannot make the world a better place if you don't understand it; if you don't make the effort to really see what it is and who it is that makes people lose their jobs; why it is that CEOs make 100 times what their employees make; why it is that downtown New Haven [in 1992] is a war zone." Consciously or not, Wojewodski gravitated toward plays that treated—to put it more mildly than Brecht or Kushner or Churchill or Shaw or Horváth or David Edgar do in their respective *St. Joan of the Stockyards*, *Slavs!*, *Serious Money*, *Mrs. Warren's Profession*, *Figaro Gets a Divorce*, and *Pentecost*—the adverse outcomes of unbridled capitalism.

Today, in a world of *Pride and Prejudice and Zombies* and *A Doll's House, Part Two*, Wojewodski's notion in 1994 to combine Beaumarchais's *The Marriage of Figaro* (1784) and Ödön von Horváth's *Figaro Gets a Divorce* (1936) into one theatrical evening wouldn't appear so odd. Well-funded theaters had occasionally created colossal "War of the Roses" projects out of Shakespeare's seven-play run from *Richard II* to *Henry VI, Part 3*, but no one had thought of linking two plays separated by 150 years and written in two different languages.

Beaumarchais's Spanish barber/factotum comes from a long line of male servants with quicker wits than their masters. A mere five years before the fall of the Bastille, Figaro had the audacity to offer this opinion of his master, Count Almaviva: "Nobility, wealth, rank, position—all that makes a man proud. But what have you ever done to earn them; you took the trouble to be born, and that's it. Otherwise you're an utterly ordinary man." The play was banned. Georges Danton, an architect of the French Revolution, claimed that "Figaro killed the aristocracy," and then Mozart and da Ponte swiftly poached Beaumarchais for their own imperishable collaboration.

As befits a French neoclassical comedy, the multiple plots of *Marriage* resolve in one day. For Horváth, writing *Figaro Gets a Divorce* in Vienna two years before the German *Anschluß*, money, not love, turns the wheel of fortune; he therefore gives his characters several years to make their way in a restive, postrevolutionary world. Figaro and Susanna, married for six years, have remained with the count

Amy Malloy and Reg Rogers in act 2 of *Figaro/Figaro* (1994)
PHOTO © T. CHARLES ERICKSON

and countess, but watching their exiled masters decline into a self-deluded oblivion, Figaro decides to take up his razor again and convinces Susanna to open a hair salon. Figaro's swift embourgeoisement disappoints his wife. They drift apart; she has an affair. Figaro crosses the border to become the new steward on Count Almaviva's old estate, which has been turned into a state-run orphanage and tourist attraction. The thoroughly modern Figaro won't bring his own children into the world, but his return to the palace and his reconciliation with Susanna do present a wary equilibrium of freedom and social responsibility.

Wojewodski had Overmyer in mind for the project. Working from a draft translation of the Horváth by the late Douglas Langworthy ('91) and several versions of Beaumarchais in the public domain, Overmyer considered himself a "text designer" who took cues from the director. He recalls today, "I think what Stan wanted and what I wanted was a contrast to match them up in an evening and see what happened. I wasn't trying to draw parallels that weren't there or be consistent. I was trying to be true to each Figaro." To avoid a six-hour event, they compressed Beaumarchais's five acts to slightly less than one. *Figaro/Figaro* (an inevitable, delightful title) does not resolve the Beaumarchais plot at intermission. The two leading couples are plunged into the darkness of a forest as the first scene of Horváth ends the first act of Overmyer's adaptation, creating, in Wojewodski's words, "a docking maneuver between the first and second play."

Derek McLane's ('84) set design was a forest of hundreds of identical chairs stacked in columns that rose out of sight around the front side of a thirty-foot-tall gilt chair standing center stage. For the French Revolution—the docking maneuver—an enormous creaking sound was heard in the darkness followed by a tinny version of "The Marseillaise." Then the giant chair tipped over backward, hit the floor, and flew up to the sound of "The Internationale," sonically moving the audience and characters from Robespierre's Reign of Terror to the fascist Europe of Franco and Hitler.

Figaro and Susanna were played by Reg Rogers ('93) and Sue Cremin ('95), and the count and countess by associate artist Byron Jennings and real-life spouse, Carolyn McCormick. The two couples are adrift in act 2, uncertain how to behave in a world in which equal rights are shared by all. For Overmyer, "the sense I retain after all these years is how wonderful the transformation was, how powerful it was, to go from the first act to the second, and see the count and countess looking lost with their fancy suitcases." Like *Mahagonny* and *Midsummer Night's Dream* and *A Lesson from Aloes* before it, *Figaro/Figaro* was a high spot for the Rep. Out of the many hundreds of Yale performances he witnessed from 1977 to 2004, Mark Bly has never forgotten Jennings as Count Almaviva, the proud, calculating aristocrat in the first part who withers into a threadbare, disoriented old man in the second. He ranks Jennings's Count alongside Priscilla Smith's Mummy in *The Ghost Sonata* and Reggie Montgomery's Foundling Father in *The America Play*.

Edward II, *St. Joan of the Stockyards*, and the *Figaro*s are not laden with preconceived baggage, but this is not the case for Chekhov's *Uncle Vanya* (1897). As we've seen, one way to defamiliarize a classic play is a metaphorical supertext (Brustein's "photographic" *Wild Duck*); another is cultural transfer (Rucker's "Mod" *Twelfth Night*); a third is point-by-point adaptation (for example, Synge's *Playboy of the Western World* becomes Mustapha Matura's *Playboy of the West Indies* [Yale Rep 1989]). Because of his extreme specificity and because he stresses character over plot and thought, Chekhov tends to outmaneuver directors bent on novelty. Chekhov is so hard to get right in his original environment that hiring David Mamet to "adapt" his texts or helicoptering Vanya and Yelena into East Hampton in 1995 feels like cheating or betrayal, or worse. But then, a curtain going up on a samovar, lamps to be lit, and a man dozing in an armchair are all too often the dreariest of enticements in the American theater. Simply put, there is nothing so bad as bad Chekhov. (With bad Shakespeare, there's at least the verse to savor.) In the wrong hands, the boredom of Chekhov's characters is more contagious than the measles, yet actors and directors will always set forth with pickaxes to excavate the subtextual mysteries inside Chekhov's characters; and theaters will always program him because of his, to quote Paul Schmidt, "extraordinary creation of human depths out of the surface banalities of everyday life."

Having Len Jenkin direct *Uncle Vanya* in 1995 was Wojewodski's way of improving the odds for Chekhov, in keeping with his intention of promoting the growth of his associate artists. As a playwright, Jenkin was another ludic, hallucinatory language-meister but with a darker outlook than Overmyer. A three-time Obie winner, he had never directed a classic text before or seen a production of *Uncle Vanya*, which he found to be a play of "passionate people trapped in a house. The pot is on the boil; the lid is rattling." The opposite of a literary stylist, Chekhov provides commonplace dialogue for ordinary Russians. American English mutates so rapidly that his plays require constant retranslation. For *Vanya*, Schmidt stepped in again: "I have to try to re-create in American English a voice that resounds within the American language the way Chekhov's voice resounds within Russian." (One example is when Marina says, "Everything's gone haywire these days." Another is when Vanya utters the line, "I just go around grumbling like an old fart.")

Vanya's physical production was casually postmodern. The stage floor was covered in straw. The period samovar and tea glasses and a fainting couch covered with a moth-eaten bearskin rug were countered by metal-framed, webbed lawn chairs from the 1960s and a portable oxygen tank for the ailing Serebryakov. Worker bee Sonya wore drab, roomy cardigans, while Helen, the indolent target of multiple erotic vectors, lay on the bearskin in silken nightwear. To keep the lid rattling, Jenkin reconceived Vanya's mother, Mrs. Voynitsky, as a ribald woman still very much in the sexual game, and pious old Marina became a devout, youthful nurse. There were also metatheatrical touches. Especially memorable was the white peacock that began the show. After a luxurious stage cross, he'd hop onto a dressing table, linger, and then disappear, magically replaced by Elaine Tse ('92) making herself up to go on as Helen. (The wire attached to the peacock's leg did not escape the notice of animal rights activists and would not pass muster today.)

Marin Hinkle, Elaine Tse, and translator Paul Schmidt in Chekhov's *Uncle Vanya* (1995)
PHOTO © T. CHARLES ERICKSON

Stan Wojewodski Jr. (1991–2002)

The actor's saw maintains that "dying is easy; comedy is hard." This applies more to the verbal than the physical mechanics of comedy. Laughs at a pratfall, a thwack of Arleccino's club, and a simple spit take are easier to generate than from any single "joke" in Touchstone's fencing speech in *As You Like It*. Unless their abstrusely clever remarks are cut or rewritten, Shakespeare's clowns die nightly in front of a contemporary audience. In other words, comedy is hard, but *wit* is even harder. It dates as quickly as social mores, so as daunting as *King Lear* or *The Bacchae* or *Death of the Last Black Man in the Whole Entire World* might be to stage, one could argue that a comedy of manners like William Congreve's *The Way of the World* (1700) makes for an even greater challenge.

World has a wildly complicated plot. Character relationships are difficult to parse, and its cast is strewn with half siblings, thwarted former lovers, present adulterers, and gleeful double crossers. Material gain, not love, is the motor of courtship, and no one role in the play elicits sympathy or identification. The characters don't evolve, a disappointment to modern audiences conditioned to crave "growth moments" in their protagonists. Three and a half hours of dialogue like "Out upon't, out upon't! At years of discretion, and comport yourself at this rantipole rate!" make *The Way of the World* a high-bar workout for the brains and ears of its spectators.

Given his embrace of knotty classics and his delight in language-centered comedy, it's not a surprise that Wojewodski would eventually visit Congreve's London, where base appetites are cloaked in exquisite diction. The tercentennial of Yale College and (very nearly almost) Congreve's play were both marked in 2001. Wojewodski agrees with a laugh today that *Way of the World* was tough to put up. "There's no beaten path to the dramaturgical door to the play. How do you make that society recognizable? How do you create a rehearsal atmosphere and encourage a way of working that makes the embodiment of that spectacular language an inevitability that's intellectually stimulating, emotionally involving and theatrically compelling—in a very short time?"

Wojewodski, when pressed, admits to being more interested in iconic than representational sets, particularly for classic works. The giant gilt chair in *Figaro/Figaro* and the Serra curlicues in *Richard III* were pieces whose placement and movement and conversions became part of the scenographic text. *Way of the World* audiences were greeted with a giant cylinder and ball, both in green neon on a yellow floor. The cylinder opened at the start to reveal a scarlet upholstered interior, an enclosed environment for Congreve's first act in a coffeehouse. Then, for the next act, the set shifted to a towering topiary in St. James Park. Production

Alicia Roper and Lee Mark Nelson in Congreve's *The Way of the World* (2001)
PHOTO © T. CHARLES ERICKSON

dramaturg Sheehy felt that the outsized scale of Scott Pask's ('97) abstract set, in juxtaposition with the highly concrete characters, helped the audience focus on the plot and—yes—the language.

Highlights of the feast would include the elegant *a vista* scene changes and the famous contract scene—a prenuptial agreement, as it were, by which romantic leads Millamant and Mirabell will, respectively, "dwindle into a wife" and prove "a tractable and complying husband." As Lady Wishfort, a killer part for an actress *d'un certain âge*, Sandra Shipley's romantic fluctuations were hilariously etched; she brought down the house when saying to her mirror, "I look like an old peeled wall."

One critic caviled that the actors relied overmuch on standing still and delivering their lines straight out to the audience, but this practice (known as park and bark) had been Western stage custom for centuries. An excess of Method acting movement and a more casual delivery would scupper the language and sink the play. The onstage string quartet and the rich period costumes might have led another critic to slight the production for a museum-like quality, but one might also point a finger at the university's gargantuan, international *Tercentennial Conference: Theatricality and Anti-Theatricality in the 18th Century*. Combined resources from the Beinecke and Walpole Libraries, the Center for British Art, the Department of English, the Program in Theater Studies, and the School of Drama underwrote a birthday celebration the weekend of February 16–18. In addition to comp tickets to a *World* performance, conference attendees could, among other offerings, view an exhibit of "Theater and the Painted Image" and hear a concert of eighteenth-century theater music at the Yale Center for British Art. Perhaps this surfeit of historical context and scholarship threw more shade than light on *The Way of the World*, making it seem a less than urgent theatrical exploration in the way that *St. Joan of the Stockyards* had been several seasons before.

Wojewodski did not champion new plays for their own sake. He didn't attend O'Neill conference readings. Apart from his associate artists, he didn't spend money to create a pipeline for new plays in the way that he commissioned new translations and adaptations for the Rep. When asked why he wasn't workshopping or developing new work à la Richards, he replied that he was focusing those resources on the nine playwriting students, who could be produced at the Rep only after graduation. Unlike peer institutions following funding signals in the 1990s, Yale Rep didn't contract a case of "premiere-itis"; every season scheduled contem-

COPRODUCING

Fourteen Yale Rep programs bear the credit "A coproduction with…" What does that mean? Most simply, nonprofit theaters, always seeking to improve their balance sheets, share the burden of production expenses—casting, rehearsal and tech time, set and costume construction, artist compensation, and so on.

The prototype for its current form was the production-sharing model engineered in the 1980s by Mordecai and his peers for the August Wilson cycle. For a new play—and twelve of the fourteen Yale Rep coproductions have been new plays—the producing partners share the risks that a work like Suzan-Lori Parks's *Venus* (1996) or David Adjmi's *Marie Antoinette* (2006) can present to an audience comfortable with more familiar titles like *Hamlet* or *The School for Scandal*. For the playwright, a coproduction doubles royalties—always a boon—but more importantly, it gives her and the director the opportunity to see and hear the play with an initial audience and then, during the hiatus between the two mountings, provides valuable time to rewrite the play into a more ideal form.

Those are the positives. As for the negatives, Victoria Nolan, who oversaw *every* Yale Rep coproduction, points out, "If the length of the two contracts (and the hiatus) is very long, you can lose cast members at the second theater. If the two stages are significantly different, design can be compromised, or more expensive because you are building two sets. Finally, the second theater gets the better production, though the staff there may not feel as much ownership or pride."

Most crucially, the collaborating theaters must share compatible artistic and fiscal points of view. Artist compensation and presence is a high priority for Yale Rep. In its history, the theater has joined forces with Baltimore's Center Stage, New York's Theater for a New Audience, and San Diego's La Jolla Playhouse four times each, the New York Shakespeare Festival three times, Berkeley Repertory Theatre five times, and A.R.T. in Boston once. ◆

porary work, but plays like *The Colored Museum*, *Oleanna*, *The Cryptogram*, *Antigone in New York*, *Thunder Knockin' on the Door*, and *Crumbs from the Table of Joy* had been recent successes elsewhere. *Escape from Happiness*, *Slavs!*, the musical *Triumph of Love*, and *Splash Hatch on the E Going Down* all began in Baltimore with coproducing partner Center Stage.

Stan Wojewodski Jr. (1991–2002)

Yale Rep continued to support the accelerating career of Suzan-Lori Parks by coproducing, with the New York Shakespeare Festival, the world premieres of *The America Play* in 1994 and *Venus* in 1996. Like *Death of the Last Black Man in the Whole Entire World*, these metaphorical meditations on huge subjects would never be for all markets. Wojewodski remembers getting a letter from a subscriber responding to a TBA listed in a season brochure: "I know it's going to be a play by that Suzan-Lori Parks, but you're just not telling us."

The press release for *The America Play* says, "Parks explores the American dream of greatness and the impulse—both creative and tragically destructive—to find one's place in the grand pattern of history." In its first act, a Black gravedigger named the Foundling Father, seeking fame and validation, has abandoned his family in favor of monetizing his close resemblance to Abraham Lincoln. For a penny, he offers customers the opportunity to shoot him in a flag-draped theater box. Customers enter as John Wilkes Booth, or whomsoever they please, fire their blanks, and deliver an imprecation or justification. Then the Foundling Father slumps in his chair. In the second act, titled "The Hall of Wonders," the Foundling Father's wife, Lucy, and their son, Brazil, dig up the hole—"The exact replica of the Great Hole of History"—where he used to perform. They take hold of objects from their own, and the country's, history (for example, George Washington's dentures) and share their memories of the Foundling Father, reconstituting the "w/hole" of him as they find his body, in order to bury him properly.

The Great Hole of History in *The America Play* marks the absence of recorded Black American history, the saga that needed to be written down and hidden under a rock in her *Death of the Last Black Man*. Short-sighted viewers wished out loud for Parks to write plays like August Wilson, whose decade-by-decade survey filled some of the same historical gaps with a radically different poetic toolbox, but, as Wojewodski remarks today, "No one ever said to Picasso to paint like Goya."

Actor Reggie Montgomery (1947–2002) was made the first Black Barnum and Bailey clown in 1969. Like all great comic actors, from Molière to Lahr to Fo, he had an ability to locate the tragic substrate in his characters. Playing a man who builds an infamous career as the Great Emancipator out of a ludicrous remark about his appearance, Montgomery, in a beard and stovepipe hat, moved—in Parks's characteristic "rep and rev" technique—from a joyous, electric pomposity through faint intimations of self-doubt to a harrowing final descent into madness before history swallows him up at the close of the first act.

The America Play marked Parks's sixth collaboration with Liz Diamond. For *Venus*, there was pressure from the Public Theater to pair Parks with the avant-garde playwright-director-designer Richard Foreman. A pre-Brustein YSD graduate ('62), Foreman, who had founded his Ontological-Hysteric Theater in 1968, had, for his thirty original works, won six Obies, been given the NEA Distinguished Artist Fellowship Award for Lifetime Achievement in Theatre in 1990, and been designated a MacArthur genius the week before the *Venus* matchup was announced to the press.

Another play about historiography, *Venus*, unlike the totems in *Death of the Last Black Man* or the factitious Foundling Father in *America Play*, uses the raw materials of the biography of Saartjie Baartman (177?–1815) as a platform to examine the ironies of fame through the transformation of a human being into an object of study, apropos for an American society that, even pre-Internet, had become obsessed with the cult of celebrity.

Parks said at the time, "*Venus* is a play about show business—the business of showing yourself. The play is also about *love*. At the center of the play is a woman with a big posterior—she's a woman with a part—a big part—in History." A mem-

Reggie Montgomery as the Foundling Father and Michael Potts as Brazil in Parks's *The America Play* (1994)
PHOTO © T. CHARLES ERICKSON

Stan Wojewodski Jr. (1991–2002)

ber of the Khoikhoi tribe, Saartjie Baartman is lured with the promise of wealth from South Africa to London, where she is sold to the Mother-Showman, who makes her a highly successful sideshow exhibit; Europeans travel from all over to see "The Hottentot Venus" and her steatopygia. In Parks's formulation, Baartman's thirst for adulation transforms her from a naïve captive to a siren complicit with the system that has colonized and exploited her. Smitten with Saartjie (and her future scientific value), the Baron Doctor takes her to Paris and has her jailed until her death, after which her skeleton and a plaster cast of her body are put on permanent display.

Rehearsals were held in New York before previews began at the UT. Foreman's design included some of his alienating Ontological-Hysteric visuals—flashing overhead lights, a stage space crisscrossed with wire cables and geometric designs, and black-and-white makeup. Surrounding the edges of the stage were large, luminous human faces shaped like flowers that blurred into one another. A flashing red light that pulsed throughout the play was added in the final three days of rehearsals. Parks said in a *New York Times* interview that she hadn't asked Foreman why he'd put it there. "You could say it's the heart of Venus that beats forever. It's Luuuv. It's ya luv lite, right there."

Adina Porter as Saartjie Baartman in Suzan-Lori Parks's *Venus* (1996)
PHOTO © T. CHARLES ERICKSON

Brustein and Richards had often produced American premieres of contemporary world playwrights (*White Marriage, Lear, A Play of Giants, Night Is Mother to the Day*, and so on). Wojewodski did it once, with David Edgar's *Pentecost*, a mammoth undertaking à la *Mahagonny* and *St. Joan of the Stockyards* that opened at the Rep four months before *Venus*. Edgar, who had won a Tony Award for his *Nicholas Nickleby* adaptation, began writing *Pentecost* during the liberation of the Eastern Bloc from Soviet rule, "when it seemed that the entire youth of Europe was marching, the "Ode to Joy" on their lips . . . through the great yawning gaps in the Berlin Wall. But the glorious dawn of 1989 waned with its promise of a unified Europe as ecstatic utopian visions gave way to militant nationalism, policies of exclusion, and the horrors of Sarajevo and Bosnia."

Pentecost takes place in an unspecified Eastern European country and is centered on the discovery of a fresco Pièta similar to but predating Giotto's *Lamentation* by a century, which if true would not only upend the history of Western art but also relocate the birth of universal European humanism dangerously close to the margins of the Arab world. The first act, which Edgar wanted to be like the Tower of Babel, behaves like a mystery, as three art historians with different agendas—a minister for the preservation of national monuments and priests of both the Orthodox and Roman Catholic Churches—debate its authenticity and ultimate value.

At the end of the act, a partially armed band of refugees enter and demand sanctuary. They hail from Kuwait, Mozambique, Ukraine, Russia, Afghanistan, and Sri Lanka; two are Roma from Bosnia. The different cultures attempt to communicate during the siege, playing instruments and swapping folk tales as they wait for news from the media circus just outside the church walls about who among them will be adopted, and who rejected, by other nations. The riddle of the fresco painter is solved just before a sudden explosion. Armed commandoes in black uniforms and balaclavas burst through a hole in the painting and kill four characters. Pentecost is not achieved.

Opening at the Other Space at the Royal Shakespeare Company, *Pentecost* moved to the Young Vic in May 1995. "The most ambitious and rewarding play all year," said the *London Observer*. Given the acclaim and its topical importance, *Pentecost* might have gone to the Public or Lincoln Center or New York Theatre Workshop for its American premiere, but as soon as Bly got wind of it in late 1994,

The company in act 1 of David Edgar's *Pentecost* (1995)
PHOTO © T. CHARLES ERICKSON

Stan Wojewodski Jr. (1991–2002)

he began pressuring Edgar's agent, Michael Imison, for the rights. Bly convinced Wojewodski to send him to England to woo Edgar and Imison. Then, according to Bly, convincing Wojewodski to direct it himself was a second siege.

Only three of the thirty characters in *Pentecost* are native English speakers; the rest communicate through dialects, gestures, and imperfect translation. They also speak Arabic, Turkish, Polish, and Russian to their colleagues. For Yale Rep speech and dialect coach Barbara Somerville ('83), the polyglot *Pentecost* was the toughest and most exhilarating assignment she had in her fourteen seasons in New Haven. She first had to find native speakers of the right age and vocal quality, which was not especially difficult in a university town. "Then I made a set of accent tapes. Then I made a set of language tapes for the foreign dialogue spoken in the play. Then," she laughs, "I had to make tapes of someone speaking Russian with an African accent. And so on and so forth. That was a *lot* of coaching."

The setting was a palimpsest of centuries of foreign invasion. Actualizing the layers was Yeargan, restoring the theater to its ecclesiastical origins. The uncovered section of the mysterious Pietà fresco, about ten feet square in dimension, was fronted by levels of work scaffolding and surrounded by a realist mural depicting cheerful Soviet drones that took up the entire back wall of the Rep.

Wojewodski recalls *Pentecost* being well received and well attended, but he doesn't remember any whispering about moving his production or any nudges from Edgar or calls from producers. "Given the scope, scale, and cast size of the play, I never thought it would 'move'—except perchance to other productions in regional theaters." As Alvin Klein wrote in his *New York Times* review, "Broadway? Only in a vital regional theatre can so rich an adventure come to life-like experience. Give thanks." Like Soyinka's *A Play of Giants*, which also, curiously, closes on an artwork and an explosion, Edgar's struggle between nationalism and globalism seems an even more urgent dramatic tocsin than ever.

Wojewodski was appointed to a second five-year term on January 15, 1996. He recalls today, "I remember in my fourth year, talking to [President] Rick Levin, who was always very supportive, about re-upping. I took an inventory of everything I was doing. Did I still have fire in my belly for all of it? I found I did. By year nine, when that conversation came up again, I knew it wasn't there anymore. It wasn't out of a sense of defeat. It was more, 'This is the arc of that.' The institution needed someone else, a new tiller to fight new battles, or revisit old ones."

Consequently, Levin announced in April 2000 that Wojewodski would step

PERSONS OF THE DRAMA: MICHAEL YEARGAN AND HIS TOP TEN

Michael Yeargan came to the Yale School of Drama from Texas in 1969, taking classes with both Donald Oenslager, who retired midyear, and fresh hire Ming Cho Lee. He returned shortly after graduation to teach (and eventually chair) in the design department and has never left the drama school, despite maintaining an international opera career, working at regional theaters across the country, designing twenty-five Broadway shows, and earning eight Tony Award nominations. Yeargan holds the record for most production credits at Yale Rep—fifty-two. Cajoling him into selecting ten favorite productions, in chronological order, was an enjoyable assignment. His first production, as costume assistant to Lawrence King ('69) on *The Rivals*, is a sentimental favorite. "I was a first year, and Larry was in his third year. I met him on *The Rivals*, and we were life partners until his death in 2009, just shy of forty years."

1. *Woyzeck* (1971). "I was a second-year student. We decided to do the play in a space with no visible entrances or doors. I created a section of a wooden tunnel piercing through a big wall, a reference to those horrible barracks and bunks I'd seen at Dachau. I thought I was going to be kicked out of the school, but Ming liked it. He thought it was a major breakthrough for me."
2. *The Frogs* (1974). "An insane experience. It was so hot, I worked in my bathing suit. You got dizzy from the chlorine fumes. There was a chemical reaction between the fumes and the fireproofing solvent, so the paint wouldn't take. The panels were peeling. We tried to repaint the doors, and the paint came up like chewing gum, it dried so fast from the chlorine. Instead of paint, we tried masking tape. Which peeled right off because the adhesive wouldn't stick. To tie it all together, I silkscreened thousands of Greek keys—like on diner cups—on contact paper. And there were miles of cheesecloth dyed saffron."

Michael Yeargan
PHOTO © ROBERT GREGSON

3. *The Tubs* (1974). "This 'gay Feydeau' set in a bathhouse needed farce doors and walls. We went to all the bathhouses in New York for research, saved the receipts, and got reimbursed. There was still the old church balcony in the Rep, so we created a second level for a beehive set. When it went to New York the following year as *The Ritz*, the set was more realistic. Working with Terrence [McNally] led me to making my Broadway debut with his *Bad Habits*."

4. *The Idiots Karamazov* (1974). "Brustein called us in during tech and said the set was *horrible*. Our purposely flattened version of a Stanislavsky set for *A Doll House* struck him as too real. So, we added photos of great Russian writers looking on in bug-eyed horror as Constance Garnett (Meryl Streep) mistranslated everything. We also split the walls apart and had branches of cherry trees invading the set like weeds. Perched on top of it all was a badly stuffed seagull. The stage braces were revealed on the sides to make it even more obvious that we were watching a play. In the end I agreed with Bob—it was fun to be more anarchic and just crazy."

5. *The Ghost Sonata* (1977). "This was my first time working with Serban, whom I'd read about before he came to Yale. Without being literal, we wanted to honor Strindberg's strange specificity in his stage directions. I came up with a set of gold-framed, tubular boxes, like aquaria or jewelry display cases. Each box was a separate stage space; they stood side by side in the first act for the street. In the second act, they were arranged in a semicircle around the banquet in Strindberg's Round Room. At the end, in the Hyacinth Room, Strindberg's enormous Buddha instantly vanished, replaced by Boecklin's painting *The Island of the Dead*. Soon thereafter, Serban started my opera career."

6. *Sganarelle* (1978). "Here we wanted a low-tech look. André and I had been doing a lot of research when we spotted a picture of a Mexican commedia troupe that used panels of white homespun linen sewn together. That's what we went with. That last piece, 'Dumb Show,' was totally improvised. Just hysterical. I handwrote the title cards. I'm pretty sure the word for sex was 'myushy pushy.'"

7. *Ah, Wilderness!* (1988). "It was so much fun working with the Lunts of the design world, Ben [Edwards] and Jane [Greenwood]. They held court

in the presidential suite at the Duncan Hotel, a space like Noël Coward crossed with *Barton Fink*. Ben was old school. I let him design *Long Day's* first, then changed the wallpaper and furnishings and drapes for *Wilderness!* The set was only sixteen feet deep, on a platform, so you could move it back for the barroom and lake scenes. I never worked on a show with a better cast."

8. *Pentecost* (1995). "I always loved working with Stan. He's just a brilliant thinker, ideal for such a huge play like *Pentecost*. I remember a very tight backstage: three gigantic flats stacked against one another at the back of the original church space. The first was the Soviet mural with a couple of feet of the fresco, which was based on one by Giotto, peeping through. That flew out for the second act, when more of the painting [is] revealed. The third flew in after the explosion."

9. *The Winter's Tale* (2012). "Everything about this show grew from Liz's [Diamond] personal experience of having adopted a baby girl. It featured one of my favorite effects ever. At the end of the first act, the infant Perdita is left alone in a basket on the beach of Bohemia. It's snowing. The prop baby was purposely made even smaller to render it more vulnerable. The character of Time passes through. We snuck in a very thin black 'bobinette' scrim on which silk flowers had been spot-glued. It flew in just as the falling snow turned into the same kind of silk flower petals. For the audience, the snowflakes instantly became flower petals. That scrim 'defined' Bohemia."

10. *These Paper Bullets!* (2014). "The idea was to conjure up the Beatles—Richard Lester–like looks from *A Hard Day's Night*, period lawn chairs and hotel furniture—without walls or panels. There wasn't time to redesign it for the Atlantic and the Geffen. Their spaces were so tiny, the set looked like a furniture store on a turntable. It definitely worked best at Yale."

Honorable mentions include *Happy End* (1971, 1975), *Don Juan* (1975), *A Lesson from Aloes* (1980), *The Resurrection of Lady Lester* (1981), *Edward II* (1991), and *Hay Fever* (1998). ◆

down at the end of the following June. Shortly thereafter, a search committee was set up, led by Yale College English and theater studies professor Joseph Roach. Joining him were Mark Bly, Liz Diamond, Ming Cho Lee, James Leverett, DFA candidate Peter Novak ('98), Evan Yionoulis, and engineering professor Gary Haller. The ArtSEARCH job listing put out by TCG concluded with the sentences "Candidates are expected to stand in comparison to the foremost leaders in the field. Candidates should be available to begin full responsibilities as of July 1, 2001."

After six months, an intensified search had gained two committee members, Ben Sammler and Deputy Provost for the Arts Diana Kleiner. Leading candidates bruited about in the press included Benjamin Mordecai, Victoria Nolan, Jon Jory, Mark Lamos, Anna Deavere Smith, Oskar Eustis, David Chambers, Kenny Leon, Anne Bogart, and Carey Perloff.

The hiring challenge began going public in January 2001. Longtime Connecticut journalist and theater critic Frank Rizzo had a loose-lipped, highly placed source and began reporting on the search for the *Hartford Courant*, as did the *Yale Daily News*. Behind the scenes, Mark Lamos had withdrawn his candidacy a couple of days after giving a strong series of interviews. Anne Bogart told the *Daily News*, "I went after it pretty hard; I was obviously not what they were looking for." JoAnne Akalaitis didn't want to live in New Haven. James Nicola, artistic director of New York Theater Workshop (NYTW), was told he would not be able to run Yale and NYTW at the same time. Trinity Rep artistic director Oskar Eustis was offered the job on January 21, but turned it down, publicly announcing two days later, "I do feel this incredible sense of obligation to Providence." Subsequent history points to a calculated risk by Eustis to wait a couple of years in order take over the New York Shakespeare Festival in 2002.

The press leaks were said to have embarrassed Levin. No one wanted this plum job. Lamos had ended a seventeen-season run at Hartford Stage in 1997 and was enjoying his freelance status. Avant-gardists like Bogart and Akalaitis might move Yale Rep even further along the sliding scale of nonnarrative experimentation than Wojewodski had, meaning more clowns of horror and no Broadway-baiting domestic realism. On February 23, President Levin circulated a letter acknowledging two realities. The following Rep season could not be chosen without a new artistic director, and certain candidates could not come to New Haven as quickly as desired. In view of that, Wojewodski agreed to stay for one more season and extend his term through June 30, 2002.

On October 1, 2001, Levin announced the appointment of James Bundy, a 1995 graduate of the YSD directing program and the current artistic director of the

Great Lakes Theater Festival in Cleveland. Like Wojewodski before him, Bundy would make fact-gathering trips to New Haven to prepare for the job, with the added advantage of knowing key institutional players from his student days.

Wojewodski went ahead with a final season as eclectic as his first. *You Never Can Tell*, Shaw's "play pleasant" about poor parenting, followed by Williams's luridly Gothic *Kingdom of Earth* (1967), directed by Rucker as the inaugural production in a new space for Yale Rep (see box). Churchill's *Serious Money* was, as previously noted, the third-year acting challenge. Works by two writers instrumental in shaping the original Rep returned after decades: Christopher Durang's *Betty's Summer Vacation* and Kenneth Cavander's new translation and adaptation of Euripides's *Iphigenia at Aulis*.

The remaining title in the 2001–2002 season was *It Pays to Advertise* by Roi Cooper Megrue and Walter Hackett, who take top honors as the most obscure authors in Yale Rep history. For subscribers, it was the final (welcome or unwelcome) entry in a five-play run of early American comedies produced during the Wojewodski years, a subspecialty as much a part of his artistic signature as Bond and Brecht had been for Brustein and Wilson and Fugard had been for Richards. If Brustein had loved burlesque, Wojewodski delighted in the ever-mutating sprawl of the American dialect as an engine for hilarity, especially when applied to dramatic studies of an evolving national character.

As noted, Sheehy had given *The Beauty Part* to Wojewodski; that play had closed his first season. Perelman's satire traces the journey of freshly minted Yale BA Lance Weatherwax, who like many a Skull and Bones man before and after, yearns to *create*. He is crammed through every portal of American culture making and mongering before he finally settles down to marriage and a life spent clipping his bond coupons. *The Beauty Part* was originally written as a vehicle for comic genius Bert Lahr, who played six different roles, from tough-as-nails magazine editor Hyacinth Beddoes Laffoon to a "fake Cambodian" known only as Wing Loo's Father. Lacking a Lahr—only a Nathan Lane or Tracy Ullman or Eddie Murphy could pull off the assignment today—director Walton Jones divided the six comic turns among several actors, which drained the play of some force and continuity.

Hilarious on the page, Perelman's dialogue, clogged with puns, patois high and low, Yiddishisms, and more syntactical switchbacks than a mountain trail, is as difficult for actors to deliver and audiences to apprehend as *The Way of the World*. Moreover, the play is tone-deaf to cultural difference; its jokes and, worse, visual gags at the expense of Southeast Asians discomfited some audiences in 1992. Today, *The Beauty Part* would be as impossible to revive as Guare's deliberately insensitive *Moon Over Miami*.

THAT THIRD THEATER

Yale Rep subscribers are familiar with both the University Theatre and the Rep, which began life as the Calvary Baptist Church, on the corner of Chapel and York Streets. Few of them probably recall that there is a third performance venue nearby. A brainchild of the Yale Arts Area Planning Committee, the New Theatre forms part of the art school complex that rose from the foundations of the long-unused Jewish Community Center at 1156 Chapel Street. Designed by emeritus chair of the YSD design department, Ming Cho Lee, and emeritus chair of technical design and production, Bronislaw Sammler, with Deborah Berke, now dean of the Yale School of Architecture, the New is a flexible black-box space that can seat up to two hundred people in multiple configurations.

Black boxes, a dream space for regional and campus theaters that can afford to build them, are ideal for plays of intimate scale, plays that do not draw or intend to command large audiences. Because contemporary theater economics encourage if not insist that playwrights create works for as few actors as possible and with modest scenic requirements, the flexible New Theatre, christened in 2000, was deemed the ideal stage for Yale Rep to present Tennessee Williams's feverish, forgotten three-person *Kingdom of Earth* (2001) and then three new works by MFA playwrights, postgraduation: Sunil Kuruvilla's *Fighting Words* (2002), Roberto Aguirre-Sacasa's *The Mystery Plays* (2004), and Marcus Gardley's *dance of the holy ghost: a play on memory* (2006). Ultimately, however, the space proved more flexible than its subscribers, who, already vexed with the deathless question "So, are we in the UT or the church tonight?," preferred knowing in advance exactly where their seats would be for every outing; thus it was decided that the New Theatre better fit the needs and aims of the YSD.

In recognition of a generous gift from Frederick Iseman (YC '74), chair and CEO of CI Capital Partners, LLC, the space was renamed the Iseman Theater in 2007. Today, it is the home of the Carlotta Festival of New Plays by graduating playwrights; the global performance series No Boundaries; the Shakespeare Repertory Project productions of the second-year directing students; and the third-year directing thesis productions. The annual array of theatrical choices at the Iseman, in a sense, duplicates (in miniature) the artistic breadth of Yale Rep. ◆

Jefferson Mays and Amy Povich in S. J. Perelman's *The Beauty Part* (1992)
PHOTO © GERRY GOODSTEIN

While tracking down a copy in the Sterling stacks of Kaufman's *George Washington Slept Here*, Sheehy spotted *First Lady*, by Katherine Dayton and George S. Kaufman, on the same shelf. It had an impressive initial run of 238 performances in 1935 but hadn't been seen since 1952. A play about two Washington doyennes vying to be first lady, it trades the smoke-filled rooms of backstage politicos for Georgetown hen parties and gave Wojewodski, so comfortable with abstract scenography, an opportunity to deploy actors on an utterly realistic set, down to the last finial and Duncan Phyfe settee (sets by John Coyne, '97). Topicality was a boost, as *First Lady*, headed by Maureen Anderman as Lucy Chase and Cecilia Hart as Irene Hibbard, the scheming wife of a dull Supreme Court justice, opened three weeks before the 1996 presidential election, a contest in which much ink was spilled over the distaff ticket choice of Hillary Rodham Clinton versus Elizabeth Dole. Reaction to the diverting *First Lady* was a template for critics everywhere assigned vintage American comedies to review; every "riotous, smartly staged look at our past" is matched by a "dreary, labored exercise in nostalgia."

As America shifted in the early twentieth century from the a-day's-pay-for-a-day's-work mindset to an urbanizing landscape of fast and easy credit, business plays began to dramatize the ethical tensions of capitalism. If Wojewodski and Sheehy had had their way, their final trio of period comedies, *A Cup of Coffee* by Preston Sturges, *Big Night* by Dawn Powell, and *It Pays to Advertise*, would have been presented in rotating repertory over two slots in the same Rep season. They

Stan Wojewodski Jr. (1991–2002)

had a subject in common: advertising, which was for Sheehy a great American art form and a great American shame. The idea was a nonstarter. Nolan knew that paying and housing and rehearsing three companies of actors as well as designing and building three sets and costume plots, not to mention weeks of daily set changeovers, would, at the very least, be cost prohibitive. It would also wreak havoc on Ben Sammler's production calendar.

One at a time would be the way to proceed, starting with *A Cup of Coffee* in 1999. Before Hollywood, Preston Sturges wrote plays. His second effort, *Strictly Dishonorable*, had been a whopping success in 1928. *A Cup of Coffee*, written in 1931, was never performed in his lifetime, although he did repurpose its story for his 1940 film *Christmas in July*. "A comedy about business," *Coffee* draws on Sturges's early managerial years of the Maison Desti, a fancy cosmetics emporium owned by his bohemian mother's fourth husband.

The enterprising Jimmy MacDonald is the youngest salesman for Baxter House, a coffee firm resisting the advertising revolution. When Jimmy wins a radio contest for best ad slogan for a rival company, the dyspeptic founder of Baxter House, Ephraim Baxter, and his two sons, J. Bloodgood and Oliver, promise him the moon if he'll stay put. All deals are off when it's discovered that the true winner is doppelgänger James MacDonald from Utica. A final unconvincing plot twist restores all romantic and commercial hopes. This deus ex machina aside, *A Cup of Coffee* is a well-structured, sharply observed brisk comedy in the school of Kaufman and Hart and Ben Hecht. What keeps it fresh after seventy years is the ceaseless snap, crackle, and pop of Sturges's dialogue. His verbal fizz tempers cockeyed hope with hard-earned cynicism. Lines like "You talk like you're the last plume on a hearse" are a joy to hear. As a critic of the system, Sturges will bite the feeding hand only so far. He's not out to kill initiative or ingenuity, since one hitch to criticizing the American dream is that people actually get rich quick here every single day.

To direct, Wojewodski hired Joe Grifasi ('75), whose most recent of *twenty-five* Yale Rep credits had been Fo's *About Face* in 1983. Grifasi cast as the Baxter brothers two MFAs of his vintage, Michael Gross ('73) and John Rothman ('75), neither of whom had been back to Yale in twenty years. In a joint interview with the *New Haven Advocate*, Grifasi and Gross recalled their early training. "I didn't even want an Equity card," said Gross. "I thought it would limit what was available to me. We were so brainwashed by Brustein that not only did we not think about going to television, we didn't even think about going to New York." To which Grifasi replied, "It was not so much brainwashing as it was dogma. We were on the neo-Grotowski, Artaud wave, groveling on the floor." The dogma had not included

John Rothman, George Hall, and Michael Gross in *A Cup of Coffee* by Preston Sturges (1999)
PHOTO © T. CHARLES ERICKSON

screwball comedy, but as Brustein grads, they had been trained to score in any part, and so they did in *A Cup of Coffee*.

The return to print of Dawn Powell (1896–1964) in the 1990s is a posthumous American lit success story to match those of Melville, Nathanael West, and Zora Neale Hurston. In addition to fifteen published novels, Powell had two plays produced in her lifetime. Her first, *The Party*, was written in 1928 in a three-week rush after her husband, a well-paid but bibulous ad man, got the sack. The prestigious Theatre Guild optioned and then sat on the play for two years. The Group Theatre then took it up, announcing the premiere of *Big Night* (its new title) in January 1933. Six months of Method-based rehearsals generated a slew of rewrites and hilarious journal entries from Powell but did the hard-boiled domestic comedy no favors. The reviews were disastrous; it closed after nine performances. Harold Clurman, who had taken over directing the play, said decades later, "We should have done it in four swift weeks, or not at all."

Big Night's plot has adman Ed Bonney pimping out his wife, Myra, a former showroom model (a part originated by Brustein's very first Yale hire, Stella Adler), to Bert Jones, head of a dress-store chain. Jones has carried a three-year torch for Myra with only a scratched face and bruised ego to show for it. To land the account, the Bonneys stage a party. It's, as they said in the 1920s, a doozy. Eight bottles of bathtub gin, Vera from upstairs who can't seem to keep her clothes on, a yapping dog, the surprise entrance of a rival ad man and his wife—and Jones is constantly drawing a bead on Myra, finally wrestling a kiss out of her at the end of act 2. Then, in the morning, a group hangover. Jones, unsure of how far things went (they didn't) with Myra, awards Ed the account. The end having justified the means, Ed rushes to work, leaving Myra, stunned and appalled by his cynicism. Jones offers marriage. Her reply? "I'm so damned unhappy. You'd understand about me, maybe." And, staking her future on one little "maybe," she's out the door with Jones, acutely aware that she's not leaving the racket; she's just traded up for a better cage.

It's a grim ending. American comedy of the period centered on the comfortable-or-better class, leaving out the money motive. The Bonneys have four dollars in the bank, and their desperate shindig, in Wojewodski's production, was the proverbial car wreck. Audience members were trapped guests, choosing pained laughter over muted screams. Without sacrificing Myra's sense of humor, Katie MacNichol captured every nuance of resignation and resistance in her dilemma. Where could a beautiful and intelligent but uneducated young woman station herself? Powell's answer is that of an even-handed, gimlet-eyed realist. The men, Matthew Mabe as Ed and Jay Patterson as Bert, created equally vivid portraits of male hunger and male flop sweat. The supporting characters, led by Jennifer Frankel as resident floozie Vera Murphy, were comic relief, yes, but their own hell-bent pursuits made for a rogue's gallery of soused chiselers. By the end, one felt sorry for all of their sorry selves. That was Powell's way, and Yale Rep's production fully honored it.

Substitute a bar of soap for a cup of coffee and you get *It Pays to Advertise*. This

Jennifer Frankel as Vera Murphy in Dawn Powell's *Big Night* (2001)
PHOTO © JOAN MARCUS

"farcical fact in three acts" hasn't the depth of the Powell or the verbal pyrotechnics of the Sturges, but its plot is swift, possessing a brace of surprise twists and more genuine laughs than one would think possible in a play written only one year before American drama "officially" began with the Provincetown Players in 1915.

As Rodney Martin, Adam Greer was the visual acme of the suave Arrow Col-

Stan Wojewodski Jr. (1991–2002)

lar Man. Sarah Rafferty played the secretary Mary, purportedly in love with Rodney but actually a rock-ribbed businesswoman on the take from Rodney's father, getting $5,000 from him to force her sweetheart to get a job in advance of their nuptials. When Peale, Rodney's press agent pal (played expertly by Broadway veteran Michael McGrath), shows up, he convinces Rodney to fight his father's soap trust by starting a rival company. Their business plan: Thirteen—at a dollar a cake, the most expensive soap the world has ever known.

Lest this upsell sound too harebrained, recall Howard Schultz's plan, launched after a trip to a housewares show in Milan, to get all of America to buy four-dollar beverages at Starbucks. Indeed, acts 2 and 3 of *It Pays to Advertise*, filled with additional double-crosses, a kited check, and ad-budget figures for Quaker Oats, Colgate's Dental Cream, Uneeda Biscuits, Postum, and Kellogg's Grape Nuts, played like a behind-the-scenes peek at a contemporary Silicon Valley IPO. The balance struck between love and lucre at the final curtain was ambiguous—and utterly American. If nothing else, Yale's once-in-a-lifetime revival of *It Pays to Advertise* demonstrated that an awareness of how money circulates in the New World didn't begin with the humorless critiques of Clifford Odets and Arthur Miller.

To this day, Sheehy indulges in a rueful Yale Rep what-if: "It would have been lovely if we had done all three together. Tracking the gentleness of *It Pays to Advertise* through the blithe satire of *A Cup of Coffee* to the corrosive wit of *Big Night*, an audience couldn't have ignored the hollowness of capitalism at the heart of the American enterprise. Their comedy offset the indictments of *St. Joan of the Stockyards*, *Pentecost*, and *Mrs. Warren's Profession*, which whipped you for three hours and made you grateful for it."

The impossibility of presenting an advertising trilogy in rotation shows that the institution had lost its original rambunctious flexibility. For Wojewodski, making theater was not like assembling a toy—building a set, inserting actors, turning on the lights, and—action! "I always felt that a production is more like a plant than a machine, and that you had to create an ecology for it. You had to recognize, or guess at, what the plant was, because the ecology could change during the gestation period." This greenhouse philosophy was at odds with Sammler's calendar, which was trying to bring order to the chaotic, simultaneous needs of Rep shows, director thesis projects, second-year Shakespeare projects, and No Boundaries offerings. Inheriting a culture where the actors onstage were more important than production values, Wojewodski had immediately ramped up production budgets and added rehearsals and tech time at both the school and the Rep. Following the enfranchisement of the sound designer as a valued collaborator for the American stage, he also regularized the use of original scores and composed soundscapes. A cue can be as

Stan Wojewodski Jr. and Catherine Sheehy at the Yale Rep fiftieth-anniversary celebration in October 2016
PHOTO © T. CHARLES ERICKSON

immense as the storm on the heath in *King Lear* or as subtle as a mimed rack of knocking milk bottles in *Our Town*. Contemporary playwrights and their directors rely on acoustic meaning in a manner unavailable to previous generations. Creating and adjusting these landscapes requires a designer trained in both text analysis and technological wizardry. In 1999, David Budries was made a full-time YSD faculty member. Under his stewardship, he moved sound design from a concentration to its own specialty in the design department, accepting three students a year.

Part of Wojewodski's legacy was that he allowed the students to experience a broader range of work and working methods. His anticommercial taste intensified in the move from Baltimore to New Haven. Neither recalls who articulated it, but both he and Sheehy remember throwing up their hands one day in a season planning meeting and saying, "Surely there are plays that they like and that we like." Left unsaid is the perception that Wojewodski's Yale Rep was indifferent to its audience, the same grievance that had dogged the less sanguine (and less taciturn) Brustein. Victoria Nolan maintains today that although the current Rep audience isn't significantly larger than it was during the Wojewodski years, she feels it's better informed and more committed to the work Yale Rep does. Her biggest regret? "I didn't have a better capacity or the institutional agility to deliver more of an audience for Stan's artistic inclinations."

For many, Wojewodski's programming had gone far enough. With hindsight, he now wishes he had gone even further: "I wish that I'd seized the opportunity to support/produce more formally challenging writing, offered more examples of ensemble-driven original work and cross-cultural interdisciplinary devising."

Resident Director Diamond, affiliated with the theater and the drama school for nearly thirty years now, recalls Wojewodski asking Suzan-Lori Parks whether Yale could produce *Death of the Black Man*. "She said yes, and he said, 'Who do you want to direct?' He could have been extremely paternalistic and insisted on his choices. She said, 'Liz Diamond.' He didn't know who the eff I was. He didn't even interview me to see if I was okay. He just said yes. Stan was great at saying, 'yes' to artists he believed in."

Years after his departure in 2004, Mark Bly remains perplexed at the shift in perceptions about Yale Rep from Richards to Wojewodski. "When Stan came in, it was sort of a strange period where nothing *appeared* to be happening, when actually there were all these great things happening that no one knew about—you had *The America Play, Pentecost, Venus, Figaro/Figaro, Children of Paradise*. . . . I mean, how many artistic directors would throw all that support behind Ralph Lemon for a global dance-theater trilogy?" Sheehy seconds Bly, adding, "Although Stan certainly didn't suffer fools gladly or well, he made little show of his intellect or his successes. He could have explained his decisions more plainly to the public, or flogged his achievements, but a hucksterish 'face of the theater' was not who he was. The work would speak for itself. In some ways, he was modest to a fault."

In other words, it might have paid to advertise. But to what end? When Wojewodski was appointed in 1991, an elderly Jesuit sent him a note of congratulations that read, "I shall continue to follow your career with pride, provided you pursue it in all humility."

It seems he had.

CHAPTER FOUR

James Bundy
(2002–)

When so much narrative experience is now on demand, there is a monkish element to making theatre in the twenty-first century. The stake we're still planting in the ground is the reverence for the written word, which was a founding principle of George Pierce Baker when he began what would become the Yale School of Drama in 1926.

—JAMES BUNDY, 2016

THE SELECTION OF THE FOURTH artistic director of Yale Rep has a *Rashomon* quality similar to that of Brewster's offer to Brustein in 1966. The name James Bundy, a surprise to the nonprofit theater community in October 2001, had occurred to some involved during the protracted eighteen-month search but not in a clear-cut chronology.

Mark Lamos, who had left Hartford Stage in 1997, had been the initial leading candidate. Search committee member Bly feels that "Mark was having too great a time as a freelancer to take the job, but he brought up James Bundy as a potential leader." Lamos, who had withdrawn postinterview because he had no desire to lead an academic institution, had worked with Bundy at the Acting Company but doesn't remember submitting his name. He does recall talking to James about the troubles with the job search and Bundy replying, "Why haven't they contacted me? I'm perfect for the job." Lamos says, "At the time, I thought he was too young. Ha! What did I know, right?"

Liz Diamond thinks that the decanal search seemed to go dormant after Oskar Eustis's leaked refusal. "Ming—who enjoyed playing kingmaker—told me that he called for a private meeting with President Levin in which he told Rick to give this young James Bundy, who had been my student in my first year of teaching, a try."

Sharing his own recollections, Bundy turns the clock back an additional twenty years. After graduating from Harvard in 1981, he went to England for actor training at the London Academy of Music and Dramatic Arts (LAMDA). A friend, Tracy Thorne, asked him in the fall of 1982 if he could have any job in the world, what would it be? He replied, "Dean of the Yale School of Drama and artistic director of Yale Repertory Theatre." A college junior when Brustein moved "his" Rep to Cambridge, Bundy had been a member of the Harvard-Radcliffe Drama Club committee that protested his appointment. His youthful qualms were allayed by watching the early Yale Rep ethos in action—a resident company engaged in rotating repertory. In Brustein's first A.R.T. seasons, Bundy saw everything—in the case of Alvin Epstein's *A Midsummer Night's Dream*, more than twice.

Like his predecessors, Bundy had worn a variety of hats before Yale. After leaving LAMDA, he became a freelance actor, working on the West Coast. He met his wife, actor-singer Anne Tofflemire, in San Francisco when they were cast as replacements in a commercial run of the satiric Ronald Reagan musical *Rap Master Ronnie*. From 1989 to 1991, he was the managing director of Cornerstone Theater Company, a site-specific, community-based theater founded by Harvard classmates Bill Rauch and Alison Carey. The following year, he entered the Yale School of Drama as a directing student, graduating in 1995. His third-year thesis was *The Three Sisters*.

James Bundy (2002–)

The fiscal lessons Bundy learned at Cornerstone served him well at his next two postings: associate producing director of the Acting Company, a classical touring company based in New York, and artistic director of Great Lakes Theater Festival in Cleveland, a job he began in 1998. Bundy was reportedly the only candidate who studied the theater's then-weak finances before his interview. He also credits his wife for her support during the hiring process, dryly observing, "Lots of people say they like me better when they meet Anne."

Bundy's three seasons in Ohio were marked by budgetary stabilization, a 30 percent growth in attendance, and an expansion in school-based theater education programs. Costume designer Ilona Somogyi ('94) nominated Bundy for the Yale job while they were working together on *Macbeth* in the fall of 2000. "I was thrilled to be nominated," says Bundy. "I recall thinking that this was the one job I would leave Cleveland for." Bundy contacted Yionoulis, who taught him the correct pronunciation of President Levin's name. Search chair Joseph Roach subsequently called Bundy. "He said to me, 'We have three groups of candidates. The nos, the maybes, and a third pool, that you are in, that we think of as the fallbacks.' Whether this was the truth, or whether it was a kind way of telling me I wasn't under serious consideration, I don't know. A year later, the search had cratered. I had meanwhile re-upped at Great Lakes when they came to me and said, 'Send your stuff.'"

Whether Levin selected Bundy that summer by fiat—à la Kingman Brewster—or let the committee choose him remains open to debate. "I do know that the interview order was reversed," says Bundy. "My first interview was with Rick; my second visit was with the search committee, which I believe was a change from the prior way."

On October 1, Yale released a letter from the president announcing both Bundy's appointment and his delayed start, on July 1, 2002, as dean and artistic director.

Much was made of Bundy's youth, reporters failing to note that at the age of forty-two, Bundy was three years older than Brustein had been in 1966. The *Yale Daily News* remarked that he was a combination of artistic creativity and political skills. Growing up in a family that believed in public service and in pursuing one's passions, Bundy was part of a long blue line: his father, McGeorge Bundy ('40), was a legendary (and legendarily young, at thirty-four) dean of the faculty of arts and sciences at Harvard before serving as national security advisor to Presidents Kennedy and Johnson, and later, as president of the Ford Foundation. There were two uncles in the Yale class of '39, a grandfather in the class of '09, and an older brother in the class of '76. Drama librarian Pam Jordan saw that "James could charm money out of people. He had both the Blue *and* the Crimson covered," meaning his background and connections would make him a savvy fund-raiser for Yale Rep as it moved forward in the new millennium.

In March 2002, Bundy, commuting between Cleveland and New Haven, announced five of six plays for his first season. A Latinx, all-male *Taming of the Shrew*, directed by Lamos; a second production for both Kia Corthron's *Breath, Boom* and Amy Freed's *The Psychic Life of Savages*; the American premiere of *Fighting Words* by recent graduate Sunil Kuruvilla ('99); and *Medea/Macbeth/Cinderella*, a devised theatrical mash-up on the scale of *The Frogs*, *Children of Paradise*, and *Geography*. The sixth offering, announced that August, was the world premiere of *The Black Monk*, a Chekhov adaptation by David Rabe, to star Sam Waterston (YC '62). A conceptualized Shakespeare, three new plays, a genre-busting extravaganza, and something Russian—all in all, very Yale Rep. (Wojewodski's signature third-year acting project had been publicly scrapped that May.)

Upon taking residence, Bundy immediately made Victoria Nolan deputy dean of the drama school, an executive partnership with a title that was more aligned with and familiar to the university hierarchy. During Bundy's hiring process, search committee members had been in agreement that the top three priorities were financial aid, faculty salaries, and the deteriorating and inadequate physical facilities. Yale's leadership position, rooted in the breadth and scope of its offerings, needed to remain competitive with less renowned programs that had more resources for its faculty and students. By the following May, Bundy and Nolan, working with interested students, devised a first (and last) strategic plan for YSD / Yale Rep to cover 2003–2009.

Academic objectives included the standardization of department chair meetings, a full curricular review, student evaluations of all courses, an increase in student and Yale Rep artist interactions, decreasing student loan debt, and admitting three playwrights and three directors each year rather than four, a decision that would partially free up the overburdened production schedule.

For Yale Rep, there would be a renewed focus on commissioning and developing new work and on the wooing of nationally and internationally prominent artists. Artist compensation would be brought in line with America's leading nonprofit theaters, and the artist housing stock would be improved (see box). For audience-building there would be a consistent coordination of publicity efforts, regular market research, improvements in accessibility services, and finally, an increase in ticket prices to the level of other major Connecticut theaters.

The strategic plan *Update*, dated November 2006, demonstrated progress on every objective except facilities. Yale Rep had produced six world premieres, commissioned seven emerging and established American playwrights, and mounted

ARTIST HOUSING

Where do the actors live when the curtain comes down? Their union, Actors' Equity, requires housing within a half mile of the rehearsal and performance facility, with a separate bedroom for each actor. If outside that range, the theater must provide transportation. Included in Equity's mandated inventory are cooking utensils, table service for four, cleaning supplies, linens, and the acme of modern essentials: Wi-Fi.

Yale Rep first housed visiting actors in the Hotel Duncan, a half block west and across the street on Chapel. Home to the oldest hand-operated elevator in Connecticut, with operators who seemed older than the crank they spun, the once-fashionable Hotel Duncan reached its centenary in 1994, a dowager with peeling paint, sloping floors, potholed mattresses, and towels like sandpaper. By that time, Yale Rep was putting its actors up either in the El Dorado next door, less dodgy as digs go, or in the Holiday Inn on Whalley Avenue, a dicey commute in the crime-ridden years when, as Anna D. Shapiro ('93), former artistic director of Steppenwolf Theater, once quipped, "downtown New Haven felt like Beirut."

Today the refurbished Duncan, now called the Graduate New Haven Hotel, has lost its funky, *Lower Depths* patina and quintupled its room rates, and since 2003, Yale Rep has been renting seventeen apartments, fifteen of them in Madison Tower at 123 Park Street and two in the Taft, at the corner of Chapel and

second productions of seven new plays. Designer, director, and actor compensation increased significantly. A student matinee program had been in place for three seasons. The average price per ticket sold had increased 44 percent, slightly trailing both Long Wharf and Hartford Stage. A second *Update* did not happen, occurring as it did during the height of the recession. Nolan remembers, "In 2009 we were in free fall, and doing drastic financial cutting, layoffs, et cetera."

Asked about his learning curve, Bundy recalls his first big surprise, ten weeks into the job. "I was sitting up late in technical rehearsals for *Medea/Macbeth/Cinderella*, a musical with a company of twenty-seven actors. There was a different feeling to the room, because of the twenty-five people sitting in this note session. I realized eighteen of them would be in class tomorrow morning at nine. There's a

James Bundy (2002–)

Church. The Yale Rep company manager, a rotating position for second-year management students, maintains a spreadsheet of available apartments for the season. In addition to actors and artistic personnel with Rep contracts, company management tries to accommodate anyone who seeks housing, whether they be directors and designers doing preproduction, actors and playwrights for Binger Center workshops, or guest artists for YSD shows. Long Wharf Theatre also has Madison Tower apartments. Yale Rep and Long Wharf used to rent from each other, but now they borrow apartments at no cost, except a cleaning fee.

As with Las Vegas, what happens in company housing stays with company management, but stories are sometimes too weird not to divulge. To wit: In 2016, Dianne Wiest was in residence to play Winnie in Beckett's *Happy Days* and brought her parakeet Gus (short for St. Augustine) with her. One day company manager Flo Lo ('17) received a call from the cleaning person to say that the bird was gone. An emergency summit was called to decide how to break the news to Wiest, working very hard on a famously demanding role. When the delegation arrived, Wiest revealed that she had already known of Gus's disappearance, and oh what a very sad turn of events it was.

Case closed, except Gus showed up just days later in the paint shop at 149 York, the building where Wiest was rehearsing. Their reunion was swift and happy. Perhaps Gus knew that his human companion needed complete and utter privacy to work on Winnie and was just giving her space. ◆

kind of split focus in tech and previews at Yale Rep that I had never twigged when I was a student. In Cleveland, for tech and previews the attention of every single person in the organization was turned, 24/7, into making that show."

This producing challenge led Bundy to change one policy in the academic "blue book" for his second year. In the case of a time conflict, Yale Rep work would take precedence over school responsibilities. "At some point in his tenure, Stan had changed it the other way," says Bundy. "Classes took precedence. Yale Rep came in second. I flipped it back, because I felt that we couldn't stand in good faith with the professionals who were coming in and devoting their full energy to the event if all of the people working on the show were in a position to say, 'I've got a class; I can't do that.'"

James Bundy (2002–)

WILL POWER!

What Shakespeare can do for the young—and what they can bring to him—is at the heart of *Will Power!* To date, over twenty-five thousand middle- and high-school students and educators throughout Connecticut have been introduced to Yale Rep via *Will Power!*, an arts-in-education initiative begun by Bundy in his first season. Whether the *Will Power!* play is a Shakespeare, like *All's Well That Ends Well*, or a work that speaks to their curricula, like *Death of a Salesman*, or to a contemporary issue that affects their lives, like *In the Continuum*, *Will Power!* subsidizes the cost of admission for school groups and presents special school-time matinee performances.

The program centers on students' attendance of a Yale Rep production and includes a variety of components to enhance their theatergoing experience before and after the show, such as study guides and postperformance discussions with members of the company. Additionally, *Will Power!* offers free teacher workshops aimed at providing educators with multiple curricular connections to the plays and artists featured in the program.

The effect of live theater on the collective consciousness of three hundred or so minds in one space at one time is unpredictable—and for Plato, Oliver Cromwell, and generations of school board officials, *dangerous*—but therein lies the power. "Taking the kids seriously, preparing them, and connecting them to performed text expands their worlds in amazing ways," says Amy Boratko. "Take *Cymbeline*: largely unknown, rarely taught, and tough as hell. On paper, Evan Yionoulis's production, which included a number of gender-swapped roles, would seem to up the

The ad copy read, "90 Costume Changes, 27 Actors, 25 Musical Numbers, 11 Murders, Three Family Squabbles, One Lost Slipper, One Extraordinary Night of Theater." *Medea/Macbeth/Cinderella* was a colossal, three-text musical circus. Rather like Wojewodski scheduling Jeune Lune's *Children of Paradise* without having seen or read a script, Bundy called Bill Rauch and said he wanted to open his first season with something unusual. He was thinking about *Medea/Macbeth/Cinderella*, which he had heard a lot about but never seen.

Rauch recalls theater and opera director Peter Sellars saying in a conversation at Harvard that the three great populist movements in the Western tradition were

James Bundy (2002–)

Three New Haven middle schoolers learning about The Comedy of Errors *(2005)*
PHOTO © RMFELDMAN, 2005

confusion ante. Yet *Cymbeline* was a big hit for *Will Power!* Local students especially responded to seeing themselves onstage in the actors of color. They followed the plot and were completely swept up."

In the 2019–2020 season, Boratko successfully piloted a program with the New Haven Public School District to provide one thousand free *Will Power!* tickets to the district's students as a way to address the systemic inequities in the state of Connecticut's schools. ◆

Greek tragedy, Elizabethan drama, and the American musical, a stray remark that stuck with the nineteen-year-old. Already obsessed with what makes something populist but also heavily influenced by the experimental methodology and company aesthetic of the Wooster Group, Rauch kept thinking about how to combine the three forms. He hit upon Euripides's *Medea*, Shakespeare's *Macbeth*, and a musical love from his childhood, Rodgers and Hammerstein's *Cinderella*. Noting, for example, that Medea's first major speech to the Female Chorus, Macbeth's first soliloquy, and Cinderella's "I Want Song" occur at the same time in their respective narratives led Rauch to the challenge of uncovering and highlighting these shared

James Bundy (2002–)

The Female Chorus in Bill Rauch and Tracy Young's *Medea/Macbeth/Cinderella* (2002)
PHOTO © JOAN MARCUS

rhythms of populist storytelling across two millennia. "I invited my favorite actors on campus to just be in a company with me for my final semester at Harvard. We worked in a basement space mostly on chunks of what became *M/M/C*. It was completely illegal. We didn't have the rights."

Some fifteen years later, LA-based playwright Tracy Young, who had written a piece for Cornerstone Theater, learned about *M/M/C*. She insisted that Rauch rework and stage the play in a coproduction with the LA Actors' Gang. Its success there even met with the cautious approval of the Rodgers and Hammerstein Organization. Four years later, once Bundy had invited Rauch and Young, who had become coadapter and codirector, to Yale, they continued their focus on creating and staging synchronicities among the three, ideally ending up with "the fourth story." Rauch remembers that "at college, all three plays largely went on at once. Its later incarnations were marked by more and more intercuts, juxtapositions, and repetitions. In Yale rehearsals, we developed the mantra, 'It's the interdependence, stupid.'"

Medea was solely cast with women; *Macbeth*, with men. The traditional villainesses—Medea, Lady M, and the Stepmother—were drawn more multidimensionally. Each seemed to absorb the choices and the consequences of the others in their respective worlds, and all of them were very invested in good-girl Cinderella's actions. Rauch and Young created a meditation on ambition, power, gender, and the bonds of family that played out on Rachel Hauck's vast tiered set of ramps, doors, and stairs as though on three overlapping channels: the witches dress Cinderella while Medea prepares the poison; the knocking on the door that the porter hears in *Macbeth* is Medea smacking Jason's breastplate.

In terms of verbal overlap—the printed text is laid out as three running columns—Medea, for example, declares she has to kill her sons at the same time as the Attendant discloses that Lady M is acting strangely and Cinderella sings "A Lovely Night." Teaching the audience how and where and when to look and listen through three hours and twenty-five scenes was a gargantuan feat. The reviews were generally laudatory, with one critic calling it "a crash-course in theater history and directing techniques of the twentieth century." Just as *Prometheus Bound, A Lesson from Aloes*, and Winterfest XII had been for his predecessors, *Medea/Macbeth/Cinderella* was the event that made the requisite splash in Bundy's inaugural season.

At the opposite end of the spectrum that season was *Fighting Words* by Sunil Kuruvilla, a Yale playwright whose *Rice Boy*, a cross-cultural coming-of-age tale of a motherless Indian boy in Canada, had made its world premiere at Yale Rep in the fall of 2000. *Fighting Words* places a real-life event at the heart of the action—a World Boxing Council Bantamweight Championship match in 1980 between Welshman Johnny Owen ("the Merthyr Matchstick") and Mexican Lupe Pintor. Owen was knocked into a coma in the twelfth round of the bout and died seven weeks later. Kuruvilla, then a Toronto teenager slipping out of the house to train as a boxer on the sly, saw a rebroadcast of the title fight the day after it happened and gave up the sport. Already a writer, he wanted to cover ring death in some way. "So I started keeping a file every time there was a boxer who was killed," he recalls. "It was only when I went to grad school, about fifteen years later, that I had a breakthrough."

The Owen-Pintor fight was held in Los Angeles; the play stays put in Merthyr Tydfil, Johnny's drab hometown. The action is confined to three women—sisters Nia and Peg, both in love with Johnny, and their landlady, Mrs. Davies—left behind in the days immediately before and after the fight. Preparing and baking

Meg Brogan, Jayne Houdyshell, and Emma Bowers in Sunil Kuruvilla's *Fighting Words* (2002)
PHOTO © JOAN MARCUS

Welsh teacakes for the victory celebration, they reveal the poverty and circumscription of their lives in dialogue that is at once mundane and lyrical without being sentimental. Partway through, Peg, a shadowboxing, rope-jumping dervish and virtual stand-in for Johnny (and the teenage Kuruvilla) hops a flight to Los Angeles. Because of spotty television reception, Nia and Mrs. Davies and the rest of the townspeople don't know the outcome of the fight until Peg returns and reports, in Greek-messenger style, of the ultimate fall of their hero. Like Hecuba at the close of *The Trojan Women*, the women of Merthyr are left to mourn and to persevere.

Resident Director Liz Diamond directed *Fighting Words* in the intimate two-hundred-seat New Theatre. Student designer Marie Davis-Green ('03) transformed the black box space into a dingy gym with a boxing-ring stage. The audience watched from all four sides. Ambient bells, buzzers, and crowd noises punctuated the scene changes. Kuruvilla had written the part of Nia for a classmate, Meg Brogan ('98), who was more than ably complemented in the produc-

238 *James Bundy (2002–)*

tion by Emma Bowers as Peg, and many years before New York caught up with her formidable talent, character actor Jayne Houdyshell as Mrs. Davies. (She had also played Medea's Nurse in *M/M/C* earlier that season.)

Bundy feels his honeymoon ended in the middle of his second season with the Olmec *King Lear*, directed by Harold Scott and starring Avery Brooks. The Olmec civilization flourished from 1200 to 400 BCE in what is now southern Mexico and Central America. Except for some colossal basalt heads, they left behind few cultural traces. In 1976, scholar Ivan Van Sertima published *They Came Before Columbus*. Its subtitle, "The African Presence in Ancient America," is his thesis: Africans sailed to Central America and settled there as early as 700 BCE. The African features on the Olmec totem heads were a major clue that led him to posit an alternative origin for their civilization. Scott shared the book with Brooks in 2001. They began collaborating on a *King Lear* set in a pre-Christian society "composed of brown-skinned people representing a convergence of cultures, including African." Once they were at Yale, much was made in the press of this first time in American history that a Black director was helming an all-Black cast in *Lear*.

Presiding stage center over this tale of the end of the Lear family line was—yes—a seventeen-foot-tall Olmec head, framed by jade panel screens that shifted for location changes. The striking costumes by Jessica Ford ('04) were a mix of African and Meso-American elements, including a fantastical feathered cape worn by Lear in the opening celebration, which featured a pageant dance performed by girls from the Betsy Ross Arts Magnet School in New Haven.

"The production was fraught," says Bundy today. There was pushback from the history of art department, which felt that the production concept was an essentially fraudulent academic premise. Graduate student James Terry hammered home this idea in the *Yale Daily News*, maintaining that Van Sertima's work had long been debunked and that the dramaturgy pages in the Yale Rep program, which were being distributed to New Haven schools for the inauguration of the *Will Power!* matinee outreach effort, were promoting "Eurocentrism in blackface," an affront to the First Peoples of the Americas.

Lear is a difficult test. Most of the critics praised the elaborate physical design and individual performances but chided Brooks for an overdone madness and a case of the fidgets. *Nihil novi sub sole*: the half-baked Olmec *Lear* turned out to be a kissing cousin to Brustein's misguided Stonehenge *Macbeth* in 1971.

Bundy recalls, "It was the rare production where an outside director working for the first time at the Yale Rep couldn't dock with the student designers, and said things that were inappropriate, and I didn't know how in that environment to defend everybody, and I couldn't defend everyone at the same time, and so I chose the artists who were onstage and the director over the designers. And I ended up literally doing an apology tour of the school afterwards."

Indeed. On the Monday morning after the *Lear* strike, Bundy went into his office, and there stood the reassembled Olmec head with the arresting addition of a foot-long pink tongue. Before going out, he told his assistant, Josephine Brown, to get technical director Neil Mulligan ('01) to remove the head, knowing that it was highly likely that Mulligan and his crew had put it there. Mulligan insists today that the gesture was not a visual referendum on Bundy's leadership. "We wanted to add levity to a tragedy in which the entire design team had been in tears every night in tech. James was on our team; he was still our leader—you only prank the people you care about."

Brustein had Bond. Richards had Wilson and Fugard. Wojewodski had Parks. With six productions of four new plays and two adaptations, Bundy had Sarah Ruhl, whose first work at Yale, the world premiere of *The Clean House*, opened his third season in 2004. Every half generation in the American theater seems to produce a playwright, essentially and profoundly comic, who manages to titrate the prevailing anxieties of their time. Their tool kit includes a poetic use of the stage space, metatheatrical elements, fantastical visuals, an adamant intellectualism, a lyrical sense of time, fractured narrative structures, and an extravagant love of the lexicon. Their characters and their moods turn on a dime. For the audience the laughs are nonstop, and the tears flow from unexpected sources. Guare was perhaps the first of these theatrical wizards, followed by Durang ('74), Craig Lucas, Richard Greenberg ('85), Paula Vogel, Nicky Silver, and Robert O'Hara. Ruhl, a protégé of Vogel's in the Brown MFA playwriting program, is very much in this line.

An original commission for the McCarter Theatre, *The Clean House* was being read everywhere in 2003, including South Coast Rep in California, where Bill Rauch, subbing last minute as director, fell for it head over heels. In the spring of 2004, *The Clean House* won the Susan Smith Blackburn Prize for the best work by a female playwright. The Yale Rep artistic politburo (Diamond, Sheehy, Yionoulis, and Bly) had been pushing the play in season planning, but Bundy initially resisted. Ruhl says today, "I'll never forget the phone call, actually. Because you know how everything has a million readings these days before getting done, and I remember James Bundy calling me and I'd never met him, and he said, 'We want

A promotional sponge for Sarah Ruhl's *The Clean House* (2004)
COURTESY OF YALE REPERTORY THEATRE

to do this play.' And I thought, 'My god, this man doesn't need to hear it out loud? He just *knows*?'"

A dinner party that Ruhl attended where a woman complained that her maid wouldn't clean provided the germ for *Clean House*. "In a metaphysical Connecticut," Matilde, up from Brazil, finds cleaning the house of married doctors Lane and Charles depressing. She'd rather devote her time to creating the perfect joke in Portuguese, so Lane's sister, Virginia, for whom daily cleaning represents daily progress, secretly takes over the job. Home and hearth are threatened when Charles falls in love with Ana, a much older breast cancer patient.

The perfect joke is discovered at the end of *Clean House*, but its price is death. Ruhl's insights into mercy, healing, the eternal mystery of one's parents, decline and decay, class anxiety, sisterhood, and the messiness of love are richly earned. An example of Ruhl's use of space: "A spice jar goes flying from Ana's balcony. A cloud of yellow spice lands in Lane's living room." Another example: "In the distance [Alaska] Charles walks across the stage in a heavy parka. He carries a pickax. On the balcony it is snowing." These images are quickly conjured; the audiences see them for a fleeting moment, and then they vanish just as swiftly.

Such "How did they do that?" moments require highly creative designers. James Mountcastle ('90), production stage manager of Yale Rep since 2004, has been the stage manager on five of the six Ruhl projects. "I love working with Sarah. She's always excited, interested, and fascinated by what and how the actors will do in service of her poetic flights, which are hung on a sturdy frame." Running the

James Bundy (2002–)

plays in performance, he sees "her images flower every night and I always sense the audience yearning hopefully for the next one."

Orpheus and Eurydice and their underworld trips have been treated by artists as diverse as Ovid, Titian, Monteverdi, and Pynchon. Two seasons after *Clean House*, in the middle of technical rehearsals at Yale for her *Eurydice*, Ruhl was awarded a MacArthur Fellowship, a.k.a. the genius grant, "for creating vivid and adventurous theatrical works that poignantly juxtapose the mundane aspects of daily life with mythic themes of love and war." The encomium certainly applies to *Eurydice*. Her reworking is one of the few told from the perspective of Eurydice; moreover, one of its essential characters, as well as the third leg of its love triangle, is Ruhl's invention: Eurydice's dead father. (Ruhl has acknowledged that *Eurydice* partly sprang from her desire to have a few more conversations with her father, who had died of cancer in 1995.)

In this play of three movements, Eurydice's father has resisted the forces of Lethe—the River of Forgetfulness—and kept his memory in the Underworld. In the Overworld, at her wedding reception to Orpheus, Eurydice is told by the Nasty Interesting Man that he has a letter for her from her father. Spurning his advances, she falls to her death through the portal to Hades, which is an elevator filled with rain. Once there, her father manages to restore Eurydice's memory and language.

When Orpheus finds the right musical pitch to enter the Underworld, he makes the grumpy chorus of stones (Big Stone, Little Stone, and Loud Stone) weep. At her father's insistence, Eurydice leaves with Orpheus, but after his fateful look backward, she dies a second time. Her father, meanwhile, dips himself into the river Lethe to forget the loss of his daughter. Eurydice writes Orpheus a final letter, giving him instructions on how to find, and treat, his next wife. She dips herself into the Lethe and lies down next to her father. In the close, Orpheus descends and sees her but, dipped in forgetfulness as well, cannot read her epistle. The play ends with the sound of water.

Eurydice's East Coast premiere at Yale Rep was a remounting of Les Waters's 2004 production at Berkeley Rep, with the same design team and largely the same cast. Waters and set designer Scott Bradley ('86) created an environment where the Underworld and the Overworld could happen simultaneously and where the Lethe could flow. "At times, the world feels Victorian or Edwardian," Waters said in the Yale Rep newsletter. "Scott researched all those old turn-of-the-century baths and swimming pools. Now, we have a tiled, bottom-of-the-pool world that can be filled with images of loss." Covering the walls were letters from the dead to the living, a reminder of the walls of the missing in Lower Manhattan after the Twin Towers fell, one of many touches that led Charles Isherwood in the *New*

Ramiz Monsef, Gian-Murray Gianino, and Carla Harting as the Three Stones in *Eurydice* (2006)
PHOTO © CAROL ROSEGG

York Times to deem *Eurydice* "the most moving exploration of the theme of loss that the American theatre has produced since the events of September 11, 2001." As with *Prometheus Bound* decades before, enchanted drama students saw *Eurydice* over and over again.

Ruhl's third show at the Rep was *Passion Play*. Dedicated to Vogel, it skips

James Bundy (2002–) 243

Company at the Last Supper in Sarah Ruhl's *Passion Play* (2008)
PHOTO © JOAN MARCUS

in time and place from a village in northern England, when Elizabeth I is trying to outlaw performances of the mystery play cycle, to the three-hundredth anniversary of Bavaria's Oberammergau Passion Play in 1934, which Hitler attended twice, to the present-day Black Hills Passion Play, which was started in Spearfish, South Dakota, in 1939 by a seventh-generation passion-play actor-émigré. Ruhl had drafted the English and German acts and then set them aside until Arena Stage asked her to write a play about America. "A daunting task," she writes in the foreword. "Until I realized that little is more American than the nexus of religious rhetoric, politics, and theatricality."

Arena audiences loved *Passion Play*, but a negative review in the *New York Times* could have ended its life in Washington, DC. "Twelve actors and three hours? No one wanted to touch it," says Ruhl. "But one of the wonderful things about James is that he doesn't have an obsession with premieres." Bundy and Robert Falls at the Goodman Theatre extended invitations for a new team to keep working. Ruhl feels they began to refine the design in the Chicago leg and that the evening finally pulled together in New Haven, with the brilliant Kathy Chalfant in the triple role of Elizabeth I, Hitler, and Ronald Reagan. "Hitler was easy to inhabit," Chalfant remembers. "But because I hated Ronald Reagan so much for what he began in this country, I couldn't impersonate him until I had the wacky insight that while I might hate Ronald Reagan, Ronald Reagan thought he was swell. It worked."

Chekhov is easy to spoil. Ruhl was fittingly modest when she adapted his *Three Sisters*, which hadn't been seen at Yale Rep since 1968. With a poet's ear and eye, she noticed—and respected—syntactical quirks in Chekhov's deliberately prosaic Russian. The following November, Ruhl, by now a Yale Rep associate artist and member of the playwriting faculty, teamed up with Waters again for the commissioned world premiere of *Dear Elizabeth: A Play in Letters from Elizabeth Bishop to Robert Lowell and Back Again*, a distillation of nearly five hundred pieces of correspondence between the two poets that stretched over their thirty-year friendship. Her most recent Yale Rep commission, *Scenes from Court Life; or the whipping boy and his prince* (2016), used a potpourri of genres and styles to dramatize "the cost of dynastic privilege." Scenes from seventeenth-century England, where the Stuarts are defending their divine rights, are intercut with scenes of the Bush family playing political hardball in twenty-first-century America. Actors doubled as their cross-temporal counterparts Charles I and George, Charles II and George W., the Whipping Boy and Jeb Bush, and the Groom of the Stool and Karl Rove. If one of comedy's purposes is "to punish customs with laughter" (*castigat ridendo mores*), Ruhl provided plenty of insightful laughs during an extremely tense election season.

In addition to *The Clean House*, Yale Rep produced two more important American plays in the 2004–2005 season. *The Intelligent Design of Jenny Chow* by Rolin Jones and *Radio Golf* by August Wilson. Like *The Idiots Karamazov* and *The Resurrection of Lady Lester*, *Jenny Chow* had begun in the classroom. Jones ('04) wrote it during his first year in a frenzied three and a half weeks for two acting students, Keiko Yamamoto and Jennifer Lim. Directing professor David Chambers saw *Jenny Chow* in Drama 47 and contacted South Coast Rep about its promise. By the spring of his second year, Jones was permitted to leave school for six weeks to work on the world premiere directed by Chambers at South Coast Rep. The Old Globe in San Diego mounted a second, different production that summer. "They both did okay, just enough to not die," Jones laughs today.

One of the first plays to deal with cyberspace communication and connectivity, *The Intelligent Design of Jenny Chow* has an outlandish premise. After losing her job at the mall, Jennifer Marcus, an agoraphobic twenty-two-year-old genius with OCD, begins working for a defense contractor. Adopted from China, she doesn't get along with her overworked mother and builds a robot replica of herself out of spare government parts in order to travel across the world to meet her birth mother. Jennifer experiences everything her flying alter ego, Jenny Chow, does via virtual gloves and special vision goggles, but as the play progresses, Jennifer begins to reject Jenny in a displacement of the anger she feels toward her birth mother. The play risks a painful, unfunny curtain after Jennifer sends Jenny away for good and begins to have a panic attack in the bedroom she never leaves.

Jenny Chow's subtitle, "An Instant Message with Excitable Music," alerts the audience to an evening comprised largely of computer message voiceovers. A risky methodology, but Jones avoids monotony with his premise, a loopy sense of humor, a lightning pace, and a deeply strange trio of characters—a Russian scientist, an aeronautics engineer, and a Mormon missionary—played by the same actor. Yet underneath the whimsy is a wrenching look at mother-daughter conflicts, one that reflects the three painful years in Jones's twenties when he and his mother had ceased speaking.

As Jones was about to graduate, Bundy told him he wanted to produce *Jenny Chow* the following season; Jones, having convinced himself by this time that it was "a chick play," thought a woman should direct. He remembered the work of Jackson Gay, who had graduated two years before him: "She was wildly unpretentious and has a great bullshit meter." He took Bundy to New York to see her production of Brecht's *Man Is Man* at a small theater on 86th Street. Gay remembers, "I was shocked to see James and Rolin on the sidewalk one night out of the blue, so I asked them, 'What are you doing here?' [They said,] 'Seeing your show.' And they hired me."

Both Gay and Jones credit the other for coming up with Jennifer's final action. "We just didn't know how to end the play," says Gay. "We tried so many different things. There was no emotional punch." Playwright or director—perhaps both simultaneously—suddenly remembered, in the kind of eureka moment theater makers cherish, the dumplings hidden in the scarf that Jenny had brought back from Jennifer's birth mother in China. The sight of Jennifer, completely alone, unwrapping the scarf and wolfing down her mother's food was a heartbreaking last gesture. At its premiere, John Guare, a hero to Jones, sought him out to tell him he'd had a great night in the theater. "I was a kid at Christmas. It was the greatest artistic ya-ya feeling I'll ever have." Like *The Clean House*, which it directly followed at Yale, *Jenny Chow* had a high-profile production in New York and became a Pulitzer Prize finalist.

Keiko Yamamoto and Seema Sueko in Rolin Jones's *The Intelligent Design of Jenny Chow* (2004)
PHOTO © T. CHARLES ERICKSON

    Mordecai and Wilson began talking to Bundy as early as 2003 about a return to Yale Rep with *Radio Golf*, the tenth and final installment of the Century Cycle and the first to feature members of the Black middle class. After *Gem of the Ocean* opened on Broadway in early December 2004, Wilson began writing the play, scheduled to begin rehearsals in a mere four months. In mid-January, Timo-

John Earl Jelks as Sterling Johnson in *Radio Golf*, the final installment of the August Wilson Century Cycle (2005)
PHOTO © CAROL ROSEGG

thy Douglas ('86), a Yale-trained actor who had understudied roles in the original *Ma Rainey*, *Fences*, and *Joe Turner's Come and Gone* and had been the associate artistic director of Actors Theatre of Louisville for four years, was announced as director for *Radio Golf*. Artists have to be flexible when there is no advance script to work from, so the idea of using student designers was rejected in favor of professionals who had worked with Wilson post–Lloyd Richards: David Gallo (sets), Susan Hilferty ('80; costumes), and Donald Holder ('86; lighting).

Bundy recalls the first full draft of the script coming off the copy machine the first day of rehearsal. At the company meet-and-greet, Wilson pointed to his friend and producing partner and told the crowd there were only two constants in the ten plays—"August Wilson and Ben Mordecai." Mordecai, frail from chemo and in a wheelchair that day, would die of cancer in May, a week before the conclusion of the *Radio Golf* run.

James Bundy (2002–)

Radio Golf was a play Wilson didn't want to write. "To my observation," he told *USA Today*, "the black middle class has failed to return the expertise and sophistication and resources that they've gained over the past fifty years back to the community." To tell its story about the dangers of assimilation, *Radio Golf* combines a Faustian bargain with the tale of a prodigal son. It's 1997. Harmond Wilks, running to be the first Black mayor of Pittsburgh, has inherited a real estate company. He and his business partner, Roosevelt Hicks, are trying to clinch a deal for their redevelopment project, which will bring high-rise apartment buildings and the chain-store trappings of consumer success to gentrify the long-neglected Hill District. The most famous address in the Century Cycle will have to be demolished: 1839 Wylie Avenue, home to Aunt Ester, the former slave and "washer of souls" who was 285 years old in *Gem of the Ocean* and 322 in *Two Trains Running* and who died in 1985 during the events of *King Hedley II*.

Harmond, who knows the house was obtained illegally, thinks building around the property will solve the dilemma; Roosevelt favors demolition. Refereeing this battle for his soul are the pragmatic neighborhood handyman, Sterling Johnson (the young hothead of *Two Trains Running*), and Elder Joseph Barlow, one of Wilson's damaged clairvoyants. Wilson said in a rehearsal interview, "So what does black America do at the end of the millennium? What should they do? Not replace or redevelop. *Transform*." At the final curtain, Harmond has picked up a brush to join the neighborhood activists holding a paint party at 1839 Wiley.

In its initial outing, *Radio Golf* was judged overlong, convoluted, and lacking focus. The play contains several signature Wilson themes, but intentionally missing was a soaring vernacular lyricism in Harmond's and Roosevelt's speeches. Material success and Ivy League educations have kept these men from discovering their own song, so central in Wilson. Unlike Elder Joseph and Sterling, they don't know what they've lost or how lost they are.

What many remember about Wilson's return to New Haven was his generosity and openness with the students, hanging out and smoking with a crowd of them for hours outside Booktrader's Café at the corner of Chapel and York or down the street at the Irish bar, once Kavanagh's and now called Sullivan's. "He loved to talk to people. And talk about the work and tell stories and give interviews," recalls Tarell Alvin McCraney ('07), then a playwriting student whom Bundy assigned to be Wilson's assistant. McCraney appreciated how Wilson had created an enormous community with his ten plays and then kept it together by using the same artists again and again. "The rehearsal community extended to me . . . , Michele Shay, Antony Chisholm, Tim Douglas; John Jelks came to my cabaret; they came to my first-year project. They spread my work throughout the country after they left. I didn't have a direct lineage to August as a writer, but I was encompassed in his community."

Yale Rep took a calculated risk with *Radio Golf*; the prestige and goodwill of completing the Century Cycle where it began outweighed the negatives of producing a hasty first draft. (The text would continue to evolve through seven subsequent productions across the country before its New York premiere.) But it wasn't a new-play process Yale Rep would want to have happen again. Indeed, just as *Radio Golf* began rehearsals, Bundy announced, after a national search, the appointment of a new associate artistic director, Jennifer Kiger, to replace Bly, who had resigned after twelve years and sixty-four productions in the position.

The literary manager at South Coast Rep since 2000, and codirector of the Pacific Playwrights Festival, Kiger had trained at Brustein's A.R.T. Conservatory at Harvard. In California, she had worked with Yale Rep directors Mark Rucker and David Chambers and dozens of emerging and established playwrights, including Ruhl and Jones.

Bundy says, "I knew we needed to get into commissioning if we wanted to build strong relationships with excellent writers, but I had precious little experience commissioning or developing new work, and I needed someone who could really run the show in that area." They couldn't know at the time of her hire how Yale Rep would become the beneficiary of the James Binger and Robina Foundation's generosity, but when the resources did arrive, the Bundy and Kiger partnership was more than ready to shape a program.

Marcus Gardley ('04) is another playwright who felt embraced by Wilson: "I remember Vicki Nolan calling to see whether I would like to attend the opening of *Radio Golf*. They sat me next to him. I could hardly pay attention to the stage. He said to me, 'I've read your play, and I love it. I'm coming to see it.'"

Wilson would not live to see Gardley's *dance of the holy ghosts: a play on memory*. Diagnosed with liver cancer a month after *Radio Golf* closed, Wilson died on October 2, 2005. Through the prism of his own impending death, Wilson wrote a tribute to Mordecai, an address that Bundy read at the memorial for Mordecai held at the University Theatre on October 25.

Like Wilson, Gardley was a poet before he became a playwright, and he also found great inspiration from the blues. Lorca and Baldwin spring to mind when reading *dance of the holy ghosts*. Unlike a Wilson play, *dance* is nonlinear, taking place at five different points in time between 1955 and 2005 but shifting most between the coming-of-age tale of Marcus G. and the coming-to-terms of his estranged grandfather, Oscar Clifton, a Delta bluesman who preferred the road to family responsibility. The play climaxes at his daughter's funeral, where, in a Wilsonesque moment, Oscar is released from the ghosts of his past. Running along a parallel track are young Marcus's fanciful adventures in Catholic school with a love interest, two mean girls, and a bizarre, Durang-like priest who at one point moonwalks like Michael Jackson.

This dramaturgical coexistence gelled better when *dance* was first staged at the school with an all-student cast. Despite a first-rate company at the Rep, with Oscar played by Chuck Cooper, who turned a first-class jerk into a fascinating patriarch, the tonally disparate halves didn't cohere, something both Gardley and director Liz Diamond concede for different reasons long after the fact. "The student production, directed by Brendan Hughes ['04], released the jubilation that we simply didn't achieve," says Diamond. "Our cast was older, arguably more 'age appropriate' to the roles, but they leaned into the minor key. They related to the melancholy of missed opportunity, failed love in the play. We got that. But failed to spring the lock on the exuberant, youthful comedy. It was Marcus's first professional production, and I knew he felt something was wrong; I did too. I was probably asking for rewrites that felt wrong to him. But I think what was not working in the production was not really a script issue. Chuck was a powerful force in that show, and—no fault of Chuck's; it's just the physics of rehearsal when a star is in the room—what he was doing in the role skewed my sense of what was needed away from the playfulness that Marcus wanted to protect."

Of the student production, Gardley remembers he had more space to explore and do whatever he wanted. When moved to the larger space, "Liz and the creative team wanted the play to have a life in the outside world. So, they were giving their best advice on how to make it well made. I felt grateful, so I took all of it instead of standing my ground. The bones of that play need to be whimsical and fun and unpredictable." Another school show lost its spark when it crossed the street. Realizing what had happened, Bundy went up to Gardley at the end of a performance of *dance* and commissioned a next play from him on the spot.

Bundy directed less often than Wojewodski or Richards had. (Brustein, an official company member, had acted more than he directed.) After his first two Rep productions, Amy Freed's *Psychic Life of Savages* (2003) and Lillian Groag's *The Ladies of the Camellias* (2004), both newish plays he had worked on elsewhere, Bundy directed only classics. "I am not an auteur," he says. "I'm genuinely interested in the restrictions when, for instance, I'm working on a Shakespeare play. I like figuring out a way to make the weird stuff *play*. I like the dig dig dig, what's the puzzle to be put together here, as opposed to how can I write over the event."

Bundy's first Shakespeare for Yale Rep was *All's Well That Ends Well*, whose central puzzle is, Why does its charismatic heroine, Helena, fall for the feckless, underscripted Bertram? Every show begins with high hopes and best intentions. Bundy felt *All's Well* needed to have contemporary music throughout, but his costume designer convinced him that the clothes should reference Dior's New Look of the late 1940s. They decided to go with both, and well, "that conceptual mash-up turned out to be a nightmare," says Bundy today.

Things would get grave. "On a Friday rehearsal three weeks in, I felt [bad]. We knocked off early, a first for me. I thought it was the flu." Feeling worse on Saturday, he stayed home and left rehearsal to his assistant. "By Sunday late afternoon, I was basically non compos mentis. I was hallucinating." His medical team diagnosed endocarditis on Monday and performed open heart surgery to replace his aortic valve. "A killer infection had seeded itself in my aortic valve. It was shredding little bits of my heart and flying into my bloodstream, which led to two embolisms."

When Bundy awoke from surgery, his thoughts were on *All's Well*. He agreed with Kiger's idea to call Mark Rucker at South Coast Rep and have him come and finish the show. Rucker hopped on a plane, and after a jittery company did a stumble-through for him, he broke the tension with a well-timed quip, "That's the best first rehearsal I've ever seen." Bundy spent twelve days in the hospital and stayed on antibiotics for six months. Opening on time, *All's Well That Ends Well* divided its critics—the problem-comedies always do. Bundy smiles today, saying, "I was well on my way to completely screwing that production up, and Rucker completely saved the theater's bacon. It would have been a disaster up there with every legendary disaster in the history of Yale Rep."

An aggressively bullish stock market fueled by the mortgage-lending bubble coincided with Bundy's first term. The Yale University endowment grew from $11 billion in his first season to $23 billion in his sixth, phenomenal growth that enabled the theater to make good on some strategic goals and become competitive with its TCG peers when it came to artist compensation. A fresh opportunity Bundy spotted early on was alumni engagement. Trust fund theater artists are common in America, and the ever-mutating entertainment boom that began with the ascent of HBO in the early 1990s has rewarded many drama alums, but the alumni culture at the drama school had never been overly philanthropic. When each directing or acting or design gig could be an artist's last, the vast majority of YSD alums are thrilled just to be able to retire their student debt someday.

"James really cared about fund-raising," says Deborah S. Berman, long-term director of development and alumni affairs for the school and the theater. In his first year, Bundy, with the help of Mordecai, sought to create a group of ambassadors chosen for their expertise in the arts and in business and tasked them with looking for ways to connect alumni to the activities of the school and the Rep. This Leadership Council began sub rosa with John Badham (YC '61, '63), John Beinecke (YC '69), Neil Mazzella ('78), and Ed Trach ('58). The Council "went public" after eighteen months in July 2004 with twenty-six members, including Yale College and drama school alumni from a variety of disciplines and all walks of life. Berman was hired the following year, and her energy and solicitation skills helped shift the Council into higher gear. By 2010, the Leadership Council changed its title to the Yale School of Drama Board of Advisors, which now stands at sixty-one members.

John Beinecke was also instrumental in creating the Beinecke Fellows Program. Since the 2005–2006 season, resources have been awarded every year to a shifting number of high-profile artists to come to Yale Rep, do a show, work alongside students, and interact with the greater Yale community in various ways: for example, lectures with or without Q and A sessions, master classes, and college teas. The roster of fellows engaged to date includes Paul Giamatti, Charles C. "Roc" Dutton, Dianne Wiest, and Kathleen Chalfant.

Bundy also supported increased audience connectivity. Interestingly, the Internet Archive Wayback Machine shows that the first search for Yale Rep (www.yalerep.org) on April 15, 1997, *preceded* the first search for the university itself (www.yale.edu) by eighteen days. Advantix, the theater's ticketing system provider, designed the initial site. The drama school (www.yale.edu.drama) had its first search that October. The next web designer, Tom Schultz, was brought on in 2000. By 2007, Yale Rep programs had begun to be posted simultaneously online, and e-blasts about season- or production-specific information and sale offers had become the theater's primary marketing tool. Yale Rep's Facebook presence began in 2009; its content is generally managed by the associate director of marketing and communications (a third-year management student) under the supervision of the director of communications, Steven Padla. "Behind the Scenes at . . ." video clips began in 2009 as well. Padla produces their content, subject to approval by the artistic department, and the videos are shot and edited by outside vendor David Kane. Yale Rep began an Instagram account at the beginning of the 2015–2016 season, with photos of the *Indecent* tech installation at the UT and a shot of *Indecent* playwright Paula Vogel wearing a "Yale Repertory Theatre—We Do It in a Church" T-shirt (www.instagram.com/yalerep/).

There was a time when one wasn't offered the option of rating an airport bathroom experience by pressing a button, and home goods stores didn't pester once a day with emailed cutlery savings alerts. As a harbinger of the "How are we doing?" perpetual feedback loop that the consumer culture demands today, Bundy's first "Welcome to Yale Rep" address in the *Eurydice* program in September 2006 was soft sell—and genuinely fresh. Brustein had always had something to say. Richards provided a formulaic greeting for his Winterfest programs but weighed in with his constituents only seven other times, most notably in a professionally empowering answer to the deathless question, What is a dramaturg?, in the *Mrs. Warren's Profession* program in 1981. Except for a page of past quotes in the *On the Verge* program and an explanatory caution for the formal experiments of Winterfest XII several months later, Wojewodski never said a word.

Bundy isn't sure why he waited so long to begin welcoming patrons. "I think I thought I had a happy obligation to be an interlocutor for the institution with anybody who wanted to engage with it in any way." It might also have coincided with a program redesign. In his first message, Bundy remembered the legacy of Richards, who had died that June at the age of eighty-seven, and dedicated the four new plays of the season to the memory of the man who'd spent his life championing new writers.

Bundy's welcomes avoided Brustein's quasi-hectoring, pedagogical stance. He doesn't tell the audience what to look for but will point out the obvious as though to calm undue alarm: "This Tartuffe is dressed in a track suit," or "This is the first book musical in more than ten years." He celebrates alumni homecomings, such as Charles S. "Roc" Dutton ('83) and Kimberly Scott ('87) in *Death of a Salesman*, belated Rep debuts (Edward Albee's *A Delicate Balance*), and the return of treasured collaborators, like Robert Woodruff and Bill Camp. He is at his most eloquent—a very high bar for those who know his way with words—when introducing repertory classics such as *Hamlet* or *The Master Builder*.

By his third welcome, Bundy was inviting audience members to tell him how they felt about what they'd seen. "The liveliness and variety of responses to our productions is one of the most gratifying parts of my life in the theatre. You can reach me at james.bundy@yale.edu. I hope you will." Bundy admits he has to dial back the urge to be combative with particularly caustic or personal comments, but he sincerely enjoys the interchange. "It's easy for theaters to see their audiences as either right or wrong. I'm concerned for that person who might feel for some reason that they don't have a place to go with their experience. I want to signal that I do care about their experiences." Bundy's surefire method for meaningful exchange is to get the mystified or disgruntled patron to simply describe what they

THE PROGRAM

Despite the relentless forward thrust of civilization, the architectural, visual, tactile, and textual traces that the theater leaves behind haven't changed all that much over the centuries. One category of ephemera is the program. A Broadway playbill has had a standardized format for nearly a century; a YRT program can, in terms of size, number of pages, and variety of information, differ from season to season and from artistic regime to artistic regime. Because of the rotating rep system, Brustein-era programs often documented three and four productions simultaneously. Ditto Winterfest programs under Richards. Wojewodski's commitment to intellectual breadth led to an expansion of the dramaturgy pages; where some saw plenitude, others saw superfluity. You can't please everyone.

Today, given that every program will contain a welcome from Bundy, donor lists, author and actor biographies, in-kind ads from local businesses, paid ads from Long Wharf and Hartford Stage and Yale art galleries, a four-page dramaturgical apparatus, notices for upcoming YSD and Yale Cabaret productions and No Boundaries events, it's not surprising how many hands are involved in its creation.

Director of Communications Steven Padla oversees program content. Graphic designer Maggie Elliott oversees the visual layout and sets a season production schedule at the beginning of August. The total page count, always a multiple of four, depends on the number of artist biographies; a Shakespeare or a musical will, without fail, require more personnel than a Binger premiere.

The management and artistic offices collaborate on billing. Actors' Equity has strict rules that management makes sure are followed. Bio requests are sent out via stage management very soon after the full company has been announced. Hard copies of bios in layout are approved and collected about two weeks before press. Literary manager Amy Boratko and the production dramaturg discuss with the director and playwright how to designate time, location, intermission (or not), character names, their order, and so on.

Boratko, the editor of the dramaturgy pages, convenes a brainstorming session at least six weeks before copy is due. This session is generated by the production dramaturg with layout and conceptual assists from Elliott, resident dramaturg Sheehy, and on a new play, input from the director and playwright. Donor recognition, production sponsorship details, and paid advertising space are the purview of director of development and alumni affairs Deborah S. Berman and the managing director, who double-checks that nothing is amiss from a legal or labor stand-

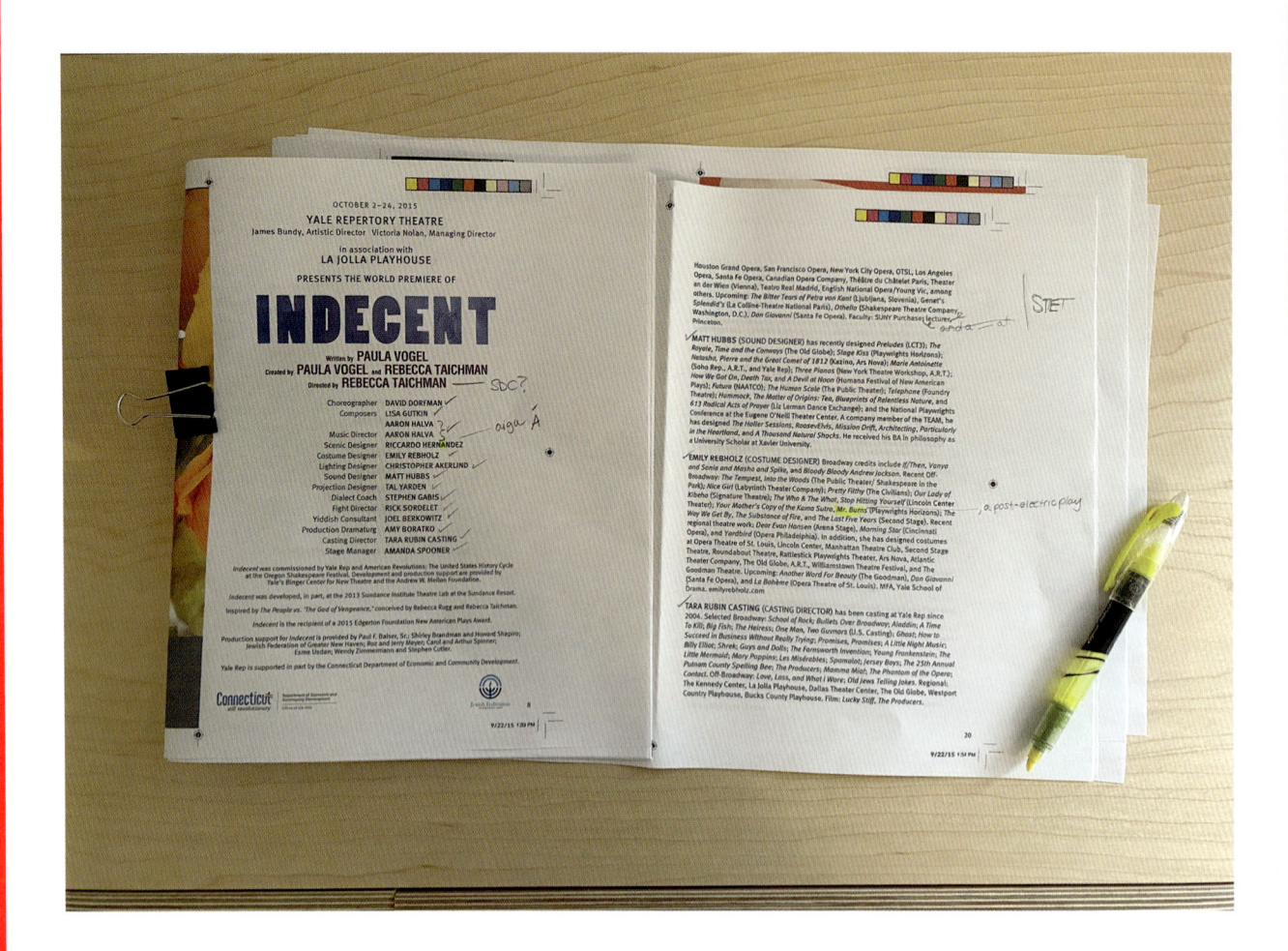

The Yale Rep program in progress for *Indecent* (2015)
COURTESY OF YALE REPERTORY THEATRE / MARGUERITE ELLIOTT

point. Sheehy and Boratko do copy-edit sweeps, and the package file is sent off to GHP Media one week before first preview. A final draft is then circulated to stage management, the production dramaturg and Sheehy, the business office, the box office, the development department, and the production office for changes and approvals three days before print date.

A clean, print-ready PDF is sent to the final set of eyes and edits—Bundy's—and the program is delivered on the morning of first preview. GHP does an average of five thousand books for its print run. Email has somewhat streamlined the once-laborious collaboration, wasting less paper and requiring fewer red pens. Today the program is duplicated on the Yale Rep website; what used to be a linked PDF download is presently loaded to a site called *Issuu*, which displays everything, ads and all, for interested visitors. True information junkies can access—and supplement—past Yale Rep, drama school, and Cabaret programs at www.ensemble @yale.com, an interactive database that relies on crowd-sourced transcription. ◆

saw. "I remember a patron's response to *The Evildoers*. 'There's water pouring down this gorgeous glass ceiling. What does that mean?' My answer is 'What do you think it means?' and a dialogue began."

Direct dialogue with the present, in the manner of *Watergate Classics*, has not been routine at Yale Rep. Playwrights embed political content in their works, directors and designers embellish their work with suggestive visuals, and dramaturgs infer mightily in their program pages, but from-the-headlines calls to action at Yale have generally been the province of solo performers and No Boundaries acts. A notable exception was *In the Continuum*, a two-character play that, to quote the Yale Rep newsletter, was "shaking loose the layers of silence around an international crisis."

The fight against AIDS made important strides beginning with the implementation of combination antiretroviral therapy in 1996. Seven years later, statistics showed that AIDS had become the leading cause of death around the globe for Black women between the ages of twenty-five and thirty-four. Moreover, Black women accounted for the highest rate of new infections in both Africa and the United States. Men were the vectors, women their victims.

Early in 2004, two students in the NYU graduate acting program, Danai Gurira and Nikkole Salter, were encouraged by a teacher to combine monologues each had been independently writing about Black, HIV-positive women. They began researching and developing characters together. Eventually Robert O'Hara joined them in the capacity of dramaturg/director. The result, *In the Continuum*, starring the two women, was an instant sensation at Primary Stages in New York, transferred for an open off-Broadway run, and then began an international tour that included the Edinburgh Fringe Festival, Zimbabwe, and South Africa.

Gurira and Salter impersonate multiple characters in *In the Continuum*, but the most important are Abigail (Gurira), a successful newsreader for the state-run Zimbabwean Broadcasting Network who has a husband and child, and Nia (Salter), a Los Angeles teenager with a flair for poetry who is in love with a basketball player. On the same day, continents apart, both discover that they are pregnant *and* HIV-positive. In alternating monologues over a forty-eight-hour period, the women suffer social scorn and isolation in their search for advice and medical treatment. A play designed to counteract ignorance, *Continuum* transcends the potential stigma of political agitprop through its gallery of characters, unexpected humor, the bone-deep details of Nia and Abigail's existences, and finally, its refusal to show the audience the ultimate fates of the two women or to answer the terrible questions it raises.

Simple premises told with simple tools can lead to shattering results. The set

Actor-writers Nikkole Salter and Danai Gurira in *In the Continuum* (2007)
PHOTO © JAMES LEYNSE

for *Continuum* was an ocher-colored back wall with a doorway, two stools, and a battered trunk. The actors wore black leotards and slacks accessorized with a swatch of fabric—Abigail's brightly hued traditional pareu and Nia's oversized blue bandanna. Two purses, a nurse's cap, a pair of eyeglasses, and a headdress for the traditional healer constituted the rest of the entire physical production. Yale Rep had never before booked a touring show, but Bundy made an exception for *Continuum*: "I saw it in NYC. It was an irresistible and important work written and performed by two extraordinary Black women, and I thought (a) these are exactly the kind of artists whose work and visibility we must advance, and (b) what a great pair of role models for our students—actors who generated their own work."

Deployed by the *Will Power!* program, Gurira and Salter performed *In the Continuum* for as many as two thousand middle and high schoolers during their monthlong run. As a harbinger of the pitched identity politics that would challenge university life in the coming decade, the usually equable local critic, Christopher Arnott, a rare dissenter in regard to the power of *In the Continuum*, published an article titled "White Chocolate" in the *New Haven Register*. He slammed both Yale Rep and Hartford Stage for cynically presenting *In the Continuum* and *Fences* during February, which is Black History Month. Bundy, about to be reappointed for a second term as dean / artistic director, wasn't amused, and in a letter to the *Register*, he cited his previous four Yale Rep choices for February: the Olmec *King Lear*; the Kushner/Sendak children's opera *Brundibar*; the über-Caucasian *Psychic Life of Savages*; and a *Comedy of Errors* set in Morocco.

Yale Rep continued its association with Gurira, presenting *Eclipsed* in 2009, a play about five women trying to survive the end of the Second Liberian Civil War. Based, like *In the Continuum*, on interviews Gurira conducted in Africa, *Eclipsed* would move to Broadway seven years later and earn six Tony nominations, including Best Play and Best Leading Actress for alumna Lupita Nyong'o ('12). *Familiar*, a Yale Rep commission that premiered in 2015, examines the tensions of cultural assimilation with a lighter heart. Transplanted to Minnesota from Zimbabwe, Marvelous and Donald Chinyaramwira are holding a wedding for their daughter, Tendi, who is marrying a local white man. Aunt Anne arrives from Harare and throws a wrench into the plans by holding a traditional bride-price ceremony in which the brother of the groom has to barter for the bride.

Gurira said in a 2007 interview that part of the impetus for creating *In the Continuum* was her frustration at how little representation there was of the contemporary African woman on the global stage. Fifty-two years before her, during the nascent period of the Civil Rights Movement, another frustrated actress/writer wrote a scathingly hilarious play about the dearth of meaningful roles for Black actors.

"Show business, it's just a business. Colored folks ain't in no theatre" is the thesis under examination in Alice Childress's *Trouble in Mind*. Its heroine, Wiletta Mayer, is a middle-aged actress whose career stretches back to shows like "Brownskin Melody" and who has played every jewel—Crystal, Pearl, and Opal—a maid might be named by a white author. This time, Wiletta has a big part, playing the mother in "Chaos in Belleville," a lynching play with a mixed-race cast set in the contemporary South. She doesn't think much of the role, but she trusts Manners, the white director with whom she's worked before. Her radicalized son is played by a Method actor still young enough to believe in capital-T Theater. Unaccustomed to analyzing her roles, by act 3, Wiletta has parsed "Chaos in Belleville" and decided that no mother would willingly send her child off to be lynched. Awakening gradually to her complicity in her own marginalization, Wiletta explodes at last into a corus-

Don Guillory, E. Faye Butler, and Natalia Paine in Alice Childress's *Trouble in Mind* (2007)
PHOTO © JOAN MARCUS

cating monologue that catalogs her history of "justifyin'" her demeaning character parts. She accuses Manners of being a prejudiced man and calls for rewrites. Before the shocked cast is dismissed for the day, Manners admits the play is a lie. "But it's one of the finest lies you'll come across for a damned long time!" At the curtain, whether the show will go on is, for once, in serious doubt.

The original reviews for *Trouble in Mind* were excellent; a Broadway transfer was in the offing, but in a dismal case of life imitating art, commercial producers got cold feet and insisted that Childress write a happier ending. She never could satisfy both them and herself, and *Trouble in Mind* largely disappeared. A rare revival at Actor's Express in Atlanta in 2003 led to a revival in the spring of 2007 at Baltimore's Center Stage, directed by Irene Lewis ('66) with dramaturgy by Sheehy, on loan from Yale, who spent a lot of time at the Schomburg Research Center for Black Culture examining the multiple drafts. "Not even her estate had

James Bundy (2002–)

a definitive copy," says Sheehy, who pitched the play to Bundy, who then invited Lewis to bring the show to Yale.

With new designers and several new cast members, *Trouble in Mind* opened in New Haven that fall to unanimous acclaim, with audiences and critics both delighting in the provocative swings in tone. Hilarious "Chaos in Belleville" scenes played to the hilt—baying bloodhounds, stick whittling, a spiritual by kerchiefed servants, a white girl's tearful pleas for tolerance, a thousand "Lawd have mercys!"—interrupted a hypnotic recollection of an actual lynching by an old character actor in the company. Underneath it all was the depressing realization that little had changed for Black actors in the intervening half century. E. Faye Butler, a dazzling Wiletta, thought *Trouble in Mind* "couldn't be updated even if it wanted to be." Playing her antagonist, Manners, Kevin O'Rourke had the courage to commit fully to the character's perpetual microaggressions. *Trouble in Mind* was the kind of experience that makes one wonder how many other forgotten American plays await rediscovery.

Tragedy struck the Rep the day after *Trouble in Mind* closed. Yale was the second leg of a *Tartuffe* coproduction with the McCarter Theatre at Princeton. A parked trailer containing set materials was being unloaded at the corner of York and Chapel Streets in the middle of the night on November 18. Thirty-two sheets of $4' \times 8'$ particle board shifted inside and pinned second-year technical and design production student Pierre-André Salim against the opposite wall. Salim, twenty-six, from Jakarta, Indonesia, was killed in the impact.

Bundy delayed *Tartuffe* for a week, in part to give the community time to come together in support of Pierre's family, friends, and colleagues. At a memorial service held for Salim on November 20, Thomas Delgado ('09), speaking for his technical design cohort, said, "This morning, as we began our first class without Pierre, I knew in my heart and soul that we are still ten. We are still ten because each of us will take Pierre with us as we continue forward with our lives."

Resident stage manager Mountcastle, assigned to *Tartuffe*, feels that Salim's death changed the school and the Rep. The university immediately mandated that there would be no more overnight load-ins and load-outs. "James and Vicki and Ben [Sammler] all rose to the occasion," says Mountcastle. The Occupational Safety and Health Administration (OSHA) report, released the following month, noted that the truck, which had been loaded by a private shipping company, could have been loaded differently to avoid the tip-over. A full scholarship was created in Salim's name, with priority for students from Southeast Asia, and area OSHA director Robert Kowalski continues to lecture on safety and standards every April.

With rare exceptions (*Lear, Moon Over Miami*), Yale Rep subscribers accept

Stephen Barker Turner and Matt McGrath in the world premiere of David Adjmi's *The Evildoers* (2008)
PHOTO © JOAN MARCUS

violence, nudity, and bad language far more readily than nonlinear dramaturgy. The full-frontal male and female nudity and blood spatters in Mark Lamos's 2007 production of *Lulu* managed to shock the public *and* the media. The *New York Times* and the *New Haven Register* refused to run ads using the poster art, a photograph of a nude female torso with an apple covering the pubic area. Perhaps this kerfuffle was on everyone's mind when David Adjmi's *The Evildoers* made its premiere the following season with the advisory "For mature audiences."

Adjmi's title refers to George W. Bush's vow on September 16, 2001: "We will rid the world of evildoers." The play has a four-character, two-couple structure akin to *Who's Afraid of Virginia Woolf?*, *Lips Together, Teeth Apart*, and *Dinner with Friends*. Adjmi's highly strung quartet, the wealthy, white, and hyperarticulate Martin and Judy and Carol and Jerry, sit astride an amoral high horse in American culture. What begins as a bitchy, drunken argument about authenticity in a posh restaurant devolves over the course of three breakneck, often hilarious acts into an Armageddon. Riccardo Hernández's ('92) set, a luxury New York apartment with an overwaxed floor and sloping, reflective black walls, splits down the middle—"The seams of the play are starting to pull" reads a stage direction— and sheets of rain pour down the glossy walls. By the end of the second act, Martin has bitten off Carol's tongue and spit it onto the stage. He slices off his own finger, and then later slits his throat, all in full, sanguineous view of the audience. At the curtain, all that remains of civilization is a plate of cheese and quince paste.

The Greek root for "theater," *teatron*, means "a place for seeing." Greek in scale, Adjmi's vision of chaos and violence was more challenging for audiences to see and process when located within recognizable souls and contemporary walls. "At the first preview the play broke," says Adjmi. "Like a leg snapping. My heart sank.... I was shocked at how bad I felt. I must have wanted the audience to experience trauma. Through the run, there was vomiting. People were holding each other up, unable to walk, as they left the theater." That they stayed the course until the end speaks to the brilliant production that director Rebecca Taichman ('00) put together with Hernández, lighting designer Strawbridge ('83), costume designer Susan Hilferty ('80), and the spectacular cast of Johanna Day, Matt McGrath, Samantha Soule, and Stephen Barker Turner. Today, Adjmi half regrets the act of violence he inflicted on the audience. "James was getting hate mail, and I said, 'I'm so sorry,' and he smiled and said, "I'm just going to get a bigger in-box."

In terms of historic moments for Yale Rep, equal perhaps to the day in 1982 that August Wilson received a telegram from the Eugene O'Neill Theater Center saying that *Ma Rainey's Black Bottom* had been accepted to the summer conference, is the day in May 2008 when Dean Bundy and Associate Artistic Director Kiger received word that the Robina Foundation had awarded the Rep a three-year grant for $2.85 million in support of the development of new works.

Since its beginnings, Yale Rep had intermittently received grants for new work from the National Endowment for the Arts, the Mellon Foundation, CBS, the Ford Foundation, and other outside sources. Drawing on her experience with South Coast Rep and its Pacific Playwrights Festival, Kiger had begun commissioning works after her arrival in 2005, but until Robina, Yale did not have a complete developmental pipeline for the creation of new plays and musicals that went from idea to commission to drafts to rewrites to readings to workshops to premiere productions.

In 2007, the then-new Robina Foundation, a Minnesota-based private grant-making foundation created by businessman, theater producer, philanthropist, and 1938 Yale College graduate James H. Binger, selected four leading institutions and invited them to "positively impact critical social issues by encouraging innovation and financially supporting transformative projects." The four were Abbott Northwestern Hospital in Minneapolis, the Council on Foreign Relations in New York, University of Minnesota Law School, and Yale University. Bundy and Kiger started brainstorming. Advocating for his alma mater in New York was Rocco Landesman ('72, DFA '76), who had been running Jujamcyn Theaters, at James Binger's express invitation, since 1987.

Kiger recalls the thinking behind Yale Rep's pitch: "We made a case for how research and development is conducted in the arts, as opposed to the sciences. How could we make a home for writers and further the scope of American drama? We were at the heart of one of the greatest universities in the world, with an already established program that trained the future leaders of the American theater. The Robina opportunity could leverage our proven competency in producing new work into a leadership model for the field. We decided we'd set out to create a program to make Yale Rep a significant home and launching pad for playwrights. The better the quality of the work at [Yale Rep], the better the conservatory training at the YSD. We would be able to grow exponentially and, over the three-year granting cycle, learn how to respond, with growing flexibility, to the needs of the writers and their gestating projects."

Once begun, the Yale New Play Program wasted no time, going from two to eight commissions in its first year alone. Funds went not only to playwrights but also to directors, composers, performers, and ensembles at any stage in their career, and with a wide aesthetic range. "What do you *need* to create this work?" Kiger would ask the artists. Each process is tailored to their response. "We can offer you quiet time in residence. You can write, you can have dramaturgical meetings, do research, meet experts, see our work, meet students, or just lay low." Unstructured time in residence may or may not lead to small, private "table reads" with Kiger and the artistic staff. Later, there might be large-scale, multiday workshops in New York—or elsewhere—with professional actors and directors. Binger funding also underwrites the production costs of commissions and other new plays at the Rep. The Binger Center's production enhancement fund provides financial support for subsequent productions—sometimes the second or third production of the same play—at other theaters. In other instances, the enhancement fund is used to help other theaters defray the costs of premiering a play that Yale Rep commissioned but elected not to produce.

The initial grant expired in its fourth year, after Yale Rep had supported more than two dozen commissioned artists. Robina paused to assess outcomes but nevertheless awarded Yale Rep $950,000 in July 2010 as bridge funding to keep the Yale New Play Program going for another two years. Money attracts money: eight days after the Robina announcement, the theater program of the Andrew W. Mellon Foundation gave a gift of $1 million to support the activities of the Yale Center for New Theatre to take artistic risks for the following five years.

The Robina Foundation then invited Yale Rep to apply for an endowment to make the program permanent. In April 2012, Bundy and Nolan announced the receipt of a staggering, transformational gift of $18 million to fund the newly renamed Binger Center for New Theatre in perpetuity, the largest single philanthropic gift to support playwriting in the history of American theater.

Despite its moniker, the Binger Center is not a building. Bundy credits Kiger as being 99 percent in charge of all Binger decision-making, and Nolan jokes that the Binger Center is Kiger's desk. At any point there are twenty commissioned projects in play, from an unwritten kernel of an idea to a work with two or more years of development behind it. "James and I have programmed eclectic seasons at Yale," says Kiger. "We have an abiding interest in theatricality. We are interested in a strong sense of play and metaphor. Because we commit to offering a variety of theatrical experiences for the students in training, we have to be okay with risk, with scale, and with challenges. Our taste is not particularly commercial. Or wildly avant-garde. We're producing American *drama* in a wide breadth of forms."

Commissioning fees are in the top decile in the nation for nonprofit organizations, made in the hopes of moving the compensation needle forward at other theaters. A permanent endowment means that the Binger Center will continue to evolve and ideas can be leveraged into practices. From its inception through the 2016–2017 season, Robina funds and the Binger endowment underwrote the development processes and premiere productions of twenty new works, from the intimate to the epic, at Yale Rep. In recent years, Binger-supported plays have comprised three-fifths of the entire season, and a large percentage of them receive second and third productions across the country.

Bundy's ego is secure enough for him to declare, "I think Yale Rep should be producing a lot of things that I can't remotely do or touch myself." Stylistic ecumenism of this sort isn't common in the nonprofit theater universe, but in addition to his personal respect and admiration for the work of Robert Woodruff, he knows it's critical for the drama students to be exposed to different aesthetics and working methods. Over a thirty-five-year span, Woodruff has directed everything from early Sam Shepard premieres to classics from Webster to Racine, making a name for himself as an artist unafraid of putting his visions on the stage without regard for propriety or convention. In other words, theaters hiring Woodruff can expect plenty of stage blood, nudity, simulated sex, walkouts, and hate mail.

Woodruff had in many ways been the ideal successor to Brustein at the director-centered A.R.T., but after five seasons in Cambridge, his contract wasn't renewed. Subscription numbers had dropped, and to deal with annual budget gaps, the theater had to draw a larger percentage from its endowment income. Yale faculty members Diamond and Chambers had convinced Bundy to hire Woodruff, known to be equally inspiring in the classroom, to come to Yale to teach and direct a show at the Rep. Woodruff and protean actor Bill Camp were commissioned to adapt Dostoevsky's *Notes from the Underground*. It opened in March 2009, the first Robina-supported work of the Yale New Play Program out of the gate.

In *Notes from the Underground*, the Underground Man, a civil servant who has withdrawn from a corrupt society, wages daily war on everyone and everything in a furious, tortured rant. Like the Ancient Mariner or Beckett's Krapp in *Krapp's Last Tape*, he relives the story of what drove him underground. His bottomless self-loathing has stood in the way of his making any human bonds.

How do you adapt what is essentially a monologue for the stage? Woodruff is revered by his design teams. Susan Hilferty ('80), who has done fifteen shows with him, has said, "Working with Woodruff, I've described, is walking on a razor blade. It's dangerous work in that you really could fail and hurt yourself, but when it works, there's something so light and perfect and for which there are no words, with always the thought, 'Did we do all we could do as a team?'"

Woodruff and Camp constructed their adaptation for the Rep space. The visual and aural team was David Zinn (sets), Moria Sine Clinton (costumes), Mark Barton (lighting), Michaël Attias (composer and sound designer), and Peter Nigrini (projections). The Underground Man's lair is a begrimed, decaying office space littered with detritus. Snow falls through missing ceiling tiles. Stage left is a table with the Man's notes. Stationed on either side of the stage were actor-musicians Merrit Janson and Attias, who were also summoned by the text to play the streetwalker, Liza, and the manservant, Apollon. Upstage of the main playing area was a raised, glassed-in bedroom with a door. Action there was shot on video and projected onto screens, as were select thoughts and locations in the Man's unraveling mind.

For Woodruff, "it was so much a music theater piece. And Bill's relationship with the performance and the text with the music. And Michael was always composing and working at the same time. And Merrit was also playing. So, it was like a really great jazz trio, in the end. I thought it was really alive, it felt alive in performance." Alive? Definitely. Life affirming? No. More like a brutal, misogynistic hallucination for the senses, but a thrilling night at the theater, with a towering, self-lacerating performance by Camp, who had first appeared at Yale Rep in 1990 as a freshly minted Troilus from Juilliard.

A second Yale Rep commission for Camp and Woodruff, an adaptation of Rainer Werner Fassbinder's 1978 film *In a Year with 13 Moons*, opened two seasons later. Fassbinder had made *13 Moons* as an existential exploration of the trauma he felt on account of the real-life suicide of his lover, but this being Fassbinder, the movie is host to a dizzy array of influences and concerns: Douglas Sirk melodramas, German history post–World War II, Schopenhauer, European immigration, capitalism, genocide, and gender dysphoria. No one coming to *Notes* or *13 Moons* could fail to apprehend that they were witnessing the powerful, if grim, vision of a theatrical auteur along the lines of Serban and Wajda thirty years before.

Unless written by Brecht and Weill, or Weinstein and Bolcom, musicals weren't

Merritt Janson and Bill Camp in Camp and Woodruff's adaptation of Dostoyevsky's *Notes from Underground* (2009)
PHOTO © JOAN MARCUS

James Bundy (2002–)

historically worth analyzing, crafting, or performing at Yale, except at the Cabaret or as a rare directing thesis. From the beginning, however, Kiger and Bundy have extended Yale Rep commissions to composers, lyricists, and librettists, aware that musicals take more time to develop, bust the budget at every turn, and rarely, if ever, succeed artistically *and* commercially at the same time. In 2009, looking to find and invest in emerging talents rather than individual musicals, Bundy and music school dean Robert Blocker founded the Yale Institute for Music Theater (YIMT), an autonomous developmental laboratory, and then hired Mark Brokaw ('86) and Beth Morrison ('05) to run it.

Brokaw recalls setting up the YIMT with a definite parameter. "The collaborative teams that applied had to be either in school or within five years of getting out of undergraduate or graduate school. The Institute experience would help them make the transition from formal study to the professional world, give them confidence and a calling card." Teams applied with a complete first draft, including at least five to seven songs, of an unproduced piece. In the two-week lab, which culminated in open-rehearsal readings, Brokaw would watch team after team—two or three each summer—enthusiastically rewrite their entire shows, sometimes twice. Because of the recession, the School of Music withdrew its commitment to the Institute in 2012, so YIMT moved under the fiscal umbrella of the Binger Center for New Theater. Continued downward pressure on the YSD / Yale Rep budget led to the painful decision to make the 2017 season its last.

After seeing a presentation of Maggie-Kate Coleman and Anna K. Jacobs's musical in vitro, *Pop!*, at the conclusion of the first summer lab, Bundy scheduled it, with Brokaw directing in the upcoming season. The most far-fetched idea can be musicalized, from a pajama-factory strike to the lives and loves of the men on the ten- and twenty-dollar bills. No reason to think that a musical couldn't be made out of the group reaction to the assassination attempt on Andy Warhol at his famous Factory on June 3, 1968. Through ceaseless self-promotion, Warhol and his menagerie of in-house "superstars" had captured a segment of the cultural imagination in their day, much as Byron and the other Romantic poets and the Bloomsbury Group had before them in England, and the way the Kardashians, in a ceaseless downward publicity spiral (made possible by Warhol), saturate social media today.

Coleman and Jacobs structured their material as a whodunnit. History shows that radical feminist Valerie Solanas shot Warhol in the torso and left him for dead because he passed on producing her play. Defying the facts, *Pop!* posits two other suspects, poor little rich girl Edie Sedgwick, who wants to make real movies, and the intellectual Viva, whose theoretical postures vex Andy. At the end, in a move reminiscent of *Murder on the Orient Express* and Sondheim's *Assassins*, the entire cast shoots Andy because they've somehow learned, contrary to his sovereign philosophy of Nothing, to want to be Something.

Pop! was a "doughnut-hole" musical, one in which the central character has no objective or action to play. Writing teams must work extra hard to arm and embellish the foils and antagonists to fill this hole in the middle, in this case, the unreadable Andy Warhol. *Pop!* gives Viva, Edie, and Valerie guns and motives, but their motives are insubstantial. Everyone wants to get inside the Factory to be with the cool kids, but no character is pleasant enough or—riskiest of all in a musical—worth rooting for.

That said, *Pop!* had its giddily entertaining sections, especially the excerpts of Solanas's play performed as an operetta, and a gunfight at the Cedar Tavern with abstract expressionists Pollock, Kline, and Motherwell. Coleman's lyrics were clever; Jacobs's melodies, referencing period pop and Broadway, were better suited

Randy Harrison and Cristen Paige as Andy Warhol and Edie Sedgwick in Coleman and Jacobs's musical *Pop!* (2009)
PHOTO © JOAN MARCUS

James Bundy (2002–)   269

for comic turns and choral numbers than the inevitable confessional solos. Among Brokaw's terrific cast of seven, the standouts were Leslie Kritzer's demanding, demented Solanas and Randy Harrison's cunningly deadpan Warhol. *Pop!* was so fleet of foot that one might have suspected Yale Rep had been producing musicals for years. The Binger Center production enhancement fund supported two future productions of *Pop!*

In 2013, Bundy and Kiger asked Jackson Gay whether she might like to direct a Shakespeare the following season. She pitched them a couple of ideas and then talked to Rolin Jones, who had been making a name for himself in episodic television. Jones shared with Gay his "stupid idea for *Much Ado about Nothing*." They successfully pitched it—*Much Ado* meets the Beatles—for Bundy and Kiger. "We had no script. They threw money, trusted us, and we were on in a year. It was a giant leap of faith," remembers Jones.

Benedick, Claudio, Balthasar, and Don Pedro, returning from battle in Shakespeare, become a pop band, the Quartos, just back from a sybaritic world tour. Beatrice becomes Bea, a Mary Quant–type fashion designer, and her cousin Hero is Higgy, a pill-popping model and heiress to the Messina fortune. The eventual title, *These Paper Bullets! A Modish Rip-off of William Shakespeare's Much Ado about Nothing*, refers to a question of Benedick's in the original: "Shall quips and sentences and these paper bullets of the brain awe a man from the career of his humour?"

Shakespeare has long been the source of hit musicals. Jones had a hitmaker in mind for the songs: Billie Joe Armstrong, front man of the Oakland-based band Green Day. Getting Armstrong to say yes was almost too easy, says Jones. "Two days later, I had three songs before I wrote a single word." Armstrong wrote the Quartos a clutch of catchy tunes in early prepsychedelic Beatles mode, with titles like "Give It All to You" and "Keeps Me Satisfied." "It was a massive sound show," recalls Gay, "mixing, mics on everybody, onstage instruments and recording."

Technical demands forced the cancellation of the first preview. Dramaturg Sheehy vividly remembers tech: "There was the meeting in which we decided rather than have the church for the wedding constituted by set pieces that the actors pushed into place, that the inside of St. Martin in the Fields could be projected. That might have been the same night when, struggling with the set change into the penthouse apartment, [stage carpenter] Janet [Cunningham] suggested that the railings, which were giving her enormous headaches, be projected instead of 'real.' [Projections designer] Nick Hussong ('13) looked up with a 'why not?' look on his face and away we went."

As with the sound designer, the ubiquity of projection designers on theater mastheads is an outcome of technical advances generated in the arena of rock concerts. Scene titles like "This Is My Sister. Celebrate Her with Strings" in *The Glass Menagerie* create mood; in Brecht's *Mother Courage and Her Children*, they designate location shifts and the passage of time, and they alert the audience to how to process the scene to follow. Today, on the one hand, scenic projections in the commercial arena can be cynically perceived as a way to reduce set budgets; on the other hand, if a playwright wants to change locations fifteen times, why deny them the opportunity to do so with projections instead of flats and furniture? The trick is not to overuse them.

Wendall Harrington, head of the projection concentration in the Yale design program, a pioneer in the field and self-described as old school, worries that young designers are too often asked to be programmers and that a "bigger is better mindset" threatens the ability of the stage to do what it does best. "Story. It's all we have.

Jeanine Serralles, Ariana Venturi, and Keira Naughton in *These Paper Bullets!*, Rolin Jones and Billie Joe Armstrong's musical riff on Shakespeare's *Much Ado about Nothing* (2014)
PHOTO © JOAN MARCUS

James Bundy (2002–)

It's what we sell. Story is our business. A six-foot actor cannot compete with a fifty-foot LED screen."

Jones's work, understandably—or inevitably—stinted the serious or melancholic aspects of *Much Ado* in favor of dotty extensions. If Shakespeare's seething Claudio says, "I wish him joy of her," Jones adds, "Love's a sack of dicks. Shove off." In such a mash-up, how can Hero's false death and entombment be anything besides Higgy vomiting in a locked bathroom until Claude spirits her out with the serenade "Regretfully Yours"?

Both *Pop!* and *Paper Bullets!* featured youth on a tear; a just-say-yes approach to acid; cameo appearances from the likes of Walter Cronkite, Clement Greenberg, Dionne Warwick, and Queen Elizabeth II; lunatic visuals; and gifted casts. *Bullets* was particularly blessed with its miniskirted women: Bea (Jeanine Serralles ['02]), Higgy (Ariana Venturi ['14]), and the hilariously potted Ursie (Keira Naughton). Because the Beatles and their sound are evergreen and because Jones could lean as he liked on Shakespeare, *Paper Bullets!* was closer to achieving its aims than was *Pop!*, although Jones, something of an Eeyore about his work, says today, "There's nothing rock-and-roll about a two-and-a-half-hour show. Like everything on that lovable dented paint can of a show . . . , I blame the playwright." *Paper Bullets!* went on to subsequent productions at the Atlantic Theatre Company in New York and the Geffen Playhouse in Los Angeles.

The 2011–2012 season featured two Binger-supported premieres that, under the roomy umbrella of realism, were similar in method, divergent in meaning, without intermission, and equivalently unsettling. Like *The Evildoers* two years before, Amy Herzog's *Belleville* and Will Eno's *The Realistic Joneses* feature two married heterosexual couples in crisis, Herzog's closer to Albee and Eno's spinning in cryptic hyperdrive toward Ionesco or Pinter.

Awful marriages make good plays, but domestic realism has maintained a poor standing at YSD / Yale Rep ever since Brustein's contempt for a box-set modality: a couch facing downstage, flanked by armchairs. A window and/or fireplace on the rear wall. A stage left exit to the hallway or outdoors. A stage right exit to the bedroom or kitchen. An imaginary television set placed in the laps of third-row ticketholders. Working lamps. Class-signaling accessories on the walls, mantels, and coffee and end tables. Fast-acting truth serum—alcohol or pot—ready at hand.

Minus the marijuana, that's an Ibsen parlor, a Chekhov drawing room, an August Wilson dining room, an O'Neill den, an Albee study. Then why such scorn for the form? It has to do with the magnitude of the problems under examination and the expressivity and intellectual heft of the playwright. Hedda and Lovborg might be on the verge of reigniting their romance, but more important to Ibsen

Gilbert Owuor and Maria Dizzia in the world premiere of Amy Herzog's *Belleville* (2011)
PHOTO © JOAN MARCUS

than their backstory is his gun pointed at the psychopathology of the nineteenth-century bourgeois mind-set. Lopakhin *doesn't* propose to Varya—devastating for the audience, yes, but Chekhov is always dramatizing how Time erodes the individual. Albee invites existential dread into his box sets. Wilson fills his rooms with poetic symphonies for the overlooked.

Grade B (or lower) domestic realism answers the once-popular *Ladies' Home Journal* column question "Can this marriage be saved?" with a yes, no, or maybe. *Belleville* takes place in a realistically detailed apartment in working-class Paris (with plenty of pot), and much of *The Realistic Joneses* is set on a back patio in a semirural area with trees and hoot owls, but Herzog and Eno sidestep running the odds on their scripted marriages by asking bigger, better questions—Can one live with a lie? Do we need other people? What are other people for? Is life merely the process of waiting to die?—and then, as would Ibsen or Albee, not answering them.

Yale Rep commissioned Herzog upon her drama school graduation in 2007;

James Bundy (2002–)   273

she remains grateful that Kiger kept the faith through the four years and three completely different drafts it took to get *Belleville* into rehearsal. In the play, Zack and Abby have moved to Paris, the dream destination for escapist Americans since Henry James. Zack, a pediatric AIDS researcher, has more purpose than Abby, who is rebooting herself as a yoga teacher in their hip, polyglot Belleville neighborhood. Rounding out the quartet are Alioune and Amina, their French-Senegalese landlords. Yoga and Doctors Without Borders are deceptive telegraph signals for who this couple really is. Why has Abby gone off her anxiety meds? How can a doctor be such a stoner? Why is the rent four months overdue? Why is there so much pressure to be happy? Why can't Abby put down her cell phone? Why is there only a butcher knife with which to cut a baguette? Why is this play getting darker and more menacing by the minute, like a Strindberg rewrite of *Barefoot in the Park*?

Herzog's Americans are approaching Christmas on a frozen lake that's begun to thaw; the cracking ice is racing to meet and take them under, but in the end, only Zack succumbs. As originally written, Zack, smoking a joint by the window, tips over the ledge and falls to his death. Julia C. Lee's ('12) set was designed for that specific capability. They tried it. Not only did Herzog, director Anne Kauffman, and dramaturg Amy Boratko find that an insufficiently passive demise for Zack, but the audience could hear a giggleworthy thud as the actor met the backstage safety cushion. They kept changing it. The butcher knife, previously used to remove a portion of Abby's toenail, was too aggressive for Zack to use onstage. It was important to Herzog that the audience intuit that Abby would be able to pick up the pieces of her life after Zack's death, but sending her into the bathroom—the site of an earlier suicide attempt—would convey the opposite message. The team finally settled on sending Abby into the bedroom on her cell phone, with Zack entering from the kitchen with the knife. He pulls a chair into the bathroom and we hear him set it against the door. We hear the bathwater run for a bit, then Zack getting into the tub, and then after a moment, the knife drop.

Running water, windows that open, baguettes, a starter Christmas tree—the buttresses of domestic realism, but Herzog's compressed use of the form is so specific in its character details that you feel you've sat in on this marriage for years instead of two days. Her dialogue "realistically" zigzags, meanders, teases, forgives, and wounds as it hits the chords to Abby's and Zack's slightest shifts in mood. They don't know what they're doing, and we don't know where the play is going, but we want them to please, please, please work it out. Kauffman superbly paced the action and the silences, and Maria Dizzia and Greg Keller had such poignant chemistry as Abby and Zack that you would be happy to see them play *Barefoot in the Park*, *Who's Afraid of Virginia Woolf?*, and *As You Like It*.

Will Eno, who came to prominence with the monologue *Thom Pain: (based on nothing)* (2004) and a bizarre riff on Wilder's *Our Town* called *Middletown* (2010), said to Kiger at the beginning of his development process, "I would like to try to write a realistic play. I have set out to do it, and it eludes me." As with Herzog, it took several drafts for Eno to put his stamp on the form.

The Realistic Joneses begins with Bob and Jennifer Jones sitting up late on their porch, listening to the night. The animal they hear rattling their metal garbage cans turns out to be their new, younger neighbors, John and Pony Jones. The four Joneses get acquainted. Starting with the identical surname, things seem more ominous than they are (very Eno, whom Charles Isherwood dubbed "a Samuel Beckett for the Jon Stewart generation" in the *New York Times*). Pony spots a dead squirrel beneath a table. Jennifer transfers the carcass with a spatula into a plastic bag that John holds open. Unexpected but realistic.

Eno makes brilliant hay from a combination of low-context dialogue among Joneses who are getting to know one another and high-context dialogue among Joneses who have been together for years, that is, a scene between Jennifer and Bob speaking in the elliptical shorthand of an old married couple, followed by a hilariously tense, overexplicated scene between Jennifer and John in the aisle of a grocery store. The blunt honesty of Eno's off-kilter chitchat reaches toward a poetry of the hyperreal. As the play progresses, there is a slow-growing pissing match between the husbands, who are both getting experimental treatment for (the invented) Harriman Leavey syndrome. *The Realistic Joneses* ends where it began, with the two couples placidly watching the nighttime sky on Bob and Jennifer's patio. An owl hoots. Jennifer says to their neighbors, "I'm glad you guys are over there." Bob, in a rare upbeat mood, offers his wife mints he picked up at the restaurant where they all had just dined together on a coupon and then puts one in his mouth. END.

A seismic shift had happened, but what was it? Early on, Jennifer offers one clue on how to approach the play: "All these different levels of not knowing anything." Whether an audience completely "got" Eno's meditation on life and mortality, they knew they were experiencing the minimal—or the granular—becoming the maximal. *The Realistic Joneses* represents an apex of its form as well as a comment on its form. Eno quoted poet Wallace Stevens in the Yale Rep program: "The real is only the base. But, it is the base."

As with *Belleville*, *Joneses* benefited from a gifted young director, Sam Gold, and a first-rate ensemble able to inflect and convey Eno-speak: Pulitzer Prize–winning playwright and actor Tracy Letts as Bob, a philosophic denialist with a long fuse; Johanna Day, who had lost her tongue nightly as the hateful Carol in *The Evildoers* four seasons before, as Jennifer, the grounded soul of spousal patience; independent-movie queen Parker Posey as the opaquely wise Pony, never so funny as when trying to talk to God for the first time in years; and Glenn Fitzgerald as the nervy, needling John.

Belleville and *The Realistic Joneses* shared one final innovation. Herzog remembers a production meeting with Kauffman and the Yale Rep staff in which they were asked what they needed for *Belleville*. "And Annie and I, sort of joking, we're like, well, can you make your theater any smaller? Because . . . it's kind of an intimate play. And the Rep is so giant it just seems a little scary." Having forgotten they'd said that, they were surprised to learn at the next meeting that the production staff had come up with a solution: the Ming Wall (see box).

As American society enlarges the image of what a family looks like, so do its playwrights. With so many commissions out to so broad a spectrum of writers, the Binger Center would have to yield a certain number of AFPs. Two produced during Bundy's tenure stretched the parameters of the form. One of them, *Lydia* (2009), was not a Yale Rep commission but represented some overdue East Coast exposure for Octavio Solis, whose plays had been consistently produced on the West Coast for nearly twenty years. The other was *War*, a Yale Rep commission (the Binger Center supported its development and production) by Branden Jacobs-Jenkins, who would win a MacArthur genius grant two years after its 2014 premiere.

Although built on family secrets that will out, *Lydia* and *War* both elude the stigma of domestic realism through the efforts at speech by women trapped in their physical bodies. Solis's Cecilia Flores was in a car accident three days before her quinceañera, and for two years she has lain in a vegetative state in her family's living room in El Paso. The rest of the family members—two immigrant parents and two brothers at opposite ends of the machismo scale—remain frozen in grief or indulge in counterproductive coping mechanisms. The outer Ceci possesses no coherent language; the inner Ceci, however, speaks to the audience with surpassing eloquence and beauty of past events and her present desires. Things change when Rose Flores hires Lydia to care for her daughter. Lydia's ability to understand Ceci as well as accurately read the pain in the male characters is uncanny, perhaps supernatural or spectral, and never explained. The accumulated secrets kept and the self-blinding partial truths the family tell one another, including the story of

THE MING WALL

Until 2011, watching a performance from the back rows of the Yale Rep church space was a different experience from sitting in the fifth row. Images of telescopes, scuba masks, ear trumpets, and the far end of a football field spring to mind. To be blunt, they were terrible seats, especially for new plays of intimate size trying to connect with audiences across the visual and aural distance.

With great windfalls come fresh solutions. The establishment of the Binger Center for New Theatre in 2008 led, as hoped, to an increased number of commissioned plays, often of small and quiet dramaturgy. The question of how Yale Rep could best serve these plays *and* enhance audience engagement was a running artistic discussion until Amy Herzog's *Belleville*, a four-character play set in a Parisian apartment, became a test case for the Ming Wall, a structural addition to the theater so named because of the design input of design chair Ming Cho Lee. Acoustical and lighting considerations were handled by faculty members David Budries

Blueprint for the Ming Wall, created for *Belleville*
PHOTO © ERIC LIN

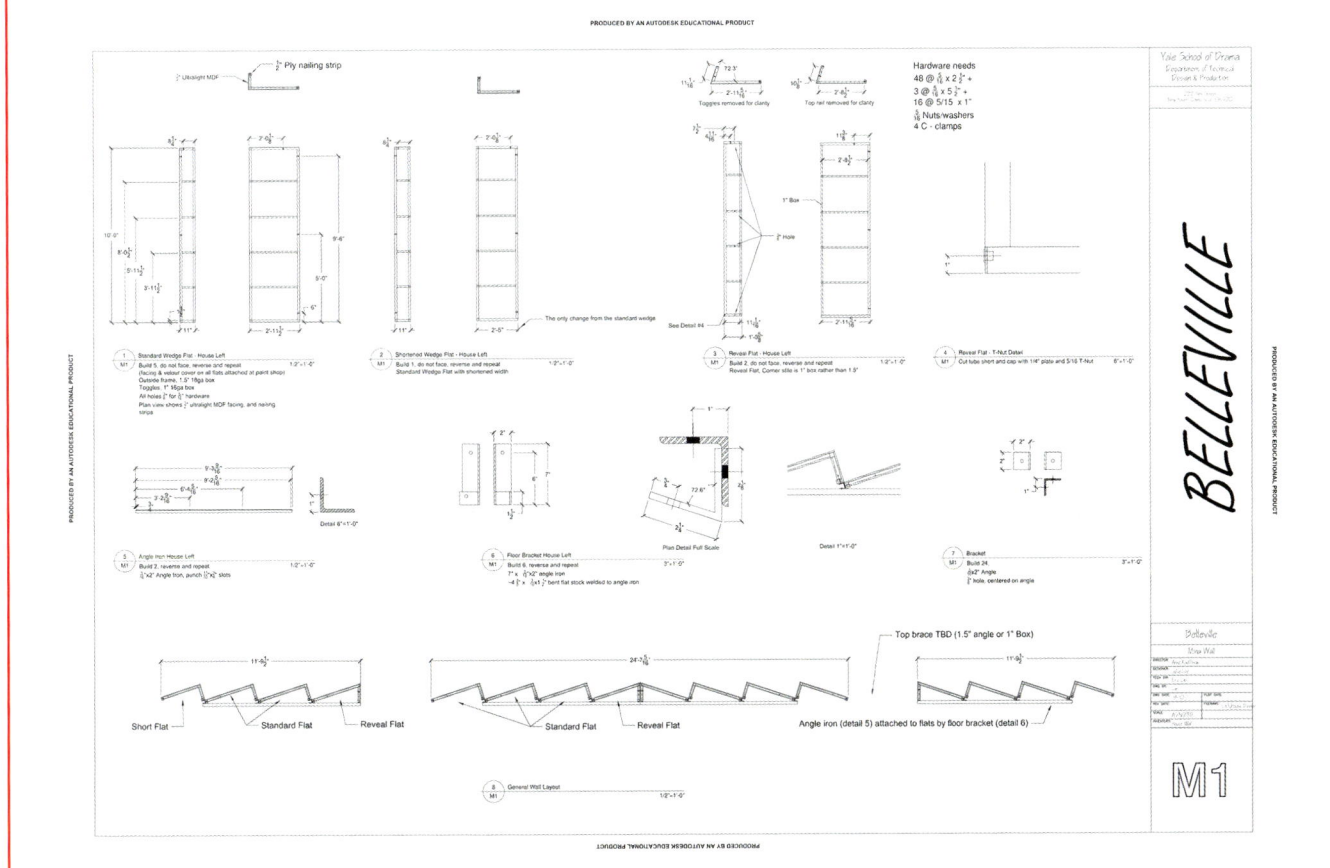

and Steven Strawbridge. Eric Lin ('12), then a student, today the Yale Rep projection supervisor, spearheaded the transition from blueprint to reality.

The Ming Wall is a set of sixteen nearly identical L-shaped panels made of square steel tube framing covered with medium-density fiberboard and wrapped in dark-blue velour to match the theater wall coverings. When assembled in an irregular pattern—to reduce the chance of echo from actor voices or the sound system—it simply blocks off the back rows of the theater. It stands ten feet tall and is in three sections—about twenty-four feet wide in the center and twelve feet wide on either side of the aisles.

The wall was a budgeted production element for *Belleville* as well as an experiment. "The result," recalls Vicki Nolan, "was wildly satisfying. There was a critical mass in the theatre at every performance; we had sold-out shows but were mostly able to accommodate patrons on other nights; and there was virtually no cost in terms of lost revenue. Not to mention the palpable upside of having a hit show that might be harder to access if patrons waited too long to buy."

No reason, then, not to keep the Ming Wall around as a permanent option. *The Realistic Joneses*, later that same season, required scenic projections; faculty member Wendall Harrington modified the initial design to create positions where projectors could be mounted behind the Wall and shot through it. When a season has been selected, Wall / no Wall decisions are made, as are the balcony / no balcony decisions for UT shows. The Wall can be moved forward or backward by a number of rows, enabling the Rep to expand seating inventory. When not pressed into service, the Wall is stored on the loading dock at 149 York Street. Its panels are numbered on the back for easier assembly and disassembly, a process that requires four people and four hours. ◆

Ceci's accident, must be revealed. The knowledge leads to violence, expulsion, and death.

What lends glory to an AFP are the details of the family under examination. The Floreses draw from the same well of love, hate, shame, guilt, regret, and loss that the Youngers or the Lomans do, but so specific are the details of this border family just getting by in the 1970s that *Lydia* approaches the universal. The younger son, Misha, wants to be a writer, but, in metaphors worthy of Tennessee Williams, the inner Ceci shines even brighter than her brother, with a recurring use of *loteria* cards she's invented for the people in her botched life. In the promotional video for *Lydia*, Solis says, "In the end, I wasn't writing about my family—

Onahoua Rodriguez as Ceci in Octavio Solis's *Lydia* (2009)
PHOTO © CAROL ROSEGG

I was writing about *your* family." Whoever his subject, New Haven had not seen this family before. *Lydia* had been commissioned and produced first by Denver Theater Center. Director Juliette Carrillo ('91) brought five of her original cast members to Yale Rep. Onahoua Rodriguez as Cecilia and Stephanie Beatriz as Lydia led an exceptional ensemble.

The notion of stasis hangs over Jacobs-Jenkins's *War*. Roberta is in a coma in a hospital bed. Her tightly wound son, Tate, feels stuck explaining himself to white people all day. Her daughter, Joanne, feels stuck in an awful dynamic with her brother. Her half nephew from Germany, Tobias, is stuck in Roberta's apartment waiting for word from his missing mother, Elfriede. We learn later that they've all been stuck (or struck) with the same genetic disposition to dementia. The biggest family secret in *War*, revealed early on, is that Roberta's father had a child with a German woman. Elfriede is a *Mischlingkinder*, a child born to white Germans and Black soldiers during the occupation of post–World War II Germany.

Trapped like Ceci in *Lydia*, Roberta is able to communicate in the space of her comatose mind with a group of six gorillas. Alpha, the leader, speaks gesturally, and his dialogue is projected onto a screen at the top of the stage. As Roberta gradually puts together the pieces of her prestroke life, she charms the gorillas. They would like her to stay among them, have a child with Alpha, and teach them how to retain memory.

Production dramaturg (and Yale Rep literary manager) Amy Boratko ('06) recalls the rehearsal evolution of the apes, who were doubling as Joanne, Tobias, Tate, and so on, as a process of subtraction. Montana Levi Blanco's ('15) initial costume ideas featured animalistic suggestions, but the need to shift instantly from human to ape and back again made bits of fur seem a silly trick. So the costume palette went more neutral, using darker colors instead of patterns. The screeching and grunting called for when Roberta first meets the apes got softer over time. "Through a series of workshops with choreographer David Neumann, the cast developed an animal language made of signs, gestures, and postures. Less was more."

Act 2 moves to Roberta's apartment, where the siblings are gathering up the Germans' belongings. Tate is given to persuasive rants to his white brother-in-law, Malcolm, about, for example, the terms "Black" and "African American" and the meaning of the Obama presidency. What finally silences Tate—breaks him open, actually—is a letter that Elfriede, who grew up *mischling* and parentless in a hostile country, has prepared in German about the importance of family, which Tobias translates to his half cousins.

Roberta, who has died alone in the hospital, is listening in the audience and enjoying the spectacle of unexpected family comity. In a final coup de théâtre, a sheet

Director Lileana Blain-Cruz and Tonya Pinkins rehearsing the world premiere of Branden Jacobs-Jenkins's *War* (2014)
PHOTO © JOAN MARCUS

of plate glass descends and separates the audience from the cast. The newly blended family is visiting the ape house at the zoo. They watch us. They see. They recognize. They laugh. It was a thrilling condemnation of white institutions (or even the American theater) using Black people for entertainment purposes.

Although it was not perfect in its first production, and some critics did fault it for didactic overreach, *War* is the rarest kind of AFP. Like a Shaw or Ibsen play, *War* bristles with contemporary arguments larger than the secrets, lies, and hurts of one family system. In German, English, and for lack of a better term, Simian, Jacobs-Jenkins wielded his scalpel to dissect received wisdom about race, privilege, causality, and human inheritance. Much credit was due to his close collaboration with recent Yale directing graduate Lileana Blain-Cruz ('12).

War took Jenkins four years to write, overwrite, and then madly rewrite in rehearsal and previews. Flexibility until the very last minute is a hallmark of the kind of support a playwright can expect from the Binger for their paper bullets of the brain. Ruhl, who has received two commissions from Yale Rep, maintains there is a slight disingenuity to many commissions from other theaters. "I think it takes a year or two years to write a play. If you get a commission for $7,000, you can't live on that for a year, so the commissioner is assuming that you're making your money another way. I think that Yale's Binger Center makes more of an effort to invest in the writer's life and in the time to produce the work."

For classic plays, Bundy tended to hire from a handful of house directors, three of whom, Diamond, Yionoulis, and Christopher Bayes, teach or taught on either the directing or the acting faculties. After saving *All's Well*, Rucker was invited back in 2008 to stage *Rough Crossing*, the Molnár/Stoppard shipboard valentine to show business, with chorines and the deliciously hammy leading pair of Reg Rogers ('93) and Susannah Schulman. Two seasons later, two years before his death, Rucker was given the tougher assignment of Williams's *A Streetcar Named Desire* with René Augesen ('96) as Blanche DuBois. The iconic movie version, which has led to audience overfamiliarity with the play, has made *Streetcar* rough going today for Blanches. Audiences laugh at her fragility, her poetic language, and her famous lines; she is too vulnerable perhaps to accept with a trusting heart. Augesen remembers, "There were sweet, tender moments taken lasciviously by the audience, who laughed at every single performance. I didn't know what to do. I tried everything. It was a very painful experience."

Diamond directed Strindberg's *Miss Julie* in a new English version by then-faculty member Richard Nelson in 2005, and Brecht's massive *Caucasian Chalk Circle* with Steven Skybell ('88) as Azdak and Shaunette Renée Wilson ('16) as Grusha. Bundy, as noted, doesn't direct every season, but in 2009 Yale pulled out the design stops for his *A Woman of No Importance*. Augesen, who had first worked with Bundy as Masha in his *Three Sisters* directing thesis, played Mrs. Allonby and now thinks, "I could have done a better job. I wasn't miscast; I don't know what it was. Oscar Wilde requires one hundred percent technique. I'm better when I'm able to surrender at least partly to the visceral." Edward Albee made his belated Yale Rep debut in 2010 after Bundy reached out to gauge Edward Herrmann's interest in playing Tobias in *A Delicate Balance*. Opposite Herrmann was Kathleen Chalfant, who had played Agnes in two other productions. She recalls, "James's was the best, because he knew those people. He didn't try to make them okay, or soften them, or try to explain them." The famously cantankerous Albee came to the first preview and was upset that Bundy had used music (recorded) in the production, but backstage after the show he told Chalfant that it had been the best first preview of one of his plays he'd ever seen.

Yionoulis staged her own valentine to show business with *Black Snow*, an adaptation of Bulgakov's satire of the Moscow Art Theatre by Keith Reddin ('81), and she also directed Shakespeare's *Richard II*. Brustein's leading company member, Alvin Epstein, was in both productions. Yionoulis recalls, "Alvin, while he was doing John of Gaunt in *Richard II*, came to speak to my acting class. I asked how he, no matter what the material, no matter how pronounced the transformation in character, managed always to speak in his own voice. He said, 'As I've gotten older, I've tried more and more not to act. Just to understand what I'm saying and say it.' He told the students, 'Just respect the text. And you can respect any text. Even the phone book.' He also sang 'Mack the Knife' for us. A capella. In German."

When Yionoulis took on *The Master Builder* in 2009, Ibsen hadn't been produced at Yale Rep since *Little Eyolf* in 1985. *Builder*, written just before *Eyolf*, is one of Ibsen's strange, final, symbolist works. Its protagonist, Halvard Solness, is, like his creator, a famous artist who fears artistic decline and displacement by the young. (Above his desk, Ibsen placed a portrait of Strindberg, twenty-one years his junior. In a letter, he said, "He is my mortal enemy. He must hang there and observe everything I write.")

Solness's fame and wealth spring from a grievous mistake that cost him his infant sons and any chance of a loving marriage with his wife, Aline. Like many an absolutist before him—recall Don Juan and Caligula in the Brustein years—Solness seeks the impossible and so must be cut down. His "demon in white" is Hilda Wangel, a freethinking young woman who has waited ten years for Solness to build with her a palace in a kingdom of their own. The artist and his new muse bond over the improper "troll spirit" they spy in each other. At the end of the play, he climbs the tower on his newly completed house to crown its spire with a wreath, the same action that had enraptured Hilda when she was thirteen, and falls to his death.

Yionoulis and her designer, Timothy Brown ('10), created a stunning set. The stage floor, pale birch in color, was the side of a house laid flat, with its perspective narrowing upward into a cloudy, smoky sky, lit by Paul Whitaker ('02). Six windows, one shuttered, were part of the floor and could be illuminated from below. The furniture was kept to a minimum, and a suspended shelf of books for Solness's library, or a row of flowers in pots for Aline, could float in from above. For his final action, Solness climbed an upstage ladder that went into a window that mirrored the house on the stage floor. Says Brown, "The set became a vision of vertigo, a tower to be climbed, driven by the fear and act of falling."

Felicity Jones Latta as Aline
Solness in Ibsen's *The Master
Builder* (2009)
PHOTO © T. CHARLES ERICKSON

The Master Builder was also fortunate in its translator, Paul Walsh, a man of the theater who has taught in the dramaturgy department since 2008 and knows Norwegian. For Walsh, *Master Builder* is, among other things, "a play about conscience and the curbing influence that guilt places upon desire. But it's also a play about moral vertigo, couched in an elusive and at times esoteric language of private reveries that both mask and reveal private desires. This creates an extra layer of difficulty for the translator. How to keep the play's allusive and elusive language afloat without drifting off into the ether or crashing down to earth?"

Leading the cast was the inspired trio of David Chandler as Solness, Felicity Jones Latta as Aline, and Susan Heyward as Hilda Wangel. Chandler, last seen at Yale as an obnoxious art historian in *Pentecost*, was unapologetically unpleasant as necessary yet vulnerable when revealing his shame and terrors. Latta, in a sixth performance for Yale Rep, was a drifting, exquisitely fragile shell, having sacrificed her life force to her husband's ambition and empty social duties. Making her Yale Rep debut as Hilda, Susan Heyward was the life force times ten—demanding, spontaneous, bewitching, tender, labile, and forthright when dealing with her idol, and like her idol, perhaps a little crazy.

The spirit of commedia dell'arte had been seen at Yale Rep in the past—Serban's *Sganarelle*, Fo's *Elizabeth*, Mump + Smoot, a lunatic musical Disneyfication of Carlo Gozzi's *King Stag* by Evan Yionoulis, Mike Yionoulis, and Catherine Sheehy in 2004—but never a Goldoni, the master chef of the form, until 2010. Director and Jeune Lune alumnus Christopher Bayes, who had been teaching clowning in the drama school for a decade (and had helmed *The Birds* for the acting class of 2001), pitched a traditional staging of *Servant of Two Masters* to Bundy, with the standard masks and costumes and a cascade of time-tested comic bits, as a means of sharing with a modern audience what has been eternally funny: food, sex, and money. The famished Truffaldino and stingy Pantalone and the pedant Dr. Lombardi and the seen-it-all Smeraldina and the young lovers aren't shy about dealing from their most animal urges. By serving two masters, Truffaldino can eat twice and get paid twice. Language is less essential than the sound of a slapstick or the sight of roasted chickens sailing across the stage.

There was only one Truffaldino for Bayes, his old friend and collaborator Steven Epp. "Working together," Bayes said, "we're different sides of each other's brain." Bayes had already acted in a *Servant* by Constance Congdon, who had adapted a literal translation by Christina Sibul ('94). She allowed Bayes and Epp to play with it further as well as add onstage musicians to the proceedings. For Bayes, the key, when building a show through improvisation, is to "have really good taste

The full company of Goldoni's *The Servant of Two Masters* (2010)
PHOTO © RICHARD J. TERMINE

about having bad taste. Let's learn in rehearsal how far we can go." When asked, "When is it too much?" Bayes answered, "I'm always too much."

Katherine Akiko Day's set evoked an Italian town square, where commedia troupes originally set up shop. Stage center was a freestanding wood frame hung with a double curtain; trunks held props, and there were sconce footlights. A cloud-strewn Tintoretto sky over the village, painted in miniature, formed the back curtain. Like Barbara Damashek and her *Story Theatre* crew decades before, the trio of composer-musicians in *Servant*, seated stage left, were involved with every beat, punctuating the comic action with Spike Jones drum rolls, buzzes, the sound of horses galloping, and so on. The music itself referenced everything from Palestrina to gospel to a hoedown. As can—and should—happen in commedia, the tone shifts to genuine pathos when the heartsick Clarice and her maid, Smeral-

286   *James Bundy (2002–)*

dina, sing a gorgeous duet about the anguish of love in the second act, reminding the audience just at the right moment that the dramatic stakes are real.

If well done, some commedia belly laughs have an underbelly. Epp said, "I think you always have to look for the other side of [the comedy]. Servants are at the mercy of higher powers in the society. Truffaldino fears beating if something goes wrong. It contains an inherent feeling of violence in it." The *New York Times* was impressed with his wily, resourceful, yet strangely innocent clown, writing, "Steven Epp manages to combine the cheerful hostility of Groucho Marx, the winsomeness of Tommy Smothers and the stupidity of Homer Simpson." All while wearing a black leather half mask, which shifts everything to the body and the voice. Epp explains the challenge: "The whole life of the character has to be in the body, because you don't have access to the facial expressions that we're all so used to using to understand. When it's working, you forget. You no longer notice the mask."

Bayes's master class in comedy was so successful that theaters across the country practically begged for a tour. After New Haven, *Servant* went to the Shakespeare Theater in Washington, the Guthrie Theater in Minneapolis, Arts Emerson in Boston, Berkeley Rep, and Seattle Rep. By the end of 2013, Bundy noted in the *Accidental Death of an Anarchist* program (directed by Bayes and starring Epp) that *Servant* had played its 175th performance since its Yale Rep opening.

As with Ibsen's final quartet of plays, Shakespeare's last four, *Pericles, Cymbeline, The Winter's Tale*, and *The Tempest*, are so dissimilar to the rest of his work that the Bardolators gave them their own category—the Romances—in the late nineteenth century. Ibsen's last are obsessed with mortality. Shakespeare's last brim with magic, miracles, nonrealistic modes of representation, and a chance at rebirth. All are tricky to stage. *Pericles* is a meandering odyssey with assists from lesser writers; *Cymbeline*'s plot is tortuous to track. For all its magic, *The Tempest* has a punitive center in Prospero. *The Winter's Tale* is a lopsided beast with a literal bear.

With *Winter's Tale,* can one really spend two hours in Sicilia watching the jealous King Leontes destroy his wife, Hermione, and his family with the violence of a winter storm on less evidence than the strawberry-spotted handkerchief that takes down Othello? Can we really, after intermission, skip sixteen years and pick up the story in Bohemia with a roster of new characters, a sheep-shearing festival, and more hey nonny-nonny than May Day in *Camelot*? Can we invest in the romance of Perdita and Florizel, who have the poetry but not the heft, color, or stage time of Romeo and Juliet, Orlando and Rosalind, or Orsino and Viola? Can the mirac-

Tim Brown and Lupita Nyong'o as Florizel and Perdita in *The Winter's Tale* (2012)
PHOTO © JOAN MARCUS

ulous reunion of parent and child and the reawakening of Hermione erase all the suffering that has gone before? Can *we* forgive the misogynistic ragebag Leontes?

No director completely "solves" a Shakespeare problem play, but Diamond went a very far distance with *The Winter's Tale* in 2012. The key for her was the idea of a lost child. "I felt the fulcrum moment in the play is when we're on the desolate wastes of the shore, and this little, swaddled baby lies alone, like a little seed pod that could be blown away at any moment." Diamond also rejected the notion that Hermione has been dead for sixteen years. "There is indeed magic in the apparent awakening to life of the stone statue of the dead Hermione. It is a flat-out miracle that cold stone becomes warm flesh again, that a dead love, a dead hope is reborn in that final scene. What died? Hermione's love, when her husband proved

James Bundy (2002–)

so utterly faithless. What was broken? Her heart, when he tore her child from her arms. She cannot be alive to her husband unless that child is returned, and until a transformation of soul occurs in Leontes."

Reaching over both worlds in the play is Leontes's transformation, a Shakespearean triumph of time. The venomous tyrant of Sicilia, now an embittered self-recluse, is granted a moment in the second half where he has the choice to be kind and not cruel to Perdita and Florizel when he promises them protection. "The entire world turns on that scene," says Diamond. "It helped that I had two ravishing actors, Lupita Nyong'o ('12) and Tim Brown ('13), in the roles." The adults were equally well cast: Rob Campbell ('91) and Susannah Schulman as Leontes and Hermione, Hoon Lee as Polixenes, and Felicity Jones Latta as Paulina.

Composing for an onstage trio of cello, percussion, and woodwinds, sound design faculty member Matthew Suttor had learned in previous collaborations that the text of the play conducts the music in Shakespeare. "The prologue opens with an idiosyncratic adaptation of Ravel's 'Le Tombeau de Couperin' for clarinet, cello, and steel-tongue drum. It's continually reinvented on different instruments as we move back and forth in location." The musicians themselves changed from white tie and tails at court to a Silk Road–riot of color in Bohemia. As for Shakespeare's most famous stage direction, the bear that pursues and kills Antigonus offstage was seven feet tall and brown with fearsome claws and teeth and was deployed mostly as a shadow effect to heighten the terror in the production.

Bundy is modest about his acting past, but Bill Rauch remembers him playing Feste in *Twelfth Night* and persuading an outdoor audience of twelve hundred to sing along with him to "O Mistress Mine" at the Oregon Shakespeare Festival. Bundy's interest in directing began after too many experiences performing in shows where everyone was acting in a different play. Getting all the actors in the same play while respecting their different rhythms as they make their character discoveries is central to Bundy's process. "My job is not to tell the actor what to do but to create the environment where the actor can do something that looks spectacular on them."

That begins with casting. Early in his tenure, Bundy had a meal with busy alumnus Charles S. "Roc" Dutton and successfully pitched him the idea of Willy Loman. It took several years for schedules to coincide. In interviews, Dutton recalled a lunch he'd had with Lloyd Richards two months before his death. "He stated very bluntly to me, 'Do not waste any more of your theater years. You've wasted too many of them. You've got to play the great roles.' And I made him a promise."

Willy, the "low man" who realizes that he has wasted his life pursuing the illusion that he has the capacity for greatness, is one of the great American roles. Bundy and Dutton decided to cast all of *Salesman* with Black actors, a transposition that August Wilson had derided in a famous speech, "The Ground on Which I Stand," at the 1996 TCG National Conference. "It is an assault on our presence, and our difficult but honorable history in America; and it is an insult to our intelligence, our playwrights, and our many and varied contributions to the society and the world at large." Dutton and his Linda Loman, alumna Kimberly Scott, respectfully disagreed. As did Bundy, who says, "We weren't reinventing the wheel—there had been Black *Salesmen* before." (In 1991, Sheldon Epps had directed it at the Guthrie with a Black Loman family, including alumna Isabell Monk ['81] as Linda. Minneapolis native Wilson was probably referring to it in his speech.) Miller himself had avoided—to mounting criticism over the years— identifying the Lomans as Jewish Americans, and there had been robust but segregated Black economies in the 1940s in America's biggest cities. It was probably a bigger surprise to the Yale community that the Rep was doing an Arthur Miller play, usually the province of Long Wharf, but for the moment it was a refreshing signal that canons don't belong to one culture.

Physically and vocally, Dutton is a powerhouse in the Lee J. Cobb (the original Willy) tradition. These traits were on full display in *Salesman*, especially in the scenes with his sons, but many remember Dutton's quieter, confessional moments with Linda, or when he begs to keep his job, as even more persuasive. The innate stillness of actors Thomas Jefferson Byrd and Stephen McKinley Henderson as Willy's brother, Ben, and loyal neighbor, Charley, proved great foils to the volcanic Dutton, allowing audiences to experience these secondary characters in a new way. Scott, although young for the part, had no trouble accepting the offer to play Linda: "A black man losing heart? I know that story. *Salesman* is about the truth we tell ourselves and the lies we tell ourselves." Playing Linda requires uncovering her strength and will in her apparent passivity. "The key is to not judge her, the suffering, the feeling of powerlessness," says Scott. "For any woman to play Linda, it takes a little piece out of you."

When it comes to acting challenges, there's Willy Loman, and then there is the Melancholy Dane. Bundy had been a year behind Paul Giamatti ('94) at the drama school and decided that if he were ever to direct *Hamlet*, it would be with him. Like Dutton, Giamatti had a very active film and television career, so Bundy would periodically check his availability. When *Hamlet* with Giamatti, a favorite son of New Haven and the literal son of the president who fired Brustein in 1979, was announced for the spring of 2013, tickets for the entire run sold out ten days before the first preview.

Howard Overshown and Charles S. "Roc" Dutton in *Death of a Salesman* (2009)
PHOTO © JOAN MARCUS

Forty-six at the time, short of stature, and with a rumpled, hangdog appearance, Giamatti didn't physically square with the tradition of matinee idol Hamlets. But Bundy was interested in taking advantage of a comedian gifted at playing malcontents to emphasize Hamlet's fish-out-of-water position in the royal family. In addition to Giamatti's erudition, which Bundy felt hadn't been tapped in Hollywood, he appreciated his "capacity to misbehave unapologetically and still draw people to him. If you're going to spend three-and-a-half hours with a character, that combination of charisma and humanity is critical." Acknowledging his offbeat casting at the annual Maynard Mack Lecture sponsored by the Yale Elizabethan Club, Giamatti said to his interlocuter, Murray Biggs, "I realized I'd be stupid not to do it. Nobody in New York would ask me to play Hamlet."

Bundy solicited advice from other directors about how to approach the play. "They said basically three things. One, you get the Hamlet that you have, and you walk through it with him shoulder to shoulder. Two, you are never going to get

James Bundy (2002–)

Jarlath Conroy and Paul Giamatti as the Gravedigger and the Danish prince in *Hamlet* (2013)
PHOTO © JOAN MARCUS

there—every time you think you've safely turned a corner and found a solution, a new question will pop up. Three, you are going to have a great time." Walking shoulder to shoulder with Giamatti meant minute comparisons of the three existing versions of the text and having him contribute to the design discussions so the production would fit him like a glove.

Giamatti had never seen a stage or film *Hamlet*. Rereading the play, he was shocked by how much "gamy, dark, intense humor" it contained. He felt Hamlet's heightened self-awareness gives him the "ability to step back and see the landscape with a piercing insight that recognizes the cosmic joke that life is. There's a sweetness and a joy to him that's being crushed; a wonderfully expansive, electric mind will be shut off at the end."

The set was suggestively Elizabethan. The costumes by Jayoung Yoon ('13) were more modern dress. Critics, for example, made much of a pair of boxer shorts and a plaid bathrobe that Hamlet spun around the court in. (Giamatti's choice to

James Bundy (2002–)

stay in constant, hyperactive motion led him to lose fifteen pounds.) Prominent among the cast of nineteen were Felicity Jones Latta and Patrick Kerr ('87) as the often overlooked Player King and Queen. Rather unimpressed with Hamlet's famous instructions, Kerr showed Hamlet how it's really done with a beautifully simple King Priam speech. Veterans Gerry Bamman and Jarlath Conroy turned in performances that made one wish that Polonius and the Gravedigger had more to say.

Giamatti's life force made rehearsals a joyous occasion. In performance, he delivered soliloquys that sounded freshly minted and was able to make the audience forget the end of the play and believe that things would turn out all right for him. Bundy says, "Paul was really, really funny in the duel, just messing around, until Laertes tells him that he's been poisoned—in death, that's when Hamlet comes most alive, and decides to take revenge on his uncle."

Because the character, like the play, contains multitudes, no single Hamlet will please everyone. He's always too much this and not enough of that. The only "too" that offended Bundy was "too old." "It drove me crazy, because Paul looked like that at twenty-five when we were in drama school." Some felt Giamatti was too antic, too much of a slacker, too much a superannuated frat boy—in other words, too funny—precisely the Hamlet that surprised others who were relieved to have him lead them on the Danish death march. Giamatti says that positive audience response to the humor egged him on during the run, and although there were certain things he felt he never got right, chief among them the "To be or not to be" soliloquy and the bedroom scene with Gertrude, it made him happy to hear from a number of people who said that his was the first Hamlet they genuinely felt sorry for at his death.

Most American nonprofit theaters schedule proven crowd-pleasers and/or prizewinners, "easier" titles that balance out the unproven new play or the thorny classic. In the earliest days, Brustein scheduled his taste, and sometimes the audience he was creating would follow him to the box office. Richards created crowd-pleasers out of Wilson and Fugard. Wojewodski had an unlikely commercial hit with his stiletto-sharp staging of *Oleanna* in 1993, but one could counter that Mamet's inflammatory two-hander about alleged misconduct between a male professor and his female student was tailor-made for Yale. That Giamatti's Hamlet or Dutton's Willy Loman set sales records was, at best, a secondary consideration. Bundy makes good on his belief that "it's more important for us to move the art needle than to ring the cash register."

Now and then one can have one's cake and eat it too, as happened with *Arcadia*, which opened Yale Rep's forty-ninth season in October 2015. The play was

Max Gordon Moore and René Augesen as "the moderns" in Stoppard's *Arcadia* (2014)
PHOTO © JOAN MARCUS

twenty years old but had never been seen in Connecticut. Like much of Stoppard's later work, the content in *Arcadia* is a vertiginous portmanteau of ideas, in this case, fractal geometry, chaos theory, the second law of thermodynamics, the history of landscaping, literary scholarship—and love and sex. *Arcadia*'s form, a whodunnit crossed with a romance, is equally dizzying as two historical time periods intersect in the same English country house.

With its intellectual rigors and a tragic ending for the earlier set of characters, *Arcadia* might not qualify as a crowd-pleaser in Dayton or Spokane, but the academic community of Yale fell hard for Bundy's lavish production. His two "moderns," Hannah (René Augesen) and Bernard (Stephen Barker Turner) were nonchalantly funny and sexy, offset by the pairing of student actor Tom Pecinka ('16), as tutor Septimus Hodge, and Rebekah Brockman's Thomasina, whose sorrowful fates haunt the play.

Felicity Jones Latta, who had done three Rep shows with Bundy, played Lady

Croom and says, "I was just full of doubt all the time. Until we started getting audiences, I thought I was going to tank in *Arcadia*." Augesen, though, hard on herself for her work in *A Woman of No Importance* and *Streetcar*, said playing Hannah and the entire *Arcadia* experience was "one for the books. Really super hard, but I had Stoppards in my past. James and I are such opposite people. He's head, and I'm heart. We trade off as we work." Latta and Augesen agree that Bundy had loosened up in the six years since their collective foray into Oscar Wilde. "James used to be more rigid," says Jones. "Maybe in the beginning he was afraid he was going to get run over. Now he's able to relax into the more nurturing thing." Responding to the comment, Bundy acknowledges his large capacity for argument in rehearsal, but says, "I talk less now. I talk more about the story and less about the performance. Unlike *Hamlet*, *Arcadia* was within reach."

Bundy was reappointed for a third term as dean/artistic director in February 2011, for a five-year period that would encompass many artistic advances. Two developments, however, one financial, the other cultural, forced Bundy and Nolan, who are both whip-smart systems analysts, to take structural action as Yale Rep approached its half-century mark.

Nolan clarified the interdependence of the Rep and the drama school this way: "We are a nine-million-dollar organization embedded in a thirty-three-million-dollar organization embedded in a multibillion-dollar corporation, but the theater and the school are so intertwined that if you closed down the Rep tomorrow, you wouldn't save nine million dollars." The Great Recession of 2008–2009 and the resulting loss of endowment income from the university were the main reasons for the enormous cuts that Yale had chosen to spread across multiple years. This belt-tightening coincided with a promise from the provost to give the drama school an additional million dollars in financial aid as well as an approved 10 percent bump in faculty salaries two years in a row. According to Bundy, when the new president, Peter Salovey, and new provost, Ben Polak, assumed their roles in 2013, "they basically set an agenda that was about getting past that problem of kicking debt down the road. That put enormous pressure on us."

Bundy and Nolan had to chop an additional million out of the budget. They laid off a couple of staff members, changed the financial aid policy to include an assessment of familial wealth, and, most visibly, removed one slot from the Rep. Beginning with the 2014–2015 season, the theater would present five, not six, mainstage productions. For Nolan, the loss of one show "was more of a symbolic gesture to say, 'Artistic will take a hit too. We're not just going to lay off people or cut material budgets.'" Doing one fewer show was also intended to combat the prevailing culture of exhaustion at the school. That was the intention. (Nolan admitted before her retirement in 2020 that the students are busier than ever.) Kiger had been concerned that the crunch would mean a loss of new plays in the season or smaller budgets, but it didn't happen. "It's harder to produce a five-play season; the calculus is trickier. But I'm very proud that new plays haven't suffered, as we're often producing three a year and two classics." Because the new-play work at Yale Rep is endowed, Bundy felt the theater needed to "keep the faith" with the Robina Foundation. One staffer let go in the crunch was Ruth M. Feldman, who was hired in Bundy's second year as education manager and had, over eleven seasons, risen to the title of director of education and accessibility services. Feldman's duties were then distributed among three staff members with already-heavy workloads. Literary Manager Boratko, who divides her duties between administering an education program and working closely with the Binger Center, laments the loss of potential innovation in the theater's pedagogical and community engagement activities.

In 2013, reacting to the acquittal of George Zimmerman in the shooting death of Trayvon Martin in Sanford, Florida, the previous year, Alicia Garza posted "A Love Note to Black People" on her Facebook account. From Garza's words, "Our Lives Matter, Black Lives Matter," Patrisse Cullors coined the hashtag *#blacklivesmatter*. Together with Opal Tometi, the three women began an online movement, calling for acts of nonviolent civil disobedience to protest police brutality against Black people. The deaths in 2014 of Michael Brown in Ferguson, Missouri, and Eric Garner in New York at the hands of police officers added strength and national visibility to the Black Lives Matter (BLM) movement. Concurrent to the growth of BLM, social media moved the concept of white privilege from academia to mainstream awareness. Despite the promises tendered and the progress made by the Obama administration, it was abundantly clear that the aims of the Civil Rights Movement remained a dream postponed. The battles over the identity politics of race, culture, and gender became ever more pitched in the run-up to the election of Donald Trump.

Events surrounding Halloween 2015 bodied forth the conflict between the Yale academic community and its social-justice warriors. It began when thirteen administrators from the Yale Intercultural Affairs Committee sent a letter to the undergraduates advising them against wearing costumes on Halloween that could be interpreted as acts of cultural appropriation or misrepresentation—for example, feathered headdresses, turbans, war paint, black- or redface, and so on. Erika Christakis, a child and developmental psychologist and Yale faculty member, sent an email to the students of Silliman College, where her husband, Nicholas Christakis, served as master. With the subject heading "Dressing Ourselves," she suggested that "we should reflect more transparently, as a community, on the consequences of an institutional (which is to say: bureaucratic and administrative) exercise of implied control over college students."

Reaction was swift and incendiary: a march on Silliman, calls for the resignations of the Christakises, a thousand-strong March of Resilience on November 9, 2015, a subsequent week of town hall meetings at Battell Chapel, and continued calls for specific actions throughout the school year. To a segment of the community, the students were coddled virtue-signalers, bullies who saw themselves as victims, unwilling to engage in rational dialogue, a hallmark of the college experience. For many students of color, queer and trans students, and students with disabilities, Halloween was a last straw. Their pain was real. Whatever one's position, it was clear that Yale, like the nation at large, needed to be doing far more to combat racial insensitivity in its citizens.

In 2013, Bundy attended the TCG summer conference in Dallas, where he participated in a session on DEI (Diversity, Equity, and Inclusion) issues led by Carmen Morgan, the founding director of artEquity. Bundy vividly recalls her saying that there were a lot of institutions that valued diversity without practicing inclusion. "The second she said it, I thought, 'That's totally us.' Diversity had had a long tradition on Yale Rep stages, but I had no idea what it was like to be inclusive. I had very little understanding of the ways in which social location operated." White, male, heterosexual, educated, and from a family of means and connections, Bundy felt a responsibility to put his privilege in service but hadn't known it was also his responsibility to acknowledge it. "I wasn't sophisticated about intersectionality or marginalization. And so, I needed to get schooled and continue to need that schooling." He also felt a responsibility to ensure that his colleagues were getting schooled. And as future leaders in the field, the drama students needed to become literate in DEI work too.

Bundy hired Morgan to work in New Haven with the MFA department chairs in November 2015. At her first meeting with the collective leadership, she was the only person of color at the table—a stunning visual for the room to acknowledge and a starting point for long-overdue conversations about race and its complications at the school, which could eventually pivot to the identification of shared values and a common language to talk about race, equity, and inclusion. Morgan was in New Haven the day of the student-led March of Resilience. "It was one of the most exciting days of my life. The energy and commitment of all those students moving in the same direction for a purpose was thrilling." She joined the march to

Battell Chapel. "It was packed to the rafters—I squeezed into a seat in the second balcony that Vicki Nolan saved for me."

That same fall semester, YSD students had begun engaging in cross-campus conversations around diversity, equity, and inclusion, with a specific focus on race. Playwright Tori Sampson, who has Black Panthers in her family, came to Yale strongly politicized and says that her class (2017) was unusually rebellious. Arriving in New Haven in 2014, she says, "There was zero activity, zero mention of diversity or EDI issues. All we had at the school was Folks, a longstanding affinity group started in 1981 by Angela Bassett ('83), as a space for Black students to exist at YSD with each other in community, fellowship, and family. A place where Black folks could be Black and joyous in peace." Sampson, accustomed to being in affinity spaces, decided after her first year that Folks should make T-shirts for themselves. "We started wearing them in the fall of 2015. The design was so cute, people wanted to buy them. Our first political argument [in Folks] was whether to sell them as a fund-raising tool."

Never underestimate the power of an excellent visual. Sampson says, "At the YSD, we withstood microaggressions constantly, and it was our job to pretend they weren't there. The white structure hadn't made space for us to exist in our blackness. The T-shirts signaled that we were a crew, and that we had each other's backs." That fall, dramaturgy student Catherine María Rodríguez ('18) started El Colectivo, an affinity group for Latinx students, followed by the creation of Asian and Asian American Theatre Coalition (Asian Potluck) and Womxn's Voices in Theatre. At a Folks event during orientation that semester, actor Patric Madden ('18) recalls third-year theater manager Libby Peterson ('16) standing up in solidarity with *Folks* and issuing a call to action for other white students. "It is one thing to theorize about how a curriculum may be ill-suited for this or that demographic," says Madden. "It is another to witness close up how a curriculum is hurting your friends." Madden answered Peterson's call and became one of the cofacilitators of what became Analyzing and Mobilizing Privilege (AMP), a learning group that aimed to unpack white privilege and leverage it to ignite change.

As planned, Morgan returned in January 2016 for Seminar Week, the week before classes resumed, to lead a three-day, fifteen-hour Beyond Diversity workshop, mandatory for all first-year students and benefited employees. "The material was brand new for a lot of people," says Kari Olmon ('18), who, coming from aggressively progressive Swarthmore College, felt that Yale—faculty, staff, and students—was five years behind on DEI issues. "Carmen and her artEquity team provided the foundations of a shared vocabulary during that first Seminar Week workshop. I remember people hearing terms like 'white privilege' and 'microaggression' for the first time, and learning what antisemitism meant." Madden grasped that "the dynamics of oppression don't wane; they just morph into new forms with each generation and situation, often ever more subtle, and therefore more effective, forms." Advising against the formation of a top-down infrastructure apparatus, Morgan encouraged letting the community decide what it wanted so that there would be more buy-in.

As a postworkshop assignment, Morgan, who believes "the activity creates the opportunity," had the entire class of 2018 draft a letter to Bundy outlining the most urgent needs to address in order to foster a more equitable and inclusive environment at the school. Chosen representatives met and crafted language that reflected the concerns and ideas generated by the workshop.

Separately but around the same time, the leaders of all the affinity groups, from all three classes, had been meeting regularly to draft a lengthier and more pointed set of demands, set in motion prior to Morgan's seminar to the deans. Madden remembers "a sense of excitement as several people pressed the 'send' key together on the email that delivered the document to the deans." This email used the word "demand" explicitly and repeatedly.

Fifty years (and two months) after the drama school students successfully petitioned Kingman Brewster en masse to fire Dean W. Curtis Canfield, a second group of student activists, seeking this time to dismantle an entrenched culture of white supremacy, presented a five-point agenda to Dean Bundy:

1. Create a working group to address racism at the school.
2. Diversify the faculty and staff.
3. Diversify the student body.
4. Review the curricula.
5. Increase wellness in marginalized drama student committees.

Bundy, Nolan, and Associate Dean Joan Channick ('88) met with a subset of the working group to discuss the agenda at the beginning of February. Channick recalls, "James was resistant to being asked to 'respond to demands,' so the first part of the [February] meeting was about what language we would all agree to use. We settled on something like a 'discussion of issues,' even though now, in retrospect, everyone, including James, refers to it as 'demands.'" For Madden, the meeting "illustrated the great paradox of institutional change. Even when leaders explicitly invite radical change, they are flustered when it arrives." As for the students, Madden felt the meeting "fractured what had been a fairly unified effort on the part of affinity group leaders. The white students in the meeting (myself included) were too eager to make peace. The students of color were there to follow through on demands. It was a learning experience for everyone."

In April, the deans held an all-school meeting to discuss the issues and demands. In that first meeting, Sampson, who rued that the legacy of August Wilson seemed to have been erased, proposed that the upstairs space at 305 Crown Street, known as Crown UP, where the first half of Wilson's Century Cycle had originally rehearsed, be renamed for Wilson—and the proposal took hold. Sampson recalls, "Another student not only supported this idea, but upped the ante by suggesting that more spaces be renamed after people who've significantly contributed to this community. An energetic dialogue ignited as folks began suggesting more names and spaces. At some point the chatter simmered, and James responded with something like 'I don't see why not.'"

The Naming Spaces Initiative canvassed students and alumni for "members of the School of Drama and Yale Rep community who represent a diverse spectrum of identity, lived experience, and contributions to the School, Yale Rep, and the field of performing arts." Ten spaces were renamed in a ceremony held in the spring of 2018.

Today at the drama school there are eight different student affinity groups with their own, often overlapping agendas, and the EDIWG, a working group that holds monthly two-hour meetings before work and rehearsal calls. Morgan continues to lead the same workshop for first-year students and new staff hires every January. Momentum has not been difficult to sustain. Morgan says, "The bar has moved distinctly; there's been wonderful progress; every year the expectation of change grows. There is always the next thing the students want to address."

As for Yale Rep, casting actors of color has always been an ad hoc proposition. Brustein wanted his repertory actors to be able to play any role, but with the exception of Carmen de Lavallade, who appeared in everything from Strindberg to *Story Theatre*, there were next to no company members of color from 1967 to 1979. Rejecting the idea of a company after his first season, Richards and the directors he hired expanded the practice of what was then known as color-blind or non-traditional casting: James Earl Jones as Judge Brack and Timon; Theresa Merritt as the matchmaker Fiokla in *Marriage*; Ben Halley Jr. ('77) and Aleta Mitchell ('84) as Time and Hermione in *The Winter's Tale*; and Gail Grate and Jane White as Eliza Doolittle and Mrs. Higgins in *Pygmalion*. Yet at the same time there were Anglo actors cast in Cuban and Native American roles in *Rum and Coke* and *Melons*, respectively. Over time, a growing awareness of insensitivities in the culture at large as well as productions of several dozen plays by writers of color and dozens more in the Binger Center pipeline have brought Yale Rep to a position of casting the best actor available for the role. The chief difference today is that the talent pool to draw from is much larger and far more diverse.

Given the priorities of the current administration, the *Operation Sidewinder* crisis of 1968 would not recur. What of the insensitive *Where Has Tommy Flowers Gone?*, *The Tubs*, *Boesman and Lena*, *Melons*, *Moon Over Miami*, *Playboy of the West Indies*, *Pentecost*, *The Beauty Part*, or *In a Year with 13 Moons*? Bundy would probably choose not to direct a black *Death of a Salesman* today. Would Diamond be permitted to direct premieres by Sunil Kuruvilla, Marcus Gardley, and Suzan-Lori Parks? Would Irene Lewis get to direct *Trouble in Mind*? Would Mark Lamos be able to stage a *Lulu* or his Latinx *Taming of the Shrew*? Would Athol Fugard be censured for writing the racially mixed–cast *Master Harold . . . and the Boys*, *A Lesson from Aloes*, *My Children! My Africa!*, and *The Blood Knot*? Would Rolin Jones feel comfortable writing *The Intelligent Design of Jenny Chow*? Such questions can only be posed in hindsight. Pendulums swing in both directions before they reach a point of equilibrium, yet stasis is inimical to an art form and an arts institution predicated on change, revolt, and social justice. All the more reason, then, for Yale School of Drama to enroll young or early-career artists in a shifting society and instill in them enough DEIB (the current Yale University–wide acronym, with "B" representing "belonging") fluency regarding all their constituencies as they prepare to take their place as the next generation of leaders.

The fiftieth-anniversary season of Yale Rep tipped toward the new, with three Binger Center–supported premieres, all of them by women playwrights and all employing women directors: Paula Vogel and Rebecca Taichman's *Indecent*, Jiehae Park's *peerless*, and Jen Silverman's *The Moors*. Completing the season were Shakespeare's gnarly *Cymbeline*, directed by Yionoulis, and *Happy Days*, Samuel Beckett's classic gauntlet thrown down for a great actress to lift, helmed by Bundy.

Indecent, to date, is the only example of a drama school project eventually winning Tony Awards (for director and coauthor Taichman ['00] and lighting designer Christopher Akerlind ['89]). Its origin story begins in the fall semester of 1997 in a class called Drama 50, a first-year collaborative project with as many pedagogical iterations over the decades as there are Goldberg Variations. Taichman and dramaturgy student Rebecca Rugg ('00) went to Professor Sheehy looking for material that was both Jewish and queer to adapt for their Drama 50 project. Sheehy suggested Sholem Asch's *The God of Vengeance* (1906), a Yiddish play that included a lesbian love affair that was shut down after two months of Broadway performances in 1923. Its cast and producers had been thrown in jail on obscenity charges, put on trial, and convicted; after a protracted legal battle, during which their producer / trial lawyer Harry Weinberger asked for amicus briefs from everyone from H. L. Mencken to the ACLU, the defendants won on appeal in 1926.

Taichman had been aware of the legal story. It was fortuitous that the Asch papers, including a handwritten copy of *The God of Vengeance*, were at the Beinecke; the Weinberger papers were in Manuscripts and Archives at Sterling; and a six-inch-thick transcript of the trial was in the Lillian Goldman Law Library. The women brought their photocopied trove to Joseph Roach in theater studies; he suggested an adaptation structure that interwove scenes from the play with segments of the trial. At the end of the semester *The People v. The God of Vengeance* debuted in Drama 50.

In their second year, Taichman and Rugg convinced the school to allow them to take Yale actors to Boston to present *The People v. The God of Vengeance* in a festival of queer theater at Abe Rybeck's Theatre Offensive. Taichman then persuaded the faculty to allow *People v. The God of Vengeance* to be her directing thesis. Due to creative differences over the direction the show was taking, Rugg and Taichman parted ways that third year. In mid-May 2000, concurrent to the show's six-day run, a symposium called "Sholem Asch Reconsidered" was held at Yale, which included lectures and discussions by Yiddish Studies scholars, queer theater theorists, and Asch's great-grandson.

Postgraduation, as Taichman built an impressive career directing classics and new work all over the country, including four shows at Yale Rep (*Iphigenia at Aulis*, *The Evildoers*, *Marie Antoinette*, *Familiar*), she never stopped thinking about the Asch material. In 2012, she connected with Paula Vogel, who had picked up a copy of *God of Vengeance* as a graduate student in 1974 and been amazed at the tender and explicit lesbian affair written in 1906. Asked if she would work on Taichman's concept, Vogel, a Pulitzer Prize–winning playwright and legendary teacher who had spent five years at the drama school as the Eugene O'Neill Professor of Playwriting, said, "It took me thirty seconds to say yes. I said, 'Can we do this as more than the obscenity trial? I think there's a larger story here.'" In 2012, the Yale Rep and Oregon Shakespeare Festival co-commissioned *Rehearsing Vengeance*, which would also be known as "The Vengeance Project" at the 2013 Sundance Theatre Lab.

Vogel wrote dozens of drafts before the play opened in the UT. Moving "as blinks in time" from Warsaw in 1907 to Connecticut in 1952, *Indecent* is performed by a troupe of seven actors brought back from the dead for this history lesson. Asch's play dramatizes a love story between Rifkele, the virginal daughter of a bourgeois brothel owner, and Manke, one of his prostitutes. Vogel retains little of Asch's original melodrama in *Indecent*, with the exception of a love scene in the rain that recurs throughout the play, as *The God of Vengeance* takes its controversial path to Russia and then across Europe before coming to America. (It should be noted that in addition to Rifkele and Manke's forbidden love, a Torah is desecrated onstage.) Posttrial, much of the troupe returns to Poland, led by the stage manager Lemml, Asch's disheartened protégé and *Indecent* narrator. We last see the actors performing in an attic in the Lodz ghetto in 1943, begging for food instead of payment.

Part of the larger story Vogel was after was "about a fiery young playwright—not just Asch, but me, too—ignored for decades and then embraced by students. I knew right from the beginning that I wanted music and a klezmer band, and Rebecca and Yale Rep brought on composers, musicians, and a choreographer." Much of the Broadway acting ensemble and all of the original creative team were brought together for the earliest Binger Center workshops.

Adina Verson and Katrina Lenk in Paula Vogel and Rebecca Taichman's *Indecent* (2015)
PHOTO © CAROL ROSEGG

James Bundy (2002–)

Indecent balances Brechtian reportage with dramatization to tell its restless, episodic story. Taichman's fluid production triumphantly demonstrated the virtues of a director conceiving and shaping a piece, beat by beat, with a writer, a design team, and an ace company of actors. Featuring choreography by David Dorfman, seven songs, and a score of twenty-two musical tracks for clarinet, violin, and accordion by Lisa Gutkin of the Klezmatics and Aaron Halva of Nu D'Lux, *Indecent* never stopped moving and brought audiences to their feet wherever it played.

The close of the fiftieth Yale Rep season brought a second triumph. "I met Dianne at a book party in New York in 2004," says Bundy, referring to two-time Oscar winner and one-time Yale Hedda and Nora, Dianne Wiest. "I asked her whether she would ever be interested in playing Winnie in *Happy Days*, and it turned out Beckett was her favorite author." Wiest's shooting schedule kept her from being able to commit to a Yale run until 2016.

The tragicomic *Happy Days* opens on an indelible image: Winnie, a woman of "about fifty," is buried up to her waist at the center of a mound of dirt. Within reach is her beloved black bag and an unfurled parasol. A bell rings. In blazing light, she blinks, wakes up, mumbles a prayer. Drawing from an array of hand props in the bag—a comb, a toothbrush, toothpaste, the last of a bottle of tonic, a hat, lipstick, a nail file, a revolver named Brownie, and a music box—she natters through another "happy day."

Listening and occasionally responding is her husband, Willie, a man of "about sixty," who lives in a hole nearby but crawls to her mound to share newspaper headlines, an erotic postcard, and a bit of a song. Knowing that Willie is there keeps Winnie going. As night descends, she puts all of her items, except the revolver, back into the bag and tells Willie how to find his way back to his hole.

Act 2 is another happy day, except Winnie is now buried up to her neck. Her hat is battered. Brownie and the bag are in place. She keeps falling asleep, but the bell wakes her. Willie, whom she cannot see, doesn't answer her calls. Finally, he crawls out from behind the mound, looking spruced up, which reminds her of the day of their engagement. She encourages his approach and is charmed when he manages to grunt out the first syllable of her name. Winnie sings "I Love You So," a music-box waltz. They look at one another, with the revolver between them, and the play ends.

Winnie's optimism in the face of an epic process of subtraction is superhuman and, depending on the actress, very comic. Brustein deemed Winnie "a hopeful futilitarian" in his *New Republic* review of the American premiere in 1961. Essentially a seventy-page monologue, Winnie is a Mount Everest of a role, a distaff Hamlet. Wiest had always wanted to play her but was terrified of the challenge.

She describes the memorization process: "Where the comma is, and the question mark, and exclamation points, where the pauses are, the long pauses, the maximum pauses. In act 1, you use the props on a particular line or pause. The first twelve pages were excruciating for me to learn—prop after prop, line after line. . . . It took a year."

Eight months prior to the start of rehearsals, Bundy scheduled a West Coast workshop with Wiest, production dramaturg Sheehy, and stage management student Vicki Whooper ('16). Half off-book when they began the workshop, Wiest memorized the rest with the help of drama alumni in Los Angeles. And then, the following April . . . , "The minute I walked into rehearsal it was all gone. As though I'd never even read the play. And I felt so badly for all these people excited to start. . . . All this work has been for nothing, so I prepared myself to create an honorable failure. By the second week, the lines began to return, but not with precision."

The rehearsal room was an operating room with six textual surgeons: Bundy; Wiest; Sheehy; Jarlath Conroy, who was playing Willie; student dramaturg Nahuel Telleria ('16, DFA '21), who was doing a comprehensive exam on Beckett; and Oxford-trained student director Lucie Dawkins ('18). Of the process Bundy recalls, "All I had to do was watch. I'd ask about a moment or a line, 'What do you think?' and all these incredible minds would just pipe up with suggestions."

Wiest gives her director more credit: "After a while he just began to read my mind. He gave me all the room and space in the world and at the same time he said, 'Put the toothbrush down.'" Bundy hadn't regarded *Happy Days* as a love story until he saw Conroy and Wiest work together in the room. For Sheehy, being in on rehearsals "was stupefying, because of Dianne's ability to make sense of every line, and all the connections among them. It was acting unlike anything I'd ever seen, it went that deep."

The team noticed a direct, if unacknowledged, line from Chekhov to Beckett, with a critical difference. "Chekhov is under the lines," says Wiest. "Beckett—you couldn't get more *on* the lines. Without the toothbrush, I'm nothing. You're not having an experience. You just are. You aren't acting. You *are*." Once she knew the part, Wiest found the biggest challenge in playing Winnie was not to succumb to her sorrow. "It's not that her sorrow is not real, or intense," she says, "but if she went completely, she would not survive. That's been the hardest thing for me to do. Smile on, smile off. Voice breaks, voice normal, instantaneous, turn on a dime."

Some Winnies dither. Other Winnies play the coquette. Many Winnies put one to sleep. Tough, funny, sexy, deeply *investigative*, Wiest's Winnie broke Beckett's code wide open and made of her palaver a riveting and ultimately consoling

James Bundy and Dianne Wiest in rehearsal for Beckett's *Happy Days* (2016)
PHOTO © JOAN MARCUS

philosophy. Audience response and critical reactions to *Happy Days* were overwhelming. The Beckettheads went again and again. After closing in New Haven, *Happy Days* played engagements at Theater for a New Audience in New York and the Mark Taper Forum in Los Angeles. The part is so rich, Wiest says she would be happy investigating Winnie for the rest of her life. Sheehy quotes Hamlet when she thinks of how Wiest, in partnership with Beckett and Bundy and Conroy, found so much freedom in the role: "'I could be bounded in a nutshell and count myself a king of infinite space'—that's Dianne's Winnie."

At a panel discussion held in October 2016 during a weekend celebration of Yale Rep's fiftieth anniversary, Yeargan, sitting two seats from Brustein with de Lavallade between them, recalled a memory of being a first-year design student, assisting on *The Rivals*, the first show directed by Alvin Epstein and the first show mounted in the church space. "We'd been up all night trying to paint the set and do all of that, and I remember Bob coming down the aisle, kind of the center aisle, and you clapped your hands and said, 'We have a theater.'"

Kingman Brewster gave Brustein the use of Calvary Baptist Church for one year. Setting aside the UT, when the nine different buildings that the theater currently occupies, wholly or partially, were constructed, no one anticipated the existence of Yale Rep. Decades later, it remains a challenge to build community interaction in a far-flung, piecemeal environment that, according to Bundy, carries over seven hundred years of deferred maintenance. No wonder, then, that a permanent dream for YSD / Yale Rep has been a new facility to cover all the needs of the school and the theater, the kind of shining, state-of-the-art edifice that colleges and state universities routinely construct.

If it is true, to quote Wojewodski quoting a former Yale Rep technical director, "that you know you're at Yale when you see the glaciers whizzing by," then it's possible to believe the rumors going all the way back to the 1980s that the new theater was definitely in the works, the architect hired, the plans drawn up, the lot found, the money very nearly practically almost entirely raised. The Yale Corporation, however, has its own timetable for building projects, and its own enigmatic matrix of variables. That said, at this writing, plans are afoot, drawings have been made, and a site has been identified on which to create a new home for Yale Rep and the David Geffen School of Drama at Yale of approximately 100,000 assignable square feet, with an additional 4,200 square feet dedicated to the Yale College Theater and Performance Studies Program and the Dramat. The DGSDY / Yale Rep portion is divided roughly into four spaces, with 25,000 square feet for a flexible four-hundred-seat theater and a one-hundred-seat studio, a doubled capacity of 25,000 square feet for production shops, 25,000 square feet for classrooms, and 25,000 square feet for office and classroom space. Some refurbishment of the University Theatre may follow.

President Salovey will determine the fate of the church space. Looking to the future with a director's eye, Diamond says with cheerful vehemence, "Give that church *back* to New Haven if they won't let us mess with it architecturally. The idea that that pile of ugly Victorian bricks should have been landmarked is beyond me." Countering her opinion is technical director Neil Mulligan ('01), who feels the irregularities of the church space create a unique set of challenges for every student—"It's an amazing teaching tool."

During the fiftieth-anniversary celebration week in October 2016, Salovey announced a fourth five-year term for James Bundy. One assumes he will remain in place until ground has at least been broken on the new theater facility, but as Diamond says, "James believes in transparency, but when it's a secret he keeps, he's like Fort Knox."

Since he remains artistic director at this writing, it's premature to describe the Bundy legacy. Associates and collaborators aren't reluctant, however, to shower him with encomia. Sarah Ruhl, who began her association with Yale with *The Clean House* in 2004, feels he's a very rare leader in terms of his ability to listen to artists. "I felt heard, I felt respected, I felt honored by him and not patronized by him, and I've felt that way ever since working with him." Felicity Jones Latta, who has worked with him on *Ladies of the Camellias*, *A Woman of No Importance*, *Hamlet*, and *Arcadia*, says, "James loves theater and he loves theater people. He's very critical, you know, but I've never known such a theater enthusiast. He still acts like a little kid. He just giggles and gets giddy when he is able to be surprised." Christopher Bayes has a theory about Bundy: "He's so smart and so sensitive that he knows he has to pretend he's not as smart as he is, so he doesn't freak people out."

Sheehy notes that Bundy and Kiger have completely reinvigorated new work at the Rep, and she appreciates his coming out in front of DEIB issues, an opinion Diamond seconds: "James has shown integrity, and great courage in pursuing the goal of dismantling white supremacist culture—at Yale of all places. Thanks to his leadership, the institution is becoming more transparent and accountable. There's a long way to go yet, to be sure, but James is determined that the entire enterprise be grounded in an antiracist ethos and he is putting tremendous energy and resources into the effort."

Although Bundy initiated *Will Power!* in his first year on the job, weak engagement with schools and the New Haven community is a legitimate current criticism. For Sheehy and Boratko, Bundy's national and student-driven focus has led him to neglect devoting attention to what is happening in New Haven, a criticism for which he takes ownership. Nolan says, "It has been a very long journey for James to his stated commitment to shared leadership. As he himself has said about his privilege, 'When you're born on third base, you don't have to hit a home run to score.'"

Bundy describes his evolution as "becoming better at taking advice that I have been giving freely to other people for years, to practice being more personal while taking things less personally." His negative reaction to the word "demands" in January 2016 he regards as a marker of his journey and now hears the word as acceptable and necessary to the work of undoing racism. Carmen Morgan says, "I'm mindful not to give white people extra credit for what they should already be doing, but James, who had the gall to decide to lead with these values, took on this task as if his life depended on it."

Asked in May 2016 during *Happy Days* previews whether he ever experienced professional burnout, Bundy responded with a smile both sly and shy: "I get a lot of pleasure in making things go." Twenty years into the job, Bundy has never been tempted to take a sabbatical, as Brustein had in 1972. The reason? "FOMO," he says, referring to the social acronym of the young, "fear of missing out."

In 2015, Robert Woodruff, musing about the upcoming half century mark for Yale Rep, said, "Somebody once said the DNA of an institution is planted the moment that it's born. And it can never ultimately change radically from that idea. And it's interesting to me whether it's indeed true, [and] therefore what does that mean in terms of evolution of an institution. Now we're fifty years on, how is it still the same, how is it responding to that same impulse? And how has it grown, diverged, fallen short, whatever?"

Working from this idea, we can say that the DNA of Yale Rep was Robert Brustein's ego, and his taste for playwrights who revolt, and his personal connections, and his eschewal of boulevard theater, and his dream of a European-style repertory company. He disrupted the slumbering Yale School of Drama with a training arm meant to model the students not for academia but for the profession. In an ideal world, Brustein graduates would save America from the middlebrow by following his Johnny Appleseed injunction to fertilize the hinterlands with repertory theaters of their own. Closer to home, the Yale Rep, following a coeval Brustein injunction, "No more masterpieces," would develop a method to reinvestigate classic texts through a more intellectual and visually metaphorical lens. These fresh takes on Shakespeare and Ibsen and Brecht would rotate in repertory with new plays that spoke to or against the urgent ideas of the day in—ideally—poetic, not prosaic, forms. Overseeing the visuals was the colossal, invisible but omnipresent hand of Ming Cho Lee, who chaired the design department for decades but designed only one set for Yale Rep (see box).

Brustein accomplished much of his project in thirteen seasons. Mark Linn-Baker (YC '76, '79) did nine shows for Brustein, who, after seeing him play Pantagleize at the Yale Dramat, invited him to apply to the acting program. On his first day, right after registration, he was fitted for a toga for *Julius Caesar*. He recalls "wildly productive years for everyone. Vital, growing, vibrant . . . a bubbling cauldron of creative activity doing work that felt important, that was the beginning of learning a craft, being surrounded by artists who continued to grow themselves." When Linn-Baker began his own theater with Max Mayer and Leslie Urdang

PERSONS OF THE DRAMA: MING CHO LEE (1930–2020)

One opinion that Brustein, Richards, Wojewodski, and Bundy all shared was the value of Ming Cho Lee. Brustein recalled, "Design was a discipline that had always been good at the drama school. I didn't have to do anything to reform that except get a hold of Ming Cho Lee."

When Donald Oenslager retired in 1970, the top student choices for his replacement were Tanya Moiseiwitsch, the founding designer of both the Stratford Shakespeare Festival in Canada and the Guthrie Theatre, and Lee. Moiseiwitsch was too busy. Lee arrived in 1969 and became head of the design department after a year.

Born in Shanghai, Lee was educated at mission schools; he also studied ink drawing and landscape painting with Chang Kwo Nyen, from whom he learned that everything begins with a line. After graduating from Occidental College in California in 1953, where he had moved from the art to the speech department in order to make theater, he moved to New York and apprenticed for four years to Broadway design legend Jo Mielziner. Lee also assisted other high-profile set designers and began designing off-off-Broadway productions. Four years of designing sets and lights for at the Peabody Institute of Music in Baltimore established him in opera as well. In 1962, he became resident designer at the Delacorte Theater in Central Park for the New York Shakespeare Festival, a position he held for ten years. Lee always believed that the theater space should be acknowledged as such and that, ultimately, the ground plan for the play *is* the play. Unlike the pictorial aesthetic and poetic scrims of his mentor Mielziner, Lee strove for dynamic, multi-leveled structural and sculptural environments.

Lee had an important design career in Broadway and nonprofit theater, opera, and dance, but during his forty-eight-and-a-half years teaching at Yale, he designed only one show for Yale Rep—Edward Bond's *Lear* in 1973. "I told Bob I'd get involved but that I wouldn't be the one designing the shows. I encouraged the best students to design for the Rep—'*if* Bob will hire you.'"

Saturday was "Ming Day" for all the first-year design students (not just set designers) and the second-year directors. From 10:00 a.m. to roughly 6:00 p.m., Lee would critique the drawings and scale models of assigned canonical works, for example, *Oedipus Rex*, *The Cherry Orchard*, *Richard III*, or *La Bohème*, one every two weeks. Costume designer Katherine Roth ('93) says, "He was riveted by what was going on in the box [the model]. For him, everything in that box had to make a kind of sense; it had to have a truthfulness to it, and a beauty to it, not in the retail sense. He gave us capital T and capital B expectations."

He was tough and didn't mince words. Former Yale Rep resident costume designer Dunya Ramicova ('77) has never forgotten Lee telling her that it looked as if she drew with her feet. "If you can survive Ming Cho Lee, you could survive anything. It wasn't that I didn't want to do what he meant, it's that I *couldn't*."

After the playwright-centered Richards years, Wojewodski immediately doubled Rep production budgets, amplifying the imaginative possibilities for student designers. Wojewodski says, "While carefully avoiding anything as limiting as a house style, Ming Cho Lee created the spirit of the atelier among the gifted young

Ming Cho Lee in the classroom (2010)
PHOTO © JOAN MARCUS

designers whose work graced the Rep stage. The result was imaginative and original design generated by passion and inspiration, informed by analysis, focused by rigorous critique, and backed by technique."

Riccardo Hernández ('92) entered Yale thinking his future would be designing operas in the painterly, Romantic style he grew up seeing in Argentina. He credits lighting teacher Jennifer Tipton for making him think not about design or location but about *space*, and Lee for telling him in his second year that he needed to stop painting, since the theater is not two-dimensional. "Ming was a born teacher," says Hernández. "He zeroed into your soul. Your strengths and your weaknesses. Somehow. So every person that he talked to was a different thing, and he could mutate into what the person was trying to do in a very precise way."

Playwrights also sat in. Julie McKee ('96) remembers, "We felt so disrespected that our production budgets were two hundred dollars that I decided to write a 'fuck-you play' that had as many characters and scene changes as I could come up with." Taking Lee's seminar her second year, she concluded that set designers could "do *anything*" and so refashioned her screenplay, *The Adventures of Amy Bock*, for the stage, using eight actors in thirty-seven roles and a couple of dozen different locations. Wojewodski and Sheehy were so impressed with the results of an in-school *Amy Bock* that it was put into the 1996–1997 season, after McKee's graduation.

In 1998, Lee was inducted into the Theater Hall of Fame. When President Bush awarded him the National Medal of Arts in 2002, mention was made of Lee's Clambake. As a way to nurture future designers, as he himself had been mentored as a young man, Lee initiated a weekend-long annual design portfolio review—the Clambake—held upstairs in the Library for the Performing Arts at Lincoln Center. Graduating students from Yale and other major theater design programs—for example, Brandeis, Southern Methodist University, North Carolina School for the Arts, NYU, and Carnegie Mellon—together with notable professional designers and directors gathered for a weekend-long review of their work and introduction to the professional community.

Bundy, who took Lee's class and benefited from his supervision of the design aspects of his thesis production, *Three Sisters*, says, "Ming was an engaged mentor on over three hundred productions, weighing in with designers, directors, and production staff on key questions with exquisite taste and discretion. Fittingly, for someone whose entire career was dedicated to the transformational possibilities of scenic design, Ming Cho Lee was a key player in the transformation of Yale Repertory Theatre, doing away with the Calvary Baptist Church seating and creating a raked auditorium in 1975, the space most associated with the Rep's history."

Alexander Dodge ('99) found designing fourteen productions a year for Ming brutal and exhausting—"Every Friday night was an all-nighter"—so much so that, after a poor critique that left him furious, beet red, and sweating, he almost didn't return for a second year. "But Ming taught me to how to look, how to see, and Saturdays were also a life class in philosophy and a search for something greater." Director Elizabeth Stevens ('99), who collaborated with Dodge at the school, laughs today. "He was much gentler on the directors. He worked hard to get us to be articulate and malleable with each other while trying to discover a place where the play could best happen *and* create the conditions where it could unfold in a beautiful way."

Jackson Gay ('02) was glad that the directing students weren't required to make models. "He wasn't shy about saying, 'Oh no, what is that?,' [and] then putting his hands into a model that a student had been up all night making and ripping parts out." She thought the highly opinionated Lee ran a class that was a heady amalgam of the poetic and deeply dramaturgical smashed up against the practical. "He cared about you as an artist and a person."

Freelance director Anne Kauffman loved watching Lee work with student Julia C. Lee ('12) on her set for *Belleville*. "We spent over four months working on this unit set for a naturalistic play. Sitting with Ming, watching him work with this young designer, watching her start to expand and grow with her ideas—and his care with her—was extraordinary."

Matt Saunders ('12) says, "The Saturday class for first years is legendary for a reason. From day one, Ming demanded that his students strike an elusive balance between designing with an inspired and personal point of view, while being careful not to 'overdesign' or even worse, 'rewrite' the text. For me, that balance is at the heart of good design, and a balance I will be chasing my entire career."

Lee sponsored his final Clambake in 2009 and taught his last Saturday class in December 2017. He was given a special Tony Award for Lifetime Achievement in 2013. (He had already won a competitive Tony in 1983 for his set design of *K2*.) At his retirement, it was estimated that he had inspired three thousand alumni across all the departments at the drama school. To this day, with his own pair of Tony Awards and after having taught alongside him for forty-two years, Yeargan still asks himself upon finishing a design, "What would Ming do? What would Ming say?"

Lee died at his home in Manhattan, three weeks after his ninetieth birthday, on October 23, 2020. ◆

('80), New York Stage and Film, which workshops new plays and musicals during the summers on the Vassar College campus, he says he took the Yale spirit with him, developing "a place where the artist could pursue the artistic impulse in the room. And let it go where it may. Don't finish. Don't try to succeed. Just follow the impulse."

Arts institutions can falter and fold when their founders depart. When Brustein was forced out in 1979, despite his fears of deprofessionalization at the hands of President Giamatti, the university did not modify the core values of the Yale Rep. Rather, Giamatti, as they say in the casting business, "went in another direction." Lloyd Richards corrected Brustein's blind spots about women playwrights, women directors, and playwrights of color. He eliminated rotating repertory after a season in favor of Winterfest, a rotating repertory of new plays that gave first breaks to several dozen playwrights. He reversed course almost instantly on Brustein's anti-Mammon edict, moving Fugard's *A Lesson from Aloes* to Broadway in 1980, to be followed by ten other commercial transfers. Richards's signature achievement was discovering August Wilson and astutely guiding him through his first six plays about Black Americans and their histories, directing them in a way that made his poetry sing from the stage. A concomitant producing arrangement dreamed up by Benjamin Mordecai and several of his managing director peers gave the Wilson plays time and spaces to refine and enhance their dramatic power and also provided the regional theater with an expense-sharing model for coproduction still in use today. The Tony Awards given to *Fences* in 1987 and the Regional Theatre Tony Award given to Yale Rep upon Richards's retirement in 1991 are simply objectives correlative to the monumental expansion of the American dramatic repertory that Wilson generated.

Sheehy, who had subbed as Richards's afternoon receptionist while still a student, adjusts Woodruff's DNA supposition this way: "There is something immutable and perpetual about the theater and the school, which is comforting in a way, which is as I think it should be. Each artistic director / dean has his own personality, his own stamp, and his own area of concentration." In 1991, Wojewodski was appointed in part to shore up the flagging morale of the students. Attempting to knit the school and the theater into the model of a teaching hospital, Wojewodski, a strong proponent of visual text, enlarged production budgets for the school and the Rep and devoted one-sixth of the Rep season to the third-year acting project. Wishing to expose the students (and patrons) to other modes of theatrical expression, he brought choreographer Ralph Lemon and the Théâtre de la Jeune Lune company in for two residencies apiece. He brought Victoria Nolan on board as managing director, and they began the Dwight/Edgewood Project. He put two female directors, Diamond and Yionoulis, on his faculty. His associate artists program replicated a slice of Brustein's resident company DNA, but not being an advocate for producing new work in its beginning stages, Wojewodski axed Richards's Winterfest after one season of "experiments in form."

Bundy remembers a Bantu saying that Wojewodski, who had been one of his teachers, kept in his office "A Person Is a Person Because of Other Persons." At the risk of overflogging the DNA metaphor, one might hazard that Bundy's Yale Rep is Bundy's Yale Rep because of Brustein's and Richards's and Wojewodski's Yale Reps. Or you could attribute Bundy's gift for balancing the demands of the school with the needs of the Rep to longevity. Whatever the reason, Bundy has had the modesty, the wisdom, and the passion to learn from the missteps and blind spots of his predecessors and expand what has worked in the past, all the while aggressively cultivating and implementing the ideas and passions of his current collaborators, be they faculty, students, staff, alumni, university officials, or outside artists. He even listens to his audience. (Feel free to weigh in at james.bundy@yale.edu.)

In an early issue of *yale/theater*, a 1968 Brustein directive now gone global, playwright Kenneth H. Brown cautioned, "Society either creates a need for theater or it doesn't. When money becomes the issue, it's already too late." Here Bundy explains the extent to which money is not the issue: "The direct charge endowment for the school and the Rep is two hundred and twenty million. The Yale University endowment is supporting us from their endowment for another three hundred million, so it's not unfair to say that we have five hundred million in endowment. Twenty-six of the thirty-seven million dollars we need to run YSD/YRT every year is coming from endowment. When you net out tuition, it's more like twenty-six out of thirty-one million, leaving five million to raise. Our relative level of stability compared to our sibling theaters is phenomenal."

So, but for that new facility, in the planning stages since Spiro Agnew resigned the vice presidency, money is not the critical issue for Yale Rep. Neither is new repertory; since its inception in 2007, the Binger Center has identified, commissioned, and supported dozens of important young and emerging artists as they develop their dream projects. Given an understanding of the resources behind its institutional stability, it is possible to imagine what the next, post-Bundy iteration of Yale Rep might be. When queried about the future of the theater, Bundy's longtime collaborators all agreed that the fifth artistic director / dean could not be a cis male. All felt that Yale Rep needed to get local again—or, in all honesty, go local for the first time—with sustained community engagement measures and redoubled educational efforts that go beyond good intentions to attain meaningful outcomes with the citizens of New Haven. Boratko feels more Binger commissions could be awarded to artists—local and national—using classical source material and possibly folding their efforts into an expansion of *Will Power!* Yionoulis and Diamond feel more Binger commissions should go to director-driven projects. Sheehy and Yionoulis wish for more challenging, less sentimental and ordinary repertory choices. Sheehy and Hernández recognize the need for canonical expansion rather than cultural cancellation so that not only new plays but also underappreciated works from the past can (re)enter the cultural imagination. Hernández is "all for dismantling the past, and the theater of illusion, but to trust your own moment and shatter the familiar again and again, as theater artists you still must be equipped to have a respectful dialogue with the past."

The constraints of the student production calendar make flexibility in the mainstage season next to impossible, but the template of a five- or six-play LORT season à la Hartford Stage, which has stood the test of fifty years, is nevertheless for Diamond a drag on the keel of the Rep. Ideally, the next version of Yale Rep should encompass far more than the restoration of the sixth slot to the regular season. Across town, Long Wharf Theatre, founded one year before the Rep, has a new artistic director. Jacob Padrón received his MFA in theater management in 2008. Post-Yale, he worked in associate producer positions at Oregon Shakespeare Festival, Steppenwolf Theatre in Chicago, and the Public Theater in New York before assuming leadership of Long Wharf in late 2018. (Bundy helped prep Padrón for his interviews.)

Since his graduation, Padrón has witnessed enormous changes in the field, changes that mirror the demographic discomforts (to put it mildly) felt by a dominant culture on the brink of losing its privilege. He looks forward to partnering with Yale Rep to forge and sustain meaningful relationships with all of New Haven's constituencies. "We'll have one city, with many stages, and not all within four walls. We'll strive to amplify the voices of the great talent that already resides here and make the city our stage." The theater ecosystem will no longer be about dividing, or duplicating, the theatrical pie with Yale Rep. Padrón wants the two institutions to make more pies together, move away from a culture of scarcity, in which ideas and artists and outputs are hoarded, and toward a culture of abundance. "We are on the path together; we're making it together; I walk next to you, not ahead of you or behind you."

Nolan feels that even a name change will soon feel appropriate: "'Repertory' is not true," she says, "and 'Yale' carries a set of expectations that limit us and/or define us in the minds of the wider community. I don't know exactly what that looks like, but theater will be interactive and not fixed in one space." Diamond wants the theater to keep an eye on its neighborhoods but not lose sight of the world: "[Yale Rep] must make a case for theater that is intellectually challenging, aesthetically daring, socially progressive, and user friendly in the most democratic sense of the word. A theater embedded in a great university with international ambitions and global reach *must* make room for great work from around the world." On the local level, Diamond envisions a next Yale Rep as a research and development lab for a communitarian enterprise that includes graduate students, undergraduates, schoolchildren, community members, and community artists with no walls between them. "The Rep could become a home for boundary-breaking theater developed not only by playwrights, but also by directors, ensembles, and individual actors. We don't know what the next thing is going to be, but we have to make room for it."

Stripping away a half century of visuals—*The Frogs* in the pool, the Olmec *Lear* head, James Earl Jones swinging a bat in *Fences*, the popcorn moon, the Black Woman with Fried Drumstick, Winnie's burning parasol—Yale Rep can be said to flourish from two foundational impulses: (1) excellence and (2) the text. Speaking to the first is Yionoulis, who left Yale in 2018 to run the training program at the Juilliard School: "I think that there's something about Yale and the School of Drama and the Repertory Theatre; there is a definite continuity. And no matter how much things change, there is something that is always the same. I think there's a desire for excellence."

Let Yeargan, in place in the Park Street design office since 1969, have the final word on the text: "I think that if there's any core thing that we do it's that we really emphasize that people always go back to the play. That it's really, how do you read a play and how do you get inside the play and work your way out, as opposed to coming up with something from the outside? And so, you make them, in a funny way, turn around and go the other way."

The impulse to make theater will never die—watch any group of children open a trunk of costumes. The capitalist consumer model of a season subscription to a nonprofit theater in a building with a lobby and a bar and one or two stages may die out sooner rather than later, but the impulse to attend theater will not. The culture is only just beginning to realize that there is something greater than dramatic content uploaded onto a wristwatch. Authentic, unmediated experiences where the terrors and joys of being alive are communicated live and in person are getting harder to find every day, which is why a theater like Yale Rep, in the perpetual show and gaze of its time, will remain one essential antidote to mendacity, data overload, artificial intelligence, and social atomization.

PRODUCTION HISTORY

Because *The Play's the Thing: Fifty Years of Yale Repertory Theatre (1966–2016)* was not conceived as a reference book, its production history includes only play titles, playwrights, composers, lyricists, translators, directors, and choreographers. A comprehensive list of all collaborators on Yale Rep productions can be found at www.yalerep.org/productions-programs/.

* World premiere
+ American premiere
\# English-language premiere

1966–1967
Dynamite Tonite!
December 6–18, 1966, University Theatre (UT)
By Arnold Weinstein
Music by William Bolcom
Directed by Paul Sills

Volpone
January 31–February 12, 1967, UT
By Ben Jonson
Directed by Clifford Williams

* Prometheus Bound
May 9–21, 1967, UT
By Aeschylus
Adapted by Robert Lowell
Directed by Jonathan Miller

Guest Companies:
   The Southwark Theatre Company at Theatre of Living Arts, Philadelphia: *Endgame*, by Samuel Beckett, September 20–25, 1966, UT
   The Open Theatre, New York: **Viet Rock*, written and directed by Megan Terry, Incidental music/accompaniment by Marianne de Pury, October 11–23, 1966, UT
   Men and Women of Shakespeare, performed by John Gielgud and Irene Worth, January 5–6, 1967, UT

1967–1968
'Tis Pity She's a Whore
October 16–28, 1967, UT
By John Ford
Directed by Kenneth Haigh

* We Bombed in New Haven
December 4–23, 1967, UT
By Joseph Heller
Directed by Larry Arrick

Henry IV
January 29–February 10, 1968, UT
By Luigi Pirandello
Translated by Eric Bentley
Directed by Carl Weber

The Three Sisters
March 4–16, 1968, UT
By Anton Chekhov

Translated by Tyrone Guthrie and Leonid Kipnis
Directed by Larry Arrick

Coriolanus
May 6–18, 1968, UT
By William Shakespeare
Directed by Jeff Bleckner, in association with Larry Arrick

Guest Company:
San Francisco Mime Troupe: *L'Amant Militaire*, by Carlo Goldoni, November 20, 1967, Yale Art and Architecture Building

1968–1969
* God Bless
October 10–26, 1968, UT
By Jules Feiffer
Directed by Harold Stone

Saved in alternation with **Yale Plays**
December 5–21, 1968, UT

+ **Saved**
By Edward Bond
Directed by Jeff Bleckner

* They Told Me That You Came This Way
By David Epstein
Directed by Michael Posnick

* The Great Chinese Revolution
By Anthony Scully
Directed by Ali Taygun

* Story Theatre
January 23–February 8, 1969, UT
Conceived by Paul Sills
Directed by Paul Sills, in association with Larry Arrick

Bacchae
March 6–22, 1969, UT
By Euripides
Translated by Kenneth Cavander
Directed by André Gregory
Associate Director: Stanley Rosenberg

* Greatshot
May 8–24, 1969, UT
Book and lyrics by Arnold Weinstein
Music by William Bolcom
Directed by Paul Sills

Guest Companies:
The Living Theatre: *Mysteries and Smaller Pieces*, *Antigone*, *Frankenstein*, *Paradise Now*, September 16–28, 1968, UT
Le Théâtre de France: *Happy Days*, by Samuel Beckett, May 12, 1969, UT; *Words and Music from the Court of the Sun King*, May 13, 1969, UT

1969–1970
The Rivals
October 16–November 8, 1969, Yale Rep
By Richard Brinsley Sheridan
Directed by Alvin Epstein

* Ovid's Metamorphoses
November 27–December 20, 1969, Yale Rep
Conceived by Paul Sills
Translated and adapted with lyrics by Arnold Weinstein
Directed by Larry Arrick
Additional material by Kenneth Cavander
Additional music by Barbara Damashek, Mark Levinson,
    Stephen Michaels, and Michael Posnick

Crimes and Crimes
January 8–31, 1970, Yale Rep
By August Strindberg
Translated by Evert Sprinchorn
Directed by Robert Lewis

The Government Inspector
February 19–March 14, 1970, Yale Rep
By Nikolai Gogol
Translated by Peter Raby
Directed by Ali Taygun

Transformations: 3 One-Acts by Yale Playwrights
April 2–25, 1970, Yale Rep
Directed by Richard Gilman

* The Rhesus Umbrella
By Jeff Wanshel

* Clutch
By David Epstein

* Iz She Izzy or Iz He Aint'zy or Iz They Both?
By Lonnie Carter

Don Juan, or the Enemy of God
May 14–June 6, 1970, Yale Rep
By Molière
A new version by Kenneth Cavander
Directed by Robert Brustein

Guest Company:
  The Negro Ensemble Company, New York: *Song of the Lusitanian Bogey*, by Peter Weiss, September 22–27, 1969, UT, translated by Lee Baxanball, Music by Coleridge Taylor Perkinson, directed by Israel Hicks

1970–1971
Story Theatre Repertory
October 8–31, 1970, Yale Rep
Conceived by Paul Sills
Directed by Larry Arrick
Music by Barbara Damashek

  * Gimpel the Fool
  By Isaac Bashevis Singer
  Adapted by Larry Arrick
  Lyrics by Barbara Damashek

  * Saint Julian the Hospitaler
  By Gustave Flaubert
  Adapted and lyrics by Kenneth Cavander

  * Olympian Games
  Based on Ovid's *Metamorphoses*
  Written and composed by Kenneth Cavander and Barbara Damashek

The Revenger's Tragedy
November 19–December 12, 1970, Yale Rep
By Cyril Tourneur
Directed by Robert Brustein
Movement and masques by Carmen de Lavallade

* Where Has Tommy Flowers Gone?
January 7–31, 1971, Yale Rep
By Terrence McNally
Directed by Larry Arrick

Macbeth
February 18–March 13, 1971, Yale Rep
By William Shakespeare
Directed by Robert Brustein

Woyzeck and **Play**
April 1–24, 1971, Yale Rep
Directed by Ron Haas

  Woyzeck
  By Georg Büchner
  Translated by Paul Butler

  Play
  By Samuel Beckett

Two by Bertolt Brecht and Kurt Weill
May 13–June 5, 1971, Yale Rep
Book and lyrics by Bertolt Brecht
Music by Kurt Weill

  The Seven Deadly Sins
  Translated by W. H. Auden and Chester Kallman
  Directed by Alvin Epstein

  + The Little Mahagonny
  Translated by Michael Feingold
  Directed by Michael Posnick

1971–1972
* When We Dead Awaken
October 14–December 8, 1971, Yale Rep
By Henrik Ibsen
Translated by Michael Feingold
Directed by Tom Haas

Production History   321

* **The Big House**
October 21–December 8, 1972, Yale Rep
By Lonnie Carter
Directed by Robert Brustein
Music composed by Maury Yeston
Choreography by Carmen de Lavallade

Caligula
November 25–December 8, 1971, Yale Rep
By Albert Camus
Adapted from the French by Justin O'Brien
Directed by Alvin Epstein

Repertory Holiday
January 20–February 12, 1972, Yale Rep

Two by Brecht and Weill
January 20–29
Adapted for this production by Ellis M. Pryce-Jones

Passion and **Stops** February 1–5
Directed by Michael Posnick

  \+ **Passion**
  By Edward Bond

  * **Stops**
  By Robert Auletta

Jacques Brel: Songs
February 8–12
English translations by Mort Schuman, Eric Blau, and the Jacques Brel Company
Directed by David Schweizer

\+ **I Married You for the Fun of It**
February 17–April 8, 1972, Yale Rep
By Natalia Ginzburg
Translated by John Hersey
Directed by Roger Hendricks Simon

Life Is a Dream
February 24–April 15, 1972, Yale Rep
By Pedro Calderón de la Barca
English version by Roy Campbell
Directed by Jacques Burdick

\+ **Happy End**
April 6–May 6, 1972, Yale Rep
Lyrics by Bertolt Brecht
Music by Kurt Weill
Original German play by "Dorothy Lane"
American adaptation and lyrics by Michael Feingold
Directed by Michael Posnick

1972–1973
* **The Bourgeois Gentleman**
October 6–December 6, 1972, Yale Rep
By Molière
Translated by Michael Feingold
Directed by Alvin Epstein

* **A Break in the Skin**
October 13–January 13, 1973, Yale Rep
By Ronald Ribman
Directed by Arthur Sherman

* **Are You Now or Have You Ever Been**
November 10–January 10, 1973, Yale Rep
By Eric Bentley
Directed by Michael Posnick

* **In the Clap Shack**
December 15–March 10, 1973, Yale Rep
By William Styron
Directed by Alvin Epstein

* **The Mirror**
January 19–March 7, 1973, Yale Rep
By Isaac Bashevis Singer
Directed by Michael Posnick
Choreography by Carmen de Lavallade

Baal
February 16–April 24, 1973, Yale Rep
By Bertolt Brecht
Translated by William E. Smith and Ralph Manheim
Directed by Tom Haas

Production History

+ Macbett
March 16–May 16, 1973, Yale Rep
By Eugène Ionesco
Translated by Charles Marowitz
Directed by William Peters, John McAndrew, and Alvin Epstein

+ Lear
April 13–May 19, 1973, Yale Rep
by Edward Bond
Directed by David Giles

1973–1974
The Tempest
October 4–December 15, 1973, Yale Rep
In association with Yale School of Music
By William Shakespeare
Music by Henry Purcell
Additional lyrics by John Dryden, William Davenant, and Thomas Shadwell
Directed by Moni Yakim and Alvin Epstein

* Darkroom
October 18–December 11, 1973, Yale Rep
By David Epstein
Directed by Michael Posnick

* Watergate Classics
November 15–January 26, 1974, Yale Rep
By Robert Barnett, Robert Brustein, Lonnie Carter, Jules Feiffer, Jeremy Geidt, Jonathan Marks, Philip Roth, Isaiah Sheffer, and Maury Yeston
Directed by Isaiah Sheffer
Choreography by Carmen de Lavallade

* The Tubs
December 20–March 27, 1974, Yale Rep
By Terrence McNally
Directed by Anthony Holland

The Rise and Fall of the City of Mahagonny
January 31–February 23, 1974, UT
In association with Yale School of Music
Text by Bertolt Brecht
Music by Kurt Weill
Translated by Michael Feingold
Directed by Alvin Epstein

Geography of a Horse Dreamer and An Evening with Dead Essex
March 7–April 27, 1974, Yale Rep

+ Geography of a Horse Dreamer
By Sam Shepard
Directed by David Schweizer

*An Evening with Dead Essex
By Adrienne Kennedy
Directed by Andre Mtumi

* Schlemiel the First
April 11–May 18, 1974, Yale Rep
By Isaac Bashevis Singer
Directed by Isaiah Sheffer
Composed by Bobby Paul

* The Frogs
March 29–May 17, 1974, Kiphuth Exhibition Pool, Payne Whitney Gymnasium
By Aristophanes
Freely adapted and directed by Burt Shevelove
Music and lyrics by Stephen Sondheim
Shakespeare and Shaw selected and arranged by Michael Feingold
Choreography by Carmen de Lavallade

1974–1975
+ The Possessed
October 3–26, 1974, UT
A new dramatization of the Dostoyevsky novel by Andrzej Wajda
Based on an adaptation by Albert Camus
Translated by Justin O'Brien
Directed by Andrzej Wajda

* The Idiots Karamazov
October 31–December 21, 1974, Yale Rep
By Christopher Durang and Albert Innaurato
Directed by William Peters

Production History

* Joseph Conrad's Victory
November 14–December 20, 1974, Yale Rep
A *Story Theatre* version by Walton Jones and Alvin Epstein
Directed by Alvin Epstein

Happy End
February 6–March 22, 1975, Yale Rep
In association with Yale School of Music
Lyrics by Bertolt Brecht
Music by Kurt Weill
Original German play by "Dorothy Lane"
American adaptation and lyrics by Michael Feingold
Directed by Michael Posnick

The Father
February 20–April 24, 1975, Yale Rep
By August Strindberg
Translated by Evert Sprinchorn
Directed by Jeff Bleckner

* The Shaft of Love
March 27–April 26, 1975, Yale Rep
By Charles Dizenzo
Directed by David Schweizer

A Midsummer Night's Dream
May 8–31, 1975, UT
In association with Yale School of Music
By William Shakespeare
Music from *The Fairy Queen* by Henry Purcell
Directed by Alvin Epstein
Choreography associate: Carmen de Lavallade

1975–1976
A Midsummer Night's Dream
October 12–October 25, 1975, UT
By William Shakespeare
Directed by Alvin Epstein

Don Juan
October 30–December 16, 1975, Yale Rep
By Molière
Translated by Kenneth Cavander
Directed by Robert Brustein

Dynamite Tonite!
November 15–December 20, 1975, Yale Rep
By Arnold Weinstein
Music by William Bolcom
Directed by Alvin Epstein and Walton Jones

* Walk the Dog, Willie
January 15–February 19, 1976, Yale Rep
By Robert Auletta
Directed by Walton Jones

Bingo
January 29–March 20, 1976, Yale Rep
By Edward Bond
Directed by Ron Daniels

General Gorgeous
February 26–May 3, 1976, Yale Rep
By Michael McClure
Directed by Lawrence Kornfeld

Troilus and Cressida
April 1–May 8, 1976, Yale Rep
By William Shakespeare
Directed by Alvin Epstein

Special Event:
    An Evening with Samuel Beckett, performed by Patrick Magee, March 24–27, 1976, Yale Rep

1976–1977
Julius Caesar
October 1–November 13, 1976, Yale Rep
By William Shakespeare
Directed by Alvin Epstein

* Suicide in B-Flat
October 14–December 17, 1976, Yale Rep
By Sam Shepard
Directed by Walton Jones

Ivanov
November 18–December 18, 1976, Yale Rep
By Anton Chekhov

Translated by Jeremy Brooks and Kitty Hunter Blair
Directed by Ron Daniels

* **The Vietnamization of New Jersey (A American Tragedy)**
January 13–February 25, 1977, Yale Rep
By Christopher Durang
Directed by Walton Jones

* **The Durango Flash**
January 27–April 1, 1977, Yale Rep
By William Hauptman
Directed by Kenneth Frankel

Mister Puntila and His Chauffeur Matti
March 3–April 2, 1977, Yale Rep
By Bertolt Brecht
Translated by Gerhard Nellhaus
Music by William Bolcom
Directed by Ron Daniels

+ **White Marriage**
April 14–May 7, 1977, Yale Rep
By Tadeusz Rozewicz
Translated by Adam Czerniawski
Directed by Andrzej Wajda

Special Holiday Production:
* **The Banquet Years**
December 30, 1976–?, Yale Rep
A celebration of turn-of-the-century Paris
Conceived by Carmen de Lavallade, Robert Gainer, Joe Grifasi, and Jonathan Marks
Directed by Robert Gainer
Choreography by Carmen de Lavallade and Joe Grifasi
Music by Erik Satie, Claude Debussy, Francis Poulenc, and Jacques Offenbach
Texts by Alfred Jarry, Pierre Louys, Max Jacob, and Erik Satie
Original text by Jonathan Marks

Guest Company:
Charles Dickens and *Dylan Thomas Growing Up*, performed by Emlyn Williams, September 14–19, 1976, Yale Rep

1977–1978

The Ghost Sonata
September 29–November 12, 1977, Yale Rep
By August Strindberg
Translated by Evert Sprinchorn
Directed by Andrei Serban

* **Reunion** and **Dark Pony**
October 13–November 28, 1977, Yale Rep
By David Mamet
Directed by Walton Jones

* **Terra Nova**
November 17–30, 1977, Yale Rep
By Ted Tally
Directed by Travis Preston

Sganarelle: An Evening of Molière Farces
January 19–February 1, 1978, Yale Rep
Translated by Albert Bermel
Directed by Andrei Serban

Man Is Man
February 16–April 11, 1978 Yale Rep
By Bertolt Brecht
Translated by Steve Gooch
Music by William Bolcom
Directed by Ron Daniels

* **Wings**
March 2–May 15, 1978, Yale Rep
By Arthur Kopit
Directed by John Madden

The Wild Duck
April 6–May 3, 1978, Yale Rep
By Henrik Ibsen
Translated by Michael Meyer
Directed by Robert Brustein

Special Holiday Production:
* **The 1940's Radio Hour**
December 28–January 7, 1978, Yale Rep
Written and directed by Walton Jones

Music director and arranger: Gary Fagin
Vocal arrangements and director: Paul Schierhorn
Choreography by Wesley Fata, Joe Grifasi, Rebecca Nelson,
    Eric Elice, and Caris Corfman

Guest Company:
    Mabou Mines, New York: *The B. Beaver Animation*, text and direction by Lee Breuer, September 16–17, 1977, UT

1978–1979
+ Tales from the Vienna Woods
September 28–November 8, 1978, Yale Rep
By Ödön von Horváth
Translated by Christopher Hampton
Directed by Keith Hack

Mistaken Identities ('Dentity Crisis and Guess Work)
October 12–December 6, 1978, Yale Rep

   * **'Dentity Crisis**
   By Christopher Durang
   Directed by Frank Torok

   * **Guess Work**
   By Robert Auletta
   Directed by Robert Gainer

Mahagonny
November 6–December 13, 1978, Yale Rep
A chamber version of *The Rise and Fall of the City of Mahagonny*
By Bertolt Brecht and Kurt Weill
Conceived and directed by Keith Hack

Buried Child
January 18–February 7, 1979, Yale Rep
By Sam Shepard
Directed by Adrian Hall

The Seagull
February 15–April 6, 1979, Yale Rep
By Anton Chekhov
A new version by Jean-Claude van Itallie
Directed by Robert Brustein

+ The Bundle: Or, New Narrow Road to the Deep North
March 1–May 2, 1979, Yale Rep
By Edward Bond
Directed by John Madden

As You Like It
April 12–May 9, 1979, Yale Rep
By William Shakespeare
Directed by Andrei Belgrader

Special Holiday Production:
Jacques Brel . . .
December 29–January 13, 1979, UT
Directed by Steve Lawson
Music direction and arrangements by Rusty Magee
Choreography by Wesley Fata

Guest Company:
    The Lucia Sturdza Bulandra Theatre Company, Bucharest, Romania: *Elizabeth I*, by Paul Foster, June 1–2, 1979; *The Lost Letter*, by Ion Luca Caragiale, June 1–2, 1979, directed by Liviu Ciulei

1979–1980
Bosoms and Neglect
October 4–November 13, 1979, Yale Rep
By John Guare
Directed by Steven Robman

+ They Are Dying Out
October 18–November 21, 1979, Yale Rep
By Peter Handke
American version by Michael Roloff, in collaboration with
    Carl Weber
Directed by Carl Weber

Measure for Measure
November 30–December 22, 1979, Yale Rep
By William Shakespeare
Directed by John Madden

Curse of the Starving Class
February 1–March 10, 1980, Yale Rep
By Sam Shepard
Directed by Tony Giordano

Ubu Rex
February 15–March 19, 1980, Yale Rep
By Alfred Jarry
Translated by David Copelin
Directed by Andrei Belgrader

+ **A Lesson from Aloes**
March 27–May 24, 1980, Yale Rep
Written and directed by Athol Fugard

Timon of Athens
April 10–May 14, 1980, Yale Rep
By William Shakespeare
Directed by Lloyd Richards
Choreography by Wesley Fata

1980–1981
Boesman and Lena
October 7–25, 1980, Yale Rep
By Athol Fugard
Directed by Walton Jones

+ **The Suicide**
November 4–22, 1980, Yale Rep
By Nikolai Erdman
Translated by Peter Tegel
Directed by John Madden

Twelfth Night
December 2–20, 1980, Yale Rep
By William Shakespeare
Directed by Bill Ludel

Winterfest I
January 10–February 21, 1981, Yale Rep

* **Domestic Issues**
By Corinne Jacker
Directed by Barnet Kellman

* **Rococo**
By Harry Kondoleon
Directed by Dana B. Westberg

* **Sally and Marsha**
By Sybille Pearson
Directed by Robert Allan Ackerman

* **The Resurrection of Lady Lester**
By OyamO
Directed by James A. Simpson
Music composed and arranged by Dwight Andrews

Hedda Gabler
March 3–21, 1981, Yale Rep
By Henrik Ibsen
Translated by Rolf Fjelde
Directed by Lloyd Richards

+ **The Magnificent Cuckold**
March 31–April 18, 1981, Yale Rep
By Fernand Crommelynck
Translated by Marnix Gijsen
Directed by Jonas Jurasas

+ **An Attempt at Flying**
April 28–May 16, 1981, UT
By Yordan Radichkov
Translated by Bogdan B. Athanassov
Directed by Mladen Kiselov

1981–1982
Uncle Vanya
October 6–24, 1981, Yale Rep
By Anton Chekhov
Translated by Constance Garnett
Directed by Lloyd Richards

Mrs. Warren's Profession
November 3–21, 1981, Yale Rep
By George Bernard Shaw
Directed by Stephen Porter

* **Rip Van Winkle, or "The Works"**
December 1–19, 1981, UT
By Richard Nelson
Directed by David Jones

Production History

Winterfest II
January 5–February 6, 1982, Yale Rep

* **Beef, No Chicken**
By Derek Walcott
Directed by Walton Jones

* **Flash Floods**
By Dare Clubb
Directed by Dennis Scott

* **Going Over**
By Stuart Browne
Directed by Jim Peskin

* **The Man Who Could See Through Time**
By Terri Wagener
Directed by David Hammond

* **Master Harold . . . and the Boys**
March 9–27, 1982, Yale Rep
Written and directed by Athol Fugard

* **Johnny Bull**
April 4–24, 1982, Yale Rep
By Kathleen Betsko
Directed by Lloyd Richards

Love's Labour's Lost
May 4–22, 1982, Yale Rep
By William Shakespeare
Directed by Mladen Kiselov

1982–1983

A Doll House
October 5–23, 1982, Yale Rep
By Henrik Ibsen
Translated by Rolf Fjelde
Directed by Lloyd Richards

Hello and Goodbye
November 2–20, 1982, Yale Rep
By Athol Fugard
Directed by Tony Giordano

The Philanderer
November 30–December 18, 1982, Yale Rep
By George Bernard Shaw
Directed by David Hammond

Winterfest III
January 4–February 5, 1983, Yale Rep

***Astapovo**
By Leon Katz
Directed by Lawrence Kornfeld

* **Coyote Ugly**
By Lynn Siefert
Directed by Christian Angermann

* **Playing in Local Bands**
By Nancy Fales Garrett
Directed by William Ludel

Much Ado about Nothing
March 8–26, 1983, Yale Rep
By William Shakespeare
Directed by Walton Jones

About Face
April 5–23, 1983, Yale Rep
By Dario Fo
English version by Dale McAdoo and Charles Mann
Directed by Andrei Belgrader

A Touch of the Poet
May 3–21, 1983, Yale Rep
By Eugene O'Neill
Directed by Lloyd Richards

1983–1984

Major Barbara
October 4–October 22, 1983, Yale Rep
By George Bernard Shaw
Directed by Lloyd Richards

A Raisin in the Sun
November 1–19, 1983, Yale Rep
By Lorraine Hansberry
Directed by Dennis Scott

Richard II
November 29–December 17, 1983, Yale Rep
By William Shakespeare
Directed by David Hammond

Winterfest IV
January 16–February 25, 1984, Yale Rep

* **Chopin in Space**
By Philip Bosakowski
Directed by James Simpson

* **The Day of the Picnic**
By Russell Davis
Directed by Tony Giordano

* **The Sweet Life**
By Michael Quinn
Directed by Robert Alford II

+ **Night Is Mother to the Day**
March 6–24, 1984, Yale Rep
By Lars Noren
Translation by Harry G. Carlson
Directed by Göran Graffman

* **Ma Rainey's Black Bottom**
April 3–21, 1984, Yale Rep
By August Wilson
Directed by Lloyd Richards

* **The Road to Mecca**
May 1–26, 1984, Yale Rep
Written and directed by Athol Fugard

1984–1985

Tartuffe
September 18–October 13, 1984, Yale Rep
By Molière
Translation by Richard Wilbur
Directed by Walton Jones

Henry IV, Part I
October 23–November 17, 1984, Yale Rep
By William Shakespeare
Directed by David Hammond

* **A Play of Giants**
November 27–December 22, 1984, Yale Rep
Written and directed by Wole Soyinka

Winterfest V
January 14–February 9, 1985

* **Between East and West**, Yale Rep
By Richard Nelson
Directed by John Madden

* **Faulkner's Bicycle**, Yale Rep
By Heather McDonald
Directed by Julian Webber

* **Rum and Coke**, UT
By Keith Reddin
Directed by Bill Partlan

* **Vampires in Kodachrome**, UT
By Dick Beebe
Directed by Evan Yionoulis

What the Butler Saw
February 19–March 17, 1985, Yale Rep
By Joe Orton
Directed by Andrei Belgrader

Talley's Folly
March 26–April 20, 1985, Yale Rep
By Lanford Wilson
Directed by Dennis Scott

* **Fences**
April 30–May 25, 1985, Yale Rep
By August Wilson
Directed by Lloyd Richards

Production History

1985–1986

The Blood Knot
September 17–October 12, 1985, Yale Rep
Written and directed by Athol Fugard

Little Eyolf
October 22–November 16, 1985, Yale Rep
By Henrik Ibsen
Translated by Rolf Fjelde
Directed by Travis Preston

Marriage
November 25–December 21, 1985, Yale Rep
By Nikolai Gogol
Translated and adapted by Barbara Field
Directed by Andrei Belgrader

Winterfest VI
January 9–February 8, 1986

* **A Child's Tale,** Yale Rep
By Carlo Capotorto
Directed by Dennis Scott

* **Crazy from the Heart,** Yale Rep
By Edit Villarreal
Directed by Mark Brokaw

* **Stitchers and Starlight Talkers,** UT
By Kathleen Betsko
Directed by William Partlan

* **Union Boys,** UT
By James Yoshimura
Directed by Steven Robman

Othello
February 18–March 15, 1986, Yale Rep
By William Shakespeare
Directed by Dennis Scott

The Importance of Being Earnest
March 25–April 19, 1986, Yale Rep
By Oscar Wilde
Directed by Alvin Epstein

* **Joe Turner's Come and Gone**
April 29–May 24, 1986, Yale Rep
By August Wilson
Directed by Lloyd Richards

Special Event:
  Dario Fo and Franca Rame, May 13–17, 1986, UT: *Mistero Buffo (Comic Mystery)*, performed by Dario Fo; *Tutta Casa, Letto, e Chiesa (All House, Bed and Church)*, performed by Franca Rame

1986–1987

Heartbreak House
September 16–October 11, 1986, Yale Rep
By George Bernard Shaw
Directed by Alvin Epstein

Neapolitan Ghosts
October 21–November 15, 1986, Yale Rep
By Eduardo De Filippo
Translated by Marguerita Càrra and Louise H. Warner
Directed by David Chambers

The Winter's Tale
November 24–December 20, 1986, Yale Rep
By William Shakespeare
Directed by Gitta Honegger

Winterfest VII
January 13–February 7, 1987

* **Apocalyptic Butterflies,** UT
By Wendy MacLeod
Directed by Richard Hamburger

* **Exact Change,** UT
By David Epstein
Directed by Jacques Levy

* **The Cemetery Club,** Yale Rep
By Ivan Menchell
Directed by William Glenn

* **The Memento,** Yale Rep
By Wakako Yamauchi
Directed by Dennis Scott

***A Walk in the Woods**
February 17–March 14, 1987, Yale Rep
By Lee Blessing
Directed by Des McAnuff

* **A Place with the Pigs**
March 24–April 18, 1987, Yale Rep
Written and directed by Athol Fugard

Elizabeth: Almost by Chance a Woman
April 28–May 23, 1987, Yale Rep
By Dario Fo
Translated by Ron Jenkins
Directed by Tony Taccone

1987–1988
Sarcophagus
September 15–October 10, 1987, Yale Rep
By Vladimir Gubaryev
Translated by Michael Glenny
Directed by David Chambers

Melons
October 20–November 14, 1987, Yale Rep
By Bernard Pomerance
Directed by Gitta Honegger

* **The Piano Lesson**
November 23–December 19, 1987, Yale Rep
By August Wilson
Directed by Lloyd Richards
Original music by Dwight Andrews

Winterfest VIII
January 11–February 6, 1988

* **The My House Play,** UT
By Wendy MacLeod
Directed by Evan Yionoulis

* **Chute Roosters,** Yale Rep
By Craig Volk
Directed by Donato J. D'Albis

* **Neddy,** UT
By Jeffrey Hatcher
Directed by Dennis Scott

* **The Wall of Water,** Yale Rep
By Sherry Kramer
Directed by Margaret Booker

The Miser
February 16–March 12, 1988, Yale Rep
By Molière
Translated by Miles Malleson
Directed by Andrei Belgrader

Eugene O'Neill Centennial Celebration
In rotating repertory March 22–May 21, 1988, UT

> **Long Day's Journey into Night**
> Directed by José Quintero

> **Ah, Wilderness!**
> Directed by Arvin Brown

1988–1989
Intermezzo
September 15–October 8, 1988, Yale Rep
By Arthur Schnitzler
Translated by Robert David MacDonald
Directed by Gitta Honegger

Kiss of the Spider Woman
October 18–November 12, 1988, Yale Rep
By Manuel Puig
Translated by Allan Baker
Directed by David Chambers

The Alchemist
October 18–November 12, 1988, Yale Rep
By Ben Jonson
Directed by John Hirsch

Production History 331

Winterfest IX
January 10–February 4, 1989

* **Phaedra and Hippolytus,** Yale Rep
By Elizabeth Egloff
Directed by Christopher Grabowski

* **The Beach,** UT
By Anthony Giardina
Directed by Amy Saltz

* **Starting Monday,** Yale Rep
By Anne Commire
Directed by Peter Mark Schifter

* **Interrogating the Nude,** UT
By Doug Wright
Directed by Gitta Honegger

Moon Over Miami
February 14–March 11, 1989, Yale Rep
By John Guare
Directed by Andrei Belgrader
Dances by Wesley Fata

* **Cobb**
March 21–April 15, 1989, Yale Rep
By Lee Blessing
Directed by Lloyd Richards

Playboy of the West Indies
April 25–May 20, 1989, Yale Rep
By Mustapha Matura
Directed by Dennis Scott

Special Event:
 Mabou Mines: *The Warrior Ant,* conceived and directed by Lee Breuer, music by Bob Telson, October 10–15, 1988, UT

1989–1990
The Solid Gold Cadillac
September 12–October 7, 1989, Yale Rep
By Howard Teichmann and George S. Kaufman
Directed by Gitta Honegger

Miss Julie
October 17–November 11, 1989, Yale Rep
By August Strindberg
Translated by Elizabeth Sprigge
Directed by Dennis Scott

Summer and Smoke
November 20–December 16, 1989, Yale Rep
By Tennessee Williams
Directed by James Simpson

Winterfest X
January 15–February 10, 1990

* **Daylight in Exile,** UT
By James D'Entremont
Directed by Amy Saltz

* **Rust and Ruin,** Yale Rep
By William Snowden
Directed by Walter Jones

* **Pill Hill,** UT
By Sam Kelley
Directed by Walter Dallas

* **Dinosaurs,** Yale Rep
By Doug Wright
Directed by Rob Barron

Troilus and Cressida
February 20–March 17, 1990, Yale Rep
By William Shakespeare
Directed by Andrei Belgrader

* **Two Trains Running**
March 17–April 21, 1990, Yale Rep
By August Wilson
Directed by Lloyd Richards

Pygmalion
May 1–26, 1990, Yale Rep
By George Bernard Shaw
Directed by Douglas C. Wager

1990–1991

Ivanov
September 18–October 13, 1990, UT
By Anton Chekhov
Translated by Robert W. Corrigan
Adapted and directed by Oleg Yefremov

Largo Desolato
October 23–November 17, 1990, Yale Rep
By Vaclav Havel
English version by Tom Stoppard
Directed by Gitta Honegger

Search and Destroy
November 27–December 22, 1990, Yale Rep
By Howard Korder
Directed by David Chambers

Winterfest XI
January 14–February 9, 1991

* **Bricklayers**, UT
By Elvira DiPaola
Directed by Walter Dallas

Ohio State Murders, UT
By Adrienne Kennedy
Directed by Gerald Freedman

* **Size of the World**, Yale Rep
By Charles Evered
Directed by Jordan Corngold

* **Ties That Bind**, Yale Rep
By Walter Allen Bennett Jr.
Directed by Walton Jones

***Underground**
February 19–March 16, 1991, Yale Rep
By Joshua Sobol
English adaptation by Ron Jenkins
Directed by Adrian Hall
Music composed, arranged, and directed by Barbara Damashek

Scapin
March 26–April 20, 1991, Yale Rep
By Molière
Translated and adapted by Shelley Berc and Andrei Belgrader
Directed by Andrei Belgrader

A Moon for the Misbegotten
April 30–May 25, 1991, Yale Rep
By Eugene O'Neill
Directed by Lloyd Richards

1991–1992

On the Verge
October 3–November 2, 1991, Yale Rep
By Eric Overmyer
Directed by Stan Wojewodski Jr.

My Children! My Africa!
November 14–December 14, 1991, Yale Rep
By Athol Fugard
Directed by Elizabeth S. Margid

Winterfest XII
January 16–March 7, 1992

Fefu and Her Friends
January 16–February 15, 1992, Yale Rep
By María Irene Fornès
Directed by Lisa Peterson

The Death of the Last Black Man in the Whole Entire World
January 22–March 7, 1992, UT
By Suzan-Lori Parks
Directed by Liz Diamond

* **Democracy in America**
January 24–March 7, 1992, UT
Developed by Colette Brooks and Travis Preston
Written by Colette Brooks
Directed by Travis Preston

Production History 333

Edward the Second
March 12–April 11, 1992, Yale Rep
By Christopher Marlowe
Directed by Stan Wojewodski Jr.

The Beauty Part
April 23–May 23, 1992, Yale Rep
By S. J. Perelman
Directed by Walton Jones

1992–1993
Hamlet
October 8–October 31, 1992, UT
By William Shakespeare
Directed by Stan Wojewodski Jr.

The Colored Museum
November 27–December 19, 1992, Yale Rep
By George C. Wolfe
Directed by Donald Douglass

Children of Paradise
January 15–30, 1993, UT
Coproduction with Théâtre de la Jeune Lune
By Steven Epp, Felicity Jones Latta, Dominque Serrand, and Paul Walsh
Directed by Dominique Serrand

* **St. Joan of the Stockyards**
February 18–March 13, 1993, Yale Rep
By Bertolt Brecht
Translated by Paul Schmidt
Directed by Liz Diamond

Escape from Happiness
March 25–April 17, 1993, Yale Rep
Coproduction with Baltimore's Center Stage
By George F. Walker
Directed by Irene Lewis

The Baltimore Waltz
April 29–May 22, 1993, Yale Rep
By Paula Vogel
Directed by Stan Wojewodski Jr.

Special Events:
   Reno, *Reno Once Removed*, November 10, 1992, Yale Rep
   Paula Poundstone, November 10, 1992, UT

1993–1994
Oleanna
October 14–November 6, 1993, Yale Rep
By David Mamet
Directed by Stan Wojewodski Jr.

The Green Bird
November 27–December 18, 1993, UT
Coproduction with Théâtre de la Jeune Lune
By Carlo Gozzi
Translated by Albert Bermel and Ted Emery
Directed by Vincent Gracieux

* **The America Play**
January 13–February 5, 1994, Yale Rep
Coproduction with New York Shakespeare Festival
By Suzan-Lori Parks
Directed by Liz Diamond

As You Like It
February 17–March 12, 1994, Yale Rep
By William Shakespeare
Directed by Stan Wojewodski Jr.

Mump + Smoot in Ferno and Caged
March 18–April 9, 1994, Yale Rep
By Michael Kennard and John Turner
Directed by Karen Hines

The School for Wives
April 28–May 21, 1994, Yale Rep
By Molière
Translated by Paul Schmidt
Directed by Liz Diamond

Special Events:
   Spalding Gray, *Gray's Anatomy*, March 24–26, 1994, UT
   Diamanda Galas, *Plague Mass*, May 14, 1994, UT

1994–1995

Antigone in New York
October 20–November 12, 1994, Yale Rep
By Janusz Glowacki and Joan Torres
Directed by Liz Diamond

*** Figaro/Figaro**
December 1–17, 1994, UT
By Eric Overmyer
Adapted from *The Marriage of Figaro* by Beaumarchais and *Figaro Gets a Divorce* by Ödön von Horváth
Translated by Douglas E. Langworthy
Directed by Stan Wojewodski Jr.

Twelfth Night
January 26–February 18, 1995, Yale Rep
By William Shakespeare
Directed by Mark Rucker

Slavs! (Thinking about the Longstanding Problems of Virtue and Happiness)
February 24–March 18, 1995, Yale Rep
Coproduction with Baltimore's Center Stage
By Tony Kushner
Directed by Lisa Peterson

* Uncle Vanya
March 30–April 15, 1995, UT
By Anton Chekhov
Translated by Paul Schmidt
Directed by Len Jenkin

Le Bourgeois Avant-Garde
April 27–May 20 1995, Yale Rep
By Charles Ludlam
Directed by Liz Diamond

Special Events:
    Eric Bogosian, *Pounding Nails in the Floor with My Forehead*, September 10, 1994, UT
    Holly Hughes, *Clit Notes*, October 1, 1994, UT
    David Cale, *Somebody Else's House*, November 13, 1994, UT
    Rhodessa Jones, *Big Butt Girls, Hard-Headed Women*, January 21, 1995, UT

1995–1996

Le Cirque Invisible
October 19–November 4, 1995, UT
Created and performed by Victoria Chaplin and Jean Baptiste Thierrée

+ Pentecost
November 9–December 2, 1995, Yale Rep
By David Edgar
Directed by Stan Wojewodski Jr.

Mrs. Warren's Profession
January 11–February 3, 1996, Yale Rep
By George Bernard Shaw
Directed by Liz Diamond

The Beaux' Stratagem
February 15–March 9, 1996, Yale Rep
By George Farquhar
Directed by Everett Quinton

* Venus
March 14–March 30, 1996, UT
Coproduction with New York Shakespeare Festival
By Suzan-Lori Parks
Directed by Richard Foreman
Songs composed by Phillip Johnston

Landscape of the Body
May 2–May 25, 1996, Yale Rep
By John Guare
Directed by Mark Rucker

Special Events:
    Donald Byrd and the Group, October 14, 1995, UT
    Don Byron, *The Scar of Shame*, February 3, 1996, UT
    Lisa Kron, *101 Humiliating Stories*, April 13, 1996, UT

1996–1997

First Lady
October 10–November 2, 1996, Yale Rep
By Katharine Dayton and George S. Kaufman
Directed by Stan Wojewodski Jr.

Production History

The Cryptogram
November 14–December 7, 1996, Yale Rep
By David Mamet
Directed by Mark Rucker

* Triumph of Love
January 16–February 8, 1997, Yale Rep
Coproduction with Baltimore's Center Stage
Adapted from Marivaux's *The Triumph of Love* by James
    Magruder
Music by Jeffrey Stock
Lyrics by Susan Birkenhead
Directed by Michael Mayer
Choreography by Doug Varone

The Skin of Our Teeth
February 20–March 15, 1997, Yale Rep
By Thornton Wilder
Directed by Liz Diamond

* The Adventures of Amy Bock
March 27–April 19, 1997, Yale Rep
By Julie McKee
Directed by Stan Wojewodski Jr.

Thunder Knocking on the Door
May 1–May 24, 1997, Yale Rep
By Keith Glover
Directed by Reggie Montgomery
Original lyrics and music by Keb' Mo'

Special Events:
   Don Byron and Existential Dred, December 14, 1996, UT
   Meredith Monk, February 8, 1997, UT
   The Dangerous Border Game, March 29, 1997, UT

1997–1998
* Geography
October 23–November 8, 1997, UT
Conceived, choreographed, and directed by Ralph Lemon
Text by Tracie Morris
Soundscores by Francisco López and Paul D. Miller, a.k.a.
    DJ Spooky

Candida
November 28–December 1997, Yale Rep
By George Bernard Shaw
Directed by Stan Wojewodski Jr.

Splash Hatch on the E Going Down
January 15–February 7, 1998, Yale Rep
Coproduction with Baltimore's Center Stage
By Kia Corthron
Directed by Marion McClinton

A Midsummer Night's Dream
February 19–March 14, 1998, Yale Rep
By William Shakespeare
Directed by Christopher Grabowski

The Cure at Troy
March 26–April 18, 1998, Yale Rep
Adapted by Seamus Heaney from Sophocles's *Philoctetes*
Directed by Liz Diamond

Petersburg
April 30–May 23, 1998, Yale Rep
Adapted by C. B. Coleman from Andrei Bely's novel
Directed by Evan Yionoulis

1998–1999
Peter and Wendy
September 17–October 3, 1998, UT
From the novel by J. M. Barrie
Adapted by Liza Lorwin
Directed by Lee Breuer
Music by Johnny Cunningham
Lyrics by Johnny Cunningham, J. M. Barrie, Lee Breuer, and
    Liza Lorwin

Galileo
October 22–November 14, 1998, Yale Rep
By Bertolt Brecht
Translated by Charles Laughton
Directed by Evan Yionoulis

Crumbs from the Table of Joy
November 27–December 19, 1998, Yale Rep
By Lynn Nottage
Directed by Seret Scott

Measure for Measure
January 28–February 20, 1999, Yale Rep
by William Shakespeare
Directed by Mark Rucker

The Glass Menagerie
March 18–April 10, 1999, Yale Rep
by Tennessee Williams
Directed by Joseph Chaikin

Hay Fever
April 29–May 22, 1999, Yale Rep
By Noël Coward
Directed by Stan Wojewodski Jr.

1999–2000
* The Imaginary Invalid
September 16–October 9, 1999, Yale Rep
By Molière
Translation and adaptation by James Magruder
Music by Gina Leishman
Directed by Mark Rucker

Betrayal
October 21–November 13, 1999, Yale Rep
By Harold Pinter
Directed by Liz Diamond

A Cup of Coffee
November 26–December 18, 1999, Yale Rep
By Preston Sturges
Directed by Joe Grifasi

Curse of the Starving Class
February 3–February 26, 2000, Yale Rep
By Sam Shepard
Directed by Jim Simpson

Richard III
March 16–April 8, 2000, Yale Rep
By William Shakespeare
Directed by Stan Wojewodski Jr.

* Tree, Part 2 of the Geography Trilogy: Asia/Belief
April 20–May 13, 2000, UT
Conceived by Ralph Lemon
Original soundscore by James Lo
Text arrangement by Katherine Profeta

Special Event:
    Hazelle Goodman, *To the Top Top Top!*, February 12, 2000, UT

2000–2001
Mump + Smoot in **Something Else with Zug**
September 14–October 7, 2000, Yale Rep
By Michael Kennard and John Turner
Directed by Karen Hines

* Rice Boy
October 19–November 11, 2000, Yale Rep
By Sunil Kuruvilla
Directed by Liz Diamond

Heaven
November 24–December 16, 2000, Yale Rep
By George F. Walker
Directed by Evan Yionoulis

The Way of the World
February 9–March 3, 2001, UT
By Willliam Congreve
Directed by Stan Wojewodski Jr.

The Birds
March 22–April 14, 2001, Yale Rep
Freely adapted from Aristophanes by Len Jenkin
Directed by Christopher Bayes
Choreography by David Neumann

Big Night
April 26–May 19, 2001, Yale Rep
By Dawn Powell
Directed by Stan Wojewodski Jr.

2001–2002
You Never Can Tell
September 20–October 13, 2001, Yale Rep
By George Bernard Shaw
Directed by Stan Wojewodski Jr.

Kingdom of Earth
October 25–December 1, 2001, New Theater
by Tennessee Williams
Directed by Mark Rucker

It Pays to Advertise
November 29–December 22, 2001, UT
By Roi Cooper Megrue and Walter Hackett
Directed by Stan Wojewodski Jr.

Betty's Summer Vacation
February 7–March 2, 2002, Yale Rep
By Christopher Durang
Directed by Doug Hughes

Serious Money
March 21–April 13, 2002, Yale Rep
By Caryl Churchill
Directed by Jean Randich

Iphigenia at Aulis
April 25–May 18, 2002, Yale Rep
By Euripides
Newly translated and adapted by Kenneth Cavander
Directed by Rebecca Taichman
Choreography by Stormy Brandenberger

2002–2003
Medea/Macbeth/Cinderella
September 20–October 12, 2002, UT
Conceived by Bill Rauch
Adapted by Bill Rauch and Tracy Young
From Euripides's *Medea*, translated by Paul Roche with music and lyrics by Shishir Kurup; Shakespeare's *Macbeth*; and *Cinderella*, with music by Richard Rodgers, book and lyrics by Oscar Hammerstein II
Directed by Bill Rauch and Tracy Young
Choreography by Sabrina Peck

Breath, Boom
October 25–November 16, 2002, Yale Rep
By Kia Corthron
Directed by Michael John Garcés

+ Fighting Words
November 15–December 21, 2002, New Theater
By Sunil Kuruvilla
Directed by Liz Diamond

The Psychic Life of Savages
February 14–March 8, 2003, Yale Rep
By Amy Freed
Directed by James Bundy

The Taming of the Shrew
March 21–April 12, 2003, Yale Rep
By William Shakespeare
Directed by Mark Lamos
Choreography by Seán Curran

* The Black Monk
May 9–June 1, 2003, Yale Rep
By David Rabe
Based on the novella by Anton Chekhov
Directed by Daniel Fish
Choreography by Peter Pucci

Special Event:
　What Ever!, written and performed by Heather Woodbury, April 9–12, 2003, New Theater

2003–2004
+ The Black Dahlia
October 17–November 8, 2003, UT
Adapted and directed by Mike Alfreds
From the novel by James Ellroy

Culture Clash in America
November 14–December 6, 2003, Yale Rep
Created, written, and performed by Richard Montoya, Ric Salinas, and Herbert Siguenza
Directed by Tony Taccone

* Rothschild's Fiddle
January 14–31, 2004, UT
Adapted and directed by Kama Ginkas
From the story by Anton Chekhov
Supertitle translation by John Freedman

King Lear
February 13–March 13, 2004, UT
By William Shakespeare
Directed by Harold Scott

* The King Stag
March 26–April 17, 2004, Yale Rep
By Carlo Gozzi
Adapted by Evan Yionoulis, Mike Yionoulis, and Catherine Sheehy
Music and lyrics by Mike Yionoulis
Directed by Evan Yionoulis

* The Mystery Plays
April 30–May 22, 2004, New Theater
Coproduction with Second Stage Theatre
By Roberto Aguirre-Sacasa
Directed by Connie Grappo

Special Events:
 Hiroshima Maiden, written and directed by Dan Hurlin, February 21, 2004, Yale Rep
 Matt and Ben, written and performed by Mindy Kaling and Brenda Withers, directed by David Warren, April 21, 2004, UT

2004–2005
* The Clean House
September 17–October 9, 2004, UT
By Sarah Ruhl
Directed by Bill Rauch

The Intelligent Design of Jenny Chow
October 22–November 13, 2004, Yale Rep
By Rolin Jones
Directed by Jackson Gay

The Ladies of the Camellias
November 26–December 18, 2004, UT
By Lillian Groag
Directed by James Bundy

The Comedy of Errors
February 11–March 12, 2005, UT
By William Shakespeare
Directed by Kenneth Albers

* Miss Julie
March 18–April 9, 2005, Yale Rep
By August Strindberg
English version by Richard Nelson
Directed by Liz Diamond
Choreography by Peter Pucci

* Radio Golf
April 22–May 15, 2005, Yale Rep
By August Wilson
Directed by Timothy Douglas

Special Events:
+ *Buwalsky, A Road Opera*, September 23–26, 2004, New Theater
 Presented in association with Nine Circles Chamber Theatre and Opera Spanga
 Music by Mel Marvin
 Libretto by Jonathan Levi, based on the screenplay by Irma Achten
 Directed by Corina Van Eijk
Ferdydurke by Witold Gombrowicz, October 22–23, 2004, UT
 Translated by Danuta Borchardt
 Adapted by Allen J. Kuharski
Grupo Cultural Yuyachkani: A Festival of Performance, Politics and Memory, April 13–19, 2005, New Theater
 Adios Ayacucho, performed by Augusto Casafranca, April 13 and 15, 2005

Production History 339

Antigona, performed by Teresa Ralli, April 14 and 16, 2005

Rosa Cuchillo, performed by Ana Correa, April 19, 2005

2005–2006

* The Cherry Orchard
October 7–29, 2005, UT
Adaptation by Alison Carey
From Anton Chekhov
As translated by Maria Amadei Ashot
Directed by Bill Rauch
Choreography by Peter Pucci

Safe in Hell
November 12–December 3, 2005, Yale Rep
By Amy Freed
Directed by Mark Wing-Davey
Choreography by Peter Pucci

The People Next Door
January 13–February 4, 2006, Yale Rep
By Henry Adam
Directed by Evan Yionoulis

Comedy on the Bridge and **Brundibar**
February 10–March 5, 2006, UT
In collaboration with Berkeley Repertory Theatre and in association with The Yale School of Music
Comedy on the Bridge
Libretto by Tony Kushner
Adapted from Vaclav Kliment Klicpera
Music by Bohuslav Martinu
Brundibar
English adaptation by Tony Kushner
After Adolf Hoffmeister's Libretto
Music by Hans Krasa
Directed by Tony Taccone

* dance of the holy ghosts: a play on memory
March 17–April 8, 2006, New Theater
By Marcus Gardley
Directed by Liz Diamond
Choreography by Peter Pucci

All's Well That Ends Well
April 21–May 20, 2006, Yale Rep
By William Shakespeare
Directed by James Bundy and Mark Rucker
Choreography by John Carrafa

Special Events:
Mabou Mines Dollhouse, copresentation with Long Wharf Theatre, conceived and directed by Lee Breuer, March 31–April 1, 2006, UT
Unbounded, choreographed by Gina Gibney, performed by Gina Gibney Dance, April 28, 2006, UT

2006–2007

Eurydice
September 22–October 14, 2006, Yale Rep
By Sarah Ruhl
Directed by Les Waters
Choreography by John Carrafa

The Mistakes Madeline Made
October 27–November 18, 2006, Yale Rep
By Elizabeth Meriwether
Directed by Mark Rucker

Black Snow
December 1–23, 2006, Yale Rep
By Mihail Bulgakov
Adapted by Keith Reddin
Directed by Evan Yionoulis

In the Continuum
January 12–February 10, 2007, Yale Rep
A Primary Stages / Perry Street Theatre Production
Written and performed by Danai Gurira and Nikkole Salter
Directed by Robert O'Hara

Lulu
March 30–April 21, 2007, Yale Rep
By Frank Wedekind
Translated by Carl R. Mueller
Adapted by Mark Lamos and Drew Lichtenberg
Directed by Mark Lamos
Choreography and musical staging by Seán Curran

The Unmentionables
May 4–26, 2007, Yale Rep
By Bruce Norris
Directed by Anna D. Shapiro

2007–2008
Richard II
September 21–October 13, 2007, Yale Rep
By William Shakespeare
Directed by Evan Yionoulis

Trouble in Mind
October 26–November 17, 2007, Yale Rep
By Alice Childress
Directed by Irene Lewis

Tartuffe
December 3–December 22, 2007, Yale Rep
Produced in association with the McCarter Theatre Center, Princeton, NJ
By Molière
Translated by Richard Wilbur
Directed by Daniel Fish

*The Evildoers
January 18–February 9, 2008, Yale Rep
By David Adjmi
Directed by Rebecca Taichman

A Woman of No Importance
March 21–April 12, 2008, Yale Rep
By Oscar Wilde
Directed by James Bundy

* Boleros for the Disenchanted
April 25–May 17, 2008, Yale Rep
By José Rivera
Directed by Henry Godinez

No Boundaries Series
    The Veiled Monologues, October 23–27, 2007, New Theater
    Peru Negro, January 30–31, 2008, UT
    Farm in the Cave Theatre Studio Presents *SCLAVI: The Song of an Emigrant*, April 3–5, 2008, UT

2008–2009
Passion Play
September 19–October 11, 2008, UT
By Sarah Ruhl
Directed by Mark Wing-Davey

+ Happy Now?
October 24–November 15, 2008, Yale Rep
By Lucinda Coxon
Directed by Liz Diamond

Rough Crossing
November 28–December 20, 2008, UT
By Tom Stoppard, from an original play by Ferenc Molnár
Directed by Mark Rucker
Choreography by Michelle Lynch

Lydia
February 6–28, 2009, Yale Rep
By Octavio Solis
Directed by Juliette Carrillo

* Notes from Underground
March 20–April 11, 2009, Yale Rep
Adapted from Fyodor Dostoevsky's novel by Bill Camp and Robert Woodruff
Based on a translation by Richard Pevear and Larissa Volokhonsky
Directed by Robert Woodruff

Death of a Salesman
April 24–May 23, 2009, Yale Rep
By Arthur Miller
Directed by James Bundy

No Boundaries Series
    A Festival of International Dance at Yale, Iseman Theater
    Yasmeen Godder, *Singular Sensation*, November 14–15, 2008
    Opiyo Okach, *No Man's Gone Now* and *Territories in Transgression*, November 11–12, 2008

Production History

Yvonne Rainer, *RoS Indexical* and *Spiraling Down*, November 11–12, 2008
Marc Bamuthi Joseph, *The Break/s: A Mixtape for Stage*, January 22–24, 2009
Mapa Teatro, +*Witness to the Ruins*, March 26–28, 2009

2009–2010

The Master Builder
September 18–October 19, 2009, UT
By Henrik Ibsen
Translated by Paul Walsh
Directed by Evan Yionoulis

Eclipsed
October 23–November 14, 2009, Yale Rep
By Danai Gurira
Directed by Liesl Tommy

* Pop!
November 27–December 19, 2009, Yale Rep
Book and lyrics by Maggie-Kate Coleman
Music by Anna K. Jacobs
Directed by Mark Brokaw
Choreography by Denis Jones

* Compulsion
January 29–February 28, 2010, Yale Rep
A coproduction with Berkeley Repertory Theatre and the Public Theater
By Rinne Groff
Directed by Oskar Eustis

The Servant of Two Masters
March 12–April 3, 2010, UT
By Carlo Goldoni
Adapted by Constance Congdon
From a translation by Christina Sibul
Directed by Christopher Bayes

Battle of Black and Dogs
April 16–May 8, 2010, Yale Rep
By Bernard-Marie Koltès
Translation and music composition by Michaël Attias
Directed by Robert Woodruff

No Boundaries Series
Wormwood, by Theatre of the Eighth Day (Teatr Ósmego Dnia), November 5–7, 2009, Iseman Theater
The Be(a)st of Taylor Mac, written and performed by Taylor Mac, directed by David Drake, January 28–30, 2010, UT
Baby-Q's MESs, by Yoko Higashino and Toshio Kajiwara, March 25–27, 2010, Iseman Theater

2010–2011

* We Have Always Lived in the Castle
September 17–October 9, 2010, UT
Book and lyrics by Adam Bock
Music and lyrics by Todd Almond
Based on the novel by Shirley Jackson
Directed by Anne Kauffman

A Delicate Balance
October 22–November 13, 2010, Yale Rep
By Edward Albee
Directed by James Bundy

* Bossa Nova
November 26–December 18, 2010, Yale Rep
By Kirsten Greenidge
Directed by Evan Yionoulis

The Piano Lesson
January 28–February 19, 2011, Yale Rep
By August Wilson
Directed by Liesl Tommy

Romeo and Juliet
March 11–April 2, 2011, UT
By William Shakespeare
Directed by Shana Cooper
Music by Gina Leishman
Choreography by Seán Curran

+ Autumn Sonata
April 15–May 7, 2011, Yale Rep
By Ingmar Bergman
Based on a literal translation by Wendy Weckwerth
Directed by Robert Woodruff

No Boundaries Series
+ *The Case of the Spectator*, created and performed by María Jerez, September 23–25, 2010, Iseman Theater
The Method Gun, written by Kirk Lynn, directed by Shawn Sides, created by Rude Mechs, February 23–26, 2011, Yale Rep
Nameless Forest, conceived and directed by Dean Moss, in collaboration with Sungmyung Chun, March 31–April 2, 2011, Iseman Theater

2011–2012

Three Sisters
September 16–October 8, 2011, UT
By Anton Chekhov
A new version by Sarah Ruhl
Based on a literal translation by Elise Thoron with Matalya Paramonova and Kristin Johnsen-Neshati
Directed by Les Waters

* Belleville
October 21–November 12, 2011, Yale Rep
By Amy Herzog
Directed by Anne Kauffman

A Doctor in Spite of Himself
November 26–December 17, 2011, Yale Rep
Coproduction with Berkeley Repertory Theatre
By Molière
Adapted by Christopher Bayes and Steven Epp
Directed by Christopher Bayes

* Good Goods
February 3–25, 2012, Yale Rep
By Christina Anderson
Directed by Tina Landau

The Winter's Tale
March 16–April 7, 2012, UT
By William Shakespeare
Directed by Liz Diamond
Composed by Matthew Suttor
Choreography by Randy Duncan

* The Realistic Joneses
April 20–May 12, 2012, Yale Rep
By Will Eno
Directed by Sam Gold

No Boundaries Series
Engagement Féminin: An Evening of West African Contemporary Dance, created and performed by Art' Dév / Compagnie Auguste-Bienvenue, November 3–5, 2011, Iseman Theater
Spectral Scriabin, piano by Eteri Andjaparidze, lighting by Jennifer Tipton, February 10–11, 2012, UT
The Rehearsal, directed by Cuqui Jerez, created in collaboration with María Jerez, Amaia Urra, Ismeni Enevold, and Thomas Kasebacher, March 23–24, 2012, Iseman Theater

2012–2013

American Night: The Ballad of Juan José
September 21–October 13, 2012, UT
By Richard Montoya
Developed by Culture Clash and Jo Bonney
Directed by Shana Cooper
Choreography by Ken Roht

* Marie Antoinette
October 26–November 17, 2012, Yale Rep
A Coproduction with American Repertory Theater
By David Adjmi
Directed by Rebecca Taichman
Choreography by Karole Armitage

* Dear Elizabeth, A Play in Letters from Elizabeth Bishop to Robert Lowell and Back Again
November 20–December 22, Yale Rep
By Sarah Ruhl
Directed by Les Waters

Stones in His Pockets
January 25–February 16, 2013 Yale Rep
By Marie Jones
Directed by Evan Yionoulis

Hamlet
March 15–April 13, 2013, UT
By William Shakespeare
Directed by James Bundy
Music composed by Sarah Pickett

* In a Year with 13 Moons
April 26–May 18, 2013, Yale Rep
Film and screenplay by Rainer Werner Fassbinder
Adapted for the stage by Bill Camp and Robert Woodruff
Directed by Robert Woodruff
Based on a literal translation by Louisa Proske
Choreography by David Neumann

No Boundaries Series
Super Night Shot, by Gob Squad, February 1–2, 2013, UT

2013–2014
A Streetcar Named Desire
September 20–October 12, 2013, UT
By Tennessee Williams
Directed by Mark Rucker

Owners
October 25–November 16, 2013, Yale Rep
By Caryl Churchill
Directed by Evan Yionoulis

Accidental Death of an Anarchist
November 30–December 21, 2013, Yale Rep
A coproduction with Berkeley Repertory Theatre
By Dario Fo
Adapted by Gavin Richards
From a translation by Gilliam Hanna
Directed by Christopher Bayes

The Fairytale Lives of Russian Girls
January 31–February 22, 2014, Yale Rep
By Meg Miroshnik
Directed by Rachel Chavkin

* These Paper Bullets! A Modish Ripoff of William Shakespeare's Much Ado about Nothing
March 15–April 5, 2014, UT
Adapted by Rolin Jones
Songs by Billie Joe Armstrong
Directed by Jackson Gay
Choreography by Monica Bill Barnes

* The House that will not Stand
April 18–May 10, 2014, Yale Rep
A coproduction with Berkeley Repertory Theatre
By Marcus Gardley
Directed by Patricia McGregor
Choreography by Paloma McGregor

No Boundaries Series
The Files, by Theatre of the Eighth Day (Teatr Ósmego Dnia), written by Ewa Wójciak and Katarzyna Madon-Mitzner, February 20–22, 2014, Iseman Theater

2014–2015
Arcadia
October 3–25, 2014, UT
By Tom Stoppard
Directed by James Bundy
Choreography by Emily Coates

* War
November 21–December 13, 2014, Yale Rep
By Branden Jacobs-Jenkins
Directed by Lileana Blain-Cruz
Choreography by David Neumann

* Familiar
January 30–February 21, 2015, Yale Rep
By Danai Gurira
Directed by Rebecca Taichman

The Caucasian Chalk Circle
March 20–April 11, 2015, UT
By Bertolt Brecht
Translated by James and Tania Stern with W. H. Auden

Directed by Liz Diamond
Music composed by David Lang
Choreography by Randy Duncan

* Elevada
April 24–May 16, 2015, Yale Rep
By Sheila Callaghan
Directed by Jackson Gay
Choreography by Kyle Abraham and Kevin Williamson

No Boundaries Series
    Now Now Oh Now, created by Rude Mechs, December 4–10, 2014, UT
    Three Acts, Two Dancers, One Radio Host, created by Ira Glass, Monica Bill Barnes, and Anna Bass, directed and choreographed by Monica Bill Barnes, December 20, 2014, UT
    Songs of Lear, by Song of the Goat Theatre (Teatre Pieśń Kozła), directed by Gergorz Bral, February 26–28, 2015, Iseman Theater

2015–2016

* **Indecent**
October 2–October 24, 2015, UT
Adapted from Sholem Asch's *God of Vengeance*
Written by Paula Vogel
Created by Paula Vogel and Rebecca Taichman
Directed by Rebecca Taichman
Original music by Lisa Gutkin and Alvin Halva
Choreography by David Dorfman

* **peerless**
November 27–December 19, 2015, Yale Rep
By Jiehae Park
Directed by Margot Bordelon

* **The Moors**
January 29–February 20, Yale Rep
By Jen Silverman
Directed by Jackson Gay

Cymbeline
March 25–April 16, 2016, UT
By William Shakespeare
Directed by Evan Yionoulis

Happy Days
April 29–May 21, 2016, Yale Rep
By Samuel Beckett
Directed by James Bundy

No Boundaries Series
    Refuse the Hour, by William Kentridge, Philip Miller, Dada Masilo, Catherine Meyburgh, and Peter Galison, November 6–7, 2015, Iseman Theater
    Escuela, written and directed by Guillermo Calderón, February 24–26, 2016, Iseman Theater

2016–2017

* **Scenes from Court Life; or the whipping boy and his prince**
September 30–October 22, 2016, UT
By Sarah Ruhl
Directed by Mark Wing-Davey

Production History   **345**

BIBLIOGRAPHIC ESSAY

Long after the scars have healed, a vast majority of MFA dramaturgy and dramatic criticism graduates of the Yale School of Drama will point to "crit class" as having been the most valuable portion of their curriculum. In each of their six semesters, students submit two criticism papers of roughly two thousand words to a subset of their peers and to a member of the dramaturgy faculty a week in advance of a workshop meeting. Feathers and fur fly in these unrestrained group critiques. Stanley Kauffmann (1916–2013) made me cry in my first-ever crit class in the fall of 1985 when he stated—as his opener—that my paper on the French film *Entre Nous* was "the very opposite of well-written." His colleague Richard Gilman (1923–2006) dinged into the heads of several decades of students his horror of footnotes and endnotes. We weren't writing for the academy. We were training to be critics. We were meant to stand or fall on our own thoughts and not rely on borrowed theoretical finery.

The Play's the Thing can be seen as my 120,000-word crit paper on the first fifty years of Yale Repertory Theatre. Artistic Director James Bundy and I conceived this book as an informed, detailed, comprehensive chronicle of events, personalities, and productions that would refrain from puffery and ideally fulfill Horace's injunction from *Ars Poetica* for the poet to instruct and delight.

The bulk of the information presented in this book derives from 127 on-the-record interviews I conducted, perhaps two-thirds of them in person with a tape recorder and one-third over the telephone without a tape recorder. Their original quotes are presented in the book in the present tense. Attributed phrases or sentences in the past tense are taken from contemporary interviews and feature stories in media outlets as diverse as the *Hartford Courant*, the *New Haven Register*, and the *Yale Bulletin*, as well as Yale Rep program notes and newsletters. Following the theatrical dictum to yield no power to one's critics, even when they shower you with praise, individual bylines in newspaper and journal reviews are routinely omitted.

Arts institutions, especially in their fledgling years, operate by triage, their leaders and administrators too preoccupied with keeping the doors open to maintain comprehensive records. Fortunately, Yale Rep has had the Yale University library system watching its back. Audio, video, and printed traces of the theater are divided between the Manuscripts and Archives Division in the Sterling Library, the Special Collections section of the Haas Family Arts Library, and the Music Library. The personal papers of Lloyd Richards and Benjamin Mordecai are housed in the Beinecke Rare Book and Manuscript Library.

Of all of these collections, I made the most extensive use of the **Pamela Jordan Yale School of Drama Scrapbook Collection**, forty linear feet of archival material, chronologically arranged, which documents the activities of Yale Repertory Theatre from the appointment of Robert Brustein as dean of Yale School of Drama in February 1966 through the end of the 2007–2008 Yale Rep season, when drama librarian Pam Jordan retired.

The scripts of the productions covered in *The Play's the Thing* from 1966 to 2009 are housed in the **Yale Repertory Theatre Scripts Collection**. While many of the works went on to commercial publication, I chose to read them as originally generated by the playwrights and the production stage managers. Amy Boratko and Jennifer Kiger supplied me with PDF drafts of post-2009 Binger Center premieres.

Anyone with an acceptance letter to the Yale School of Drama will eventually lay hands on Robert Brustein's *Making Scenes*. First published in 1981, two years after he "moved" Yale Rep to Harvard, the book is subtitled "A Personal History of the Turbulent Years at Yale 1966–1979" and chronicles the learning curve he underwent to put his ideals into practice. Founding a repertory company *and* remaking the hidebound Yale School of Drama into a professional training program worthy of its name during the explosive late 1960s with a chronic lack of resources and physical space was a Sisyphean task that makes for a fascinating read. As with all insider memoirs, its author could be accused of disingenuousness and score settling, but art is a tough sell in America.

In September 2017, when I interviewed Henry "Sam" Chauncey (YC '57), special assistant to President Kingman Brewster from 1963 to 1977 who later founded the Yale Health Management Program at the Yale School of Public Health, he told me over lunch at Mory's that he believed every institution at Yale merited its own chronicle. I'd like to believe that I took his words to heart with *The Play's the Thing*, a dissertation *à mon insu*. I also hope that my words and thoughts would pass muster with my three crit class professors, Dick Gilman, Stanley Kauffmann, and Gordon Rogoff (1931–2024), who were tougher critics than Horace.

LIST OF INTERVIEWEES

Mark Linn-Baker, Kristine Nielsen, Catherine Sheehy, Bill Rauch, Victoria Nolan, Jennifer Kiger, Frank Rizzo, Michael Feingold, Mark Bly, Gordon Rogoff, James Bundy, Joe Grifasi, Lee Blessing, Robert Woodruff, Bill Camp, Robert Brustein, Eric Overmyer, Christopher Bayes, Felicity Jones Latta, Kimberly Scott, Evan Yionoulis, Carmen de Lavallade, Edward Martenson, Frank Torok, Meg Simon, Fran Kumin, Tara Rubin, Pam Jordan, James Mountcastle, Teresa Eyring, Henry Chauncey, Charles Long, Arthur Nacht, Merle Nacht, David Adjmi, Kenneth Cavander, Doug Wright, Marcus Gardley, Rolin Jones, Tarell Alvin McCraney, Keith Reddin, Jeffrey Wanshel, David Epstein, Rocco Landesman, Joel Schechter, Jonathan Marks, Mark Brokaw, Liz Diamond, Gordon Edelstein, Jackson Gay, Irene Lewis, Mitchell Kurtz, Tony Taccone, Darko Tresjnak, Stan Wojewodski Jr., David Budries, Jess Goldstein, Jane Greenwood, Wendall Harrington, Susan Hilferty, Stephen Strawbridge, Jennifer Tipton, William Ivey Long, Michael Yeargan, Catherine Zuber, Katherine Burgueño, Joan Channick, Ruth Schmitt, Steven Padla, Robin Hirsch, Robert Wildman, Alma Cuervo, Barbara Damashek, Elizabeth Parrish, Reg E. Cathey, Reg Rogers, Tony Shalhoub, Tom Walker, Dianne Wiest, Frances McDormand, Jim Simpson, Timothy Douglas, Rick Elice, Wesley Fata, Walton Jones, Wendy MacLeod, Andrei Belgrader, Dunya Ramicova, Ben Cameron, John Conklin, Riccardo Hernández, Sherry Mordecai, Christopher Walken, Julie McKee, Amy Boratko, Kim Sherman, Anne Kauffman, Katherine Roth, Constance Grappo, David Schweizer, John Guare, Lisa Peterson, Alexander Dodge, Barbara Somerville, Elizabeth Stevens, Kathy Chalfant, Ricardo Morris, Elizabeth Bolster, Marguerite Elliott, Jacob Padrón, Neil Mulligan, Neil Mazzella, Paul Giamatti, Tori Sampson, Kari Olmon, Carmen Morgan, René Augesen, Matt Saunders, Paul Walsh, Tom McAlister, Deborah Berman, Patric Madden, Nahuel Telleria, Chad Kinsman, Lonnie Carter, Amy Aquino, and Courtney B. Vance.

    I also made grateful use of interviews previously held and transcribed by Jeffrey Sweet and Martha Wade Steketee with Athol Fugard, Jane Kaczmarek, David Clennon, Kate Burton, Henry Winkler, Nicholas Hormann, Michael Gross, Honor Moore, Jonathan Miller, Arvin Brown, Michael Posnick, Bronislaw Sammler, David Chambers, Christopher Durang, Amy Herzog, Gitta Honegger, James Earl Jones, Steven Epp, Meryl Streep, Alvin Epstein, Katherine Profeta, Ralph Lemon, Sarah Ruhl, David Shookhoff, and Lizbeth Mackay.

ACKNOWLEDGMENTS

First and foremost, I'd like to thank James Bundy and Victoria Nolan for entrusting this project to me. James and Vicki, as well as Deborah Berman, Joan Channick, and Catherine Sheehy, always made terrific first responders to my questions, the sweeping and the picayune. My apologies for abusing their availability. For deeper dives into the Brustein era, I relied on the crackerjack memories of Jonathan Marks, Michael Yeargan, and Lonnie Carter. Current Yale staffers Amy Boratko, Steven Padla, Jennifer Alzona, Josephine Brown, Emalie Mayo, Florie Seery, and Susan Clark also cheerfully responded to a constant stream of queries. I was fortunate throughout the process to have research assistants Kari Olmon and Charles O'Malley for handholding and hard facts from Manuscripts and Archives at Sterling Memorial Library. A gracious enfilade of company managers, starting with Flo Low and followed by Rachel Shuey, Lisa Richardson, Caitlin Cromblehome, Markie Gray, Dani Barlow, Eliza Orleans, and Oakton Reynolds, ensured my physical comfort at Madison Towers.

Thanks to Ed Surato of the Whitney Library at the New Haven Museum for the early visuals of Calvary Baptist Church, and to Lindsay King, former associate director for access and research services at the Haas Family Arts Library. Special thanks to María Zapata and the rest of her staff, Jodee London, Molly Bailey Dillon, Dana Eckstein Berkowitz, Shawana Snell, and Teresa Mensz, in Special Collections at the Haas for their many kindnesses and for extending their hours when possible for me, and to the collective editorial acumen and assistance of Adina Popescu Berk, Ashley Lago, Eva Skewes, and Ann-Marie Imbornoni at Yale University Press, and Gretchen Otto, Alison Rainey, and Christine Gever at Motto Publishing Services.

Photo editor Marguerite Elliott and associate photo editor Samuel Ruff provided crucial assistance in a late-breaking, highly involved, and wildly attenuated scavenger hunt for images and photographer releases in the midst of the pandemic.

A MacDowell residency in New Hampshire in December 2018 awarded me the time and the space to discover that I could—and really would—write this book. Finally, no prose flows from these fretful, fitful fingers without the support and love of my husband, Stephen G. Bolton.

INDEX

Page numbers in italics indicate illustrations.

Aarn, Kimberleigh: *Joe Turner's Come and Gone* (actor), *141*
About Face (April 5–23, 1983), 328
Abscam sting (1980), 150
Accidental Death of an Anarchist (November 30–December 21, 2013), 148, 344
Acito, Tim: *Zanna Don't!* (author/composer), 30
Ackroyd, David, 93
Actors' Equity Association, 121, 232, 255
Actor's Express (Atlanta), 260
Actor's Studio Company: *Dynamite* (production), 15
Actors Theatre of Louisville, 85, 99, 160
Adjmi, David (author): *The Evildoers*, 257, *262*, 262–63, 272, 341; *Marie Antoinette*, 207, 343
Adler, Stella, xii, 11–12, 222
The Adventures of Amy Bock (March 27–April 19, 1997), 336
Aeschylus, 75, 79, 81; *The Oresteia* (author), 192; *Prometheus Bound* (author), 12–13, 16–19, *18*, 319
AFP. *See* American family play
African Americans. *See* race, diversity, and inclusion; headings starting with "Black"
Age of American Confession, 182
Aguirre-Sacasa, Roberto: *The Mystery Plays* (author), 218, 339

Ah, Wilderness! (March 22–May 21, 1988), 132–33, 144, 214–15, 331
Ahern, James, 28
AIDS/HIV, 182, 257
Akalaitis, JoAnne, 169, 216
Akerlind, Christopher: *Indecent* (lighting designer), 301
Albee, Edward, 272–73; *A Delicate Balance* (author), 35, 254, 282–83, 342
The Alchemist (October 18–November 12, 1988), 124, 331
Alexander, Elijah: *Le Bourgeois Avant Garde* (actor), *75*
Allende, Salvador, 184
Alley Theatre (Houston), xii, 9
All's Well That Ends Well (April 21–May 20, 2006), *123*, 252, 282, 340
alumni engagement, 252–53, 254
The America Play (January 13–February 5, 1994), 202, 208–9, *209*, 226, 334
American family play (AFP), 88, 90, 276–82
American Ibsen Theater (Pittsburgh), 128
American Night: The Ballad of Juan José (September 21–October 13, 2012), 343
American Repertory Theater (A.R.T., Cambridge), 84, 101, 207; *Archangels Don't Play Pinball*, 150; Broadway and, 159; Brustein and, 50, 229; *Marie Antoinette*, 343; Woodruff and, 266

Americans with Disabilities Act (1990), 120
American Theatre (magazine), 39, 159, 197
Analyzing and Mobilizing Privilege (AMP), 298
Anderman, Maureen: *First Lady* (actor), 219
Anderson, Judith, 172
Andrews, Dwight: *The Piano Lesson* (composer), 331; *The Resurrection of Lady Lester* (composer/arranger), 112, 327
Andrew W. Mellon Foundation. *See* Mellon Foundation
Annals, Michael: *Prometheus Bound* (set designer), 17–18
Antigone (September 16–28, 1968), 26, 320
Antigone in New York (October 20–November 12, 1994), 207, 335
Antoinette Perry Awards. *See* Tony Awards
Apocalyptic Butterflies (January 13–February 7, 1987), 115, 330
Aquino, Amy, 114, 160
Aranha, Ray: *A Play of Giants* (actor), *147*
Arcadia (October 3–25, 2014), 293–95, *294*, 344
Arden, John: *Armstrong's Last Goodnight*, 13
Arena Stage (Washington, DC), xii, 9, 84, 172, 244

353

Are You Now or Have You Ever Been (November 10–January 10, 1973), 322
Aristophanes: *The Birds* (author), 178, 337; *The Frogs* (author), 49, 75, 79–82, *80*, 323
Aristotle, 88, 195; *Poetics* (author), 14
Armstrong, Billie Joe: *These Paper Bullets!* (composer), 270, 344
Arnott, Christopher, 259
Arrick, Larry, 23, 44, 93, 320; *Coriolanus* (associate director), 320; *Gimpel the Fool* (adaptation), 44, 321; *Ovid's Metamorphoses* (director), 44, 320; *Story Theatre* (associate director), 23, 40, 320; *Story Theatre Repertory* (director), 23, 40, 44, 321; *The Three Sisters* (director), 320; *We Bombed in New Haven* (director), 22–23, 319; *Where Has Tommy Flowers Gone?* (director), 23, 321
A.R.T. *See* American Repertory Theater
Artaud, Antonin, 26
Asch, Sholem: *God of Vengeance* (author), 301–3, 345
Asian and Asian American Theatre Coalition (Asian Potluck), 298
associate artists program, 161, 162–63, *163*
Astapovo (January 4–February 5, 1983), 328
As You Like It (April 12–May 9, 1979), 35, 326
As You Like It (February 17–March 12, 1994), 35, 174, 334
Atkinson, Jayne, 114
Atkinson, Linda: *A Midsummer Night's Dream* (actor), 61–62
An Attempt at Flying (April 28–May 16, 1981), 327
Attias, Michaël: *Battle of Black and Dogs* (translation/composer), 342; *Notes from the Underground* (composer/sound designer), 266
Auden, W. H., 321, 344
auditions, 121–23, *123*
Augesen, René: *Arcadia* (actor), 294–95, *294*; *A Streetcar Named Desire* (actor), 282, 295; *Three Sisters* (actor), 282;

A Woman of No Importance (actor), 282, 295
Auletta, Robert (author), 105; *Guess Work*, 326; *Stops*, 322; *Walk the Dog, Willie*, 324
Autumn Sonata (April 15–May 7, 2011), 342
avant-garde staging, 170, 171
Azenberg, Emanuel, 114

The B. Beaver Animation (September 16–17, 1977), 184, 326
Baal (February 16–April 24, 1973), 322
Baartman, Saartjie, 209–10
Bacchae (March 6–22, 1969), 36–38, *39*, 320
Backstage, 121
Bacquie, Dwight: *A Play of Giants* (actor), *147*
Badham, John, 253
Baker, Blanche: *White Marriage* (actor), *71*
Baker, Dylan, 114; *Rum and Coke* (actor), 34
Baker, Earl: *Hamlet* (actor), *173*
Baker, George Pierce, 5, 228
The Baltimore Waltz (April 29–May 22, 1993), 182, 334
Bamman, Gerry: *Hamlet* (actor), 293
The Banquet Years (December 30, 1976–?), 183, 325
Barrault, Jean-Louis, 9, 11; *Happy Days* (actor), 183
Barreca, Christopher: *Democracy in America* (set designer), 170
Barrie, J. M.: *Peter and Wendy* (adaptation by Lorwin), 336
Barton, Mark: *Notes from the Underground* (lighting designer), 266
Bassett, Angela, 114, 298
Bataille, Georges, 44
Battle of Black and Dogs (April 16–May 8, 2010), *131*, 342
Bausch, Pina, 170
Baxley, Barbara: *Major Barbara* (actor), 127; *Mrs. Warren's Profession* (actor), 127
Bayes, Christopher, 282, 308; *Accidental Death of an Anarchist* (director), 287,

344; *The Birds* (director), 178, 285, 337; *A Doctor in Spite of Himself* (director), 343; *The Servant of Two Masters* (director), 285–87, 342
The Beach (January 10–February 4, 1989), 332
Bearden, Romare, 138–40
The Be(a)st of Taylor Mac (No Boundaries Series, January 28–30, 2010), 184, 342
Beatles, 215, 270, 272
Beatriz, Stephanie: *Lydia* (actor), 280
Beaumarchais, Pierre: *The Marriage of Figaro* (author), 9, 75, 200–201, 335
The Beauty Part (April 23–May 23, 1992), 197, 217, 219, *219*, 301, 334
The Beaux' Stratagem (February 15–March 9, 1996), 176, 335
Bechdel, Alison, 165
Beck, Julian, 25–28
Beckett, Samuel, 8, 12, 76, 90, 161, 266, 275, 305, 324; *Endgame* (author), 183, 319; *Happy Days* (author), 9, 183, 233, 301, 304–6, *306*, 320, 345; *Play* (author), 321
Beebe, Dick, 113; *Vampires in Kodachrome* (author), 30, 112, 329
Beef, No Chicken (January 5–February 6, 1982), 328
Behan, Brendan: *The Hostage* (author), 15
Beinecke, John, 253
Beinecke Fellows Program, 253
Belgrader, Andrei (director), xiii; *About Face*, 328; *As You Like It*, 101, 326; *Marriage*, 101, 129–30, 330; *The Miser*, 331; *Moon Over Miami*, 152, 332; *Scapin* (translation), 333; *Troilus and Cressida*, 101, 332; *Ubu Rex*, 101, 152, 327; *What the Butler Saw*, 329
Belleville (October 21–November 12, 2011), 272–78, *273*, *277*, 313, 343
Bellow, Saul, 21
Bely, Andrei: *Petersburg* (author), 68, 336
Benjamin, Walter, 169, 171
Bentley, Eric, xi, 14; *Are You Now or Have You Ever Been* (author), 52, 322; *Henry IV* (translation), 319
Berke, Deborah, 218

Berkeley Repertory Theatre, 99, 207; *Accidental Death of an Anarchist*, 344; *Brundibar*, 340; *Comedy on the Bridge*, 340; *Compulsion*, 342; *A Doctor in Spite of Himself*, 343; *Eurydice*, 242; *The House that will not Stand*, 344; *The Servant of Two Masters*, 287
Berman, Deborah S., 253, 255
Bernhardt, Sarah, 172
Betrayal (October 21–November 13, 1999), 35, 337
Betsko, Kathleen (author): *Johnny Bull*, 328; *Stitchers and Starlight Talkers*, 330
Betsy Ross Arts Magnet School (New Haven), 239
Betty's Summer Vacation (February 7–March 2, 2001), 338
Between East and West (January 14–February 9, 1985), 329
Big Bang (Britain, 1986), 179
Biggs, Murray, 291
The Big House (October 21–December 8, 1972), 75, 322
Big Night (April 26–May 19, 2001), 219, 221–22, *223*, 224, 338
Binger, James H., 250, 264
Binger Center for New Theatre, xiv, 184, 233, 264–65, 268, 270, 272, 276–78, 281–82, 296, 301, 303, 315–16
Bingo (January 29–March 20, 1976), 324
The Birds (March 22–April 14, 2001), 285, 337
Blackall, Clapp, and Whittemore (architects), 20
The Black Dahlia (October 17–November 8, 2003), 338
Black Hills Passion Play, 244
Black History Month, 134, 259
Black Horizon Theater (Pittsburgh), 134
Black Lives Matter (BLM) movement, 296
The Black Monk (May 9–June 1, 2003), 68, 231, 338
Black Panthers, xi, 25, 34, 67, 298
Black Snow (December 1–23, 2006), 68, 283, 340
Blain-Cruz, Lileana: *War* (director), 281, *281*, 344

Blanco, Montana Levi: *War* (costume designer), 280
Bland, John: *Twelfth Night* (actor), *175*
Blau, Herbert, 10
Bleckner, Jeff (director): *Coriolanus*, 320; *The Father*, 324; *Operation Sidewinder*, 34; *Saved*, 31, 320
Blessing, Lee (author), 152; *Cobb*, 332; *A Walk in The Woods*, 118, 144–46, 331
Blocker, Robert, 268
The Blood Knot (September 17–October 12, 1985), 109, 127, 330
Bly, Mark, 52, 174, 178, 182, 185, 198, 202, 211–12, 216, 226, 229, 240, 250; *Hamlet* (dramaturg), 172; *The Production Notebooks* (editor), 193
Boesman and Lena (October 7–25, 1980), 105, 301, 327
Bogart, Anne, 216
Bogosian, Eric: *Pounding Nails in the Floor with My Forehead* (author/performer), 183, 335
Bokassa, Jean-Bédel, 146
Bolcom, William, 47, 267; *Dynamite Tonite!* (composer), 15, *16*, 319, 324; *Greatshot* (composer), 38, 320; *Man Is Man* (composer), 325; *Mister Puntila and His Chauffeur Matti* (composer), 325
Boleros for the Disenchanted (April 25–May 17, 2008), 341
Bond, Edward, 35, 92, 217, 240; *Bingo* (author), 32, 324; *The Bundle: Or, New Narrow Road to the Deep North* (author), 32, 326; *Lear* (adaptation), 32, 63, 75, 87, 104, 310, 323; *Passion* (author), 32, 322; *Saved* (author), 13, 25, 28–32, *31*, 106, 150, 320
Boratko, Amy (dramaturg), 234–35, 255–56, 296, 308, 315–16; *Belleville*, 274; *War*, 280
Bosoms and Neglect (October 4–November 13, 1979), 100, 326
Bossa Nova (November 26–December 18, 2010), 342
Le Bourgeois Avant Garde (April 27–May 20, 1995), 75, *75*, 335

The Bourgeois Gentleman (October 6–December 6, 1972), 322
Bowers, Emma: *Fighting Words* (actor), *238*, 239
Bowles, Jane: *In the Summer House* (author), 8
Boyd, Julie, 114
Bradley, Scott: *Eurydice* (set designer), 242
A Break in the Skin (October 13–January 13, 1973), 322
Breath, Boom (October 25–November 16, 2002), 231, 338
Brecht, Bertolt (author), 14, 32, 35, 76, 104, 126, 171, 182, 188, 217, 267, 309; *Baal*, 198, 322; *The Caucasian Chalk Circle*, 282, 344–45; *Galileo*, 188, 336; *Happy End*, 47–48, 50, 51, 322, 324; *Man Is Man*, 246, 325; *Mister Puntila and His Chauffeur Matti*, 50, 325; *Mother Courage and Her Children*, 15, 271; *The Rise and Fall of the City of Mahagonny*, 47–49, *48*, 51–53, 321, 323, 326; *St. Joan of the Stockyards*, 198–200, *199*, 334; *Seven Deadly Sins*, 47, 321; *The Threepenny Opera*, 50, 64
Brel, Jacques, 183
Brenneman, Amy: *St. Joan of the Stockyards* (actor), 199, *199*
Breuer, Lee: *The B. Beaver Animation* (dramaturg/director), 326; *Mabou Mines Dollhouse* (creator/director), 340; *Peter and Wendy* (director/lyricist), 336; *The Warrior Ant* (creator/director), 183, 332
Brewster, Kingman, xi, xiii, 3–4, 6, 9–11, 42, 45, 53, 56, 91–93, 229–30, 299, 307
Bricklayers (January 14–February 9, 1991), 333
Brockman, Rebekah: *Arcadia* (actor), 294
Broeker, Tom: *Edward II* (costume designer), 197
Brogan, Meg: *Fighting Words* (actor), 238, *238*
Brokaw, Mark, 268; *Crazy from the Heart* (director), 330; *Pop!* (director), 268, 270, 342
Brook, Peter, 19

Index

355

Brooks, Avery: *King Lear* (actor), 239
Brooks, Colette: *Democracy in America* (creator/author), 164, 169–70, 333
Brown, Arvin, 45–46; *Ah, Wilderness!* (director), 132, 331
Brown, Brennan: *Richard III* (actor), *177*
Brown, Josephine, 240
Brown, Kenneth H., 315
Brown, Leon Addison: *The Death of the Last Black Man in the Whole Entire World* (actor), *168*
Brown, Michael, 296
Brown, Robert: *Mrs. Warren's Profession* (actor), *127*
Brown, Tim: *The Winter's Tale* (actor), *288*, 289
Brown, Timothy: *The Master Builder* (set designer), 283
Brown, Zack: *A Midsummer Night's Dream* (costume designer), 61
Browne, Stuart, 114; *Going Over* (author), 328
Brundibar (February 10–March 5, 2006), 259, 340
Brustein, Norma, 7, 52, 93
Brustein, Robert, as dean and artistic director, 1–93, *18*; accomplishments of, 11–13, 52–53, 84, 309; acting preferred over directing by, 251; American family plays and, 88–90; appointment as dean and artistic director, 3, 11; at A.R.T. (Cambridge) after departure, 50, 229; artistic objectives vs. financial success, ix, xi, xiii, 52–53, 293, 309; background of, 1–11; Brecht and Weill productions and, 47–52, 217; casting and auditions, 121–23, *123*; celebrity talent and, 52–53, 62–67; classic repertory and, xiii, 19–20, 120, 195; compared to Bundy, 230, 239, 254; compared to Richards, 98, 120, 127, 154, 182, 314; compared to Wojewodski, 210, 226; core company of, 52; de Lavallade and, 47–48, 50, 52, 62–66; departure from Yale Rep, 91–93, 314; director's theater created by, xiii; European theaters and playwrights as models for, xi, 8, 11, 309; fears of deprofessionalization, 92, 98–99, 314; final season at Yale Rep, 92, 93; first two seasons at Yale Rep, 13–23; as founder and DNA of Yale Rep, ix, xiv, 3, 11, 309, 315; funding and, 53; Giamatti vs., 91–92; guest companies used to jump-start the Rep, 183; Honegger and, 114; Ibsen and, 128; Kiger and, 250; Lee and, 310; legacy of, xiii, 84–85, 87–88, 93, 100; The Living Theatre and, 24–28, 36; on Long Wharf Theatre, 45–46; NEA and, 153; negativity toward Broadway commercialism, xi, 84–85, 90, 105, 220, 272; objective for Rep actors to be able to play any role, 171, 300; outstanding offerings at Yale Rep of, 19, 79, 309; OyamO and, 112; personality of, xii, xiii, 92; production metaphors and, 56–62; the program during era of, 255; public communications of, 67, 254; Rogoff and, 12, 84; Russian works produced by, 68, 214; sabbatical (June 1972–June 1973), 67, 309; Story Theater productions and, 40–47; Sunday Series and, 64–66; tenth season with retrospective productions, 66–67; Vietnam War and, 5, 15, 19, 21, 25, 64–66, 87; violence as theme and, 23–39, 74; Walken and, 54, 59–61; *Watergate Classics*, actor in, 74–75, *77*, 323; Yeargan's memories of, 306–7; writings by: "Broadway Tail Wagging Yale Rep Dog" article, 159; *Happy Days* review, 304; as *London Observer* guest critic, 67; *Making Scenes: A Personal History of the Turbulent Years at Yale 1966–1979* (memoir), 23, 26, 45, 87, 91, 348; "Message from the Director" (1974), 88; *New Republic* reviews, xi; "Oedipus Nix," 74; Parks's *The Death of the Last Black Man in the Whole Entire World* review, 169; *The Theatre of Revolt: An Approach to the Modern Drama*, xi, 3, 14, *14*, 124, 126; *Watergate Classics*, 74–75, *77*, 323

Brustein, Robert, as director: *The Big House*, 54, 75, 322; *Don Juan*, 66, 324; *Don Juan, or the Enemy of God*, 21, 56, 57, 59, 321; *Macbeth*, 21, 239, 321; *The Revenger's Tragedy*, 321; *The Seagull*, 93, 326; *The Wild Duck*, 128, 202, 325
Büchner, Georg (author), 161; *Danton's Death*, 10; *Woyzeck*, 321
Budries, David, 225, 277
Bulandra Theatre Company (Bucharest), 183, 326
Bulgakov, Mihail (author): *Black Snow*, 68, 283, 340; *Monsieur de Molière, or a Cabal of Hypocrites*, 82
The Bundle: Or, New Narrow Road to the Deep North (March 1–May 2, 1979), 32, 326
Bundy, James, as dean of Yale School of Drama, 227–317, *306*; academic objectives of, 231, 233; as actor in *Twelfth Night* (Oregon Shakespeare Festival), 289; alumni engagement and, 252–53, 254; American family plays (AFPs) and, 276; appointment of, 4, 216–17, 229–30; art of more importance than commercial success, 293; background of, 229–30; casting decisions of, 122–23; classics and, 251–52, 254; commissioning new works, xiv, 231, 250, 264–65, 281–82, 308, 316; compared to Brustein, 230, 239, 254; compared to Richards, 251; compared to Wojewodski, 251; dedication to Richards's memory, 254; directors, choice of, 282–95; diversity and inclusion issues, discussion of, 299–300, 308; domestic realism and, 272–76; end of honeymoon for, 239–40; first season of, 231–37; funding and budget for Rep, 263–66, 315; growth in job, 295; illness and surgery, 252; Lee and, 311; legacy of predecessors apparent in, 315; as listener and open to opinion of others, xiv, 308, 315; loss of Yale University endowment in Great Recession and, 295–96; market research by, 179; Nolan appointed as deputy dean, 181,

356 Index

231; praise for, 308; prominent artist recruitment and compensation, 231–32, 252; Robina Foundation grant and, 250, 263–66, 296; Ruhl and, 240–46; Russian works produced by, 68; special events scheduled by, 183; third-year acting project discontinued by, 179; ticket prices and, 179, 231–32; touring show of *In the Continuum* and, 258; *Update* strategic plan of, 231; windfall from Yale University endowment and, 252; youth of, discussion of, 230

Bundy, James, as director, 251–52, 289; *All's Well That Ends Well*, 252, 340; *Arcadia*, 294–95, 308, 344; *Death of a Salesman*, 154, 289–90, 301, 341; *A Delicate Balance*, 254, 282–83, 342; *Hamlet*, 254, 290–93, 308, 344; *Happy Days*, 301, 304–6, *306*, 309, 345; *The Ladies of the Camellias*, 251, 308, 339; *The Psychic Life of Savages*, 231, 251, 259, 338; *The Three Sisters*, 229, 282, 312; *A Woman of No Importance*, 282, 295, 308, 341

Bundy, McGeorge, 230

Bunraku (puppet theater), 183

Burgtheater (Vienna), 7

Buried Child (January 18–February 7, 1979), 88–90, *89*, 101, 326

Burrows, Tom, 49

Burton, Kate, 159–60

Bush, George W., 262, 312

Butler, Dan, 114

Butler, E. Faye: *Trouble in Mind* (actor), *260*, 261

Button, Jeanne, 12

Byrd, Thomas Jefferson: *Death of a Salesman* (actor), 290

Cabaret. *See* Yale Cabaret

Cadden, Michael, 100, 114

Caged. See Mump + Smoot in *Ferno* and *Caged*

Calderón, Guillermo: *Escuela* (author/director), 184, 345

Caldwell, L. Scott: *A Play of Giants* (actor), *147*

Cale, David: *Somebody Else's House* (author/performer), 183, 335

Caligula (November 25–December 8, 1971), 59–61, *60*, 322

Calvary Baptist Church, 20, 42–43, *42–43*, 57, 218, 307, 312

Cameron, Ben, 124

Camp, Bill, 254; *In a Year with 13 Moons* (adaptation), 267, 344; *Notes from Underground* (adaptation/actor), 68, 266–67, *267*, 341

Campbell, Rob: *The Winter's Tale* (actor), 289

Camus, Albert: *Caligula* (author), 54, 59–61, *60*, 322; *The Possessed* (French adaptation), 67, 323

Candida (November 28–December 1997), 336

Canfield, W. Curtis, 3, 5, 299

Carlotta Festival of New Plays, 13, 178, 218

Carné, Marcel: *Les Enfants du Paradis (Children of Paradise)* (film), 185

Carrillo, Juliette: *Lydia* (director), 280, 341

Carter, Lonnie (author), 16–17, 25, 93; *The Big House*, 54, 322; *Iz She Izzy or Iz He Ain'tzy or Iz They Both?*, 321; *Watergate Classics*, 76, 323

Cartier, Jacques, 160

casting and auditions, 121–23, *123*, 172; color-blind casting, 300–301

Cathey, Reg E. (actor), 154; *Le Bourgeois Avant Garde*, *75*; *The Death of the Last Black Man in the Whole Entire World*, 169, 171; *Democracy in America*, 171; *The Resurrection of Lady Lester*, 112, *113*

The Caucasian Chalk Circle (March 20–April 11, 2015), 282, 344–45

Cavander, Kenneth, 44; *Bacchae* (translation), 36–37, 320; *Don Juan* (translation), 324; *Don Juan, or the Enemy of God* (revision), 53, 321; *Iphigenia at Aulis* (translation/adaptation), 217, 338; *Jason and the Argonauts* (Long Wharf Theatre), 47; *Olympian Games* (author/composer), 44, 321; *Ovid's Metamorphoses* (adaptation), 44, 320; *Saint Julian the Hospitaler* (adaptation/lyricist), 44, 321; *Story Theatre/Story Theatre Repertory* (adaptation/lyricist), 40, 44

CBS Foundation, 85, 87, 263

The Cemetery Club (January 13–February 7, 1987), 330

Center Stage (Baltimore), 6, 160–62, 169, 180, 207, 260; *Escape from Happiness* (coproduction), 197, 334; *Slavs!*, 335; *Splash Hatch on the E Going Down*, 336; *Triumph of Love*, 336; *Trouble in Mind* (revival), 260

Chalfant, Kathleen (actor), 253; *A Delicate Balance*, 282–83; *Passion Play*, 178, 245

Chambers, David (director), 154–55, 160, 216, 245, 250, 266; *Kiss of the Spider Woman*, 154, 331; *Neapolitan Ghosts*, 154, 330; *Sarcophagus*, 154, 331; *Search and Destroy*, 154, 333

Chandler, David (actor), 114; *The Master Builder*, 285; *Pentecost*, 285; *St. Joan of the Stockyards*, 199, *199*

Channick, Joan, 299

Chauncey, Henry ("Sam"), 4, 11

Chekhov, Anton, ix, 14, 35, 68, 88, 104, 126, 128, 162, 171, 202–3, 273, 305; *The Black Monk*, 68, 231, 338; *The Cherry Orchard*, 72, 340; *Ivanov*, 35, 68, 324, 333; *Rothschild's Fiddle*, 68, 339; *The Seagull*, 9, 326; *The Three Sisters*, 35, 245, 319–20, 343; *Uncle Vanya*, 35, 90, 126, 202–3, *204*, 327, 335

The Cherry Orchard (October 7–29, 2005), 72, 340

Children of Paradise (January 15–30, 1993), 185–86, 226, 334

Childress, Alice: *Trouble in Mind* (author), 259–61, *260*, 341

A Child's Tale (January 9–February 8, 1986), 330

Chisholm, Antony, 249

Chopin in Space (January 16–February 25, 1984), 329

choregoi/choregos, 7, 9, 11

Christakis, Erika, 296–97

Christakis, Nicholas, 297

Index

357

Churchill, Caryl (author), 126; *Owners*, 344; *Serious Money*, 179, 200, 217, 338; *Top Girls*, 165
Chute Roosters (January 11–February 6, 1988), 331
Cinderella. See Medea/Macbeth/Cinderella
Le Cirque Invisible (October 19–November 4, 1995), 335
Ciulei, Liviu, 101, 183; *The Lost Letter* (director), 326
Civic Repertory Theatre (New York), 8
Clambake (annual weekend for designers hosted by Ming Cho Lee), 312, 313
Clarke, Bill: *A Walk in the Woods* (set designer), 145–46
Clarke, Caitlin: *Mrs. Warren's Profession* (actor), 127
Clarkson, Patricia, 114
Classic Pornography (Sunday Series, 1971), 64
classic repertory, xii, xiii, 120, 124–31, 195, 251–52, 254
The Clean House (September 17–October 9, 2004), 240–41, *241*, 245, 246, 308, 339
Clennon, David, 18–19; *Saved* (actor), *31*
Cleveland Playhouse, 9
Clift, Montgomery, 9
Clinton, Sine Moria: *Notes from the Underground* (costume designer), 266
Close, Glenn: *Uncle Vanya* (actor), 126
Clurman, Harold: *Big Night* (director), 222
Clutch (April 2–25, 1970), 321
Cobb (March 21–April 15, 1989), 332
Cocteau, Jean, 8, 74
Colantoni, Enrico: *Hamlet* (actor), *173*
Coleman, Maggie-Kate: *Pop!* (author/lyricist), 268–70, *269*, 272, 342
color-blind casting, 300–301
The Colored Museum (November 27–December 19, 1992), 207, 334
Comédie-Française (France), 7, 9–10
comedy, difficulty of, 82, 100, 150, 203–4, 222, 286–87
The Comedy of Errors (February 11–March 12, 2005), *235*, 259, 339
Comedy on the Bridge (February 10–March 5, 2006), 340

commedia dell'arte, 82, 148, 182, 285–87
Commire, Anne, 100; *Starting Monday* (author), 332
community engagement, 188–89, 308, 315
community theaters, 9. *See also* regional theater movement
Compulsion (January 29–February 28, 2010), 342
Congdon, Constance: *The Servant of Two Masters* (adaptation), 285, 342
Congreve, William, 195, 204; *The Way of the World* (author), 178, 204–6, *205*, 217, 337
Conklin, John, 5
Conrad, Joseph: *Victory*, 44–46, 324
Conroy, Frances, 114
Conroy, Jarlath (actor): *Hamlet*, *292*, *293*; *Happy Days*, 305–6
Cooper, Chuck: *dance of the holy ghosts: a play on memory* (actor), 251
Cooper, Roy: *A Moon for the Misbegotten* (actor), 133
coproductions, xiv, 145, 185–86, 197, 207–8, 261, 314, 334, 339
Corbalis, Brendan (actor): *Hamlet*, 172–73; *St. Joan of the Stockyards*, 200
Coriolanus (May 6–18, 1968), 23, 320
Corthron, Kia (author): *Breath, Boom*, 231, 338; *Splash Hatch on the E Going Down*, 336
costuming, 13, 58, 61–62, 69, *73*, 83–84, 130–31, 172, 173, 176, 177–78, *177*, 197, 252, 258, 292
Cotsirilos, Stephanie, 48
Coward, Noël: *Hay Fever* (author), 35, 337
Coyne, John: *First Lady* (set designer), 219
Coyote Ugly (January 4–February 5, 1983), 328
Crazy from the Heart (January 9–February 8, 1986), 112, 330
Cremin, Susan (actor): *Figaro/Figaro*, 202; *Mrs. Warren's Profession*, 127
Crimes and Crimes (January 8–31, 1970), 320
Crommelynck, Fernand: *The Magnificent Cuckold* (author), 120–24, 327
Cronin, Lauren: *Moon Over Miami* (actor), 152

Cronyn, Tandy: *The Philanderer* (actor), 127
Crosby, B. J.: *King Stag* (actor), 178
cross-dressing, 29, 59
Croxton, Darryl: *The Resurrection of Lady Lester* (actor), *113*
Crumbs from the Table of Joy (November 27–December 19, 1998), 207, 337
The Cryptogram (November 14–December 7, 1996), 207, 336
Cuervo, Alma: *The Frogs* (chorus), 81
Cullors, Patrisse, 296
Culman, Peter C., 160
Culture Clash in America (November 14–December 6, 2003), 339
Cummings, Constance: *Wings* (actor), 91
Cunningham, Janet: *These Paper Bullets!* (stage carpenter), 270
A Cup of Coffee (November 26–December 18, 1999), 219–21, *221*, 224, 337
The Cure at Troy (March 26–April 18, 1998), 336
Curse of the Starving Class (February 1–March 10, 1980), 101, 326
Curse of the Starving Class (February 3–26, 2000), 337
Cymbeline (March 25–April 16, 2016), 235, 301, 345
Czyzewska, Elzbieta: *The Possessed* (actor), 70

Dadaism, 15, 184
Damashek, Barbara: *Don Juan, or the Enemy of God* (actor), *58*; *Gimpel the Fool* (lyricist), 44, 321; *Jason and the Argonauts* (Long Wharf Theatre), 47; *Olympian Games* (author/composer), 41, 44, 321; *Ovid's Metamorphoses* (composer), 41, 44, 320; *Story Theatre* (composer), 40–41, 46–47, 286; *Story Theatre Repertory* (composer), 40–41, 44, 46–47, 321; *Three Sisters* (musician), 40; *Underground* (composer), 333
Dana Charitable Trust, 120
dance of the holy ghosts: a play on memory (March 17–April 8, 2006), 218, 250–51, 340

Daniels, Ron (director): *Bingo*, 324; *Ivanov*, 325; *Man Is Man*, 325; *Mister Puntila and His Chauffeur Matti*, 50, 325

Danton, Georges, 200

Darkroom (October 18–December 11, 1973), 323

Davenant, William, 323

Davenport, Barbara, 100, 114–15

David Geffen School of Drama at Yale (DGSDY), 307

Davidson, Gordon, 114

Davis, John M., 42

Davis, Rick, 161

Davis-Green, Marie: *Fighting Words* (set designer), 238

Day, Akiko: *The Servant of Two Masters* (set designer), 286

Day, Johanna (actor): *The Evildoers*, 263; *The Realistic Joneses*, 276

The Day of the Picnic (January 16–February 25, 1984), 329

Daylight in Exile (January 15–February 10, 1990), 332

Dayton, Katharine: *First Lady* (author), 219, 335

Dear Elizabeth, A Play in Letters from Elizabeth Bishop to Robert Lowell and Back Again (November 20–December 22, 2012), 245, 343

Death of a Salesman (April 24–May 23, 2009), 35, 106, 290, *291*, 301, 341

The Death of the Last Black Man in the Whole Entire World (January 22–March 7, 1992), 167–69, *168*, 204, 208–9, 226, 333

Debussy, Claude, 325

Decroux, Étienne, 38

De Filippo, Eduardo: *Neapolitan Ghosts* (author), 124, 154, 330

de Lavallade, Carmen, xii, 47–48, 50, 52, 62–66, 109, 300, 306; *The Banquet Years* (creator/choreographer), 325; *The Big House* (choreographer), 322; *Crimes and Crimes* (actor), 63; *Don Juan, or the Enemy of God* (actor), 58–59; *An Evening with Dead Essex* (actor), *86*, 87; *The Frogs* (choreographer), 81, 323; *King Lear* (actor), 63; *Life Is a Dream* (actor), 63; *Macbett* (actor), 63; *Mahagonny* (actor), 63; *A Midsummer Night's Dream* (choreographer/actor), 61–62, *63*, 66, 324; *The Mirror* (choreographer), 322; *Ovid's Metamorphoses* (actor), *41*, 44; *The Revenger's Tragedy* (choreographer), 321; *The Seven Deadly Sins* (actor), 48; *The War Show* ("The Creation") (creator/choreographer), 63–65; *Watergate Classics* (choreographer), 323

Delgado, Thomas, 261

A Delicate Balance (October 22–November 13, 2010), 282, 342

Democracy in America (January 24–March 7, 1992), 169–71, *170*, 194, 333

Dempsey, Jerome, 50, 52

'Dentity Crisis (October 12–December 6, 1978), 30, 326

D/EP. *See* Dwight/Edgewood Project

Derricks, Cleavant, 112

Descartes, René, 169, 171, 194

de Tocqueville, Alexis: *Democracy in America*, 7–8, 169–71, *170*, 194, 333

Devine, George, 3

DeVries, Jon, 114

Dewhurst, Colleen (actor): *Ah, Wilderness!*, 132; *Long Day's Journey into Night*, 132, *132*; *A Moon for the Misbegotten*, 132

Diabaté, Djeli Moussa: *Geography* (actor), *193*

Diamond, Liz (director), 216, 229, 240, 266, 301, 307–8, 314, 315, 316–17; *The America Play*, 208, 334; *Antigone in New York*, 335; *Betrayal*, 337; *Le Bourgeois Avant Garde*, 335; *The Caucasian Chalk Circle*, 345; *The Cure at Troy*, 336; *dance of the holy ghosts: a play on memory*, 251, 340; *The Death of the Last Black Man in the Whole Entire World*, 130–31, 167, 198, 226, 333; *Fighting Words*, 238, 338; *Happy Now?*, 341; *Miss Julie*, 282, 339; *Mrs. Warren's Profession*, 127, 335; *Rice Boy*, 337; *St. Joan of the Stockyards*, 198–200, 334; *The School for Wives*, 334; *The Skin of Our Teeth*, 176, 336; *The Winter's Tale*, 215, 288–89, 343

Dickens, Charles, 325; *David Copperfield*, 104

Didier, Akpa Yves: *Geography* (actor), 193

Dinosaurs (January 15–February 10, 1990), 118, 332

diversity. *See* race, diversity, and inclusion

Dizzia, Maria: *Belleville* (actor), *273*, 274–75

A Doctor in Spite of Himself (November 26–December 17, 2011), 343

Doctorow, E. L., 21

Dodge, Alexander, 313

A Doll's House (October 5–23, 1982), 119, 126, 214, 328

Domestic Issues (January 10–February 21, 1981), 66, 110, 327

domestic realism, 272–76

Don Juan (October 30–December 16, 1975), 66, 215, 324

Don Juan, or the Enemy of God (May 14–June 6, 1970), 56–59, *58*, 321

Dorfman, David: *Indecent* (choreographer), 304, 345

Dostoevsky, Fyodor: *Notes from Underground*, 68, 266–67, *267*, 341; *The Possessed*, 67–70, *69*, 323

Douglas, Timothy, 134, 249; *Radio Golf* (director), 134, 247–48, 339

Downer, Herb: *A Play of Giants* (actor), *147*

Drama 50 project, 301–2

Draper, Polly: *Measure for Measure* (actor), 101

Dryden, John, 323

Dukakis, Olympia: *Elizabeth: Almost by Chance a Woman* (actor), 149

A Dumb Show (Sganarelle farces by Molière, January 19–February 1, 1978), 82–84, *83*, 214, 325

Dunnock, Mildred, 63, 90–91; *Bacchae* (actor), 37, 63

Durang, Christopher, 76, 105, 240, 251; *Betty's Summer Vacation* (author), 217, 338; *'Dentity Crisis* (author), 30, 326; *The Idiots Karamazov* (author/actor), 68, 76–79, 323; *The Vietnamization of*

Durang, Christopher (*continued*)
New Jersey (A American Tragedy) (author), 75, 88, 325
The Durango Flash (January 27–April 1, 1977), 33, 325
Dutton, Charles S. ("Roc") (actor), 114, 124, 253, 289; *Death of a Salesman*, 106, 254, 289–90, *291*, 293; *Ma Rainey's Black Bottom*, *135*, 136
Dwight/Edgewood Project (D/EP), 162, 189–91, *191*, 314
Dynamite Tonite! (December 6–18, 1966), 13–16, *16*, 21, 49, 319
Dynamite Tonite! (November 15–December 20, 1975), 16, 66, 324

Eckert, Sarah: *Twelfth Night* (costume designer), 174
Eclipsed (October 23–November 14, 2009), 259, 342
Edgar, David: *Nicholas Nickleby* (adaptation), 210; *Pentecost* (author), 200, 210–12, *211*, 224, 226, 301, 335
Edinburgh Fringe Festival, 257
Edward II (March 12–April 11, 1992), 162, 164, 195–97, *196*, 202, 215, 334
Edwards, Ben (set designer): *Ah, Wilderness!*, 214–15; *Long Day's Journey into Night*, 133, 215
Efremov, Yuri: *Ivanov* (adaptation/director), 68
El Colectivo (affinity group), 298
Elevada (April 24–May 16, 2015), 345
Elizabeth: Almost by Chance a Woman (April 28–May 23, 1987), 146, 148–50, *149*, 285, 331
Elliott, Maggie, 255
Endgame (September 20–25, 1966, Southwark Theatre Company production), 183, 319
Eno, Will: *The Realistic Joneses* (author), 122, 272, 273, 275–76, 278, 343
Epp, Steven: *Accidental Death of an Anarchist* (actor), 287; *Children of Paradise* (author), 185, 334; *A Doctor in Spite of Himself* (adaptation), 343; *The Servant of Two Masters* (actor), 285, 287

Epps, Sheldon, 290
Epstein, Alvin, 38–39, 47, 50, 53, 63, 66; *Bacchae* (actor), 38, *39*, 63; *Black Snow* (actor), 38, 283; *The Bourgeois Gentleman* (director), 322; *Caligula* (director), 59–60, 322; *Don Juan, or the Enemy of God* (actor), 58, *58*; *Dressing Room Stories: The Making of an Artist* (memoir), 62; *Dynamite Tonite!* (director/actor), 16, *16*, 38, 324; *Greatshot* (actor), 38; *Heartbreak House* (director), 38, 127, 330; *The Importance of Being Earnest* (director), 38, 330; *In the Clap Shack* (director), 322; *Joseph Conrad's Victory* (director), 44, 324; *Julius Caesar* (director), 324; *A Kurt Weill Cabaret* (actor), 29; *Macbett* (director), 323; *A Midsummer Night's Dream* (director), 38, 61, 229, 324; *The Possessed* (actor), 70; *Richard II* (actor), 38, 283; *The Rise and Fall of the City of Mahagonny* (director), 52, 323; *The Rivals* (director), 306, 320; *The Seven Deadly Sins* (director), 48, 321; *Story Theatre* (actor), 38, 48; *The Tempest* (director/actor), 38, 61, 323; *Troilus and Cressida* (director), 324; *The War Show* (actor), 64; *Watergate Classics* (actor), 76; *White Marriage* (actor), 71
Epstein, David (author), 16; *Clutch*, 321; *Darkroom*, 323; *Exact Change*, 330; *They Told Me That You Came This Way*, 31–32, 320
Ervin, Sam, 74
Escape from Happiness (March 25–April 17, 1993), 197, 207, 334
Essex, Mark ("Jimmy"), 85–86
Eugene O'Neill Centennial Celebration (March 22–May 21, 1988), 331
Eugene O'Neill Theater Center (Waterford, Connecticut), 50, 99, 144, 263
Euripides, 75, 81; *Bacchae*, 36–38, *39*, 320; *Iphigenia at Aulis*, 217, 338; *Medea*, 72, 235, 338
Eurydice (September 22–October 14, 2006), 242–43, *243*, 254, 340

Eustis, Oskar, 4, 216, 229; *Compulsion* (director), 342
Evans, Edith, 76
An Evening with Dead Essex (March 7–April 27, 1974), 85–88, *86*, 99, 150, 323
The Evildoers (January 18–February 9, 2008), 257, 262–63, *262*, 272, 302, 341
Exact Change (January 13–February 7, 1987), 330
Exxon Corporation, operating gift from, 120
Eyring, Teresa, 146

Facebook, 253
The Fairytale Lives of Russian Girls (January 31–February 22, 2014), 344
Falls, Robert, 244–45
Falwell, Jerry, 153
Familiar (January 30–February 21, 2015), 259, 302, 344
family dramas, 88, 110, 132–33, 144, 276–82. *See also* domestic realism
The Fantasticks (musical), 41
Farquhar, George, 195; *The Beaux' Stratagem* (author), 176, 335
Fassbinder, Rainer Werner: *In a Year with 13 Moons* (filmmaker), 267, 344
Fata, Wesley (choreographer): *Jacques Brel...*, 326; *Master Harold... and the Boys*, 109; *Moon Over Miami*, 332; *The 1940's Radio Hour*, 326; *Timon of Athens*, 327
The Father (February 20–April 24, 1975), 324
Faulkner's Bicycle (January 14–February 9, 1985), 329
Fefu and Her Friends (January 16–February 15, 1992), 164–67, *165*, 185, 333
Feiffer, Jules (author): *God Bless*, 21, 38, 320; *Little Murders*, 85; *Watergate Classics*, 323
Feingold, Michael, 16, 24, 47, 49–50, *50*, 62, 65–66, 74, 93; *The Bourgeois Gentleman* (translation), 49, 322; *The Frogs* (adaptation), 49, 81, 323; *Happy End* (adaptation/lyricist), 49, 51, 64, 322, 324; *Little Mahagonny* (translation),

49, 321; *Mister Puntila and His Servant Matti* (adaptation), 50; *The Possessed* (English adaptation), 67; *The Rise and Fall of the City of Mahagonny* (translation/adaptation), 49, 52, 323; *The Threepenny Opera* (translation), 50; *When We Dead Awaken* (translation), 49, 54, 321
Felder, Clarence: *Buried Child* (actor), 89
Feldman, Ruth M., 296
Fellini, Federico, 39, 174
Fences (April 30–May 25, 1985), 136–39, *137*, 144, 259, 314, 317, 329
Ferno. See Mump + Smoot in *Ferno and Caged*
A Festival of International Dance at Yale (No Boundaries Series, November 14–15, 2008), 184, 341
Feydeau, Georges, 214
Fichandler, Zelda, xii, 9
52nd St. Project (New York), 162, 188–89
Figaro/Figaro (December 1–17, 1994), 75, 200–202, *201*, 226, 335
Fighting Words (November 15–December 21, 2002), 218, 231, 237–39, *238*, 338
Finley, Karen, 152
First International Festival of the Arts (New York), 144
First Lady (October 10–November 2, 1996), 219, 335
Fisher, Lydia: *Ovid's Metamorphoses* (actor), *41*
Fitzgerald, Glenn: *The Realistic Joneses* (actor), 276
Fjelde, Rolf (translation): *A Doll's House*, 328; *Hedda Gabler*, 327; *Little Eyolf*, 330
Flash Floods (January 5–February 6, 1982), 328
Flaubert, Gustave: "The Legend of St. Julian the Hospitaler," 44, 321
Fleck, John, 152
Flink, Stanley, 91
Fo, Dario, 148, 183, 330; *About Face* (author), 148, 328; *Accidental Death of an Anarchist* (author), 148, 344; *Elizabeth: Almost by Chance a Woman* (author), 146, 148–50, *149*, 285, 331; *Mistero Buffo* (author/performer), 148, 330
Folks (affinity group), 298
Ford, Jessica: *King Lear* (costume designer), 178, 239
Ford Foundation, x, 9, 53, 72, 97, 167, 230, 263
Foreman, Richard, 5, 170; *Venus* (director), 208–10, 335
Fornès, María Irene, 148, 164, 167; *Fefu and Her Friends* (author), 164, *165*, 166, 333
Foster, Paul: *Elizabeth I* (author), 326
Foxworth, Bo: *As You Like It* (actor), 174
Frankel, Jennifer: *Big Night* (actor), 222, 223
Frankenstein (September 16–28, 1968), 26, 320
Freed, Amy (author): *The Psychic Life of Savages*, 231, 251, 259, 338; *Safe in Hell*, 340
Freud, Sigmund, 44, 88, 129, 186
The Frogs (March 29–May 17, 1974), 49, 79–82, *80*, 116, 174, 213, 317, 323
Frohnmayer, John, 153
Fugard, Athol, 24, 35, 101–9, 120, 122, 152, 217, 240, 293, 301; *The Blood Knot* (actor/author/director), 102, 109, 127, 330; *Boesman and Lena* (author), 102, 105, 327; *Dimetos* (author/performer), 66; *Hello and Goodbye* (author), 109, 119, 328; *A Lesson from Aloes* (author/director), 54, 101–5, *103*, 314, 327; *Master Harold . . . and the Boys* (author/director), *108*, 108–9, 328; *My Children! My Africa!* (author), 162, 164, 333; *A Place with the Pigs* (author/director/actor), 109, 331; *The Road to Mecca* (author/director), 109, 119, 144, 329
Funn, Carlos: *Geography* (dancer), 192

Galas, Diamanda: *Plague Mass* (performer), 183, 334
Galileo (October 22–November 14, 1998), 188, 336
Gallo, David: *Radio Golf* (set designer), 248

Gardley, Marcus (author), 250–51, 301; *dance of the holy ghosts: a play on memory*, 218, 250–51, 340; *The House that will not Stand*, 344
Garner, Eric, 296
Garnett, Constance, 76–77, 79, 214; *Uncle Vanya* (translation), 327
Garrett, Melody J.: *Hamlet* (actor), 172–73, *173*
Garza, Alicia, 296
Gassner, John, 3
Gates, Linda: *Lear* (actor), 37
Gay, Jackson (director), 246, 313; *Elevada*, 345; *The Intelligent Design of Jenny Chow*, 246, 339; *Man Is Man*, 246; *The Moors*, 345; *These Paper Bullets!*, 270, 344
Geidt, Jeremy, 50, 52, 93; *The Nixon Show: The Bug Stops Here* (creator), 74; *The Rise and Fall of the City of Mahagonny* (actor), *48*; *Watergate Classics* (author), 323
gender equality. See women
General Gorgeous (February 26–May 3, 1976), 75, 324
Genet, Jean, 14, 35; *The Balcony* (author), 147
Gentles, Avril: *A Play of Giants* (actor), 147
Geography (October 23–November 8, 1997), 130, 192–95, *193*, 336
Geography: Tree, Part 2 (April 20–May 13, 2000), 194–95, 337
Geography of a Horse Dreamer (March 7–April 27, 1974), 85, 87–88, 323
German expressionism, 170
Gervais, Djédjé Djédjé: *Geography* (actor), 193, *193*
Geva Theater (Rochester), 138
The Ghost Sonata (September 29–November 12, 1977), 72–74, *73*, 121–22, 214, 325
Giamatti, A. Bartlett, 91–92, 97–98, 290, 314
Giamatti, Paul, 253; *As You Like It* (actor), 174; *Hamlet* (actor), 290–93, *292*
Giamatti, Toni, 91

Index   361

Gianino, Gian-Murray: *Eurydice* (actor), 243

Gibney, Susan: *Little Eyolf* (actor), 128

Gibson, Thomas: *Edward II* (actor), 196

Gielgud, John: *Men and Women of Shakespeare* (actor), 183, 319

gifts and funding, 53, 120, 180–81, 188, 263–66. *See also* National Endowment for the Arts; *specific foundations*

Giles, David: *Lear* (director), 36, 323

Gilman, Richard (director), xi, xii; *Clutch*, 321; *Iz She Izzy or Iz He Aint'zy or Iz They Both*, 321; *The Rhesus Umbrella*, 321; *Transformations: 3 One-Acts by Yale Playwrights*, 320

Gimpel the Fool (October 8–31, 1970), 44, 321

Ginkas, Kama: *Rothschild's Fiddle* (adaptation/director), 68, 339

Ginzburg, Natalia, 85; *I Married You for the Fun of It* (author), 322

Giordano, Tony (director): *Curse of the Starving Class*, 326; *The Day of the Picnic*, 329; *Hello and Goodbye*, 328

Gister, Earle, 100, 152, 159, 172

Glaspell, Susan, 8

The Glass Menagerie (March 18–April 10, 1999), 3, 271, 337

Glover, Danny: *Master Harold . . . and the Boys* (actor), 108, 109

Gob Squad: *Super Night Shot* (collective of authors), 184, 344

God Bless (October 10–26, 1968), 21, 320

Goethe, Johann Wolfgang von, 79, 198, 199

Gogol, Nikolai: *The Government Inspector*, 68, 320; *Marriage*, 68, 101, 129–31, 300, 330

Going Over (January 5–February 6, 1982), 328

Gold, Sam: *The Realistic Joneses* (director), 275, 343

Goldoni, Carlo (author), 8; *L'Amant Militaire*, 320; *The Servant of Two Masters*, 285–87, *286*, 342

Goldstein, Jess, 172, 177

Good Goods (February 3–25, 2012), 343

Goodman Theatre (Chicago), 9, 137, 138

Gordimer, Nadine, 103

Gorman, Mari: *Saved* (actor), 31

The Government Inspector (February 19–March 14, 1970), 68, 320

Gozzi, Carlo (author): *The Green Bird*, 334; *The King Stag*, 285, 339

Graduate New Haven Hotel, 232

Granville-Barker, Harley, 28

Grappo, Connie, 133; *The Mystery Plays* (director), 339

Grate, Gail: *Pygmalion* (actor), 300

Gray, Hanna, 91

Gray, Spalding, 183; *Gray's Anatomy* (performer), 334

The Great Chinese Revolution (December 5–21, 1968), 32, 320

Great Lakes Theater Festival (Cleveland), 230

Great Recession (2008–2009), 295

Greatshot (May 8–24, 1969), 38, 320

Green, Fanni: *The Death of the Last Black Man in the Whole Entire World* (actor), *168*, 169

Green, Jamiah, *191*

Greenberg, Richard, 240

The Green Bird (November 27–December 18, 1993), 334

Greenwood, Jane (costume designer), 172; *Ah, Wilderness!*, 214–15; *Hay Fever*, 178

Greer, Adam: *It Pays to Advertise* (actor), 223

Gregory, André: *Bacchae* (director), 36–38, 320

Grier, David Alan (actor), 13; *Love's Labour's Lost*, *35*; *Measure for Measure*, 101; *The Resurrection of Lady Lester*, 113

Grifasi, Joseph G.: *The Banquet Years* (creator/choreographer), 325; *A Cup of Coffee* (director), 220–21, 337; *Lear* (actor), *37*; *A Midsummer Night's Dream* (actor), 62; *The 1940's Radio Hour* (choreographer), 326

Grimes, Tammy: *Elizabeth: Almost by Chance a Woman* (actor), 149

Grimm's Fairy Tales, 40–41

Griswold, Alfred Whitney, 4

Groag, Lillian: *The Ladies of the Camellias* (author), 251, 339

Gross, Michael (actor), 46; *A Cup of Coffee*, 220, *221*; *Sganarelle: An Evening of Molière Farces*, 83

Grosz, George, 48

Grotowski, Jerzy, 38

Group Theater (New York, 1931–1941), 8, 222

Group 20 (Wellesley College's Theatre on the Green), 10

Guare, John (author), 5, 15, 114, 195, 240, 246; *Bosoms and Neglect*, 100, 326; *Landscape of the Body*, 335; *Moon Over Miami*, 146, 150–52, 217, 332

Guess Work (October 12–December 6, 1978), 326

guest companies: Gielgud, John, and Irene Worth, 183, 319; The Living Theatre (New York), 26–28, *27*, 320; The Lucia Sturdza Bulandra Theatre Company, Bucharest, 326; Mabou Mines (New York), 183–84, *184*, 326, 332; The Negro Ensemble Company (New York), 183, 321; Open Theatre (New York), 13, 49, 183, 319; San Francisco Mime Troupe, 320; Southwark Theatre Company (Philadelphia), 183, 319; Le Théâtre de France, 320; Williams, Emlyn Williams, 325

Guillory, Don: *Trouble in Mind* (actor), *260*

Gulder, Linda: *Ovid's Metamorphoses* (actor), *41*

Gurira, Danai: *Eclipsed* (author), 259, 342; *Familiar* (author), 259, 344; *In the Continuum* (author/actor), 234, 257–59, *258*, 340

Gussow, Mel, 124, 127

Guthrie, Tyrone, xii, 9; *The Three Sisters* (translation), 320

Guthrie Theater (Minneapolis), xii, 3, 9, 38, 160, 172, 287, 290, 310

Gutkin, Lisa: *Indecent* (composer), 304, 345

Haas, Tom (director), 76–77; *Baal*, 322; *When We Dead Awaken*, 321
Haas Family Arts Library, 23, 107, 348
Haberle, Sean: *Hamlet* (actor), *173*
Hack, Keith: *Mahagonny* (creator/director), 52, 326; *Tales from the Vienna Woods* (director), 326
Hackett, Walter: *It Pays to Advertise* (co-author), 217, 219, 222–24, 338
Haff, Stephen, 197
Hagerty, Julie: *Moon Over Miami* (actor), 152
Hahn, Kathryn: *The Birds* (actor), 178
Haigh, Kenneth: *Henry IV* (actor), 23; *Prometheus Bound* (actor), 18, 23; *'Tis Pity She's a Whore* (director), 319
Halberstam, David, 70
Halévy, Ludovic: *La Vie Parisienne* (author), 9
Hall, Adrian (director): *Buried Child*, 89, 326; *Underground*, 333
Hall, Ed: *Joe Turner's Come and Gone* (actor), *141*
Hall, George: *A Cup of Coffee* (actor), *221*
Hall, Paavo, 112
Haller, Gary, 216
Hallet, James: *Hamlet* (actor), *173*
Halley, Ben, Jr. (actor): *St. Joan of the Stockyards*, 200; *The Winter's Tale*, 300
Halloween 2015, 296–97
Halva, Alvin: *Indecent* (composer), 304, 345
Hambleton, T. Edward, 8
Hamlet (October 8–31, 1992), 35, 162, 172–73, *173*, 334
Hamlet (March 15–April 13, 2013), 35, 254, 290–93, *292*, 344
Hammerstein, Oscar, II: *Cinderella* (author), 235, 338
Hammett, Dashiell, 44
Hammond, David (director): *Henry IV, Part I*, 329; *The Man Who Could See Through Time*, 328; *The Philanderer*, 328; *Richard II*, 329
Handke, Peter: *They Are Dying Out* (author), 66, 100, 164, 326

Hansberry, Lorraine: *A Raisin in the Sun* (author), 88, 97, 119, 124, 329
Happy Days (May 12, 1969), 183, 320
Happy Days (April 29–May 21, 2016), 233, 301, 304–6, *306*, 345
Happy End (April 6–May 6, 1972), 47–51, 64, 215, 322
Happy End (February 6–March 22, 1975), 52, 215, 324
Happy Now? (October 24–November 15, 2008), 341
Hare, David, 161
Harkness, Edward S., 5, 20
Harrington, Wendall, 271–72, 278
Harris, Julie, 5
Harrison, Randy: *Pop!* (actor), *269*, 270
Hart, Cecilia: *First Lady* (actor), 219
Hart, Moss, 151
Hartford Courant, 3, 161, 216
Harting, Carla: *Eurydice* (actor), *243*
Hauck, Rachel: *Medea/Macbeth/Cinderella* (set designer), 237
Hauptmann, Elisabeth. *See* Lane, Dorothy (pseud.)
Havel, Vaclav, 161; *Largo Desolato* (author), 333
Hawthorne, Nathaniel, 17
Hay Fever (April 29–May 22, 1999), 35, 178, 215, 337
Hays, Carole Shorenstein, 138
Heaney, Seamus, 195; *The Cure at Troy* (adaptation), 336
Heard, John (actor): *Ah, Wilderness!*, 132; *Long Day's Journey into Night*, 133
Hearn, George: *Ah, Wilderness!* (actor), 132
Heartbreak House (September 16–October 11, 1986), 38, 127, 147, 330
Heaven (November 24–December 16, 2000), 197, 337
Hedda Gabler (March 3–21, 1981), 13, 124, *125*, 195, 327
Heller, Joseph, 21; *Catch-22*, 15, 21; *We Bombed in New Haven*, 21–23, 319
Hellman, Lillian, 159
Hello and Goodbye (November 2–20, 1982), 109, 119, 328
Helms, Jesse, 153, 188

Henderson, Jo, 114
Henderson, Stephen McKinley: *Death of a Salesman* (actor), 290
Henry IV (January 29–February 10, 1968), 23, 319
Henry IV, Part I (October 23–November 17, 1984), 329
Hernández, Riccardo (set designer), 130–31, 312, 316; *The Death of the Last Black Man in the Whole Entire World*, 130–31, 167, 170; *The Evildoers*, 263; *On the Verge*, 164
Herrero, Mercedes: *Twelfth Night* (actor), *175*
Herrmann, Edward: *A Delicate Balance* (actor), 282
Herzog, Amy: *Belleville* (author), 272–78, *273*, 343
Heyward, Susan: *The Master Builder* (actor), 285
Higgenbottom, Jeffrey, 57
Hilferty, Susan (costume designer), 266; *The Evildoers*, 263; *Radio Golf*, 248
Hill, Darryl: *An Evening with Dead Essex* (actor), *86*
Hines, Karen (director): Mump + Smoot in *Ferno* and *Caged*, 334; Mump + Smoot in *Something Else with Zug*, 337
Hinkle, Marin: *Uncle Vanya* (actor), *204*
Hoftheater (Germany), 7
Holder, Donald: *Radio Golf* (lighting designer), 248
Holder, Geoffrey, 63–64
Holiday, Billie, 112
Holland, Anthony: *Henry IV* (actor), 23; *The Tubs* (director), 323; *We Bombed in New Haven* (actor), 23
Hollar, Lloyd: *A Play of Giants* (actor), *147*
Holst, Gustav: *The Planets* (composer), 64
Homer: *The Iliad*, 9; *The Odyssey*, 9
Honegger, Gitta (director), 114–15, 197; *Intermezzo*, 331; *Interrogating the Nude*, 332; *Largo Desolato*, 333; *Melons*, 331; *The Solid Gold Cadillac*, 332; *The Winter's Tale*, 330
Hormann, Nicholas: *The War Show* (actor), 64, 66

Horváth, Ödön von (author), 161; *Figaro Gets a Divorce*, 75, 200–201, 335; *Tales from the Vienna Woods*, 66, 93, 326
Hotel Duncan (New Haven), 232
Houdyshell, Jayne (actor): *Fighting Words*, 238, 239; *Medea/Macbeth/Cinderella*, 239
Houghton, Norris, 8
The House that will not Stand (April 18–May 10, 2014), 344
housing for visiting actors, 231–33
Howard, Sidney: *Madam, Will You Walk?*, 8–9
Hoyle, Geoff, 186
Hudson, Earnest L.: *An Evening with Dead Essex* (actor), *86*
Hughes, Brendan, 251
Hughes, Holly: *Clit Notes* (author/performer), 152, 182–83, 335
Humana Festival of New American Plays (Actors Theatre, Louisville), 85, 99
Hunter, Kim, 114
Hurok, Sol, 9
Hurst, David, *18*
Hurt, William: *Ivanov* (actor), 68
Hussong, Nick: *These Paper Bullets!* (projections designer), 270

Ibsen, Henrik, 8, 14, 35, 72, 124, 128, 171, 281, 287, 309; *A Doll's House*, 119, 126, 328; *Ghosts*, 88; *Hedda Gabler*, 13, 124–25, *125*, 195, 327; *Little Eyolf*, 127–31, *128*, 283, 330; *The Master Builder*, 283–85, *284*, 342; *When We Dead Awaken*, 49, 54, 321; *The Wild Duck*, 61, 325
The Idiots Karamazov (October 31–December 21, 1974), 68, 75, 76–79, *78*, 110, 178–79, 214, 245, 323
The Imaginary Cuckold (in Sganarelle farces by Molière, January 19–February 1, 1978), 82–83, 120
The Imaginary Invalid (September 16–October 9, 1999), 337
I Married You for the Fun of It (February 17–April 8, 1972), 322
Imison, Michael, 212

The Importance of Being Earnest (March 25–April 19, 1986), 38, 330
In a Year with 13 Moons (April 26–May 18, 2013), 267, 301, 344
inclusion. *See* race, diversity, and inclusion
Indecent (October 2–24, 2015), 253, *256*, 301–4, *303*, 345
Innaurato, Albert, 76; *The Idiots Karamazov* (author/actor), 68, 76, *78*, 79, 178–79, 323
Instagram, 253
The Intelligent Design of Jenny Chow (October 22–November 13, 2004), 245–46, *247*, 339
Intermezzo (September 15–October 8, 1988), 124, 331
Interrogating the Nude (January 10–February 4, 1989), 118, 332
In the Clap Shack (December 15–March 10, 1973), 21, 322
In the Continuum (January 12–February 10, 2007), 234, 257–59, *258*, 340
Ionesco, Eugène (author), 8; *Macbett*, 75, 323; *Le Piéton de l'air*, 9
Iphigenia at Aulis (April 25–May 18, 2002), 302, 338
Irving, Jules, 10
Iseman Theater, 218
Isherwood, Charles, 242–43, 275
Itallie, Jean-Claude van: *The Seagull* (revision), 326; *The War Show* (composer), 66
It Pays to Advertise (November 29–December 22, 2001), 217, 219, 222–24, 338
Ivanek, Željko: *Master Harold . . . and the Boys* (actor), *108*, 109
Ivanov (November 18–December 18, 1976), 35, 324–25
Ivanov (September 18–October 13, 1990), 35, 68, 333
Izenour, George C., 20
Iz She Izzy or Iz He Aint'zy or Iz They Both? (April 2–25, 1970), 321

Jacker, Corinne, 100; *Domestic Issues* (author), 66, 110, 327

Jackson, Leonard: *Ma Rainey's Black Bottom* (actor), 135
Jacobs, Anna K.: *Pop!* (composer), 268–70, 342
Jacobs-Jenkins, Branden: *War* (author), 276, 280–81, *281*, 344
Jacques Brel . . . (December 29–January 13, 1979), 183, 326
Janson, Merritt: *Notes from Underground* (actor), 266, *267*
Jarry, Alfred: *The Banquet Years* (dramaturg), 325; *Ubu Rex* (author), 101, 327
Jelks, John Earl, 249; *Radio Golf* (actor), *248*
Jenkin, Len: *The Birds* (adaptation/author), 178, 337; *Uncle Vanya* (director), 203, 335
Jenkins, Richard: *Melons* (actor), 34
Jenkins, Ron: *Elizabeth: Almost by Chance a Woman* (translation), 331; *Underground* (translation/adaptation), 333
Jennings, Byron (actor): *Edward II*, 162, *196*, 197; *Figaro/Figaro*, 202
Jiwakanon, Ritirong: *Twelfth Night* (set designer), 174
Joe Turner's Come and Gone (April 29–May 24, 1986), 138–42, *141*, 144, 330
Johnny Bull (April 4–24, 1982), 328
Johnson, James Weldon: "The Creation" (poet), 64–65
Jones, James Earl, 97, 109, 114, 137–38, 139; *The Blood Knot* (actor), 102; *Fences* (actor), *137*, 138–39, 317; *Hedda Gabler* (actor), 124–25, *125*, 300; *A Lesson from Aloes* (actor), 54, 101, 103, *103*, 105; *Timon of Athens* (director/actor), 101–2, 300; *You Can't Take It with You* (actor), 102
Jones, Rhodessa: *Big Butt Girls, Hard-Headed Women* (author/performer), 183, 335
Jones, Rolin, 250, 301; *The Intelligent Design of Jenny Chow* (author), 245–46, *247*, 339; *These Paper Bullets!* (adaptation), 270–72, *271*, 344
Jones, Walton: *The Beauty Part* (director), 217, 334; *Beef, No Chicken* (director),

364 *Index*

328; *Boesman and Lena* (director), 105, 327; *Dynamite Tonite!* (director), 324; *Joseph Conrad's Victory* (adaptation), 44, 324; *Much Ado about Nothing* (director), 105, 328; *The 1940's Radio Hour* (author/director), 183, 325; *Reunion and Dark Pony* (director), 325; *Suicide in B-Flat* (director), 324; *Tartuffe* (director), 105, 329; *Ties That Bind* (director), 333; *The Vietnamization of New Jersey (A American Tragedy)* (director), 325; *Walk the Dog, Willie* (director), 324
Jonson, Ben: *The Alchemist*, 124, 331; *Volpone*, 319
Jordan, Pam, 106–7, *107*, 230–31, 348
Jory, Jon, 160, 216
Joseph Conrad's Victory (November 14–December 20, 1974), 44, 324
Judd, Robert: *Ma Rainey's Black Bottom* (actor), *135*
Julius Caesar (October 1–November 13, 1976), 309, 324

Kaczmarek, Jane, 114; *Love's Labour's Lost* (actor), *35*
Kafka, Fyodor, 77
Kalb, Jonathan, 169, 171
Kane, David, 253
Kani, John, 102
Kasznar, Kurt: *The Rise and Fall of the City of Mahagonny* (actor), *48*
Katsioula, Elina: *Little Eyolf* (set designer), 128–29
Kauffman, Anne (director), 313; *Belleville*, 274, 276, 343; *We Have Always Lived in the Castle*, 342
Kauffman, Stanley, xi, xii
Kaufman, George S., 146, 150; *First Lady* (author), 219, 335; *The Solid Gold Cadillac* (author), 332
Kazan, Elia, 5, 10, 142
Keach, Stacy (actor): *Henry IV*, 23; *We Bombed in New Haven*, 23
Keagy, Grace: *The Rise and Fall of the City of Mahagonny* (actor), *48*
Keller, Greg: *Belleville* (actor), 274–75

Kellerman, Sally: *Moon Over Miami* (actor), 152
Kelley, Sam: *Pill Hill* (author), 115, 332
Kelley-Dodd, Linda, 178
Kennard, Michael (author/actor): Mump + Smoot in *Ferno* and *Caged*, 186–87, 334; Mump + Smoot in *Something Else with Zug*, 187, *187*, 337
Kennedy, Adrienne (author), 85, 88, 167; *An Evening with Dead Essex*, 85–88, *86*, 99, 150, 323; *Funnyhouse of a Negro*, 85; *Ohio State Murders*, 115, 333
Kentridge, William: *Refuse the Hour* (librettist), 184, 345
Kerr, Patrick, 114; *Hamlet* (actor), 293
Kerr, Philip: *A Midsummer Night's Dream* (actor), *63*
Kerr, Walter, xiv, 3, 19, 32–36, 60
Kierkegaard, Søren: "The Immediate Stages of the Erotic" (author), 56
Kiger, Jennifer, 250, 252, 263–65, 268, 270, 274, 296, 308; *No Boundaries* (curator/producer), 184
King, Lawrence, 213
King, Martin Luther, Jr., 23–24, 143
Kingdom of Earth (October 25–December 1, 2001), 218, 338
King Lear ("Olmec Lear," February 13–March 13, 2004), 239–40, 259, 317, 339
The King Stag (March 26–April 17, 2004), 178, 285, 339
Kinsman, Chad, 190
Kiss of the Spider Woman (October 18–November 12, 1988), 154, 331
Kittle, Frederick August, Jr., 134
Klein, Alvin, 212
Kleiner, Diana, 216
Kleist, Heinrich von, 161
Knowlton, Sarah (actor): *Le Bourgeois Avant Garde*, 75; *St. Joan of the Stockyards*, 199
Koernig, Steven, *191*
Koltès, Bernard-Marie: *Battle of Black and Dogs* (author), 131, 342
Kondoleon, Harry, 114; *Rococo* (author), 110, 115, 327

Kopit, Arthur: *Wings* (author), 85, 90–91, 325
Kouakou, Angelo: *Geography* (actor), *193*
Kowalski, Robert, 261
Kritzer, Leslie: *Pop!* (actor), 270
Kron, Lisa: *101 Humiliating Stories* (author/performer), 183, 335
Kumin, Fran, 121–23
Kunst, Rick: Mump + Smoot in *Ferno* and *Caged* (actor), 187
A Kurt Weill Cabaret (1968), 29
Kuruvilla, Sunil (author), 301; *Fighting Words*, 218, 231, 237–39, *238*, 338; *Rice Boy*, 237, 337
Kushner, Tony, 126, 195; *Angels in America* (author), 147; *Brundibar* (adaptation/translation), 259, 340; *Comedy on the Bridge* (librettist), 340; *Slavs! (Thinking about the Longstanding Problems of Virtue and Happiness)* (author), 68, 200, 335
Kwon, John Woo Taak: *Richard III* (actor), *177*

The Ladies of the Camellias (November 26–December 18, 2004), 251, 308, 339
Lahr, Bert, 217
La Jolla Playhouse (San Diego), 207; *A Walk in the Woods* (coproduction), 145
Lamos, Mark, 216, 229, 301; *Lulu* (adaptation/director), 262, 340; *The Taming of the Shrew* (director), 231, 338
Landesman, Rocco, ix–xiv, 24, 98, 159, 264
Landscape of the Body (May 2–25, 1996), 335
Lane, Dorothy (pseud.): *Happy End* (collaborator), 50–51, 322, 324
Langella, Frank, 59
Langworthy, Douglas E.: *Figaro/Figaro* (translation), 201, 335
Largo Desolato (October 23–November 17, 1990), 333
Larkins, Elihu, 42
La Tour, Chalia, *191*
Latta, Felicity Jones, 308; *Arcadia* (actor), 294–95, 308; *Children of Paradise* (author), 185–86, 334; *Hamlet* (actor), 293, 308; *Ladies of the Camellias* (actor),

Latta, Felicity Jones (*continued*)
308; *The Master Builder* (actor), *284*, *285*; *The Winter's Tale* (actor), 289; *A Woman of No Importance* (actor), 308

Leadership Council, 253

League of Resident Theatres (LORT), x, 316

Lear (April 13–May 19, 1973), 32–36, *37*, 87, 104, 210, 225, 310, 323

Lecoq, Jacques, 182

Lee, Hoon: *The Winter's Tale* (actor), 289

Lee, Julia C.: *Belleville* (set designer), 274, 313

Lee, Ming Cho, 12, 56–57, 159–60, 164, 172, 213, 216, 218, 229, *311*; Clambake (annual weekend for designers) held by, 312, 313; *King Lear* (set designer), 310; life and influence of, 310–13; Ming Day (Saturday) and, 310–11, 313; Ming Wall and, 277; National Medal of Arts (2002) awarded to, 312

Lee, Richard: *Ophelia Kline* (author/performer), 66

Le Gallienne, Eva, 8, 38, 172

Leicht, Alan, 6

Lemon, Ralph, 180, 314; *Geography* (creator/choreographer/director), 130, 162, 189–92, 194–95, 226, 336, 337

Lenk, Katrina: *Indecent* (actor), *303*

Lenya, Lotte, 47, 49, 51

Leon, Kenny, 134, 216

Lerner, Neal: *Greater Tuna* (actor), 29

A Lesson from Aloes (March 27–May 24, 1980), 101–6, *103*, 109, 115, 119, 202, 215, 237, 327

Letts, Tracy: *The Realistic Joneses* (actor), 276

Leverett, James, 98, 114, 216

Levin, Charles, 93

Levin, Rick, 212–16, 229–30

Lewis, Irene (director), 5, 6, 301; *Escape from Happiness*, 334; *Trouble in Mind*, 260–61, 341

Lewis, Robert, xii; *Crimes and Crimes* (director), 320

Libetti, Robert: *Richard III* (actor), *177*

Liebman, Ron: *Prometheus Bound* (actor), 18

Life Is a Dream (February 24–April 15, 1972), 63, 116, 322

Life magazine, 38

Lim, Jennifer: *The Intelligent Design of Jenny Chow* (actor), 245

Lin, Eric, 278

Lincoln Center for the Performing Arts (New York), 10, 188

Lindo, Delroy, 114

Linn-Baker, Mark, *Sganarelle: An Evening of Molière Farces* (actor), *83*, 309, 314; *Julius Caesar* (actor), 309

Little Eyolf (October 22–November 16, 1985), 127–31, *128*, 283, 330

The Living Theatre (New York), xi, 24–28, 36; *Mysteries and Smaller Pieces, Antigone, Frankenstein, Paradise Now*, 320; *Paradise Now*, 26–28, *27*, 320

Lloyd, Christopher (actor): *A Midsummer Night's Dream*, 61–62; *The Possessed*, 69

Lo, Flo, 233

Lo, James: *Geography* (composer), 337

Logan, Lael: *Richard III* (actor), *177*

Logan, Lisa, 177–78

Lombard, Michael (actor): *Henry IV*, 23; *We Bombed in New Haven*, 23

London Observer, 67, 211

Long, Charles ("Chip"), 92–93

Long Day's Journey into Night (March 22–May 21, 1988), 132–33, *132*, 144, 215, 331

Long Wharf Theatre (New Haven), 45–47, 84–85, 132, 139–40, 179, 232, 233, 255, 290, 316, 340

López, Francisco: *Geography* (composer), 192, 336

Loquasto, Santo: *Bacchae* (set designer), 38

Lorca, Federico, 10

Lorenz, Konrad: "On Aggression," 44

Lortel, Lucille, 102, 120

Losch, Tilly, 47

Louis XIV (French king), 7, 183

Love's Labour's Lost (May 4–22, 1982), *35*, 172, 328

Lowell, Robert, 17, 44; *Old Glory* (author), 17; *Prometheus Bound* (adaptation), 13, 16–19, 319

Lowry, W. McNeil. ("Mac"), 9

Lucas, Craig, 240

Lucille Lortel Fund for New Drama, 120

Ludlam, Charles, 176; *Le Bourgeois Avant Garde* (author), 75, *75*, 335

Lulu (March 30–April 21, 2007), 262, 340

Lydia (February 6–28, 2009), 276, 278–80, *279*, 341

Mabe, Matthew: *Big Night* (actor), 222

Mabou Mines Dollhouse (special event, March 31–April 1, 2006), 184, 340

Mabou Mines (New York): *The B. Beaver Animation*, 184, 326; *Mabou Mines Dollhouse*, 184, 340; *Peter and Wendy*, 184, 336; *The Warrior Ant*, 183–84, *184*, 332

Mac, Taylor: *The Be(a)st of Taylor Mac* (author), 184, 342

Macbeth (February 18–March 13, 1971), 75, 239, 321

Macbeth (in conjunction with *Medea* and *Cinderella*). See *Medea/Macbeth/Cinderella*

Macbett (March 16–May 16, 1973), 63, 75, 323

MacIntosh, Joan: *Elizabeth: Almost by Chance a Woman* (actor), 149

Mackay, Lizbeth: *A Midsummer Night's Dream* (actor), 61

MacLeod, Wendy (author), 115–18; *Apocalyptic Butterflies*, 115, 330; *The My House Play*, 115, 331

MacNichol, Katie: *Big Night* (actor), 222

Madden, John (director): *The Bundle: Or, New Narrow Road to the Deep North*, 326; *Between East and West*, 329; *Measure for Measure*, 326; *The Suicide*, 327; *Wings*, 325

Madden, Patric, 298–300

The Magnificent Cuckold (March 31–April 18, 1981), 120–24, 327

Mahagonny ("Little" *Mahagonny*, May 13–June 5, 1971), 47–49, 87, 202, 321

Mahagonny ("Medium" *Mahagonny*, November 6–December 13, 1978), 47, 326
Mailer, Norman, 21
Major Barbara (October 4–22, 1983), 127, 328
Malina, Judith, 25–28
Malle, Louis, 150
Malloy, Amy: *Figaro/Figaro* (actor), *201*
Mamet, David (author), 105, 167, 195; *The Cryptogram*, 336; *Oleanna*, 293, 334; *Reunion and Dark Pony*, 325
Manhattan Theatre Club, 110, 160, 188
Manheim, Camryn: *St. Joan of the Stockyards* (actor), 200
Man Is Man (February 16–April 11, 1978), 325
The Man Who Could See Through Time (January 5–February 6, 1982), 328
Mapplethorpe, Robert, 153
Ma Rainey's Black Bottom (April 3–21, 1984), 50, 119, 134–36, *135*, 154, 329
March of Resilience (2015), 297–98
Mardirosian, Tom: *Elizabeth: Almost by Chance a Woman* (author), *149*, 150
Marie Antoinette (October 26–November 17, 2012), 302, 343
Marks, Jonathan, 93, 100, 103; *The Banquet Years* (creator/author), 325; *The Nixon Show: The Bug Stops Here* (creator), 74; *Sganarelle: An Evening of Molière Farces* (actor), 82, *83*, 84; *Watergate Classics* (author), 323
Mark Taper Forum (Los Angeles), 84, 306
Marlowe, Christopher, 195; *Edward II* (author), 162, 164, 195–97, *196*, 202, 334
Marriage (November 25–December 21, 1985), 68, 101, 129–31, 300, 330
Martenson, Edward, 100, 105, 109, 119, 154
Martin, Trayvon, 296
Marx, Karl, 198
Marx, Robert, 24
Marx Brothers, 54, 75
Mary Alice: *Fences* (actor), 138, *139*
The Master Builder (September 18–October 19, 2009), 254, 283–85, *284*, 342
Master Harold . . . and the Boys (March 9–27, 1982), 108–9, *108*, 119, 328

Mathers, Craig: *Hamlet* (actor), *173*
Matura, Mustapha: *Playboy of the West Indies* (author), 202, 332
Mayeda, Cynthia, 189
Mayer, Max, 309
Mayhew, David, 139–40, *139*
Mays, Jefferson: *The Beauty Part* (actor), *219*
Mazzella, Neil, 105, 253
McAlister, Tom, 178
McAnuff, Des: *A Walk in The Woods* (director), 145, 331
McCarter Theatre Center (Princeton, NJ), 105, 240; *Tartuffe* (coproduction), 261, 341
McCarthy, Tom: *Hamlet* (actor), *173*
McCormick, Carolyn: *Figaro/Figaro* (actor), 202
McCraney, Tarell Alvin, 249–50
McDormand, Frances (actor), 13, 114; *A Moon for the Misbegotten*, 133; *Mrs. Warren's Profession*, 127, *127*
McGowan, Tom, 114
McGrath, Matt: *The Evildoers* (actor), *262*, 263
McGrath, Michael: *It Pays to Advertise* (actor), 224
McHattie, Stephen: *Little Eyolf* (actor), 129
McIntosh, Joan: *Elizabeth: Almost by Chance a Woman* (actor), *149*
McKee, Julie, 312; *The Adventures of Amy Bock* (author), 312, 336
McLane, Derek: *Figaro/Figaro* (set designer), 202
McNally, Terrence (author): *Bad Habits*, 214; *The Tubs*, 34, 85, 214, 323; *Where Has Tommy Flowers Gone?*, 23, 85, 321
McNamara, Robert, 21
Meadow, Lynne, 160
Measure for Measure (November 30–December 22, 1979), 61, 100–101, 326
Measure for Measure (January 28–February 20, 1999), 337
Medea/Macbeth/Cinderella (September 20–October 12, 2002), *ii*, 231, 232, 234–37, *236*, 338

Megrue, Roi Cooper: *It Pays to Advertise* (co-author), 217, 222–24, 338
Meier, Gustav, 47–48
Mellon Foundation, 53, 120, 263, 265
Mellor, Steve: *Le Bourgeois Avant Garde* (actor), *75*
Melons (October 20–November 14, 1987), 34, 182, 300–301, 331
Melville, Herman, 17, 221
The Memento (January 13–February 7, 1987), 112, 331
Men and Women of Shakespeare (January 5–6, 1967), 183, 319
Merrick, David, 19
Merritt, Theresa (actor), 114; *Ma Rainey's Black Bottom*, 135; *Marriage*, 300
Method acting, 206, 222
A Midsummer Night's Dream (May 8–31, 1975), 35, 61–62, *63*, 66–67, 79, 89, 130, 202, 324
A Midsummer Night's Dream (October 12–25, 1975), 66, 79, 324
A Midsummer Night's Dream (February 19–March 14, 1998), 35, 336
Mielziner, Jo, 310
Miles, Sylvia, 114
Milhaud, Darius, 15
Miller, Arthur, 8, 159, 224; *After the Fall*, 10; *All My Sons*, 22, 139; *The Crucible*, 45; *Death of a Salesman*, 35, 88, 234, 290, *291*, 341
Miller, Jonathan: *Beyond the Fringe* (actor), 17; *Prometheus Bound* (director), 13, 17–19, *18*, 319
Miller, Paul D. (DJ Spooky): *Geography* (composer), 192, 336
Miller, Philip: *Refuse the Hour* (composer), 184, 345
Miller, Sam, 189
Miller, Tim, 152, 182
Miner, Jan, 114
Ming Wall, 276–78, *277*
Minnesota Theater Company, 9
The Mirror (January 19–March 7, 1973), 21, 322
The Miser (February 16–March 12, 1988), 331

Index 367

Miss Julie (October 17–November 11, 1989), 332

Miss Julie (March 18–April 9, 2005), 282, 339

Mistaken Identities ('Dentity Crisis and Guess Work) (October 12–December 6, 1978), 30, 326

The Mistakes Madeline Made (October 27–November 18, 2006), 340

Mistero Buffo (Comic Mystery) (special event, May 13–17, 1986), 148, 330

Mister Puntila and His Chauffeur Matti (March 3–April 2, 1977), 50, 325

Mitchell, Aleta: *The Winter's Tale* (actor), 300

Mnouchkine, Ariane, 170

modern dance, 189–92

modernists, 8, 88

Moiseiwitsch, Tanya, 310

Mokae, Zakes (actor): *The Blood Knot*, 102, 109; *Boesman and Lena*, 105; *Master Harold . . . and the Boys*, 108, 109

Molière, 8, 35, 56, 101, 129, 162, 208, 325; *The Bourgeois Gentleman*, 49, 52, 75, 322; *A Doctor in Spite of Himself*, 343; *Don Juan*, 53–59, *58*, 321, 324; *The Imaginary Invalid*, 337; *The Miser*, 331; *Scapin*, 333; *The School for Wives*, 334; *Sganarelle*, 82, 91; *Tartuffe*, 35, 329, 341

Molina, Tirso de: *The Joker of Seville* (author), 100

Molnár, Ferenc: *Rough Crossing* (author), 282, 341

Monk, Debra, 114

Monk, Isabell, 114, 290

Monk, Meredith (special event, February 8, 1997), 183, 336

Monsef, Ramiz: *Eurydice* (actor), *243*

Montgomery, Reggie: *The America Play* (actor), 202, 208, *209*; *Thunder Knocking on the Door* (director), 336

Montoya, Richard: *American Night: The Ballad of Juan José* (author), 343; *Culture Clash in America* (creator/author), 339

A Moon for the Misbegotten (April 30–May 25, 1991), 124, 132–33, 162, 333

Moon Over Miami (February 14–March 11, 1989), 146, 150–52, *151*, 217, 301, 332

Moore, Harvey Gardner: *Richard III* (actor), *177*

Moore, Honor, 24

Moore, Max Gordon: *Arcadia* (actor), *294*

The Moors (January 29–February 20, 2016), 301, 345

Mordecai, Benjamin ("Ben") (managing director), 119, 138–39, 142, 152, 154, 159, 207, 216, 247–48, 250, 253, 314; as de facto Hollywood ambassador, 180–81; *Fences*, 138; *Two Trains Running*, 143

Mordecai, Sherry, 119

Morenzie, Leon: *A Play of Giants* (actor), *147*

Morgan, Carmen, 297–300, 308

Morris, Ricardo, 189, 191

Morris, Tracie: *Geography* (dramaturg), 192, 336

Morrison, Beth, 268

Morton, Joe: *Elizabeth: Almost by Chance a Woman* (author), *149*, 150

Moscow Art Theatre, 7, 10, 68, 283

most-produced playwrights, 35

Motherwell, Robert, 19

Mountcastle, James, 241; *Tartuffe* (stage manager), 261

Mrs. Warren's Profession (November 3–21, 1981), 35, 126–27, *127*, 224, 254, 327

Mrs. Warren's Profession (January 11–February 3, 1996), 35, 127, 335

Mtumi, Andre: *An Evening with Dead Essex* (director), 87–88, 323

Much Ado about Nothing (March 8–26, 1983), 328

Mulligan, Neil, 130, 240, 307

Mump + Smoot in *Ferno and Caged* (March 18–April 9, 1994), 54, 186–87, 285, 334

Mump + Smoot in *Something Else with Zug* (September 14–October 7, 2000), 54, 187–88, *187*, 285, 337

Munch, Edvard, 124

Munk, Erika, 24

music: Albee's *A Delicate Balance* and, 282–83; *Indecent*, 303–4; musicals, performance of, 267–68, 270; original scores and sound design, 224–25; *The Tempest*, 289; trio of composer-musicians in *The Servant of Two Masters*, 286–87; Yale Institute for Music Theater (YIMT), 268

My Children! My Africa! (November 14–December 14, 1991), 162, 164, 333

The My House Play (January 11–February 6, 1988), 115, 331

Mysteries and Smaller Pieces, Antigone, Frankenstein, Paradise Now (September 16–28, 1968), 26, 320

The Mystery Plays (April 30–May 22, 2004), 218, 339

Naming Spaces Initiative, 300

Nation (magazine), 72

National Endowment for the Arts (NEA), x, 10, 17, 53, 97, 119, 152, 153–54, 182, 188, 209, 263

National Public Radio (NPR) Earplay series, 90

Naughton, Keira: *These Paper Bullets!* (actor), *271*, 272

NEA. *See* National Endowment for the Arts

Neapolitan Ghosts (October 21–November 15, 1986), 124, 154, 330

Neddy (January 11–February 6, 1988), 331

The Negro Ensemble Company (New York), 183; *Song of the Lusitanian Bogey*, 321

Nelson, Lee Mark: *The Way of the World* (actor), *205*

Nelson, Novella: *Boesman and Lena* (actor), 105

Nelson, Richard: *Between East and West* (author), 329; *Miss Julie* (translation), 282, 339; *Rip Van Winkle, or "The Works"* (author), 327

Nemirovich-Danchenko, Vladimir, 7

Neumann, David (choreographer): *The Birds*, 337; *In a Year with 13 Moons*, 344; *War*, 280, 344

New Haven Advocate, 220

New Haven (Connecticut), 191, 198–200, 232, 308, 315

New Haven public school program. *See* Dwight/Edgewood Project

New Haven Register, 26–27, 48–49, 54, 89, 97, 103, 139–40, 143, 150, 161, 259, 262

Newman, Paul, 5

New Republic (magazine), xi, 3, 10, 159, 304

Newsweek, 6, 59, 72

New Theatre (later Iseman Theater), 218, 238

New Vaudeville, 186

New York Shakespeare Festival, 9, 207, 216, 310; *The America Play* (coproduction), 208, 334; *Venus* (coproduction), 208, 335

New York Times, xi, 4, 9, 19, 79, 91, 105–6, 122, 124, 127, 144, 150, 152, 169, 212, 244, 262, 287

Nguema, Francisco Macías, 146

Nichols, Mike, 15

Nicola, James, 216

Nielsen, Kristine (actor), 101–2; *The Ghost Sonata*, 73; *Measure for Measure*, 100; *Timon of Athens*, 102; *Ubu Rex*, 101; *You Can't Take It with You*, 102

Nigerian Civil War (1967–1970), 146

Night Is Mother to the Day (March 6–24, 1984), 210, 329

Nigrini, Peter: *Notes from the Underground* (projectionist), 266

The 1940's Radio Hour (December 28–January 7, 1978), 183, 325–26

Nivola, Alessandro: *St. Joan of the Stockyards* (actor), *199*

Nixon, Richard, 25, 64, 74–76

No Boundaries Series, 184, 218, 224, 255, 257; *Baby-Q's MESs* (March 25–27, 2010), 342; *The Be(a)st of Taylor Mac* (January 28–30, 2010), 184, 342; *The Break/s: A Mixtape for Stage* (January 22–24, 2009), 342; *The Case of the Spectator* (September 23–25, 2010), 343; *Engagement Féminin: An Evening of West African Contemporary Dance* (November 3–5, 2011), 343; *Escuela* (February 24–26, 2016), 184, 345; *A Festival of International Dance at Yale* (November 14–15, 2008), 184, 341; *The Files* (February 20–22, 2014), 344; *The Method Gun* (February 23–26, 2011), 343; *Nameless Forest* (March 31–April 2, 2011), 343; *No Man's Gone Now* (November 11–12, 2008), 341; *Now Now Oh Now* (December 4–10, 2014), 345; *Refuse the Hour* (November 6–7, 2015), 184, 345; *The Rehearsal* (March 23–24, 2012), 343; *RoS Indexical and Spiraling Down* (November 11–12, 2008), 342; *Singular Sensation* (November 14–15, 2008), 341; *Songs of Lear* (February 26–28, 2015), 345; *Spectral Scriabin* (February 10–11, 2012), 343; *Super Night Shot* (February 1–2, 2013), 184, 344; *Territories in Transgression* (November 11–12, 2008), 341; *Three Acts, Two Dancers, One Radio Host* (December 20, 2014), 345; *Witness to the Ruins* (March 26–28, 2009), 342; *Wormwood* (November 5–7, 2009), 342

Nolan, Victoria (Vicki), 180–82, *181*, 188–89, 191, 194, 207, 216, 220, 226, 231–32, 250, 261, 265, 278, 295–96, 298–99, 308, 314, 316

Norcia, Patrizia: *Sganarelle: An Evening of Molière Farces* (actor), 84

Norment, Elizabeth: *Sganarelle: An Evening of Molière Farces* (actor), *83*

Norris, Frank, 198

Notes from Underground (March 20–April 11, 2009), 68, 266–67, *267*, 341

Noth, Christopher, 114; *Rum and Coke* (actor), 34

Novak, Peter, 216; *Geography* (dramaturg), 192

Ntosha, Winston, 102

Nunn, Trevor, 159

Nyong'o, Lupita (actor): *Eclipsed*, 259; *The Winter's Tale*, *288*, 289

Obama, Barack, 280, 296

Odets, Clifford, 8, 159, 224; *Waiting for Lefty* (author), 28

Oenslager, Donald, 6, 213, 310

off-Broadway, 8, 84–85

Offenbach, Jacques, 325; *La Vie Parisienne* (composer), 9

O'Hara, Robert, 240; *In the Continuum* (director), 257, 340

Ohio State Murders (January 14–February 9, 1991), 115, 333

Oleanna (October 14–November 6, 1993), 207, 293, 334

Olivier, Laurence, 28

Olmecs (*King Lear*), 239–40, 259, 317, 339

Olmon, Kari, 298–99

Olympian Games (October 8–31, 1970), 41, 44, 321

O'Neill, Eugene, 8, 14, 88, 114, 124, 132–33; *Ah, Wilderness!*, 132–33; *A Long Day's Journey into Night*, 88, *132*, 132–33; *A Moon for the Misbegotten*, 124, 132–33, 333; *A Touch of the Poet*, 328

O'Neill Playwriting Conference (Connecticut), 97–98, 110, 112, 114–15, 133–34, 136, 146, 159, 206, 263

one-person shows, 182

On the Verge (October 3–November 2, 1991), 161, 163–64, 254, 333

Open Theatre (New York), 12; *Viet Rock* (production), 13, 49, 183, 319

Operation Sidewinder (never opened, 1968), 32–34, 40, 88, 301

Ophelia Kline (Sunday Series, 1980), 66

Orchard, Robert (Rob), 53, 56, 116

Oregon Shakespeare Festival, 289, 302

O'Rourke, Kevin: *Trouble in Mind* (actor), 261

Othello (February 18–March 15, 1986), 330

Overmyer, Eric (author), 161–62, 195, 203; *Figaro/Figaro*, 75, 201–2, 335; *In Perpetuity Throughout the Universe*, 161; *Native Speech*, 161; *On the Verge, or the Geography of Yearning*, 161, 163–64, 254, 333

Overshown, Howard: *Death of a Salesman* (actor), *291*

Ovid's Metamorphoses (November 27–December 20, 1969), 40–41, *41*, 44, 320

Owen, Johnny, 237

Index   369

Owens, Wilfred, 64
Owners (October 25–November 16, 2013), 344
Owuor, Gilbert: *Belleville* (actor), *273*
OyamO, 112; *The Resurrection of Lady Lester* (author), 30, 110, 327

Padla, Steven, 253, 255
Padrón, Jacob, 316
Paige, Cristen: *Pop!* (actor), *269*
Paine, Natalia: *Trouble in Mind* (actor), *260*
Papp, Joseph, xii, 9, 72
Paradise Now (September 16–28, 1968), 26–28, *27*, 320
Paraiso, Nicky: *St. Joan of the Stockyards* (actor), *199*
Park, Jiehae: *peerless* (author), 301, 345
"park and bark," 206
Parks, Suzan-Lori, 162, 189, 195, 240, 301; *The America Play* (author), 202, 208, *209*, 334; *The Death of the Last Black Man in the Whole Entire World* (author), 130, 164, 167, *168*, 204, 208–9, 226, 333; *Venus* (author), 207–10, *210*, 335
parody, 75
Parrish, Elizabeth ("Betsy"), 36, 47, 50, 52; *The War Show* (actor), 64
Pask, Scott: *The Way of the World* (set designer), 206
Passanante, Jean, 133
Passion (February 1–5, 1972), 32, 322
Passion Play (September 19–October 11, 2008), 178, 243–45, *244*, 341
Patterson, Jay: *Big Night* (actor), 222
Payton-Wright, Pamela: *Little Eyolf* (actor), 129
pay-what-you-can performances, 180
Pearson, Sybille: *Sally and Marsha* (author), 110, 115, 327
Pearthree, Pippa: *Fefu and Her Friends* (actor), *165*, 166
Peaslee, Richard (composer): *Bacchae*, 38; *Don Juan, or the Enemy of God*, 57; *The War Show*, 66
Pecinka, Tom: *Arcadia* (actor), 294

peerless (November 27–December 19, 2015), 301, 345
Penney, Hannibal, Jr.: *An Evening with Dead Essex* (actor), *86*, 88
Penny, Rob, 134
Pentecost (November 9–December 2, 1995), 200, 210–12, *211*, 215, 224, 226, 301, 335
The People Next Door (January 13–February 4, 2006), 340
Pepine, Arthur, 120
Perelman, S. J.: *The Beauty Part* (author), 162, 164, 197, 217, 219, *219*, 301, 334
Perloff, Carey, 216
Perry Street Theatre: *In the Continuum* (production), 340
Peter and Wendy (September 17–October 3, 1998), 184, 336
Peters, William (director): *The Idiots Karamazov*, 79, 323; *Macbett*, 323
Petersburg (April 30–May 23, 1998), 68, 336
Peterson, Libby, 298
Peterson, Lisa (director): *Fefu and Her Friends*, 166, 333; *Slavs!*, 335
Phaedra and Hippolytus (January 10–February 4, 1989), 332
The Philanderer (November 30–December 18, 1982), 61, 119, 124, 127, 328
Philips, Marjorie, 66
Phoenix Theatre, 8–9
The Piano Lesson (November 23–December 19, 1987), 35, 142, 331
The Piano Lesson (January 28–February 19, 2011), 35, 342
Pill Hill (January 15–February 10, 1990), 115, 332
Pinkins, Tonya: *War*, 281
Pinter, Harold, 148; *Betrayal* (author), 35, 337
Pintilie, Lucian, 101
Pintor, Lupe, 237
Pirandello, Luigi, 14, 22, 126; *Henry IV*, 23, 319; *Six Characters in Search of an Author*, 22
A Place with the Pigs (March 24–April 18, 1987), 109, 331
Platt, Oliver: *Moon Over Miami* (actor), 152

Play (April 1–24, 1971), 321
Playboy of the West Indies (April 25–May 20, 1989), 202, 301, 332
The Player's Guide, 122
Playing in Local Bands (January 4–February 5, 1983), 328
A Play of Giants (November 27–December 22, 1984), 146–48, *147*, 210, 329
Plimpton, George, 19
Pochinko, Richard, 186
Poggi, Gregory, 119
Polak, Ben, 295
political satires, 146–52
Pomerance, Bernard: *Melons* (author), 182, 331
Pop! (November 27–December 19, 2009), 268–70, *269*, 272, 342
Porter, Adina: *Venus* (actor), *210*
Porter, Jimmy: *Prometheus Bound* (actor), 18
Porter, Stephen: *Mrs. Warren's Profession* (director), 127, 327
Posey, Parker: *The Realistic Joneses* (actor), 276
Posnick, Michael (director), 11–12, 93; *Are You Now or Have You Ever Been*, 322; *Darkroom*, 323; *Happy End*, 51, 322, 324; *Little Mahagonny*, 48, 321; *The Mirror*, 322; *Ovid's Metamorphoses* (composer), 320; *Passion*, 322; *Stops*, 322; *They Told Me That You Came This Way*, 32, 320
The Possessed (October 3–26, 1974), 67–70, *69*, 78, 323
postmodernism, 172
Potts, Michael (actor), 114; *The America Play*, *209*; *The Death of the Last Black Man in the Whole Entire World*, 169
Poulenc, Francis, 325
Poundstone, Paula (special event, November 10, 1992, at University Theatre), 182, 334
Povich, Amy: *The Beauty Part* (actor), *219*
Powell, Dawn, 221–23; *Big Night* (author), 219, 221–22, *223*, 224, 338; *The Party* (author), 222
Powers, Kim, 135

"premiere-itis," 85, 206
Preston, Travis: *Democracy in America* (creator/director), 169–70, 333; *Little Eyolf* (director), 128, 170, 330; *Terra Nova* (director), 325
Price, Lonny, 109
Primary Stages: *In the Continuum* (production), 257, 340
Prince, Harold, 114
Profeta, Katherine: *Dramaturgy in Motion* (author), 192; *Geography* (dramaturg), 192–94, 337
the program, 255–56, *256*
projection designers, 270–72, 278
Prometheus Bound (May 9–21, 1967), 12–13, 16–19, *18*, 23, 38, 61, 79, 237, 243, 319
prop shop, 130–31, *131*
protests of 1968, 23–25
Provincetown Players, 8, 223
Psacharopoulos, Nikos, 5
The Psychic Life of Savages (February 14–March 8, 2003), 231, 251, 259, 338
public school programs. *See* Dwight/Edgewood Project; *Will Power!*
Public Theater (New York), xii, 208; *Compulsion*, 342; *Wings*, Yale Rep production at, 91
Pucci, Peter (choreographer): *The Black Monk*, 338; *The Cherry Orchard*, 340; *dance of the holy ghosts: a play on memory*, 340; *Miss Julie*, 339; *Safe in Hell*, 340
Purcell, Henry (composer): *The Fairy Queene*, 62, 324; *The Tempest*, 61, 323
Purdy, Claude, 134
Pygmalion (May 1–26, 1990), 127, 300, 332

Quintero, José (director): *Long Day's Journey into Night*, 132–33, 331; *A Moon for the Misbegotten*, 132
Quinton, Everett: *The Beaux' Stratagem* (director), 176, 335

Rabe, David: *The Black Monk* (adaptation/author), 231, 338; *Sticks and Bones* (author), 75, 88, 338

race, diversity, and inclusion: absence of recorded Black American history, 208; accessibility issues, ways to address, 120; AIDS and, 257; all-Black cast in *Death of a Salesman*, 290, *291*; all-Black cast in *King Lear*, 239–40; Analyzing and Mobilizing Privilege (AMP), 298; antisemitism, 299; Asian and Asian American Theatre Coalition (Asian Potluck), 298; Beyond Diversity workshop (2016), 298; Black History Month presentations, 134, 259; Black Lives Matter (BLM) movement, 296; Black women playwrights, 164–67, 257–59; in Brustein era, 33–34, 85, 88, 99, 300; color-blind casting, 300–301; Diversity, Equity, and Inclusion (DEI) issues, 297–300; Diversity, Equity, Inclusion, and Belonging (DEIB), 34, 301, 308; El Colectivo (affinity group), 298; emergence of Black playwrights, 98–99, 112, 154, 314; *An Evening with Dead Essex* (March 7–April 27, 1974), 85–88; Folks (affinity group), 298; Fugard and, 102; March of Resilience (2015), 297–98; microaggressions, 298–99; mixed-race characters, 280; Naming Spaces Initiative, 300; New Haven public school students seeing actors of color, 235; no company members of color from 1967 to 1979 (de Lavallade as exception), 300; *Rainbow Series* (1995), 188; *The Resurrection of Lady Lester*, 110–12, *113*, 245, 327; Richards and diversity, 154; Richards as first Black to head a professional school at Yale, 97, 157; Wajda and, 67; white supremacist culture, 281, 308; Wilson cycle and, 133–43, 154, 207, 208, 249–50, 293, 300, 314; Wilson on casting all-Black productions of white plays, 290; Womxn's Voices in Theatre, 298; Yale Intercultural Affairs Committee and Halloween 2015, 296–97. *See also* Fugard, Athol; Wilson, August; women
Racine, Jean, 265; *Andromaque* (author), 9

Radio Golf (April 22–May 15, 2005), 134, 143, 245, 247–50, *248*, 339
Rafferty, Sarah: *It Pays to Advertise* (actor), 224
Rainbow Series (1995), 188
Rainey, Ford: *Buried Child* (actor), *89*
Rainey, Gertrude ("Ma"), 135. *See also Ma Rainey's Black Bottom*
A Raisin in the Sun (November 1–19, 1983), 119, 124, 329
Rame, Franca, 148, 183, 330; *Tutta Casa, Letto, e Chiesa (All House, Bed and Church)* (author/performer), 148, 330
Ramicova, Dunya (costume designer), 130–31, 311; *The Ghost Sonata*, 73; *Marriage*, 130; *Sganarelle: An Evening of Molière Farces*, 84
Randich, Jean: *Serious Money* (director), 179, 338
Rauch, Bill, 229, 289; *The Cherry Orchard* (director), 340; *The Clean House* (director), 240, 339; *Medea/Macbeth/Cinderella* (creator/adaptation/director), 234–37, *236*, 338
Re: Play series (1994), 188
Rea, Oliver, 9
Reagan, Ronald, 120, 150, 152–53, 229, 245
Reale, Willie, 162, 188–89
The Realistic Joneses (April 20–May 12, 2012), 122, 272, 273, 275–76, 278, 343
Reddin, Keith, 112; *Black Snow* (adaptation), 283, 340; *Rum and Coke* (author), 34, 329
Redpath, Ralph: *The Idiots Karamazov* (actor), *78*
regional theater movement, x, 84–85, 99, 139, 152, 212
Rehearsing Vengeance (2012), 302
Renaud, Madeleine, 9; *Happy Days* (actor), 183
Reno Once Removed (special event, November 10, 1992), 182, 334
the Rep. *See* Yale Repertory Theatre
Repertory Theater of Lincoln Center, 10
Resident Theatre Movement, xii

Index 371

The Resurrection of Lady Lester (January 10–February 21, 1981), 110–12, *113*, 215, 245, 327

Reunion and Dark Pony (October 13–November 28, 1977), 325

The Revenger's Tragedy (November 19–December 12, 1970), 321

Revolutions of 1989, 210

Reynolds, Bill, 120

The Rhesus Umbrella (April 2–25, 1970), 321

Ribman, Ronald: *A Break in the Skin* (author), 52, 322

Rice Boy (October 19–November 11, 2000), 237, 337

Rich, Frank, 109, 152

Richard II (November 29–December 17, 1983), 35, 329

Richard II (September 21-October 13, 2007), 35, 283, 341

Richard III (March 16–April 8, 2000), 176, *177*, 337

Richards, Lloyd, as dean and artistic director, 95–155, *143*; accessibility issues addressed by, 120; appointment of, 3–4, 46, 97; background of, 97; Kate Burton on, 159–60; Carlotta Festival plays and, 178; casting and auditions, 122, 300–301; classic repertory, choices of, 120, 124–31, 195; compared to Brustein, 98, 120, 127, 154, 182, 314; compared to Bundy, 251; compared to Wojewodski, 161, 206, 210; developing playwrights and diversity, 98–100; Dutton and, 289; exit interview with *American Theatre*, 159; final Yale Rep production of *A Moon for the Misbegotten*, 133, 162; financial rewards from regional and Broadway productions, 142; as first Black to head a professional school at Yale, 97, 154; Fugard's plays and, 101–9, 217, 293, 314; gifts and funding in mid-1980s, 120, 188; growth of Yale Rep under, 119–20, 152–54; Honegger and, 114; honors bestowed on, 152; legacy of, 152–54, 164, 254; as listener to student frustrations, 160; most Brustein-like offering of Rep tenure, 100; NEA and, 153–54; as O'Neill Theater Center artistic director, 97–98; the program during era of, 255; public communications of, 254; rotating rep for his first season, 54; Russian works produced by, 68; special events scheduled by, 183; Tony awards and, 139–40, 152; transfer of plays to Broadway and, xiv, 105, 139, 142, 144, 314; Wilson Cycle of plays and, 133–43, 154, 207, 208, 217, 240, 293, 314; writing advice of, 155. *See also Winterfest*

Richards, Lloyd, as director, 251; *Cobb*, 332; *A Doll's House*, 126, 328; *Fences*, 137–39, 142, 160, 314, 329; *Hedda Gabler*, 124, 195, 327; *Joe Turner's Come and Gone*, 140–41, 160, 330; *Johnny Bull*, 328; *Major Barbara*, 124, 127, 328; *Ma Rainey's Black Bottom*, 114–15, 134, 329; *A Moon for the Misbegotten*, 124, 133, 162, 333; *The Piano Lesson*, 142, 331; *Timon of Athens*, 101–2, 124, 327; *A Touch of the Poet*, 124, 328; *Two Trains Running*, 142–43, *143*, 332; *Uncle Vanya*, 124, 126, 327

Rip Van Winkle, or "The Works" (December 1–19, 1981), 327

The Rise and Fall of the City of Mahagonny (January 31–February 23, 1974), 47–49, *48*, 51–53, 87, 202, 210, 323

The Rivals (October 16–November 8, 1969), 12, 43–44, 213, 306, 320

Rizzo, Frank, 112, 127, 216

Roach, Joseph, 183–84, 216, 230, 302

The Road to Mecca (May 1–26, 1984), 109, 119, 144, 329

Robards, Jason, Jr. (actor): *Ah, Wilderness!*, 132; *Long Day's Journey into Night*, 132–33, *132*

Robbins, Laila (actor), 114; *Major Barbara*, 127; *Summer and Smoke*, 178

Robertson, Pat, 153

Robina Foundation, 250, 263–66, 296

Robinson, Andrew: *Battle of Black and Dogs* (actor), *131*

Robinson, Marc, 168–69

Robinson, Roger: *A Play of Giants* (actor), *147*, 148

Rockefeller, John D., 10

Rockefeller Foundation, x, 11, 164

Rococo (January 10–February 21, 1981), 110, 115, 327

Rodgers, Richard (composer): *Cinderella*, 235, 338; *No Strings*, 38

Rodgers and Hammerstein Organization, 236

Rodríguez, Catherine María, 298

Rodriguez, Onahoua: *Lydia* (actor), *279*, 280

Rogers, James Gamble (architect), 20

Rogers, Michael: *A Play of Giants* (actor), *147*

Rogers, Reg (actor): *Figaro/Figaro*, 201, 202; *Rough Crossing*, 282

Rogoff, Gordon, 11–13, 19, 24, 37, 84, 92, 197–98

Romeo and Juliet (March 11–April 2, 2011), 342

Romero, Constanza: *The Piano Lesson* (costume designer), 142

Root, Melina: *Summer and Smoke* (costume designer), 178

Roper, Alicia: *The Way of the World* (actor), *205*

Rosato, Mary Lou: *Elizabeth: Almost by Chance a Woman* (author), *149*, 150

Rosen, Robert, 185

Rosenberg, Stanley: *Bacchae* (associate director), 37, 320

Rosenthal, Todd (set designer): *August: Osage County*, 173; *Hamlet*, 173

Roth, Katherine (costumer designer), 311; *Hamlet*, 173; *Richard III*, 176; *The Way of the World*, 178

Roth, Philip, 19, 21, 44; *Watergate Classics*, 323; *Zuckerman*, 134

Rothman, John: *A Cup of Coffee* (actor), 220, *221*

Rothschild's Fiddle (January 14–31, 2004), 68, 339

Rough Crossing (November 28–December 20, 2008), 282, 341

Royal Danish Theater, 7
Rozewicz, Tadeusz: *White Marriage* (author), 70–74, *71*, 325
Rubin, Tara, 122–23
Rucker, Mark (director), 250, 252; *All's Well That Ends Well*, 252, 282, 340; *The Cryptogram*, 336; *The Imaginary Invalid*, 337; *Kingdom of Earth*, 217, 338; *Landscape of the Body*, 335; *Measure for Measure*, 337; *The Mistakes Madeline Made*, 340; *Rough Crossing*, 282, 341; *A Streetcar Named Desire*, 344; *Twelfth Night*, 174–75, 179, 202, 335
Rugg, Rebecca, 301–3
Ruhl, Sarah (author), 35, 122, 240–46, 250, 282, 308; *The Clean House*, 240–41, *241*, 245, 246, 308, 339; *Dear Elizabeth, A Play in Letters from Elizabeth Bishop to Robert Lowell and Back Again*, 245, 343; *Eurydice*, 242–43, *243*, 254, 340; *Passion Play*, 178, 243–45, *244*, 341; *Scenes from Court Life; or the whipping boy and his prince*, 245, 345; *The Three Sisters* (revision), 245
Rum and Coke (January 14–February 9, 1985), 34, 300, 329
Russell, Rufus G., 42
Russian works, 68, 214, 231. *See also specific Russian authors*
Rust and Ruin (January 15–February 10, 1990), 332

Saarinen, Eero, 7
Safe in Hell (November 12–December 3, 2005), 340
St. Joan of the Stockyards (February 18–March 13, 1993), 198–200, *199*, 202, 206, 224, 334
Saint Julian the Hospitaler (October 8–31, 1970), 44, 321
St. Laurent, Yves, 9
Salim, Pierre-André, 261
Salinas, Ric: *Culture Clash in America* (creator/author), 339
Sally and Marsha (January 10–February 21, 1981), 110, 115, 327

Salovey, Peter, 295, 307
Salter, Nikkole: *In the Continuum* (author/actor), 234, 257–59, *258*, 340
Sammler, Bronislaw (Ben), 115–18, *117*, 216, 218, 220, 224, 261; *The Frogs* (technical director), 116; *Geography* (technical director), 194; *Life Is a Dream* (carpenter), 116; *Structural Design for the Stage* (author), 118; *Technical Design Solutions for Theatre* (author), 118
Sammler, Laraine, *117*
Sampson, Tori, 298, 300
Sarcophagus (September 15–October 10, 1987), 68, 154, 331
Sassoon, Siegfried, 64
Satie, Erik, 325
Saunders, Matt, 313
Saved (December 5–21, 1968), 13, 25, 28–32, *31*, 106, 150, 320
Saxe-Meiningen Troupe, 7
Scapin (March 26–April 20, 1991), 333
scene and prop shops, 130–31, *131*
Scenes from Court Life; or the whipping boy and his prince (September 30–October 22, 2016), 245, 345
Schechter, Joel, 24, 100, 114–15, 150, 197
Scher, Adam: *St. Joan of the Stockyards* (set designer), 200
Schiller, Friedrich, 199
Schlamme, Marthe: *A Kurt Weill Cabaret* (actor), 29
Schlemiel the First (April 11–May 18, 1974), 21, 87, 323
Schmidt, Benno C., 152, 160
Schmidt, Paul, 162, 203; *St. Joan of the Stockyards* (translation), 198–99, 334; *The School for Wives* (translation), 334; *Uncle Vanya* (translation/actor), *204*, 335
Schnitzler, Arthur: *Intermezzo* (author), 124, 331
The School for Wives (April 28–May 21, 1994), 334
Schreiber, Liev, 114
Schrider, Tommy: *Battle of Black and Dogs* (actor), *131*

Schulman, Susannah: *Rough Crossing* (actor), 282; *The Winter's Tale* (actor), 289
Schultz, Howard, 224
Schultz, Karen: *Hedda Gabler* (set designer), 124
Schultz, Tom, 253
Schutzel, Laura, 122
Schweizer, David (director): *Geography of a Horse Dreamer*, 88, 323; *Jacques Brel: Songs*, 322; *The Shaft of Love*, 324
Scott, Campbell: *Ah, Wilderness!* (actor), 132
Scott, Dennis (director): *A Child's Tale*, 330; *Flash Floods*, 328; *The Memento*, 331; *Miss Julie*, 332; *Neddy*, 331; *Othello*, 330; *Playboy of the West Indies*, 332; *A Raisin in the Sun*, 329; *Talley's Folly*, 329
Scott, Harold: *King Lear* (director), 178, 239, 339
Scott, Kimberly (actor), 155; *Death of a Salesman*, 254, 290; *Joe Turner's Come and Gone*, 140, *141*, 142
Scott, Seret, 114; *Crumbs from the Table of Joy* (director), 337
Scully, Anthony: *The Great Chinese Revolution* (author), 32, 320
The Seagull (February 15–April 6, 1979), 9, 93, 326
Search and Destroy (November 27–December 22, 1990), 154, 333
Seattle Repertory Theatre, 138, 172, 287
Second City (Chicago), 15, 22, 186
Seitz, John, 114
Seko, Mobutu Sese, 146
Sellar, Tom, 24
Sellars, Peter, 234–35
Seneca, Joe: *Ma Rainey's Black Bottom* (actor), *135*
Serban, Andrei, xiii, *73*, 101, 267; *The Ghost Sonata* (director), 72–74, *73*, 121–22, 214, 325; *Sganarelle: An Evening of Molière Farces* (director), 82–83, 285, 325
Serious Money (March 21–April 13, 2002), 179, 200, 217, 338

Serpent Players (South Africa), 102
Serralles, Jeanine: *Serious Money* (actor), 179; *These Paper Bullets!* (actor), 271, 272
Serrand, Dominique: *Children of Paradise* (director/author), 185, 334
Serrano, Andres, 153
The Servant of Two Masters (March 12–April 3, 2010), 285–87, *286*, 342
set design: avant-garde, 170, 171; Lee's life and influence, 310–13, *311*; Olmec *King Lear* and, 239–40; postmodernism, 172, 173; Yeargan's top ten, 213–15
7 Days of Action: A Community Response to AIDS, 182
The Seven Deadly Sins (May 13–June 5, 1971), 47–48, 321
Sganarelle: An Evening of Molière Farces (January 19–February 1, 1978), 82–84, *83*, 91, 214, 285, 325
The Shaft of Love (March 27–April 26, 1975), 75, 324
Shakespeare, William, 12, 17, 49, 79–81, 104, 106, 154, 171, 188, 199–200, 224, 251, 255, 309; *All's Well That Ends Well*, 123, 234, 252, 282, 340; *As You Like It*, 35, 203, 326, 334; *The Comedy of Errors*, 339; *Coriolanus*, 9, 320; *Cymbeline*, 235, 287, 301, 345; *Hamlet*, 9, 35, 162, 172–73, *173*, 290–93, *292*, 334, 344; *Henry IV, Part I*, 329; *Julius Caesar*, 309, 324; *King Lear*, 32–36, *37*, 75, 203, 239–40, 310, 323, 339; *Love's Labour's Lost*, 35, 172, 328; *Macbeth*, 235, 321, 338; *Measure for Measure*, 61, 100–101, 326, 337; *Men and Women of Shakespeare*, 183, 319; *A Midsummer Night's Dream*, 7, 35, 61–62, *63*, 66–67, 79, 89, 229, 324, 336; *Much Ado about Nothing*, 270–72, *271*, 328, 344; *Othello*, 330; *Pericles*, 287; *Richard II*, 35, 196, 283, 329, 341; *Richard III*, 176, *177*, 196, 337; Romances of (last four plays), 287–88; *Romeo and Juliet*, 342; *The Taming of the Shrew*, 231, 301, 338; *The Tempest*, 38, 53, 61, 101, 287, 323; *Timon of Athens*, 54, 101–2, 300, 327; *Troilus and Cressida*, 35, 101, 324, 332; *Twelfth Night*, 35, 174–76, *175*, 179, 202, 289, 327, 335; *Will Power!* education program, 234–35, *235*, 239, 258, 308, 316; *The Winter's Tale*, 35, 101, 287–89, *288*, 300, 330, 343

Shakespeare Repertory Project, 218, 224
Shalhoub, Tony (actor): *Buried Child*, 89, 90; *Measure for Measure*, 101; *Moon Over Miami*, *151*, 152
Shapiro, Anna D., 232; *The Unmentionables* (director), 341
Shaw, George Bernard, 14, 24, 28, 35, 49, 79–81, 88, 124, 126–28, 188, 281; *Candida*, 336; *Don Juan in Hell*, 56, 64; *Heartbreak House*, 38, 127, 147, 330; *Major Barbara*, 127, 198, 328; *Mrs. Warren's Profession*, 35, 126–27, *127*, 200, 327, 335; *The Philanderer*, 61, 119, 124, 127, 328; *Pygmalion*, 127, 300, 332; *You Never Can Tell*, 88, 217, 338
Shawn, Wallace, 161
Shay, Michele, 249
Shea, John V.: *Lear* (actor), 37
She Barged Down the Nile and Sank (Sunday Series, 1973), 64
Sheehy, Catherine, 169, 197–98, 206, 217, 219–20, 224, *225*, 226, 240, 255–56, 270, 301, 308, 312, 314, 316; *Happy Days* (dramaturg), 305–6; *The King Stag* (adaptation), 285, 339; *Trouble in Mind* (dramaturg), 260–61
Shepard, Sam (author), 72, 88, 105–6, 164, 166–67, 265; *Buried Child*, 88–90, *89*, 101, 326; *Curse of the Starving Class*, 101, 326, 337; *Geography of a Horse Dreamer*, 85, 88, 323; *Operation Sidewinder*, 32–34, 88; *Suicide in B-Flat*, 88, 324
Sheridan, Jamey: *Long Day's Journey into Night* (actor), 133
Sherman, Kim D., 162–63, *163*; *Twelfth Night* (composer), 174
Sherriff, R. C.: *Journey's End* (author), 15
Shevelove, Burt: *The Frogs* (adaptation/director), 79–81, *80*, 323

Shipley, Sandra: *The Way of the World* (actor), 206
Shookhoff, David, 12, 19
Shubert Theatre (New Haven), 10, 22
Sibul, Christina: *The Servant of Two Masters* (translation), 285, 342
Sills, Paul, 40–44, 47; *Dynamite Tonite!* (director), 15, 319; *Greatshot* (director), 320; *Ovid's Metamorphoses* (creator), 40–44, 320; *Story Theatre* (creator/director), 40–41, 320; *Story Theatre Repertory* (creator), 44, 321
Silver, Nicky, 240
Silverman, Jen: *The Moors* (author), 301, 345
Simon, Meg, 122–23; *Long Day's Journey into Night* (casting director), 133
Simpson, James A. (director): *Chopin in Space*, 329; *Curse of the Starving Class*, 337; *The Resurrection of Lady Lester*, 110–12, 327; *Summer and Smoke*, 332
Sinclair, Upton, 198
Singer, Isaac Bashevis, 93; *Gimpel the Fool*, 44, 321; *The Mirror*, 21, 322; *Schlemiel the First*, 21, 323
Singles Series (1995), 188
Sirk, Douglas, 267
Size of the World (January 14–February 9, 1991), 333
The Skin of Our Teeth (February 20–March 15, 1997), 35, 176, 336
Skybell, Steven, 114; *The Caucasian Chalk Circle* (actor), 282
Slavs! (Thinking about the Longstanding Problems of Virtue and Happiness) (February 24–March 18, 1995), 68, 200, 207, 335
Smith, Adam, 169, 171
Smith, Anna Deavere, 216
Smith, Mary Alice. *See* Mary Alice
Smith, Priscilla: *The Ghost Sonata* (actor), 202
Smith-Cameron, J., 114
social media, 253
Solanas, Valerie, 268–70
The Solid Gold Cadillac (September 12–October 7, 1989), 332

Solis, Octavio: *Lydia* (author), 276, 278–80, *279*, 341
Somerville, Barbara: *Pentecost* (speech/dialect coach), 212
Something Else with Zug. *See* Mump + Smoot in *Something Else with Zug*
Sommer, Josef: *A Walk in The Woods* (actor), *145*
Somogyi, Ilona, 230
Sondheim, Stephen, 70; *Assassins* (author), 269; *Finishing the Hat* (author), 79; *The Frogs* (composer/lyricist), 79–81, *80*, 323; *A Funny Thing Happened on the Way to the Forum* (composer), 79; *A Little Night Music* (composer), 70, 79
Sontag, Susan, 19; *On Photography* (author), 128
Soule, Samantha: *The Evildoers* (actor), 263
sound design. *See* music
South Africa, first integrated cast performance in, 102
Southwark Theatre Company (Philadelphia): *Endgame* (production), 183, 319
Soyinka, Wole, 100; *Madmen and Specialists* (author), 146; *A Play of Giants* (author/director), 146–48, *147*, 210, 212, 329
special subscription series, 188
Spence, Hunter (props): *Lear*, 36; *White Marriage*, 106
Spender, Stephen, 19
Spielberg, David: *Bacchae* (actor), 37
Splash Hatch on the E Going Down (January 15–February 7, 1998), 207, 336
Spolin, Viola, 40, 47
Sprinchorn, Evert (translation): *Crimes and Crimes*, 320; *The Father*, 324; *The Ghost Sonata*, 72, 325
Stadlen, Lewis J.: *Moon Over Miami* (actor), 152
Stadtheater (Germany), 7, 9
Stanislavski, Konstantin, 7–8
Stanley, Karma: *An Evening with Dead Essex* (visuals designer), 88
Starting Monday (January 10–February 4, 1989), 332

Stary Teatr (Cracow): *The Possessed* (production), 67, 70
Stein, Gertrude, 161, 167
Stein, Howard, 12, 76
Stein, Peter, 170
Stern, Edward, 119
Stevens, Elizabeth, 313
Stevens, Wallace, 275
Stitchers and Starlight Talkers (January 9–February 8, 1986), 330
Stoker, Bram: *Dracula* (author), 44
Stone, Harold: *God Bless* (director), 320
Stones in His Pockets (January 25–February 16, 2013), 343
Stoppard, Tom, 126; *Arcadia* (author), 293–95, *294*, 344; *Largo Desolato* (translation), 333; *Rough Crossing* (adaptation/author), 282, 341
Stops (February 1–5, 1972), 322
Story Theatre (January 23–February 8, 1969), 23, 38, 40–47, 129, 286, 320
Story Theatre Repertory (October 8–31, 1970), 44, 321
Straiges, Tony, 93; *A Midsummer Night's Dream* (set designer), 61, 67
Strasberg, Lee, 11
Strathairn, David: *A Moon for the Misbegotten* (actor), 133
Strawbridge, Stephen (lighting designer), 278; *Democracy in America*, 170; *The Evildoers*, 263
Streep, Meryl (actor), 12, 66; *The Idiots Karamazov*, 77, *78*, 79, 214; *A Midsummer Night's Dream*, 62, 67; *The Possessed*, *69*, 70
A Streetcar Named Desire (September 20–October 12, 2013), 282, 344
Strehler, Giorgio, 170
Strickland, Michael: *Twelfth Night* (actor), 174
Strindberg, August, 8, 10, 14, 35, 72, 88, 171, 283, 300; *Crimes and Crimes*, 63, 320; *The Father*, 324; *The Ghost Sonata*, 72–74, *73*, 214, 325; *Miss Julie*, 35, 282, 332, 339
Studio 7, 10
Sturges, Preston (author), 134, 223; *Christ-

mas in July*, 220; *A Cup of Coffee*, 219–21, *221*, 224, 337; *Strictly Dishonorable*, 220
Styron, William, 21; *In the Clap Shack* (author), 21, 322
subscription sales: flex-pass subscription, 180; as outdated model, 317; Richards and, 152, 179; special subscription series, 188; Wojewodski and, 179
Sueko, Seema: *The Intelligent Design of Jenny Chow* (actor), *247*
The Suicide (November 4–22, 1980), 68, 327
Suicide in B-Flat (October 14–December 17, 1976), 88, 324
Summer and Smoke (November 20–December 16, 1989), 35, 178, 332
Sundance, 99, 302
Sunday Series, 49, 63–66, *65*, 110, 112
surrealism, 21, 52, 90, 100
Susan Smith Blackburn Prize, 240
Suttor, Matthew: *The Winter's Tale* (composer), 343; *The Winter's Tale* (sound designer), 289
Swados, Elizabeth, 73, 82
The Sweet Life (January 16–February 25, 1984), 329

Taccone, Tony (director): *Brundibar*, 340; *Culture Clash in America*, 339; *Elizabeth: Almost by Chance a Woman*, 149–50, 331
Taichman, Rebecca (director): *The Evildoers*, 263, 302, 341; *Familiar*, 302, 344; *Indecent*, 301, 304, 345; *Iphigenia at Aulis*, 302, 338; *Marie Antoinette*, 302, 343; *The People v. The God of Vengeance*, 301–2
Talbott, Strobe: *Deadly Gambits* (author), 144
Tales from the Vienna Woods (September 28–November 8, 1978), 66, 93, 326
Talley's Folly (March 26–April 20, 1985), 144, 329
Tally, Ted: *Terra Nova* (author), 99, 325
The Taming of the Shrew (March 21–April 12, 2003), 231, 301, 338

Tantolo, Joe: *Richard III* (actor), *177*
Tartuffe (September 18–October 13, 1984), 35, 105, 254, 329
Tartuffe (December 3–22, 2007), 35, 261, 341
Taubman, Howard, 3
Tavel, Ronald, 44
Taygun, Meral: *Ovid's Metamorphoses* (actor), *41*
Taylor, Markland, 150
Taylor, Robert E., 6
TCG. *See* Theater Communications Group
Technically Speaking series (1994), 188
Telleria, Nahuel, 190; *Happy Days* (dramaturg), 305
The Tempest (October 4–December 15, 1973), 38, 53, 61, 323
Tercentennial Conference: Theatricality and Anti-Theatricality in the 18th Century, 206
Terra Nova (November 17–30, 1977), 99, 325
Terry, James, 239
Terry, Megan, 85; *Viet Rock* (author/director), 13, 183, 319
Tetrault, Patricia, 56
Theater Communications Group (TCG), 9, 146, 185, 216, 252, 290, 297
Theater for a New Audience (New York), 207, 306
Theater Hall of Fame, 38, 152, 312
Theater magazine, 24, 100, 134, 148, 167, 187
Theater of the Ridiculous (New York), 176
Theatre Crafts, 83
Le Théâtre de France, 9, 11; *Happy Days*, 320; *Words and Music from the Court of the Sun King*, 320
Le Théâtre de la Jeune Lune, 182–85, 189, 314; *Children of Paradise* (coproduction), 185–86, 234, 334; *The Green Bird* (coproduction), 334
Theatre Guild (New York), 8, 222
Le Théâtre Libre (Paris), 7
Theatre of Living Arts (Philadelphia): *Endgame* (production), 13, 319

The Doctor in Spite of Himself, 82, 84
The Great Migration (1910–1970), 138
These Paper Bullets! A Modish Ripoff of William Shakespeare's Much Ado about Nothing (March 15–April 5, 2014), 215, 270–72, *271*, 344
They Are Dying Out (October 18–November 21, 1979), 100, 102, 164, 326
They Told Me That You Came This Way (December 5–21, 1968), 32, 320
Thorne, Tracy, 229
The Three Sisters (March 4–16, 1968), 8, 23, 35, 319–20
Three Sisters (September 16–October 8, 2011), 35, 245, 343
Thunder Knocking on the Door (May 1–24, 1997), 207, 336
ticket prices, 26, 179, 188, 231–32
Ties That Bind (January 14–February 9, 1991), 333
Time magazine, 185
Timon of Athens (April 10–May 14, 1980), 54, 101–2, 300, 327
Tipton, Jennifer (lighting designer), 160, 312; *St. Joan of the Stockyards*, 200; *Spectral Scriabin*, 343; *A Walk in the Woods*, 118
'Tis Pity She's a Whore (October 16–28, 1967), 319
Tocqueville, Alexis de. *See* de Tocqueville, Alexis
Tofflemire, Anne, 229
Tometi, Opal, 296
Tony Awards, 138–40, *139*, 152, 301, 313–14
A Touch of the Poet (May 3–21, 1983), 124, 328
Trach, Ed, 253
Transformations: 3 One-Acts by Yale Playwrights (April 2–25, 1970), 320–21
Triumph of Love (January 16–February 8, 1997), 207, 336
Troilus and Cressida (April 1–May 8, 1976), 35, 324
Troilus and Cressida (February 20–March 17, 1990), 35, 101, 332
Troobnick, Eugene, 50, 52; *Dynamite Tonite!* (actor), *16*

Trouble in Mind (October 26–November 17, 2007), 259–61, *260*, 341
Tse, Elaine: *Uncle Vanya* (actor), 203, *204*
The Tubs (December 20–March 27, 1974), 34, 85, 87, 214, 301, 323
Tucci, Maria: *A Lesson from Aloes* (actor), *103*, 105
Tucci, Stanley: *Moon Over Miami* (actor), *151*, 152
Tuesday Night Discussions (1994), 188
Tunick, Jonathan: *The Frogs* (orchestrator), *80*, 81
Turner, John (author/actor): Mump + Smoot in *Ferno* and *Caged*, 186–87, 334; Mump + Smoot in *Something Else with Zug*, 187, 337
Turner, Stephen Barker (actor): *Arcadia*, 294; *The Evildoers*, 262, 263
Turturro, John, 114
Tutta Casa, Letto, e Chiesa (All House, Bed and Church) (special event, May 13–17, 1986), 148, 330
Twelfth Night (December 2–20, 1980), 35, 327
Twelfth Night (January 26–February 18, 1995), 35, 174–76, *175*, 335
Two by Bertolt Brecht and Kurt Weill (May 13–June 5, 1971), 47–48, 321
Two by Brecht and Weill (January 20–29, 1972), 322
Two Trains Running (March 17–April 21, 1990), 142–43, *143*, 332

Ubu Rex (February 15–March 19, 1980), 101, 152, 327
Uccello, Paolo: *The Battle of San Romano* (painting), 61, 67
Uncle Vanya (October 6–24, 1981), 35, 90, 126, 327
Uncle Vanya (March 30–April 15, 1995), 35, 203, *204*, 335
Underground (February 19–March 16, 1991), 333
Union Boys (January 9–February 8, 1986), 112, 330
University Theatre (UT), 5, 19–20, *20*, 32, 52, 120, 177, 182, 218, 250, 307

The Unmentionables (May 4–26, 2007), 341
Updike, John, 21
Urdang, Leslie, 309

Valdes, Ching, 114
Valle-Inclán, Ramón de, 161
Vallejo, Antonio Buero, 161
Vampires in Kodachrome (January 14–February 9, 1985), 30, 34, 112, 329
Vance, Courtney B., 114, 155; *Fences* (actor), 137–38, *137*
Vance, Nina, xii, 9
Van Sertima, Ivan: *They Came Before Columbus* (author), 239
Variety (magazine), 23, 105, 119, 140, 159, 169, 172
vaudeville, 182
"The Vengeance Project," 302
Venora, Diane, 172
Venturi, Ariana: *These Paper Bullets!* (actor), *271*, 272
Venus (March 14–30, 1996), 208–10, *210*, 226, 335
Verson, Adina: *Indecent* (actor), *303*
The Vietnamization of New Jersey (A American Tragedy) (January 13–February 25, 1977), 75, 88, 325
Vietnam War, 5, 15, 19, 21, 25, 64–66, 87
Viet Rock (October 11–23, 1966, Open Theatre production), 13, 319
The Village Voice, 49–50, 96, 169, 171
Villarreal, Edit: *Crazy from the Heart* (author), 112, 330
violence, depiction of, 15, 23–39, 87, 144, 197, 198, 262–63
Vivian Beaumont Theatre (Lincoln Center), 10
Vogel, Paula, 240, 243; *The Baltimore Waltz* (author), 182, 334; *Indecent* (author/creator), 253, 301–4, *303*, 345
Volpone (January 31–February 12, 1967), 319
Vonnegut, Kurt, 21

Wajda, Andrzej (director), xiii; *The Possessed*, 67–70, 323; *White Marriage*, 70, 166–67, 325

Walcott, Derek: *Beef, No Chicken* (author), 328; *The Joker of Seville* (adaptation), 100
Walken, Christopher (actor): *Caligula*, 54, 59–60, *60*; *Measure for Measure*, 61, 101; *The Philanderer*, 61, 119, 127; *The Wild Duck*, 61
Walker, George F. (author): *Escape from Happiness*, 197, 334; *Heaven*, 197, 337
Walker, Tom, 26, 28, 38
A Walk in The Woods (February 17–March 14, 1987), 118, 144–46, *145*, 331
Walk the Dog, Willie (January 15–February 19, 1976), 324
The Wall of Water (January 11–February 6, 1988), 331
Walsh, Paul: *Children of Paradise* (author), 185, 334; *The Master Builder* (translation), 285, 342
War (November 21–December 13, 2014), 276, 280–81, *281*, 344
Ward, Nari: *Geography* (set designer), 192–94
Ward, Tony: *As You Like It* (actor), 174
Warfel, William, 56, 93
Warhol, Andy, 51, 268–70, *269*
Warren, Robert Penn, 3
The Warrior Ant (special event, October 10–15, 1988), 183–84, *184*, 332
The War Show (Sunday Series, 1972–1973), 63–66, *65*
Watergate Classics (November 15–January 26, 1974), 53, 74–76, *77*, 257, 323
Watergate scandal (1972–1974), 74
Waters, Les (director), 242; *Dear Elizabeth, A Play in Letters from Elizabeth Bishop to Robert Lowell and Back Again*, 245, 343; *Eurydice*, 242, 340; *The Three Sisters*, 245, 319–20
Waterston, Sam: *The Black Monk* (actor), 231
The Way of the World (February 9–March 3, 2001), 178, 204–6, *205*, 217, 337
We Bombed in New Haven (December 4–23, 1967), 21–23, 85, 319
Webster, John, 265

Wedekind, Frank, 10; *Lulu* (author), 340
We Have Always Lived in the Castle (September 17–October 9, 2010), 342
Weill, Kurt, 29, 35, 50, 76, 267; *Happy End*, 47–48, 51, 322, 324; *The Rise and Fall of the City of Mahagonny*, 47–49, *48*, 51–53, 321, 323, 326; *Seven Deadly Sins*, 47, 321
Weinberger, Harry, 302
Weinstein, Arnold, 11, 47, 93, 267; *Dynamite Tonite!* (librettist), 13–15, *16*, 49, 319, 324; *Greatshot* (author/lyricist), 38, 320; *Ovid's Metamorphoses* (translation/lyricist), 40, 320; *The Red Eye of Love* (off-Broadway), 15
Weiss, Peter: *Song of the Lusitanian Bogey* (author), 321
Welles, Orson: *King Lear* (actor), 38
Welsh, Kenneth: *A Walk in The Woods* (actor), *145*
Werner-Mueller, Otto (conductor), 52; *Happy End*, 62; *Mahagonny*, 52, 62; *A Midsummer Night's Dream*, 62
What the Butler Saw (February 19–March 17, 1985), 329
Wheeler, Hugh, 70
Wheeler, Scott Rickey: *The Resurrection of Lady Lester* (actor), *113*
When We Dead Awaken (October 14–December 8, 1971), 54, 321
Where Has Tommy Flowers Gone? (January 7–31, 1971), 23, 85, 301, 321
Whitaker, Paul: *The Master Builder* (lighting designer), 283
Whitaker, Thomas, 159
White, George C., 99, 114
White, Jane: *Pygmalion* (actor), 300
White Marriage (April 14–May 7, 1977), 70–74, *71*, 106, 166–67, 210, 325
white privilege. *See* race, diversity, and inclusion
Whooper, Vicki: *Happy Days* (stage manager), 305
Wiest, Dianne (actor), 233, 253; *A Doll's House*, 119, 125–26; *Happy Days*, 233, 304–6, *306*; *Hedda Gabler*, 124–26, *125*

Index 377

The Wild Duck (April 6–May 3, 1978), 61, 128, 202, 325
Wilde, Oscar: *The Importance of Being Earnest*, 330; *A Woman of No Importance*, 282, 295, 308, 341
Wilder, Thornton, 8, 21; *Our Town*, 88, 275; *The Skin of Our Teeth*, 35, 88, 176, 336
Wildman, Robert, 139–40, *139*
Willard, Carol: *White Marriage* (actor), 71
Williams, Tennessee, 8, 106, 142, 195, 278; *Camino Real*, 8; *The Glass Menagerie*, 3, 88, 337; *Kingdom of Earth*, 218, 338; *A Streetcar Named Desire*, 282, 344; *Summer and Smoke*, 35, 332
Williamstown Theater Festival: *Moon Over Miami* (1987 production), 150–51
Will Power! (programs for middle- and high-school students), 234–35, *235*, 239, 258, 308, 316
Wilson, August, 24, 34, 35, 50, 106, 109, 120, 122, 133–43, 152, 154, 159, 167, 217, 240, 249–50, 290, 293, 314; cycle of plays, 133–43, 154, 207, 208, 217, 240, 249–50, 293, 300, 314; *Fences*, 136, *137*, 138–39, 160, 329; *Joe Turner's Come and Gone*, 138–40, *141*, 142, 160, 330; *Ma Rainey's Black Bottom*, 50, 114, 119, 133–36, *135*, 154, 263, 329; *The Piano Lesson*, 35, 142, 159, 331, 342; *Radio Golf*, 134, 143, 245, 247–50, *248*, 339; *Two Trains Running*, 142–43, *143*, 332
Wilson, Elizabeth: *Ah, Wilderness!* (actor), 132
Wilson, Mary Louise, 114
Wilson, Robert, 170–71
Wilson, Shaunette Renée: *The Caucasian Chalk Circle* (actor), 282
Wing-Davey, Mark (director): *Passion Play*, 341; *Safe in Hell*, 340; *Scenes from Court Life; or the whipping boy and his prince*, 345
Wings (March 2–May 15, 1978), 85, 90–91, 325
Winkler, Henry (actor), 52–53; *Don Juan, or the Enemy of God*, 58; *The Government Inspector*, 68

Winterfest, 24, 30, 54, 105, 110–15, 118, 120, 122, 162, 171, 254–55, 314–15; *Winterfest I* (January 10–February 21, 1981), 110–12, *111*, 327; *Winterfest II* (January 5–February 6, 1982), 328; *Winterfest III* (January 4–February 5, 1983), 114, 328; *Winterfest IV* (January 16–February 25, 1984), 112, 329; *Winterfest V* (January 14–February 9, 1985), 112, 329; *Winterfest VI* (January 9–February 8, 1986), 113, 330; *Winterfest VII* (January 13–February 7, 1987), 113, 115, 330; *Winterfest VIII* (January 11–February 6, 1988), 113, 115, 331; *Winterfest IX* (January 10–February 4, 1989), 113, 332; *Winterfest X* (January 15–February 10, 1990), 113, 153, 332; *Winterfest XI* (January 14–February 9, 1991), 113, 333; *Winterfest XII* (January 16–March 7, 1992), 164, 167, 169, 179, 237, 254, 333
The Winter's Tale (November 24–December 20, 1986), 35, 330
The Winter's Tale (March 16–April 7, 2012), 35, 215, 287–89, *288*, 300, 343
Wohl, Bess: *Cats Talk Back* (author), 30
Wojewodski, Stan, Jr., as dean and artistic director, 157–226, *225*; all-student cast in *Hamlet* and, 172; anticommercial choices of, 161, 226; appointment of, 4, 160; associate artists program launched by, 161, 162–63; background of, 160–61; *Le Bourgeois Avant-Garde* as social parody, 75; comedy as artistic signature of, 178–79, 182, 199, 208, 217, 222; community engagement and, 188–89, 308; compared to Brustein, 210, 226; compared to Bundy, 251; compared to Richards, 161, 206, 210; coproductions, 207–8, 314; departure of, 212–16; Diamond hired as resident director, 198; Dwight/Edgewood Project and, 162, 189–91, *191*, 314; extending term for additional year, 216–17; final season of, 217; funding and, 180–81, 188; Jennings and, 197; language-centered productions of, 195, 204, 217;

Lee and, 311–12; legacy of, 225–26; Lemon and, 130, 162, 189–92, 194–95, 226, 336, 337; most Richards-like offering of Rep tenure, 164; NEA and, 182–83; need for new facility acknowledged by, 307; Nolan and, 180, 314; open-door policy of, 197; original scores and sound design introduced by, 224–25; Parks and, 162, 167, 189, 195, 240; patronage of Ralph Lemon's *Geography* trilogy, 189–92; pay-what-you-can performances and, 180; personality of, 161; production budgets and, 224, 314; the program during era of, 255; public communications of, 254–55; reconfiguration of Rep space, 164; regrets of, 226; renovation of theater and, 57; Russian works produced by, 68; sole premiere given to contemporary world playwright, 210; special subscription series and, 188; student focus of, 161, 172, 233, 314; Le Théâtre de la Jeune Lune and, 182–85, 189, 234, 314; third-year acting project and, 172, 176, 179, 217, 231, 314; translations of foreign classics and, 195, 203; *Winterfest* and, 162, 164, 254, 315; workshopping not of interest to, 206–7, 315
Wojewodski, Stan, Jr., as director, 251; *The Adventures of Amy Bock*, 312, 336; *As You Like It*, 174, 334; *The Baltimore Waltz*, 334; *Big Night*, 219, 222, 338; *Candida*, 336; *Edward II*, 162, 164, 197, 334; *Figaro/Figaro*, 75, 200–201, 204, 226, 335; *First Lady*, 219, 335; *Hamlet*, 162, 172, 197, 334; *Hay Fever*, 337; *It Pays to Advertise*, 217, 219, 338; *Oleanna*, 293, 334; *On the Verge*, 162, 254, 333; *Pentecost*, 200, 210, 212, 215, 226, 335; *Richard III*, 176, 197, 204, 337; *The Way of the World*, 178, 204, 337; *You Never Can Tell*, 217, 338
A Woman of No Importance (March 21–April 12, 2008), 282, 295, 308, 341
women: all-female production of *Fefu and Her Friends*, 164–65; Black, HIV-positive women, 257; Black women

playwrights, 257–59; as directors, 34, 113, 301, 314, 315; Honegger as first woman to teach in dramaturgy and dramatic criticism program, 34; as playwrights, 85, 99, 100, 112, 240, 314; in Wilder's *The Skin of Our Teeth*, 176; Womxn's Voices in Theatre, 298. *See also* race, diversity, and inclusion

Woodruff, Robert, xiv, 254, 265–66, 309, 314; *Autumn Sonata* (director), 342; *Battle of Black and Dogs* (director), 342; *In a Year with 13 Moons* (adaptation/director), 267, 344; *Notes from Underground* (adaptation/director), 68, 266–67, *267*, 341

Wooster Group, 170, 235; *Brace Up!*, 128

World Performance Project (WPP), 184

World Theater Festival (London), 67

Worth, Irene (actor): *Men and Women of Shakespeare*, 183, 319; *Prometheus Bound*, 18, *18*

Woyzeck (April 1–24, 1971), 213, 321

Wright, Doug (author), 155; *Dinosaurs*, 118, 332; *I Am My Own Wife*, 118; *Interrogating the Nude*, 118, 332

Wright, Garland, 160

www.ensemble@yale.com, 256

X-rated production, 150

Yakim, Moni: *The Tempest* (director), 323

Yale Cabaret, 25, 29–30, *30*, 52, 63, 74, 76, 105, 112, 120, 174, 255, 268

Yale CBS Fellows, 85, 87

Yale Center for British Art, 206

Yale Collegium Musicum, 52

Yale Corporation, 307

Yale Daily News, 11, 25, 98, 216, 230, 239

Yale Dramatic Association, 20

Yale Elizabethan Club, 291

Yale Institute for Music Theater (YIMT), 268

Yale Intercultural Affairs Committee, 296

Yale New Play Program, 264–66

Yale Repertory Theatre (Yale Rep): alumni engagement, 252–53, 254; artist housing, 231–33; associate artists program, 161–63, *163*; budget process, 116–17, 131, 295–96; casting, 121–23, *123*, 172, 300–301; coproductions, xiv, 145, 185–86, 197, 207–8, 261, 314, 334, 339; costume shop, 177–78; creation of, 4; excellence as foundational impulse of, 317; facilities, challenges of configuration, 20, 307; fears of deprofessionalization (Brustein), 92, 98–99, 314; first federal grant from NEA, 17; future of, 315–17; income from regional and Broadway productions of shows, 142; interdependence with drama school, 295–96; Leadership Council, 253; "Let's get these people out!" (agenda, 1965), 6, *6*; literary management office, 114; merger with Long Wharf and, 46; most-produced playwrights, 35; name change, possibility of, 316; new home for Yale Rep and David Geffen School of Drama at Yale, plans for, 307; Nolan as longest-serving managing director, 180; online and e-blasts, 253; parodies, 75; production calendar, 117–18, 224; the program, 255–56, *256*; renovation (1975), 53, 56–57, *57*; rotating repertory, 54–55, *55*; Russian works produced by, 68; scene and prop shops, 130–31, *131*; Scripts Collection, 348; social media presence, 253; sound design, 224–25; special subscription series, 188; student role in, 12–13, 92, 161, 232–33, 299–300; text as foundational impulse of, 317; ticket prices, 26, 179, 188, 231–32; *Update* (strategic plan, 2006), 231–32; website, 253, 256; www.ensemble@yale.com (database), 256. *See also* names of *specific facilities and grant programs*; *specific artistic directors*: Brustein, Robert; Richards, Lloyd; Wojewodski, Stan; Bundy, James

Yale Repertory Theatre Associate Artists, 93

Yale School of Architecture (formerly Yale School of Art and Architecture), 4, 10

Yale School of Drama (YSD): Board of Advisors, 253; Diversity, Equity, Inclusion, and Belonging (DEIB) and, 301, 308; Dwight/Edgewood Project (D/EP), 162, 189–91, *191*, 314; founding and history of, 5, 228; Jordan as drama librarian, 106–7, *107*; Pamela Jordan Scholarship, 107; Pamela Jordan Yale School of Drama Scrapbook Collection (1966–2008), 106–7, 348; patron confusion over relationship with the Rep, 179; proposed new facility of DGSDY/Yale Rep, 307; students and curriculum, 12–13; *Tercentennial Conference: Theatricality and Anti-Theatricality in the 18th Century*, 206; third-year acting project, 172, 176, 179, 217, 231, 314. *See also specific deans*

Yale School of Fine Arts, 20

Yale School of Music, 268; *Brundibar*, 340; *Comedy on the Bridge*, 340; *Happy End*, 324; *A Midsummer Night's Dream*, 324; *The Rise and Fall of the City of Mahagonny*, 47, 323; *The Tempest*, 323; *Two by Bertolt Brecht and Kurt Weill*, 47

Yale Summer Repertory (East Hampton, NY, 1970), 44

yale/theatre magazine, 23–24, *24*, 49, 52, 74, 100, 315. *See also Theater* magazine

Yale University, 46, 75, 142, 152, 188, 191, 252, 264

Yale University News Bureau, 33

Yamamoto, Keiko: *The Intelligent Design of Jenny Chow* (actor), 245, *247*

Yamauchi, Wakako: *The Memento* (author), 112, 331

Yeargan, Michael (set designer), 20, 52, 56–59, 69, 93, 172, 213–15, *213*, 306, 313, 317; *Ah, Wilderness!*, 214–15; *Don Juan*, 215; *Edward II*, 197, 215; *The Frogs*, 213; *The Ghost Sonata*, 214; *Happy End*, 215; *Hay Fever*, 215; *The Idiots Karamazov*, 214; *A Lesson from Aloes*, 105, 215; *Pentecost*, 212, 215; *The Resurrection of Lady Lester*, 215; *The Rivals* (costume assistant), 213, 306–7; *Sganarelle: An Evening of Molière Farces*, 82–83, 214;

Yeargan, Michael (*continued*)
These Paper Bullets!, 215; *The Tubs*, 214; *Winterfest*, 110; *The Winter's Tale*, 215; *Woyzeck*, 213

Yiddish theater, 301–2

YIMT (Yale Institute for Music Theater), 268

Yionoulis, Evan (director), 172, 216, 230, 240, 282–83, 314, 315, 316–17; *Black Snow*, 38, 283, 340; *Bossa Nova*, 342; *Cymbeline*, 234–35, 301, 345; *Galileo*, 336; *Heaven*, 337; *The King Stag* (adaptation), 285, 339; *The Master Builder*, 282–83, 342; *The My House Play*, 331; *Owners*, 344; *The People Next Door*, 340; *Petersburg*, 336; *Richard II*, 38, 283, 341; *Stones in His Pockets*, 343; *Vampires in Kodachrome*, 34, 112–13, 329

Yionoulis, Mike: *The King Stag* (adaptation/composer), 285, 339

Yoon, Jayoung: *Hamlet* (costume designer), 292

Yoshimura, James: *Union Boys* (author), 112, 330

You Never Can Tell (September 20–October 13, 2001), 217, 338

Young, Lester, 110–12

Young, Tracy: *Medea/Macbeth/Cinderella* (adaptation/director), *236*, 236–37, 338

YSD. *See* Yale School of Drama

Yulin, Harris (actor): *A Lesson from Aloes*, *103*, 105; *Uncle Vanya*, 126

Zachwatowicz, Krystyna (set designer): *The Possessed*, 69; *White Marriage*, 70–71

Zeisler, Peter, 9

Zimmerman, George, 296

Zimmerman, Mary: *Metamorphoses* (author), 47

Zinn, David: *Notes from the Underground* (set designer), 266

Zou, Nai: *Geography* (actor), *193*